RACE TO THE FRONTIER:

"WHITE FLIGHT"
AND WESTWARD EXPANSION

RACE TO THE FRONTIER:
"WHITE FLIGHT"
AND WESTWARD EXPANSION

John V. H. Dippel

Algora Publishing
New York

No portion of this book (beyond what is permitted by
Sections 107 or 108 of the United States Copyright Act of 1976)
may be reproduced by any process, stored in a retrieval system,
or transmitted in any form, or by any means, without the
express written permission of the publisher.
ISBN: 0-87586-395-7 (softcover)
ISBN: 0-87586-396-5 (hardcover)
ISBN: 0-87586-397-3 (ebook)

Library of Congress Cataloging-in-Publication Data —

Dippel, John Van Houten, 1946-
    Race to the frontier : white flight and westward expansion / John V.H.
Dippel.
        p. cm.
    Includes bibliographical references and index.
        ISBN 0-87586-395-7 (trade paper: alk. paper) — ISBN 0-87586-396-5
(hard cover: alk. paper) — ISBN 0-87586-397-3 (ebook)
        1. Frontier and pioneer life—United States. 2. Frontier and pioneer life—
West (U.S.) 3. United States—Territorial expansion. 4. Whites—Migrations—
United States—History. 5. United States—Race relations. 6. Racism—United
States—History. I. Title.

    E179.5.D57 2005
    978'.02—dc22

                        2005024143

Front Cover: Bierstadt, Albert - Emigrants Crossing the Plains. 1867.
Oil on canvas
67 x 102 in. (170.2 x 259.1 cm)
National Cowboy Hall of Fame and Western Heritage Center,
Oklahoma City, Oklahoma

Printed in the United States

To the victims of slavery

ACKNOWLEDGEMENTS

Archivists and reference specialists at a number of libraries across the country assisted me in locating source materials for this book, and for this help I am very grateful. In particular I would like to thank Lori A. Bain, in the newspaper library of the State Historical Society of Missouri; Dennis Hardin, preservation imaging director, Indiana Historical Society; David Wendell, reference archivist at the Oregon State Archives; David Smolen, special collections librarian at the New Hampshire Historical Society; and Anne Prichard, special collections librarian at the University of Arkansas Libraries. In addition, staff at the Missouri State Archives; Ohio Historical Society; Young Library, University of Kentucky; National Archives and Research Administration, Washington, D.C.; Beinecke Rare Book and Manuscript Library, Yale University; Sterling Library, Yale University; Firestone Library, Princeton University; the New York Public Library; and Butler Library, Columbia University have provided me with invaluable guidance in tracking down primary and secondary materials relating to the settlement of the Western frontier.

I would also like to thank my sister, Elizabeth Archambeault, for locating material relating to Peter H. Burnett at the Stanford University Library; James Kurz, for insights and suggestions pertaining to both the Jamestown Colony and the settlement of Kentucky; Prof. Wali R. Kharif, at Tennessee Tech University, for permission to cite a 1999 conference paper of his dealing with free blacks in Tennessee; and Glenna Marra, for allowing me to quote from a letter written by one of her pioneer forebears in Oregon. Finally, I owe a debt of gratitude to Martin DeMers and the editorial staff at Algora Publishing for guiding this manuscript successfully through the production process into its present form.

TABLE OF CONTENTS

INTRODUCTION

At the end of Mark Twain's classic novel *Huckleberry Finn*, his eponymous young hero, Huck, makes up his mind to leave all his troubles behind, escape the constraints and woes of society, and forge a new life for himself by heading west: "I reckon I got to light out for the Territory ahead of the rest," Huck confides to the reader, "because Aunt Sally she's going to sivilize [*sic*] me and I can't stand it. I been there before." For Huck, the vast, nebulous mass of land on the far side of the Mississippi stands for all that the world of kindly aunts, riverboat pirates, fast-talking charlatans, fugitive-slave hunters, and cutthroat murderers he has come to know lacks — freedom, independence, a kind of radical innocence. To him, the West offers a fresh start, a new beginning. Moreover, it seems to Huck a place where he and his companion, the former slave Jim, can become true friends — where hatred between the races does not exist, and where blacks and whites can travel and live together, and no one else will object, send the law after them, or take Jim away, sobbing, in chains.

It was a grand but delusory hope — 19th-century American optimism at its fullest — faith in the untrammeled natural world *out there* somewhere, far beyond the corrupting taint of civilization, where people were still good, and good to each other, no matter what the color of their skin. Blithely impervious to the true nature of the continent stretching all the way to the shores of the Pacific, oblivious to the fact that it was already populated — by people of many races already warring with one another over its land and other resources, a character like Huck saw the West as a *tabula rasa*. In his eyes, the frontier was a romantic refuge, a postlapsarian Garden of Eden. To many Americans of his era, it beckoned like a shimmering phantasmagoria, irresistibly alluring yet forever retreating into the mists as one came closer and hesitantly reached out to touch

1

it. For the frontier was, by definition, what always lay one step ahead — on the back side of the next mountain, or across the next stream, or over in the next territory. It could be pursued, but never possessed. The frontier was all about the quest. It was, as the historian Frederick Jackson Turner once wrote, a process, not a place. But still they came west, to find their destiny and a better life there — the young and the restless like Huck, the luckless and the penniless disgorged from cities and towns back east, the misfits and outcasts of society, the dreamers and the downtrodden, all mingling their boots in the same dust, with their eyes steadfastly fixed on the stars.

But the romantic allure of the frontier represented only one aspect of its appeal. The West also beckoned as a refuge. Like Huck, most pioneers were as much running away from their old lives as looking to build new ones. They were as apt to have been *pushed* out of their homes and villages, or off their farms, by dire circumstances that would not allow them to stay any longer — bad debts, failing crops, famine or flood, an angry neighbor with a loaded rifle — as *pulled* westward by visions of bison stretching as far as the eye could see, stately wheat stalks tossing above rich, black loam, or nuggets of gold glinting in a roaring California riverbed. For most, the Western frontier was the nation's backdoor — the unlocked exit through which one could slip quietly and undetected, leaving all one's woes behind. Contrary to what F. Scott Fitzgerald would maintain, there *was* a second act in Americans' lives, and it unfolded with a flourish on the immense, sweeping stage of the West, where the past was as easily stamped out as last night's campfire, and Everyman was his own invention. Horace Greeley's admonition, "Go west, young man," resonated with hope and promise and opportunity, but it also whispered a darker message: *All is not well, here; you are better off striking out on your own.* Thus, the frontier served as a kind of safety valve, siphoning off those who faced failure, or the fear of failure, and needed to escape. It was their sanctuary.

One of the factors pushing pioneers westward was race. This was particularly so for one of the largest migratory streams to cross the continent — poor, non-slaveholding farmers who came originally from the Upper South. For them, chronically losing out to slave labor in a fluctuating, tobacco-dominated economy was the driving force. Indeed, racial prejudice and unsuccessful competition for jobs were closely related. In order to survive, these "plain folk" farmers had to flee further west. So, in the decades leading up to the Civil War, did a number of workers in cities like New York and Philadelphia, who were fearful of losing their jobs to former slaves then migrating northward out of the Deep South. But anti-black bias was not only economically based. Many white settlers — from the North as well as the South — found the presence of blacks socially intolerable — "degrading" and threatening. For them, a major attraction of the West lay in its racial exclusivity: slaves and free blacks had not moved to this region in large numbers (except to a few states, such as Missouri, Arkansas, and Texas). Thus, whites bound for the frontier could entertain hopes of settling on land where future contact and conflict with blacks could be avoided. In the open spaces of the West, these pioneers could create enclaves that would safeguard and preserve their racial identity and unity.

Starting in colonial days, the presence of blacks on the continent presented white Americans with an intractable dilemma. On the one hand, the black race embodied The Other — in its very blackness, in its "heathen" and "savage" nature, it was the antithesis of how these whites viewed themselves. On the other hand, blacks were an integral, indeed, essential element of the Europeans' world — the wellspring of wealth and power in the Southern part of their expanding domain. For this reason, blacks could not simply be driven out or eliminated, like Native Americans. Rather, whites somehow had to figure out how to coexist with these dark-skinned people they considered so alien and inimical to their own way of life.

Ironically, this dilemma was of the white settlers' own making, although a sense of this irony does not appear to have entered much into their tortured thinking about how to resolve it. Blacks had first been brought to the English colonies along the South Atlantic coast to save a fragile tobacco industry from collapse and white landowners from the ignominy of having to perform this lowly work themselves. But these blacks, stripped of their humanity and rendered virtually powerless, became the colonists' Trojan horse — ushered into the latter's midst as a welcomed "gift," slaves confounded other white needs as strong, if not stronger, than the pressing one for economic survival and well being. Chief among these was a sense of security. As much as they might oppress, brutalize, and dehumanize the blacks they owned, whites could never be sure the dark day of reckoning might not eventually come: emboldened by their sheer numbers, slaves might rise up and lay their masters low. Worse, at least in the short term, was the inevitable "mixing" of the two races, with whites being debased by contact with a people they considered innately inferior to them, and being dragged down, by some reverse evolutionary process, to their level. Such "commingling" would include the most intimate of forms — blacks and whites succumbing to animal impulses in the heat of the moment and producing offspring belonging to neither race, whose proliferation would gradually efface the color line and thus spell the doom of the whites.

Enslaved blacks also posed a grave economic threat. For every slaveholder who prospered in the Southern colonies off the sweat of his chattel, there were many more whites who paid a high price for the planter to live so pampered.

Struggling yeoman farmers who could afford small tracts of land but not slaves, were often financially marginalized by the more efficient and profitable agribusiness sustained by the labor of black farmhands. As land prices rose and their profits fell, these small, independent farmers often found themselves left with no option other than to pack up what few belongings they had, hoist their families onto wagons, and trek westward in search of cheaper acreage where the slave system had yet to take root. This displacement, repeated over several generations, left these "plain folk" whites with an abiding disdain — not for the planter class itself, but for the blacks who had taken their places in the fields and forced them to move on. As they did so, the poor whites carried this racial animus with them and planted it, along with their crops, wherever they ended up settling.

They did not settle alone, however. The slave owners soon arrived, too. They had reasons of their own for moving west — mainly because their way of growing tobacco quickly depleted the soil and fueled a chronic appetite for more, but also because the growing numbers of slaves under their control required work to avoid the dangerous idleness that bred conspiracy and revolt. So, across the continental landscape, the competition between slaveholders and non-slaveholders was reenacted, with territory after territory embroiled in a bitter struggle to determine its status as a prospective state in the Union. (Mark Twain knew what his naïve hero, Huck, did not: the fabled West offered no respite from racial strife. Conflict only grew worse there.) Rather than a contest between "free" and "slave" states, this running battle to decide the fate of the West is more properly seen as one fought by whites who needed the presence of black laborers in order to survive and those whose future depended on being "free" of this unwanted element.

Bitter hostility toward blacks did not end with their emancipation because, ultimately, race, not status, defined their "otherness" and made them contemptible in white eyes. Blacks who gained their freedom presented a disconcerting anomaly, much like mulattoes (of which there were many): how could a member of a race incapable of attaining equality with whites be considered "free"? For many whites, living north or south of the Mason Dixon Line, the answer was simple — they could not. The term "free black" was an oxymoron. Moreover, black freemen moving about the country without an overseer at their heels could "amalgamate" with whites more easily than their manacled brethren, and so the risks for whites were geographically (if not numerically) far greater. Slavery itself might be contained in the South, but the black race could only be held back by more subtle means — the withholding of jobs, the denial of rights, ostracism, antagonism, and fear.

As non-slaveholding white settlers continued to wend their way west during the late 18th and 19th centuries, they took whatever steps lay in their power to assure that blacks — whether slave or free — would not follow in their wake. For, while their movement to the frontier was largely driven by economic aspiration and necessity, this exodus could not succeed unless it was essentially a *white flight*: true freedom and prosperity in the West hinged upon keeping blacks out. Thus, expansion of the nation was inherently a withdrawal from the complexities of a biracial world — a retreat in both time and space — in order to preserve an endangered racial identity.

This book tells the story of this historic migration across the continent, viewed from the perspective of race — starting with the colonial era in Virginia and ending with the settlement of Oregon at the conclusion of the antebellum period. It shows how economics, the need for territorial expansion, and racial conflict were closely intertwined in this process. *Race to the Frontier* seeks to explain what circumstances motivated white pioneers to head west, how racial feelings and rivalries figured in these decisions, what steps non-slaveholding white pioneers took to prevent blacks from settling near them, and how the ensuing clashes between the whites' need to keep the West off limits to the black race and the equally strong need of slave owners to open up new territories to the "peculiar institution" created much of the political conflict in this country, up to and including the Civil War.

Any assessment of why people migrate quickly runs afoul of human complexity. Throughout history, individuals and groups have frequently left one spot on the planet and moved to another for a myriad of reasons — many of them unknown even to themselves. The same holds true for the flow of settlers across North America, and so to ascribe too great a role to race in their movement would simplify and falsify this phenomenon. However, it is my contention that racial factors *were* inextricably bound up with the economic well being of these white pioneers — slaveholder or not — and, therefore, did contribute significantly to their decisions to migrate and influence the social and political outlook that took hold on the frontier. Accounts of the settlement of the West have largely ignored this linkage and thus have given an incomplete account of the migratory dynamic.

To back up this contention has required an indirect approach. Migrating farmers in the 18th and 19th centuries did not accommodate future historians by writing down detailed accounts describing why they elected to move their families west. Some did keep diaries and journals, which offer some insights into the conditions they faced and their state of mind. But few wrote letters back home discussing their views of blacks. In order to gauge their motives, I have therefore had to rely heavily on other sources. These include federal and state census data, as well as such ethnographic evidence as the size, location, and movement of slave plantations, and the settlement patterns, landholdings, and wealth of yeoman farmers. Other important primary sources dealing with the racial attitudes of Western pioneers are letters and opinion pieces published in local newspapers. The records of territorial and state legislatures and constitutional conventions provide candid testimony about prevailing views on blacks, as do the actions taken by these bodies to restrict the rights of blacks or limit their entry. Similarly, an analysis of voting on race-related issues at the county and state level, correlated with data on the origins of people living in these states, has helped to elucidate how regional and socioeconomic background influenced popular sentiment. The correspondence, memoirs, and public statements of prominent politicians on race and the expansion of slavery also yield insights into how anti-black bias helped to shape their national agendas and policies. Finally, numerous secondary sources — articles and books on migration westward and on economic, social, and political conditions within particular territories and states — have provided a wealth of valuable material about the role of race in the settlement of the United States.

Taken together, all of this evidence reveals a disturbing pattern of white prejudice, hatred, anxiety, fear, and revulsion toward African Americans who posed an economic or social threat and a concomitant pattern of white escape from these dangers by moving further and further west. More than a quest for adventure, a new life, or material prosperity, this 18th and 19th century migration to the frontier bespoke the desperation of many white Americans at realizing they were trapped in a society with the black race — a situation they could not abide.

I. WHITE NEGROES IN THE TIDEWATER

Black-white relations in the United States have had a long, tortuous history. In many respects, this is a sad and painful story, replete with bigotry, hatred, fear, oppression, degradation, violence, and slavery. But it is also a geographically dynamic story — one of people of two races moving across the continent in search of a better life, or being forced to move on, and, in the process of doing so, coming again and again into conflict with one other. For many whites — primarily, those who did not own slaves — competition with blacks undermined the promise of a better life on the frontier. Other whites felt threatened by social contact with this other race. Their best chance for survival — racially as well as economically — lay in moving on, further inland. But while the vastness of the North American continent may initially have appeared to make it impervious to racial "mixing," the relentless advance of the slave system proved this view to be erroneous. Indeed, the populating of frontier was a biracial undertaking: from the Virginia fall line to the far banks of the Mississippi, blacks either accompanied or followed whites inexorably, and the animosity between them was renewed with greater intensity at different junctures on this long journey west. For much of the way, white hopes of finding an escape from the complexities of racial coexistence came to naught. Settlement of the West turned out to be not an antidote to the problem of race, but a battleground for its resolution.

This cycle of conflict and flight dates back to colonial days. It originates with the coming of slavery and reverberates down through the centuries to the present day with that institution's deep psychic scars — the contempt of whites for blacks coexisting uneasily with dependence upon the latter's labor, fear of their latent power, and shame for having so brutally dehumanized them. This complex relationship between the two races developed in the Southern colonies of Virginia and Maryland. There, not long after Europeans built their first out-posts in the New World, the enslaving of blacks and the growing of tobacco became inextricably entwined. The consequences of this long-term codependence would prove fateful not only for blacks and their white masters, but also for whites who stood outside the slave system, and whose position in society was gravely endangered by it.

Tobacco was the salvation of those Southern colonies. Initially preoccupied with a futile quest for gold and silver, British settlers at Jamestown had nearly all succumbed to disease or starvation.[1] A severe drought lasting several years and the lack of adequate resupply from England had contributed to making their survival in this New World outpost doubtful. But, gradually, the colonists had learned to support themselves. They no longer had to depend upon food shipped over the Atlantic or obtained by trading with local Native Americans.[2] Overcoming their initial distaste, the settlers started to eat the unfamiliar local diet and learned from the neighboring Algonquian-speaking Powhatan tribe how to grow corn. But simply living off the land was not enough. To justify their continued presence to the Virginia Company of London that had dispatched them to this spot on the banks of the James River, the new arrivals had to find some way of making their colony profitable. Fortuitously, they soon came upon the solution. From the days of the lost Roanoke colony, English settlers in Virginia had known that nearby Indians grew and smoked (on ceremonial occasions) a form of nightshade known as tobacco. Smoking this dried leaf in pipes had recently become tremendously popular throughout most of Europe. It occurred to the colonists that if they could not discover any buried treasure, perhaps they could create some "brown gold" by digging in the soil. In 1614, after two years of experimenting, John Rolfe — an enterprising planter from Norfolk who would also leave his mark in history as the white man who apparently won the heart of the Algonquian princess Pocahontas — determined that the rich Tidewater soils were ideally suited to the large-scale growing of a milder, Spanish form of

---

1. Only 38 of the original 105 Jamestown colonists survived the first nine months in the New World. Most succumbed to famine and diseases such as malaria. (Many of these diseases the English settlers brought with them.) John Steele Gordon, *An Empire of Wealth: The Epic History of American Economic Power* (New York: HarperCollins, 2004), 12. Ignoring instructions from the Virginia Company, the settlers had chosen a marshy location on the James, and this decision made them vulnerable to mosquito-borne maladies as well. David A. Price, *Love & Hate in Jamestown: John Smith, Pocahontas, and the Start of a New Nation* (New York: Vintage, 2003), 48.
2. Thomas B. Abernethy, *Three Virginia Frontiers* (Baton Rouge: Louisiana State University Press, 1940), 7. See also Edmund S. Morgan, *American Slavery/American Freedom: The Ordeal of Colonial Virginia* (New York: W.W. Norton, 1975), 73. Starting in 1614, local Indians provided the Virginia colonists with 1,000 bushels of corn annually in exchange for iron hatchets. R. Douglas Hurt, *Indian Agriculture in America: Prehistory to the Present* (Lawrence: University of Kansas Press, 1987), 39.

tobacco preferred by Europeans but grown (until then) only in the West Indies. This discovery would not only make the Virginia colony prosperous, but also impel regional growth and shape the South's character for hundreds of years to come.[1]

Sir Walter Raleigh had introduced the practice of smoking tobacco to Queen Elizabeth's court, and the English upper classes had quickly adopted it as a sign of their worldly sophistication.[2] They instigated a tobacco buying frenzy. By 1572, there were 7,000 tobacconists operating in London alone, with an annual business amounting to some 300,000 pounds sterling.[3] Merchants were more than eager to grab up whatever good quality leaf they could lay their hands on. They were already importing Spanish tobacco from the Caribbean. The struggling Virginia colonists decided to help meet the growing demand for this crop. By 1615, tobacco plants were sprouting like weeds in the gardens and fields, on the fortifying palisade, and along the walkways of Jamestown. Competition for nearby fertile soil developed after the Virginia Company allowed lands to be privately owned, offering each settler 100 acres.[4] Well-to-do English gentlemen bought up large plantations — some of them over 2,000 acres — along both sides of the James and nearby creeks in the coastal region known as the Tidewater.[5] To reduce the amount of labor required, they first laid claim to land that had already been cleared but was now abandoned by local tribes: the Indians had wisely chosen the most fertile spots for their own farming. Less affluent, yeoman farmers purchased cheaper, inland tracts, and soon the Chesapeake area of Virginia was widely populated. For example, across from Jamestown, in Surry County, some 398 patents were issued between the 1620s and the 1690s. A number of these lands were purchased for purposes of speculation, but most were soon under cultivation.[6]

---

1. For details on the introduction of commercial tobacco, see Thomas J. Wertenbaker, *The Planters of Colonial Virginia* (Princeton: Princeton University Press, 1922), 17, 24.
2. Parke Rouse, Jr., *Planters and Pioneers: Life in Colonial Virginia* (New York: Hastings House, 1968), 20.
3. W.F. Axton, *Tobacco and Kentucky* (Lexington: University of Kentucky Press, 1975), 24.
4. David Hackett Fischer and James C. Kelly, *Bound Away: Virginia and the Westward Movement*, (Charlottesville: University of Virginia Press, 2000), 27. The amount of land granted under a headright was subsequently reduced to 50 acres.
5. John Solomon Otto, *The Southern Frontiers, 1607-1860: The Agricultural Evolution of the Colonial and Antebellum South* (Westport: Greenwood Press, 1989), 18. This led to disparities in landholdings. By 1626, 20 percent of the patents granted (for the largest tracts, encompassing 200 acres or more) accounted for half of all those issued by the Virginia Company. Theodore M. Allen, *The Invention of the White Race* (London: Verso, 1994), vol. 2, 79.
6. Kevin P. Kelly, "'In dispers'd Country Plantations': Settlement Patterns in Seventeenth-Century Surry County, Virginia," in *The Chesapeake in the Seventeenth Century: Essays on Anglo-American Society*, ed. Thad W. Tate and David L. Ammerman (Chapel Hill: University of North Carolina Press, 1979), 184, 190.

Tobacco growing was a labor-intensive, year-round occupation performed almost entirely by hand. Copying the Indians' method of sowing seed in the early spring months, transplanting seedlings during April and May, harvesting and cutting the large, fully grown leaves in the fall, and drying them first in the sun and then hung from rafters in barns, the colonists soon became adept at cultivating the crop.[1] The yield was prodigious. A single farmer could grow about 10,000 plants on a three- to four-acre plot.[2] Abandoning their previous professions and aspirations, colonists of all walks of life became tobacco planters. Despite the misgivings of the Virginia Company about banking exclusively on one crop, this outpost in the New World had found its economic destiny.[3]

In 1615, the first hogsheads of premium Virginia tobacco were rolled on board a sailing vessel headed across the Atlantic to England, where the cured leaf sold for the relatively affordable price of three shillings a pound.[4] Three years later, some 20,000 pounds of colonial tobacco reached the London markets.[5] Buoyed by this new supply, the demand for tobacco continued to soar, and colonial planters decided to enlarge their holdings. But they faced a major challenge: the fledgling Virginia colony had a severe shortage of labor. Nearly half of the first Jamestown settlers were "gentlemen" — six times the percentage to be found back in English society — unaccustomed to working with their hands and disinclined to change their idle, dissipated ways.[6] Thus, almost from the outset, the colonists had to resort to advertising in England for manual workers willing to till their fields and perform household chores. But this labor pool was too small — and too costly[7] — to tackle the more demanding tasks of clearing the largely forested land and planting, cutting, curing, and packing tobacco for export. Soon, Virginia planters hit upon a novel solution. They would recruit unemployed English farmers and laborers, pay their way across the Atlantic, and employ them as indentured servants on their Tidewater estates. Those bonded in

---

1. Otto, *Southern Frontiers*, 11-12. Cf. Axton, *Tobacco and Kentucky*, 28-29.
2. Rouse, *Planters and Pioneers*, 22.
3. James R. Perry, The *Formation of a Society on Virginia's Eastern Shore, 1615-1655* (Chapel Hill: University of North Carolina Press, 1990), 17. The Virginia Company's owners feared that the settlers would neglect subsistence farming by focusing so much on tobacco growing. King James was personally opposed to tobacco and recommended that the colonists grow wine and silkworms instead. Edward T. Price, *Dividing the Land: Early American Beginnings of Our Private Property Mosaic* (Chicago: University of Chicago Press, 1995), 91.
4. Morgan, *American Slavery*, 11. At that time, tobacco from the West Indies was selling at the much higher price of 18 shillings per pound.
5. Axton, *Tobacco and Kentucky*, 25.
6. Early Jamestown settlers wasted their time bowling in the streets and drinking. Anthony S. Parent, Jr., *Foul Means: The Formation of a Slave Society in Virginia, 1660-1740* (Chapel Hill: University of North Carolina Press, 2003), 13.
7. Scarce colonial laborers could command four to five times the wages paid for similar work in England. Wertenbaker, *Planters of Colonial Virginia*, 30.

servitude would work for a period of seven years without wages to make up for the costs of their transatlantic passage, and then be given their freedom.

This happened to be a propitious time to be seeking out such a new work-force. Thanks to decades of relative peace, good health, and prosperity, England's population had been steadily growing, ending a period of stagnation.[1] Unable to support themselves in the countryside at a time when many farms were being sold to sheep graziers, thousands of young persons were now thronging into cities like London, crowding into workhouses and looking for jobs.[2] There was not enough work to go around. Unemployment led to mischief, and urban crime and social disorder began to increase. This state of affairs alarmed law-abiding burghers, and city officials were more than happy to embrace any plan that would take these idle troublemakers off their hands. The idea of packing them off to the New World for a prolonged stay had a decided appeal. Indeed, indentured servitude appeared to solve the problems of all parties concerned — bourgeois English society, its poor, and the colonial planters. It also brought a welcome source of income to the merchants, speculators, ship captains, and others who procured servants and sold them on the other side of the Atlantic.[3] The only ones unhappy with this solution to the colonial labor shortage were the Cavaliers — those loyal to Charles I. They disliked the element of social mobility built into indenture: once servants fulfilled their contracts, they would be given tracts of land and allowed to enter the landowning class. Aristocrats like the Calverts, who ruled over Maryland, wanted a more rigidly hierarchical order to evolve in the colonies.[4]

While indentureship was not practiced in England at that time, this form of labor was not without historical precedent.[5] A bill adopted by Parliament in the 16th century had made bonded servitude legal.[6] Under what circumstances these workers would be brought across the Atlantic did not appear to cause any concern. What mattered was ridding England of a surplus, undesirable population. Thus, in 1618, London officials rounded up 100 vagrant youths barely in their teens, paid for their steerage, and marched them down to the Thames, where

1. By the end of the 17th century, England's population had surpassed four million, having increased nearly 50 percent over the preceding six decades.
2. In some rural areas, as many as 30 percent were unemployed. Wertenbaker, *Planters of Colonial Virginia*, 31.
3. A merchant could purchase a servant for between four and ten pounds in England and then profitably sell this person for 6-30 pounds in the colonies. Abbott Emerson Smith, *Colonists in Bondage: White Servitude and Convict Labor in America, 1606-1776* (Gloucester: Peter Smith, 1965), 39.
4. Alan Kulikoff, *Tobacco and Slaves: The Development of Southern Cultures in the Chesapeake, 1680-1800* (Chapel Hill: University of North Carolina Press, 1986), 31.
5. Morris Talpalar, *The Sociology of Colonial Virginia*, 2nd, rev. ed. (New York: Philosophical Library, 1968), 352-3
6. Allen, Invention of White Race, 20.

they were hustled on board ships as apprentices bound for Virginia. Prostitutes and other social undesirables were also shipped off against their will: working-class women, in fact, made up almost a third of these first indentured servants.[1] Large numbers of imprisoned paupers as well as more dangerous criminals, plucked from the gallows and bound in shackles, joined this forced exodus to the New World, adding to its somewhat unsavory cast.[2] So did many Scotch and Irish prisoners of war — human bounty from England's latest wars. (For instance, of the 1,600 Scots captured by Cromwell's victorious forces at the Battle of Worchester in 1651, at least 150 of them ended up later that year in Virginia.) An odd assortment of individuals drawn from all classes and walks of life was coaxed, tricked, or coerced into signing up. As one historian has summed up, "People of every age and kind were decoyed, deceived, seduced, inveigled, or forcibly kidnapped and carried as servants to the plantations."[3]

Others came out of necessity — Protestants from France, Germany, and Switzerland, as well as Catholics, and Quakers, hounded out of their own countries by religious intolerance. But many more — namely, yeoman English farmers — opted to undertake the voyage to the New World of their own free will. For several years during the 1630s and 1640s they had suffered disastrously poor harvests, and the prospect of a recurrence of these calamities made the distant fields of Virginia a tempting alternative. These impoverished farmers saw this rich, distant land as the key to their future security and prosperity. They thronged to the ports with abandon. As evidence, one historian has found a close correlation between crop failures in England and upswings in the migration of indentured servants to the Southern colonies in the 17th century.[4] Equally attracted to

1. David W. Galenson, *White Servitude in Colonial America: An Economic Analysis* (Cambridge: Cambridge University Press, 1981), 11, 23.
2. The Virginia Company paid five pounds each to import convicts to the colony. Jonathan Hughes and Lewis B. Cain, *American Economic History*, 4th ed. (New York: Harper Collins, 1994), 22. From 1661 to 1700, roughly 4,500 convicts came to the New World. Smith, *Colonists in Bondage*, 96. According to another estimate, no fewer than 10,000 felons were released from the Old Bailey prison for shipment to the American colonies between 1717 and 1775. James Davie Butler, "British Convicts Shipped to American Colonies," *American Historical Review* 2 (Oct. 1896), 14. Thousands of convicts were sent to the colonies as indentured servants under the Transportation Act of 1718. Thomas Jefferson estimated that only about 2,000 criminals ever reached the Virginia coast (see Rouse, *Planters and Pioneers*, 43); but this appears to be a gross undercounting. According to recent estimates, a more likely figure is 60,000.
3. Smith, *Colonists in Bondage*, 3. According to some sources, a majority of the servants who initially crossed the Atlantic did so against their will. See, for example, Talpalar, *Sociology of Colonial Virginia*, 362. However, other scholars contend this was not the case. See James Horn, "Servant Emigration to the Chesapeake in the Seventeenth Century," in *The Chesapeake in the Seventeenth Century*, 65, passim. See also Wertenbaker, *Planters of Colonial Virginia*, 33.
4. Wesley Frank Craven, *White, Red, and Black: The Seventeenth-Century Virginian* (Charlottesville: University of Virginia Press, 1971), 22.

America were unskilled male workers, who, together with farmers, made up the preponderance of emigrating servants.[1] Agreeing to sail to the colonies was their ticket out of poverty. The chance to own land after serving a term of four or five years gave these poor laborers a compelling reason to sign a contract. Unfortunately, all too often, the grandiose promises turned out to have been exaggerated, but by the time this became obvious it was too late for the disappointed and frustrated migrants to change their minds.[2] For most, their fate was sealed when they walked up the gangplank.

The demand for helping hands in Virginia's steamy, sun-drenched tobacco fields was so great that all newcomers were welcome. What mattered to the planters was harvesting a good crop. During these years of rapid economic expansion, planters who did not add to their holdings and secure a greater share of the tobacco trade were quickly outstripped by those who did. Additional workers made such expansion possible. Hence, most indentured servants arriving without contracts were auctioned off to the highest bidder as soon as they set foot on dry land, assuring those who had paid their way a solid return on their investment. (In the mid-1600s, it cost three pounds sterling to recruit and transport a servant across the Atlantic.[3]) Tobacco growers had another incentive for importing servants: starting in 1618, colonists received a headright grant of 50 additional acres for every person whose transatlantic passage they had purchased.[4]

In short order, the trickle of indentured servants across the Atlantic turned into a tidal wave. The colonists' appetite for hired help was insatiable, bespeaking their desire for higher social status as much as for field hands. Luckily for them, the supply was just as limitless. In 1625, there were only 464 white servants in all of Virginia but that number rose to 6,000 by 1671.[5] For most of the 17th century, an estimated 1,500-2,000 bonded individuals reached Virginia's shores annually.[6]

1. This view is held by most recent historians. See Horn, *Servant Migration*, 57. See also Kenneth Morgan, *Slavery and Servitude in North America, 1607-1800* (Edinburgh: Edinburgh University Press, 2000), 19. Cf. Galenson, *White Servitude*, 49. The agricultural background of many indentured servants is suggested by their largely rural origins. See "Places of Origin of Chesapeake Indentured Servants," Fischer and Kelly, *Bound Away*, 48.
2. T. H. Breen and Stephen Innes, "*Myne Owne Ground*": *Race and Freedom on Virginia's Eastern Shore, 1640-1676* (New York: Oxford University Press, 1980), 60. The authors assert, however, that a majority of indentured servants did come willingly.
3. Ulrich B. Phillips, *Life and Labor in the Old South* (Boston: Little, Brown, 1951), 23. Another source says the transatlantic passage alone cost at least six pounds. Wertenbaker, *Planters of Colonial Virginia*, 32.
4. Otto, *Southern Frontiers*, 17.
5. Philip A. Bruce, *Economic History of Virginia in the Seventeenth Century: An Inquiry into the Material Condition of the People, Based on Original and Contemporaneous Records* (New York: Macmillan, 1896), vol. 1, 572.
6. Wertenbaker, *Planters of Colonial Virginia*, 35. One register of immigration shows that 5,000 servants came to Virginia between 1654 and 1678. David Hackett Fischer, *Albion's Seed: Four British Folkways in America* (New York: Oxford University Press, 1989), 227.

(Other tallies put the total number of indentured servants arriving in the Chesapeake colony from 1630 to 1680 at between 39,000 and 56,000 — that is, one half to three-quarters of the overall white immigration.[1]) Even though a large percentage of newly arrived servants succumbed to mosquito-borne malaria, typhoid fever, and other diseases,[2] the ratio of servants to masters steadily increased. But ownership was highly concentrated: just ten landowners owned half of the bonded servants.[3] By 1625, the wealthiest planters maintained household and field staffs numbering between 10 and 39 persons.[4] Most small farmers — including former servants — had to get by without such help.

Having so much cheap labor available to respond to their every whim made life in Virginia almost idyllic for its landed gentry. On the shores of this vast, bountiful continent, thousands of miles from home, they could replicate the idle, carefree existence their forebears had enjoyed for centuries on English country estates. At the same time, the presence of so many poor and uneducated servants radically changed the colony's demographics. Moving away from its middle-class, egalitarian origins under the early leadership of John Smith, son of a Lincolnshire tenant farmer,[5] the colony was transformed into a highly stratified society with a few powerful, well-connected families at the top, a large group of yeoman farmers and landless freemen in the middle, and an even larger servant class occupying the bottom.[6] Indeed, during the long reign of Charles I (1625-1649), Tidewater Virginia came to resemble nothing so much as a feudal fiefdom. This vertical social structure sustained attitudes, lifestyles, and patterns of behavior that would make the colony receptive to an even more hierarchical arrangement in the years ahead.

---

1. Kulikoff, *Tobacco and Slaves*, 32. Cf. Galenson, *White Servitude*, 4. The latter cites two different historians who put the proportion of servants arriving after 1630 at between half and two-thirds of the total white immigration, respectively. Other scholars content that four of every five colonists arriving in Virginia and Maryland were indentured servants. See, for example, Douglas J. Deal, *Race and Class in Colonial Virginia: Indians, Englishmen, and Africans on the Eastern Shore During the Seventeenth Century* (New York: Garland Publishing, 1993), 87.
2. At one point, the mortality rate among servants along the James reached 75 percent. Wertenbaker, *Planters of Colonial Virginia*, 39.
3. Fischer and Kelly, *Bound Away*, 28.
4. Morgan, *American Slavery*, 119.
5. Smith, who took over leadership of the Jamestown colony in 1608, had demanded that all colonists perform manual labor in order to stave off starvation, thus creating resentment among the resident gentry.
6. Only about one in 15 planters owned 1,000 acres or more. See Pierre Marambaud, *William Byrd of Westover, 1674-1744* (Charlottesville: University of Virginia Press, 1971), 5. An incomplete list of land titles from 1625 shows that 182 of 198 were for properties of 1,000 acres or less. Price, *Dividing the Land*, 96. According to Wertenbaker, *Planters of Colonial Virginia*, 54, 90 percent of Virginia planters in the 17th century were yeoman farmers. Cf. T.H. Breen, *Tobacco Culture: The Mentality of the Great Tidewater Planters on the Eve of the Revolution* (Princeton: Princeton University Press, 1985), 32.

Whatever its social consequences, the massive infusion of labor enabled the Tidewater plantations to expand — and prosper. This was essential because tobacco was literally a "growth industry." Because the English settlers had adopted the Indians' labor-saving method of planting tobacco for three or four years, seeding corn or another crop for a couple more, and then abandoning the land[1] (instead of replenishing the soil with manure), they constantly had to seek out new holdings with high quality loam further up Virginia's coastal rivers — the Rappahannock, York, Roanoke, and Potomac, as well as the James.[2] Those planters with the most wealth, social stature, and political clout grabbed up the choice locales, near navigable waterways, and they grew the most tobacco, sold the most hogsheads, and cemented their position as members of the colony's ruling elite. But during the early decades of settlement, there was enough available cultivable land so that all could thrive.

As early as 1627, planters managed to sell 500,000 pounds of tobacco in Europe.[3] Fifty years later, the amount shipped in bulky hogsheads (each weighing half a ton) had multiplied 50 times to 24 million pounds.[4] In good years, planters could sell their tobacco for about three pence per pound.[5] This meant that even a small farmer, growing between 1,000 and 2,000 pounds of tobacco in a season, could earn enough to stay in business. Indentured servants — released from their contracts with grants of 100 acres (including a house built for them on that tract), a year's allotment of grain, some clothing, and a musket — could rise to the ranks of landowners.[6] Approximately one third of the servants who survived to the end of their contracts made this transition to economic independence. They swelled the class of yeoman farmers, which, in terms of sheer numbers if not wealth, dominated the colony's economy. The fact that the average land grant during the second half of 17th century was for only 674 acres suggests the extent of their impact.[7] As Virginia grew wealthy, both small farmers and large planters reaped its rewards.

But the good times did not last. Instead, a sequence of unfavorable events nearly brought about an economic collapse. Around 1630, the local price for

---

1. Land used for growing tobacco and other crops was usually left to lie fallow for 20 years. See Kulikoff, *Tobacco and Slaves*, 47.
2. Overseers of the plantations received more compensation if they cultivated additional land, so this arrangement also encouraged the tilling of new lands, rather than fertilizing of old ones. See Bruce, *Economic History*, vol. 1, 429-30.
3. Wertenbaker, *Planters of Colonial Virginia*, 25.
4. Axton, *Tobacco and Kentucky*, 25. According to another source, the amount exported from Virginia in the 1670s was 15 million pounds. See Otto, *Southern Frontiers*, 17.
5. Bruce, *Economic History*, vol. 1, 354.
6. Philip A. Bruce, *Economic History of Virginia in the Seventeenth Century* (New York: Macmillan, 1896), vol. 2, 41. However, a servant would lose this entitlement if he had attempted to escape or otherwise violated the terms of his contract.
7. Wertenbaker, *Planters of Colonial Virginia*, 47, 80.

tobacco plummeted from a third of a shilling per pound to less than a penny, largely due to a worldwide glut.[1] Depressed and uncertain prices would persist for much of the next three decades, causing Virginia farmers to switch from growing tobacco almost exclusively to cultivating other crops such as corn and wheat, as well as raising livestock. Planters with the largest holdings managed to make this agricultural transition successfully (even increasing their acreage by outright purchase or through headright or indentures) and maintain their status in the colony during this period of stagnation, but smaller farmers fared less well. With diminishing income, they could ill afford to import indentured servants to replace those whose contracts had expired or who had died from disease. Without such bonded help, these yeoman farmers could not grow enough on their lands to make ends meet. In order to support their families, they had to go deeply into debt and still only managed to eke out a subsistence-level existence.

Under these adverse conditions, the gulf between small and large planters widened. The Virginia colony became even more socially and economically stratified, with land, power, and other assets being consolidated in fewer hands. An elite of several hundred landowners soon consolidated their control over the Tidewater. Between 1626 and 1704, the proportion of privately owned property that was encompassed in estates of 1,000 or more acres rose from 10.2 to 40.1 percent.[2] This trend was accelerated by the actions of the colonial governor, Sir William Berkeley. In an effort to keep Virginia's social system more in line with his Royalist sentiments, Berkeley encouraged his fellow Cavaliers to migrate to the colony in the 1650s, after Oliver Cromwell came to power and hostility toward supporters of the monarchy intensified.[3] (Berkeley himself was removed from office at that time, but was allowed to remain in Virginia.) Almost all the newcomers during his 35-year tenure as governor were Royalists, and they constituted the colony's upper echelon. After Berkeley regained his post, following the Restoration in 1660, he allocated the most fertile tracts of lands to settlers of his own social class and forced small planters out.[4]

The burden of these hard times during the 1640s and 1650s fell inordinately on former indentured servants trying to rise in the social order and establish themselves as free landowners. These once-bonded laborers faced a steep uphill

---

1. *Ibid.*, 134. Records of tobacco prices show that a sharp decline actually started in the 1620s. See Russell R. Menard, "The Tobacco Industry in the Chesapeake Colonies, 1617-1730: An Interpretation," in *Research in Economic History*, ed. Paul Uselding (Greenwich: JAI Press, 1980), vol. 5, 113.
2. Allen, *Invention of White Race*, 167. During the same period, the percentage of estates of 100 acres or less declined from 24.9 to 4.9.
3. Berkeley recruited mainly the younger sons of well-to-do landed families. Fischer, *Albion's Seed*, 214.
4. Fischer and Kelly, *Bound Away*, 35, 47.

struggle. Many of them ended up after a year or so sliding back down out of the landowning class into tenancy.[1] In fact, after 1660, only about five percent of former servants succeeded in lifting themselves up into the landowning ranks.[2] They simply lacked the resources and the wherewithal to gain a foothold in an increasingly competitive colonial economy. Virginia's stratified society became even more so: it is estimated that between 60 and 70 percent of all males in the colony owned no land, getting by as tenant farmers, laborers, or servants.[3] Even though some 2.75 million additional acres were made available for purchase between 1650 and 1675, few recently freed servants were in a position to take advantage of the opportunity. Furthermore, after Charles II assumed the throne in 1660, opportunities for upward social mobility were more limited. The newly crowned king promptly reduced the power of Parliament and reinstated many Royalist prerogatives. In the colonies, authorities reinforced class lines by lengthening the term of indenture for all servants and doubling it as punishment for those who ran away or indulged in illicit sexual relations.[4]

Life for indentured servants in the 17th century was harsh enough without these additional penalties and restrictions. First of all, they had to survive an often stormy and unhealthy passage across the Atlantic, which lasted between eight and ten weeks.[5] Then, once on Virginia soil, they had to endure the ravages of disease, poor food, and long hours in the fields, as well as the harsh and often brutal treatment meted out by their owners.[6] (Servants had the right to petition county courts with complaints over beatings and other abuse they had suffered, but few of them were sufficiently well informed or educated to take advantage of this right.[7]) Overcome by the harsh environment, as many as half of the servants arriving in a given year did not live to see the end of their terms.[8] Those who had emigrated freely from England were dismayed to find conditions worse in North America than what they had known back home. A large percentage ended up deserting their owners and running off into the interior, despite the ever-lurking

1.According to one estimate, in nearby Maryland only about half of former servants succeeded in becoming landowners. Deal, *Race and Class*, 94. Other records show that, during the years 1670-80, of the 5,000 servants who came to Maryland, only 1,249 secured 50 acres as "freedom dues." Smith, *Colonists in Bondage*, 299. Smith estimates that no more than seven percent of New World servants ever exercised their right to own land.
2. Wertenbaker, *Planters of Colonial Virginia*, 98.
3. Fischer, *Albion's Seed*, 374.
4. See, for example, Bruce, *Economic History*, vol. 2, 23. Whipping captured servants at the post was also a frequent way of punishing them.
5. Approximately 10-15 percent of servants died en route to the New World. Smith, *Colonists in Bondage*, 118.
6. Morgan, *American Slavery*, 127. Cf. T.H. Breen, "A Changing Labor Force and Race Relations in Virginia, 1660-1710," *Journal of Social History* 7 (1973), reprinted in *Colonial Southern Slavery*, ed. Paul Finkelman (New York: Garland, 1989), 16.
7. Breen and Innes, *"Myne Owne Ground,"* 62.
8. Talpalar, *Sociology of Colonial Virginia*, 375.

danger of Indian attacks.[1] Many who did manage to complete their contracts left the colony afterwards, thoroughly disenchanted with the New World.[2] Coping with all these hardships required toughness and self-reliance. Poor whites — the overwhelming majority of colonial Virginia's population — learned a stern code of survival: each person had to look out for himself and depend upon no one else. Occupying the bottom rung of society created an enduring sense of exploitation and vulnerability. It also engendered resentment — anger at the frustrating of their dreams for a better life and at the inequitable social and economic system that held them back. White servants were driven by an overriding desire to escape this precarious and demeaning position — to claw their way upward by scrambling over the backs of others to achieve their goal of becoming independent yeoman farmers.

The grim reports about colonial life that filtered back across the Atlantic made would-be servants less eager to sign contracts of indenture. Partially as a result of this, the number of applicants declined during the mid-17th century. However, of more importance in stemming the migration of servants to the Chesapeake were several developments in England that reduced the supply of available labor. The first was a recurrent outbreak of plague. In 1625, a virulent, uncontrollable epidemic killed over 40,000 persons, and 40 years later, it returned with an even greater vengeance. This time, the plague claimed at least 70,000 victims, reaching its height in the summer of 1665, when more than 7,000 Londoners died within the space of a single week.[3] This fearful loss of life had scarcely come to an end when the city of London was struck by another great tragedy. A fire that started in a baker's shop near the Thames on the night of September 2, 1666, burned out of control for five days, blown across the tinder-dry city by gale-force winds. When the flames finally died out, four-fifths of medieval London lay in ashes, including some 13,000 houses, nearly 90 churches, and historic treasures such as St. Paul's Cathedral.[4] The diarist Samuel Pepys declared the view from the top of a surviving church tower "the saddest sight of desolation that I ever saw."[5] The Great Fire necessitated a massive reconstruction effort during the 1670s, entailing the construction of some 8,000 homes in

---

1. Large numbers of servants ran off when tobacco prices fell, during the late 1660s. See Deal, *Race and Class*, 51. For more details on the hardships faced by these servants, see John Van der Zee, *Bound Over: Indentured Servitude and American Conscience* (New York: Simon & Schuster, 1985), 29-51.
2. Kulikoff, *Tobacco and Slaves*, 39.
3. Another estimate puts the total loss of life in London alone at 100,000. Leonard W. Cowie, *Plague and Fire: London 1665-66* (New York: G.P. Putnam's Sons, 1970), 56.
4. For more details on the Great Fire, see *The City Remembrancer: Being Historical Narratives of the Great Plague, at London, 1665; Great Fire, 1666; and Great Storm, 1703* (London: W. Nicoll, 1769), vol. 2, and Stephen Porter, *The Great Fire of London* (London: Sutton, 1996).
5. Quoted in Porter, *Great Fire*, 53.

addition to several dozen public buildings. This metamorphosis of London into a thoroughly modern city, with structures made of brick and tile replacing flammable wooden ones, kept skilled craftsmen and laborers busy for many years. (Other employment in England was provided by the burgeoning wool industry.[1] By 1660, wool accounted for two-thirds of the country's exports.) To attract workers, wages started to rise in the 1680s. These factors, coupled with a falling birth rate after 1650, effectively did away with England's unemployment problem and the concomitant need to go abroad to find jobs.[2] And, on top of this, persons who still wanted to emigrate to the New World now had other, more attractive destinations to ponder — including the Caribbean, where the term of service was shorter, and the recently created colonies of Pennsylvania and the Carolinas.[3]

The net result was a shortage of persons willing to become indentured servants in the Tidewater.[4] This created a dilemma for Virginia's planters. Having largely depleted nearby alluvial soils over the past several decades, they badly needed to push further up the coastal estuaries where they could find sufficient virgin soil to grow enough tobacco so that they could continue making a good return on their investments.[5] Now, in a time of lower tobacco prices and rising costs for imported goods, their vast commercial enterprise was imperiled.[6] Charles II added to the planters' economic woes by requiring them to sell all of their tobacco first in England (or another British colony), under the Navigation Acts of 1660 and 1663, and then imposing a levy of a half a penny per pound on these imports. These additional revenues pushed many small planters to the brink of bankruptcy.[7] At the same time, war with the Dutch restricted foreign trade, leading to overproduction. Surplus tobacco piled up in London and Bristol

---

1. Abernethy, *Three Virginia Frontiers*, 30. England's wars with the Dutch and Spanish during the 1650s also discouraged many would-be servants from migrating. See Menard, "From Servants to Slaves," 379.
2. Menard, "Tobacco Industry," 121. England's population declined by about 400,000 between 1656 and 1686.
3. Russell Menard, "British Migration to the Chesapeake Colonies in the Seventeenth Century" in *Colonial Chesapeake Society*, ed. Lois G. Carr, Philip D. Morgan, and Jean B. Russo (Chapel Hill: University of North Carolina Press, 1988), 110-14.
4. For a recent discussion of the various reasons why fewer indentured servants came to Virginia in the late 17th century, see Parent, *Foul Means*, 56-8. In neighboring Maryland, the number of arriving servants decreased sharply in the late 1670s. See Menard, "From Servants to Slaves," Fig. 1, "Pattern of Immigration from Maryland Headright Entries, 1634-1681," 364.
5. It was believed that good-quality tobacco could only be grown on previously untilled soil. Depleted tobacco fields were often allowed to lie fallow for up to 20 years.
6. Tobacco prices in Maryland reached a low of less than one pence per pound in 1666. Series Z 583-584, "Farm Prices of Maryland Tobacco, 1659 to 1710, and Chesapeake Tobacco, 1618 to 1658," *Historical Statistics of the United States: Colonial Times to 1790* (Washington: U.S. Bureau of the Census, 1975), part 2, 1198.
7. A small planter who grew approximately 1,200 pounds of tobacco in 1667 was left with earnings of only 50 shillings after having paid all his taxes. See Breen, "Changing Labor Force," 18.

warehouses, driving prices further down.[1] Under these worsening conditions, only the wealthiest could afford to pay the higher cost of increasingly hard-to-find servants. Unless the plantation owners could find a new source of cheap workers, fields would go uncultivated, tobacco would go unharvested, and profits would evaporate. But who would rescue them from this impending disaster?

The colonists had already made some attempts to employ neighboring Powhatan Indians. In the early years, a small number of them had worked as household domestics, hunted for the Europeans, or labored in their fields. But white wariness toward this native people kept the number of such servants low. The Powhatans had demonstrated their hostility by rising up against the colonists on March 22, 1622, killing 400 men and women, or a third of Jamestown's inhabitants. Since the colonists were greatly outnumbered by the Indians and lacked the military force to conquer them, they adopted a defensive strategy of keeping the Powhatans at a safe distance. Moreover, the Virginia Company expressly prohibited enslaving these "heathens" out of hopes of baptizing them.[2] But renewed violence would cause a change in this policy. In April 1644, after a bloody uprising that led to the deaths of as many as 500 settlers, Indians taken as prisoner were sold into slavery, although most of them left Virginia.[3] And, after another attack on the western frontier in 1676, enslavement was made legal within the colony itself. In addition, some men from local tribes were hired to work on the tobacco plantations. But these efforts to utilize Native American labor largely failed. Indian males considered farming to be women's work and displayed little willingness to plant or harvest the crop. This recalcitrant attitude, coupled with their demonstrated "untrustworthiness" and refusal to convert to Christianity, made the Indians appear inassimilable. Hence, their presence in the colony was undesirable, and their rapid removal from the Tidewater inevitable.[4] In short, with the coming of tobacco, "the doom of the Powhatans was sealed."[5]

Thus, in the late 1660s, Virginia planters saw only one feasible solution to their labor shortage: import black slaves. Introducing chattel seemed as good a

---

1. Alf J. Mapp, Jr., *The Virginia Experiment: The Old Dominion's Role in the Making of America, 1607-1781*, 3rd ed. (New York: Hamilton Press, 1987), 138.
2. This policy did not change until 1676, in the wake of renewed attacks by Indians.
3. After 1660, the Virginia Assembly ruled that Indians could only be sold as servants. Previously, some Indians had worked as slaves in English households despite an official ban on this practice. Deal, *Race and Class*, 51.
4. By 1670, virtually no Indians remained in the Virginia lowland.
5. Helen C. Rountree and E. Randolph Turner III, "On the Fringe of the Southeast: The Powhatan Paramount Chiefdom in Virginia," in *The Forgotten Centuries: Indians and Europeans in the American South, 1521-1704*, ed. Charles Hudson and Carmen Chaves Tesser (Athens: University of Georgia Press, 1974), 366. After 1667, many other Indians died from smallpox.

way to meet their need for cheap workers as shipping over indentured servants had earlier in the century. A number of reasons made bringing in blacks as slaves a logical decision. For one thing, slavery was already a well-established and accepted practice in the New World. The first slaves had been brought to Latin America by Spanish and Portuguese colonists, after indigenous peoples had proven to be physically incapable of carrying out the exhausting work demanded of them and nearly died out as a result. By the 17th century, slaves could be found as far afield as Brazil and New Amsterdam. European settlers in the Southern colonies had seen the economic advantages of slave labor when they traveled to places where the system had already taken hold.[1] Blacks also seemed ideally suited to working in Virginia's tobacco fields: they tolerated the hot climate and long working hours well. They were also considered docile and submissive to their white masters. But, perhaps most important, black slaves cost less to keep than any other workers and thus offered planters the best hope for remaining solvent when hard times returned.

Blacks were not unknown in the Tidewater. The first ones — some 20 in number — had arrived without fanfare or even prior notice in August 1619, on board a Dutch man-of-war which docked at Point Comfort, near the mouth of the York River. Those blacks were sold by its captain as bonded servants to local planters in exchange for badly needed food and other supplies. This human cargo had most likely been abducted from an island in the Caribbean.[2] At first, the English colonists found little use for slaves, and only two more of them entered the colony over the next five years. Other blacks were subsequently hired as servants "for life" — and, incidentally, were treated no worse than their white counterparts. In fact, servants of both races faced equally harsh working conditions. A small number of these blacks continued to live and work in the colony as freemen after having been emancipated by their owners. Many of their offspring remained, as well. Planters had reluctantly come to accept the presence of blacks as a necessary evil, part of a servile labor system they had come to depend upon. Furthermore, in stratified Southern society, servants and slaves were a widely acknowledged indicator of wealth and power. Yeoman farmers with growing incomes aspired to employ such workers in their fields and households as a way of moving up a notch on the social ladder. Ultimately, the race of these underlings mattered less than the status they bestowed upon their owners. As workers, the planters tended to regard black and white field hands as interchangeable inferiors. Furthermore, the exploitation of these workers helped psychologically condition wealthy landowners for the introduction of an even more oppressive

---

1. Winthrop D. Jordan, *White Over Black: American Attitudes toward the Negro, 1550-1812* (Chapel Hill: University of North Carolina Press, 1968), 56.
2. Deal, *Race and Class*, 163.

system of labor. When the supply of white servants began to dry up, Virginia planters had little hesitation about enslaving blacks in their stead.[1]

Moral considerations did not enter into the planters' thinking. The decision about whether or not to employ slaves was dictated largely by economics. This was also the case throughout much of the New World. For example, in New England, farmers tilled small, self-sustaining plots of land and could neither afford nor use slave labor. A few wealthy settlers in the Northern colonies did own slaves during the 17th century, but mostly as household servants. And the predominance of Puritan values stressing independence and hard work further discouraged the importing of chattel labor.[2] The situation in the South was quite different. Commercial agriculture as practiced on sprawling tobacco plantations required a much larger workforce. Farming on this scale could only be made profitable by paying workers little or nothing.

While the English had not kept slaves for centuries, they were by no means adverse to the buying and selling of other human beings.[3] Since the second half of the 16th century, British ships had vied with Spanish ones to supply slaves to the South America colonies. This had been a highly lucrative enterprise. Involvement in the slave trade also familiarized at least some sectors of the English public with the practice of slavery and gave it a stamp of legitimacy. Consequently, most had come to think of slavery as a normal condition for black people. Prevailing racial attitudes backed up this practice: blacks were widely regarded as a subhuman species — a form of savage not worthy of human dignity or respect. Their very color marked them as inferior and set them apart. In the eyes of a typical Englishman of the Elizabethan age, "white" was identified with purity and innocence, whereas "black" connoted ugliness and sin.[4] Black skin was a mark of Cain, a curse placed by God upon the African people for ancient transgressions unknown but unmistakable. Their lowly stature in the Great Chain of Being justified both ostracism and oppression on the part of whites: the sons and daughters of Ham deserved no better fate. They certainly did not merit the fruits of their own labor.[5] That belonged properly — and solely — to their white masters. Because of these pre-existing prejudicial assumptions, colonists in Virginia could readily justify their introduction of slavery.

---

1. Russell Menard makes a strong case for the dwindling supply of white servants being the chief cause of a transition to slave labor in the Virginia colony. He notes that the decline in available servants preceded the mass importing of slaves by a decade or more. See Menard, "From Servants to Slaves," 368.
2. Puritan theology also opposed slavery. See Jordan, *White Over Black*, 69-70.
3. There had been slaves in Mercia, Wessex, and Sussex during the early Middle Ages. Fischer, *Albion's Seed*, 241.
4. Winthrop D. Jordan, *The White Man's Burden: Historical Origins of Racism in the United States* (New York: Oxford University Press, 1974), 8.
5. Bruce, *Economic History*, vol. 2, 65.

There was another reason why Chesapeake landowners were willing to employ black slaves. In recent years, white servants had caused their owners considerable trouble. Many had escaped from the plantations and had to be hunted down or else replaced by new recruits from England. (And, in general, the chronic need to hire more servants when contracts expired made indenture an expensive practice.) Those servants with a rebellious and criminal past were wont to break the rules, cause mischief, and challenge the colony's rigid social order. By contrast, slaves were thought to be reliable and hard-working field hands.[1] Generally, this tendency of white servants to challenge authority was confined to the local level and thus did not cause a great deal of concern. However, in 1676, Virginia's planters faced a more severe threat. By then, the search for affordable land had brought a number of former servants some 100 miles inland from Jamestown, well beyond the protection of colonial forts, where they staked out claims, planted tobacco, hunted, and traded with Indians to make a living. But the Tidewater grandees coveted this virgin territory for themselves, and tensions between the two white classes mounted. These erupted into open conflict in the aftermath of an Indian attack, which left one settler dead. A band of Virginia colonists set off in hot pursuit of the responsible Doeg warriors, but then, after crossing the border into Maryland, killed members of another tribe by mistake. This massacre triggered a series of violent clashes on the frontier. Local landowners appealed to the colonial governor, Berkeley, for help, but he declined, being anxious to restore both peace and good trading relations without having to fire a shot. Outraged by this inaction, a 29-year-old, newly arrived gentleman planter named Nathaniel Bacon (whose overseer was one of the settlers slain) assembled an army of 300 men and led them off into the hinterlands to seek revenge.

In the capital of Jamestown, Bacon's audacity was considered an act of insubordination against colonial authorities. Berkeley — who happened to be a second cousin of Bacon's — issued a proclamation ordering the rebel commander to return at once. When Bacon eventually did come back to Jamestown, after defeating the warring Indians, he was seized and brought before the governor and the colony's Council. After admitting his crime of disobedience on bended knee, he was pardoned. But then, fearing that he would be arrested again, Bacon fled into the countryside and regrouped his forces. For them, the issue now was more than fighting Indians. This was a struggle between the haves and the have-nots — a foreshadowing of the American Revolution. Berkeley's rule of the colony was widely regarded as corrupt, riddled with cronyism. Instead of providing

---

1. Timothy James Lockley, *Lines in the Sand: Race and Class in Lowcountry Georgia, 1750-1860* (Athens: University of Georgia Press, 2001), 18.

security against Indian raids, the governor was constantly raising taxes, including a head tax of 60 pounds of tobacco per poll, and slipping much of these monies into his own pockets.[1] These taxes were crippling for many small planters, eating up as much as half of their yearly income. Some of those in New Kent County had already taken the provocative step of refusing to pay the new levies.[2] Backcountry farmers were also angry that the planter elite had grabbed up most of the good tobacco-growing tracts and driven up land prices.[3] Furthermore, the colonists had no say in choosing their rulers — Berkeley had not called elections since he had resumed power fifteen years before — and thus no way to express their unhappiness with the situation. On a personal level, yeoman farmers resented the governor's great wealth and lavish lifestyle, which was sustained by an annual income of 1,400 pounds sterling.[4]

On June 23, 1676, Bacon led a rowdy throng of 400 farmers, laborers, and backwoodsmen through the streets of Jamestown, forcing Berkeley to flee, and taking control of the capital. (When governor and rebel leader met, a crowd voiced its sentiments with shouts of "No levies!"[5]) The rebel band looted much of the town and nearby arsenals, and Bacon declared a state of civil war, demanding numerous financial and political reforms, including the restoration of voting rights to landless colonists. This uprising lasted until that September, when Berkeley returned from the Eastern Shore (where he had ignominiously fled) accompanied by a small fleet of six warships, bristling with British soldiers and local mercenaries. Realizing he could not hold out against such a seaborne force, Bacon hastily beat a retreat inland after setting fire to Berkeley's five houses and other buildings belonging to the colony's aristocrats, but he was soon captured. He died shortly thereafter, of dysentery, and the rebellion collapsed. Some 23 of his followers were hanged without trial, and the property of many more was confiscated.[6]

This somewhat murky incident, known thereafter as Bacon's Rebellion, lay down a direct challenge to Virginia's ruling elite. For several years afterwards, up

---

1. Some 5,000 of the approximately 7,000 pounds collected ended up in Berkeley's hands. Stephen Saunders Webb, *The End of American Independence* (Cambridge: Harvard University Press, 1985), 18.
2. Mapp, *Virginia Experiment*, 145.
3. Parent, *Foul Means*, 39. This was one of the findings of the royal commission that investigated Bacon's revolt.
4. Mapp, *Virginia Experiment*, 140.
5. *Ibid.*, 159.
6. For more details of Bacon's rebellion, see Webb, *End of American Independence*, 3-83; *Narratives of the Insurrections, 1675-1690*, ed. Charles M. Andrews (New York: Charles Scribner's Sons, 1915), 11-33; Nathaniel Bacon, *Bacon's Declaration in the Name of the People* (30 July 1676), Project Gutenberg (Champaign, Ill.): *emedia.netlibrary.com/reader.asp?product_id=1028100*; T.H. Breen, "Changing Labor Force," 15-23; Abernethy, *Three Virginia Frontiers*, 25; and Morgan, *American Slavery*, 262-69

until 1682, violent unrest flared up throughout the colony and in neighboring Maryland and the Carolinas as a "giddy multitude" of recently released servants, other freemen, and small planters protested policies that only served the interests of the well connected and the well to do.[1] This continuing disorder threatened to overturn the colonial power structure. Virginia's planter elite now looked at their white indentured servants with growing suspicion and apprehension. They quickly tightened policies governing the entry of servants into the colony. Starting in the 1680s, Jamestown authorities required all persons intending to emigrate from England to possess signed contracts, thus weeding out those unwilling "spirits" who often turned into troublemakers once they reached the colony.[2] This more restrictive policy left well-off colonists in even greater need of an alternative labor force.

Thus, without weighing the full implications of their momentous decision, Tidewater planters elected to solve their short-term labor problem by creating an enduring racial one.[3] In the coming decades, that decision would fundamentally alter the nature of colonial society, turning a white, class-based hierarchy into one defined by race and sustained by black subjugation. This change would, in turn, undermine the status of poor, non-slaveholding white farmers and force thousands who could not compete with slave labor to move to the backcountry and build new homesteads on that frontier.

***

Given the choice, wealthy Chesapeake tobacco growers would probably have preferred white workers to black workers — well-established class distinctions delineated them from the former, whereas the presence of an alien race in their midst was disconcerting. But economic realities had forced a reassessment of this attitude. The requirements of tobacco production also induced a fundamental change in the relationship between blacks and whites in colonial Virginia. As the number of slaves — mostly males — imported from the Caribbean increased, discomfort with having blacks in the colony increased as a consequence. The ruling Cavaliers were already concerned about white servants crossing class lines and disrupting the highly stratified social order. But the potential impact of black bondsmen on the status quo in Virginia was far more serious — and more dreaded. Blacks were generally considered "primitives," outside the civilized world. Any extensive contact between the two races was thus

---

1. Breen, "Changing Labor Force," 16.
2. *Ibid.*, 26. Convicts were barred from emigrating to Virginia and Maryland after 1713. Smith, *Colonists in Bondage*, 110.
3. Planters were worried that slaves would overproduce tobacco and thus drive prices down. See Marambaud, *William Byrd*, 170.

unthinkable. Having a few blacks employed in the fields or as household servants — or even taking one as a mistress — might be tacitly accepted, but if thousands were brought into the colony, how could white society protect itself against being overwhelmed? Concentrated in large numbers, slaves might rise up against their masters. Blacks might also join forces with indentured white servants to overthrow the colonial regime. Previously, white servants — who were relatively free of racial prejudice — had formed friendships with free blacks working in the same fields or households, and black and white servants had frequently run away together from their masters.[1] Even more alarming, blacks and poor whites had colluded during Bacon's uprising. Emancipated blacks, black servants, and as many as one in ten Virginia slaves had joined his ragtag army and, in the final showdown with Berkeley's forces, 80 of the 100 final holdouts had been blacks.[2] The prospect of downtrodden whites and blacks aligning against them in the future was more than the colonial elite could countenance. Some historians have suggested it was fear of this eventuality that prompted greater repression of Virginia's slaves in the coming decades.[3] Governor Berkeley and his successors would seek to drive a wedge between poor whites and poor blacks by devaluing the latter and building racial solidarity among whites of all classes.[4] To preserve white control and security, black servitude evolved into slavery, and many of the limited rights previously enjoyed by Virginia's blacks were taken away. In the 1640s, planters began to refer to their black workers as "slaves" and to treat them accordingly.[5]

By 1650, the black population had reached 500.[6] By the early 1660s, a number of other ships arriving from the West Indies had deposited their human cargoes of naked, frightened, ebony-skinned captives at wharves on the James and other Tidewater rivers, and slaves were working in scattered groups in the surrounding tobacco fields. Ten years later, the colony's black population had swelled to 2,000, although these numbers were still relatively small in compari-

---

1. Breen and Innes, *"Myne Own Ground,"* 28, 35.
2. Webb, *End of American Independence*, 6.
3. The most recent to do so is Thomas Allen, in his polemical two-volume study, *The Invention of the White Race*. He argues that Bacon's uprising led the planters to divide black and white workers and that because "'race' consciousness superseded class consciousness . . . the continental plantation bourgeoisie was able to achieve and maintain the degree of social control necessary for proceeding with capital accumulation on the basis of chattel bond-labor." Allen, *Invention of White Race*, vol. 2, 240.
4. See, for example, Ira Berlin, *Generations of Captivity: A History of African-American Slaves* (Cambridge: Harvard University Press, 2003), 55. After a royal commission castigated Berkeley over his handling of Bacon's Rebellion, he was forced to give up his position and return to England.
5. Winthrop, *White Over Black*, 73. The first statutes institutionalizing slavery were adopted in 1660.
6. Morgan, *American Slavery*, 154.

son to the 6,000 white indentured servants then employed.[1] However, the mounting costs associated with importing and keeping new white servants after their predecessors completed their terms of indenture soon accelerated the changeover to a black labor force. Steadily, the number of slaves in Virginia increased, reaching 14.3% of the colony's population of approximately 40,000 by 1677, while the population of white servants remained essentially unchanged. The price for slaves rose with demand: by the mid-1650s, planters were prepared to put up between 4,000-5,000 pounds of tobacco for each one — considerably more than white servants could command.[2] Planters were willing to pay this much more because they calculated that making a lifetime investment in one black slave was less costly than having to hire a new white servant every four or five years.[3] The bottom line was that slaves produced tobacco more cheaply.

But, this greater racial complexity of the colony brought new problems. With the arrival of so many slaves, Virginia's planters increasingly feared an inevitable mingling of blacks and whites, politically, socially, and sexually. Concern deepened about a full-fledged slave rebellion — an uprising that would make Bacon's recent backwoods skirmish with colonial authorities pale by comparison. The prominent planter William Byrd would warn of the day when "a man of desperate courage" might incite his fellow blacks to slay their white masters and "tinge our rivers, as wide as they are, with blood...."[4] Virginia's colonists could tolerate living among blacks as long as they — the whites — were in the majority, and blacks were widely dispersed on the plantations. The isolation of slaves and the overwhelming numerical superiority of whites helped to reinforce the latter's power and control. But a large influx of slaves threatened to undo this compartmentalized social structure. The "blacker" the colony became, the more precarious the whites' position in it. With slaves so prevalent, the two races could no longer be physically kept apart. Subjugation had to take the place of separation. In order to maintain their dominance, the planters had to increase the psychological distance between themselves and their chattel. Racial bias had to be transformed into racial ideology. Whites emphasized the "otherness" of blacks so that they could oppress and brutalize them without experiencing any pangs of conscience.[5] European settlers had already developed such an outlook

1. *Ibid.*, 79. However, the *Historical Statistics of the United States* estimates Virginia's black population to have been 405 in 1650 and 950 in 1660.
2. Deal, *Race and Class*, 175. By 1674-76, slaves cost nearly three times as much as servants — 23 versus 8 pounds. See Menard, "From Servants to Slaves," Table 7, "Prices of Servants and Slaves, 1641-1720," 372. This price differential subsequently narrowed as the number of available servants declined.
3. Slaves cost more to buy, but maintaining an indentured servant was more expensive — between two and four pounds annually. Wertenbaker, *Planters of Colonial Virginia*, 127.
4. Marambaud, *William Byrd*, 172.

to justify their hostile actions toward Native Americans, defining them as "savages" or "heathens" to rationalize their attempts to enslave, drive off, or annihilate this other race.

To draw clear lines between whites and blacks, a series of rigid, race-based legal changes was enacted. These laws explicitly codified blacks' subordinate, impotent status. For example, Virginia's General Assembly passed a bill in 1640 barring slaves from possessing firearms and other weapons. To prevent the arousal of dangerous tribal emotions, they were not allowed to blow horns, or beat drums. Slaves were to be severely punished for striking a white person, even if they did so in self-defense. They were denied the freedom to travel alone without permission, or to gather in groups without a white person being present. Nor could they be taught how to read or write.[1] To justify these and other such flagrantly discriminatory measures, the colonial government revised the Virginia Code in 1661 and 1662, giving slavery legal status and designating slaves a form of personal property.[2]

But the Europeans' greatest fear was miscegenation. They dreaded the purported "bestial" sexual potency of black males, while tacitly acknowledging that black females presented an irresistible, if distasteful, temptation to male colonists. What was worse, in their eyes, some free black householders living along the Eastern Shore had had the audacity to marry white women.[3] All forms of interracial intercourse destroyed the rigid separation of whites from blacks that the dehumanizing system of slavery required. Miscegenation also undermined white identity. In a futile effort to discourage such sexual congress, the colonial government imposed harsh penalties for it. As early as 1630, a white settler in Virginia was publicly whipped for "defiling his body in lying with a Negro," and in 1662, the fine for such fornication was doubled.[4] That same year the colonial government declared that any child born of a black female would be classified as a slave — reversing a centuries-old practice of awarding legal status on the basis of paternity.[5] Two years later, neighboring Maryland made marriage between blacks and whites a criminal offense.[6]

---

5. Colonies in which the black population exceeded the white population tended to treat slaves more harshly. See, for example, Trevor Burnard, *Master, Tyranny, and Desire: Thomas Thistlewood and His Slaves in the Anglo-Jamaican World* (Chapel Hill: University of North Carolina Press, 2004).
1. Phillips, *Life and Labor*, 163.
2. Talpalar, *Sociology of Colonial Virginia*, 355.
3. Parent, *Foul Means*, 116. This was in the 1660s.
4. Carter G. Woodson, "The Beginnings of the Miscegenation of the Whites and Blacks," *Journal of Negro History* 3:3 (Oct. 1918), 339.
5. Deal, *Race and Class*, 180.
6. *Ibid.*,180. Winthrop, *White Man's Burden*, 44.

These laws were passed with a sense of urgency. Starting around 1690, slavery emerged as the driving engine behind economic growth in the Chesapeake, and blacks came pouring into the region.[1] Sufficient new land for growing tobacco commercially simply could not be cleared and cultivated without them. Planters also benefited from gaining a headright grant of 50 acres for every slave they imported.[2] As large landowners invested heavily in this growing workforce, the proportion of slaves to white servants reached one-to-three.[3] In order to keep up with incessant demand for more slaves, the Royal African Company was formed. Instead of combing the islands of the Caribbean (primarily Barbados) for chattel, this euphemistically named British enterprise purchased blacks in Africa, primarily from ports along the western coast where they had been collected for sale, and then shipped them across the Atlantic. Colonists began submitting to the company requests to buy slaves in exchange for tobacco or specie, and a brisk transoceanic trade quickly developed. By the early 1680s, the Royal African Company was transporting several thousand slaves to the Southern colonies each year. Ships sailed up Tidewater estuaries and docked at various wharves before throngs of expectant buyers. Young men and women who had survived both a long captivity in Africa and then a perilous sea journey were led away blinking and uncomprehending to a life of degrading servitude.

Many of them did not even make it across the Atlantic. Crammed into low-ceilinged, foul-smelling decks like so many sacks of flour, often deprived of adequate food, and felled by fevers and dysentery, large numbers of slaves perished during the Middle Passage, their bodies summarily dumped into the sea. During one typical eight-year period, the Royal African Company lost nearly a quarter of its human freight en route to the Chesapeake.[4] That percentage might well have been higher but for the fact that most slaves brought over from Africa were young (only in their teens) and healthy. Conditions for them on terra firma were somewhat better, if only because their new masters wanted to safeguard this newly acquired property. Slaves worked in the fields for 16 or more hours at a stretch, resting only on Sundays, and enjoying only three holidays — Christmas, Easter and Whitsuntide — during the entire year.[5] Their living quarters were primitive, with little in the way of sanitation; they were fed barely nutritious

---

1.Virginia records show an importation of 229 slaves in 1700, followed by a sharp increase to 1,639 in 1705. See Menard, "From Servants to Slaves," Table 6, "Slaves Imported to Maryland and Virginia from Africa, 1695-1709," 370.

2. For this purpose, slaves were classified as "servants." Hughes and Cain, *American Economic History*, 33.

3. Bruce, *Economic History*, vol. 2, 85.

4. *Ibid.*, 123.

5. Isaac Rhys, *The Transformation of Virginia, 1740-1790* (Chapel Hill: University of North Carolina Press, 1982), 44.

rations and received almost no medical attention if they were injured or taken sick. (Many, in fact, died shortly after arrival as the result of respiratory infections against which they had no immunity.[1]) Still, Africans brought to Virginia survived reasonably well — in fact, they tolerated New World conditions better than their fellow slaves in the Caribbean and the white servants who labored beside them in the tobacco fields. Although the early cargoes of slaves arriving in the colony contained few females, importation combined with natural increase enabled the black population to grow relatively rapidly, doubling in size every 25 years up until 1710.[2]

But even this burgeoning supply of slaves could scarcely keep up with demand. By the 1670s, Virginia was annually sending some 15 million pounds of tobacco back to England, and to sustain this high level of exports, more and more slave labor had to be acquired.[3] The roughly 2,000 blacks then living in the colony were not sufficient.[4] More and more slave traders docked on the banks of coastal rivers during the next few decades, bringing an estimated 2,000 slaves in the 1680s, over 1,300 in the following decade, another 8,000 between 1700 and 1710, and over 11,000 from 1718 to 1725.[5] Meanwhile, the migration of white indentured servants virtually came to a halt by the second decade of the 18th century.

In fact, turning Virginia into a slave colony had a strong, negative impact on all working-class whites. As the number of slaves increased, the need for white help declined. Virginia's proletariat was radically transformed: in 1674, slaves made up only a fifth of those in servitude, but this percentage grew to one third in 1686.[6] By the last decade in the 17th century, blacks had numerically surpassed white servants as the chief source of labor in the colony.[7] From then on, the "Africanization" of Virginia proceeded apace. In 1710, one in five persons was enslaved;[8] within a decade, slaves made up more than 30 percent of Virginia's total population of 87,757.[9] (Viewed in a broader perspective, the proportion of the colony's blacks grew from about 7 percent in 1680 to more than 30 percent in

1. Kulikoff, Alan, "A 'Prolifick' People: Black Population Growth in the Chesapeake Colonies, 1700-1790," *Southern Studies* 16 (1977), reprinted in *Colonial Southern Slavery*, 130.
2. Hughes and Cain, *American Economic History*, 19.
3. Otto, *Southern Frontiers*, 17.
4. See Bruce, *Economic History*, vol. 1, 572.
5. Berlin, *Generations of Captivity*, 55. Menard, "From Servants to Slaves," 367. Richard L. Morton, *Colonial Virginia*, vol. 2, *Westward Expansion and Prelude to Revolution, 1710-1763* (Chapel Hill: University of North Carolina Press, 1960), 492.
6. Morgan, *American Slavery*, 306.
7. Deal, *Race and Class*, 87. Cf. Morgan, *American Slavery*, 306.
8. Menard, "From Servants to Slaves," 381.
9. Deal, *Race and Class*, 175. This population statistic comes from Series Z 1-10, "Estimated Population of American Colonies: 1610-1780," *Historical Statistics of the United States*, part 2, 1168.

1730, and more than 40 percent by the 1750s.[1]) This headlong rush to import slaves is reflected in the continuing rise in prices planters were willing to pay for them: these doubled from approximately 18 pounds sterling in 1676 to 35 pounds in 1700.[2] Virginia's well-to-do planters handed over this much of their hard-earned money for slaves even though they remained almost twice as expensive to purchase as increasingly costly white servants.[3] As a result of this racial changeover, opportunities for poor young English men and women to seek social and economic advancement across the Atlantic were effectively eliminated.

From the plantation owners' perspective, switching over to black labor was far less painful. For them, it was mostly a matter of psychological adjustment. They had to come to terms with their role of racial oppressors. This was eased by the changing make-up of the colony's black population. As slaves imported directly from Africa grew in number, their alien nature — their strange and "primitive" customs, their unfamiliar, incomprehensible languages, their exotic appearance and behavior — helped to confirm the whites' belief that the black race was wholly different from, and vastly inferior to, their own. In the late 1600s, white Europeans did not think of human beings in any biologically or philosophically all-embracing manner. (This was a decade before John Locke articulated the notion of "natural law" in his *Two Treaties on Government*, and fully a century before Thomas Jefferson's penned the Declaration of Independence.) Rather, they measured an individual's humanity by his or her racial identity. Some "superior" races — for example, the English — possessed moral as well as intellectual capabilities that set them apart from other peoples and enabled them to abide by God's will, lead principled lives, create civilizations, conquer the wilderness, and spread goodness and light around the globe. This was, indeed, their collective mission. Other races played secondary parts in the divine scheme of the universe, and some — notably, blacks — were destined by their dark hue and "heathen" nature to bow down and serve the white man.

Some social historians have argued that the demonizing of other races in the New World — whether by the Puritans in the Massachusetts Bay Colony or by Virginia tobacco planters — represented an external projecting of the whites' own dark, uncontrollable impulses. Native Americans and blacks symbolically assumed the roles— to borrow a literary phrase — of "objective correlative" for the colonists' moral shortcomings and guilt. In psychological terms, the English settlers could overcome their own failings by mercilessly "punishing" their mani-

---

1. Wertenbaker, *Planters of Colonial Virginia*, 131.
2. Talpalar, *Sociology of Colonial Virginia*, 388. Cf. Bruce, *Economic History*, vol. 2, 92.
3. The prices for indentured servants increased from 1,435 pounds of tobacco in 1659-61 to 2,000 lbs. in 1761-73, to 3,200 lbs. in 1686-88, to 3,600 lbs. in 1704-06. Menard, "From Servants to Slaves," 372.

festation in others. As one scholar has put it, by placing chains around the necks and ankles of blacks and treating them like animals, "white men were attempting to destroy the living image of primitive aggressions which they said was the Negro but was really their own."[1]

To preserve a barrier separating blacks from whites called for even more drastic changes in laws as well as attitudes. Colonies with the greatest concentration of slaves, notably Virginia, raised these barriers the highest. Restrictions on the rights and freedoms of slaves enacted earlier in the 17th century were gradually tightened, so as to deny these blacks virtually all vestige of human stature. Virginia's slave code, originally adopted in 1680, was bolstered a quarter century later, with stiffer penalties, including castration and death, for running away and other major transgressions. Blacks were forbidden to marry and kinship ties were torn asunder by the common practice of selling of slaves individually to new masters. Interracial marriage, which had previously been legal, was banned by a 1691 vote of the General Assembly. The preamble to this new law made clear the reasons behind it:

> And for the prevention of that abominable mixture and spurious issue which hereafter may increase in this dominion, as well by negroes, mulattoes, and Indians intermarrying with English, or other white women, as by their unlawful accompanying with one another, Be it enacted by the authoritie aforesaid, and it is hereby enacted, That for the time to come, whatsoever English or other white man or woman being free shall intermarry with a negro, mulatto, or Indian man or woman bond or free shall within three months after such marriage be banished and removed from this dominion forever, and that the justices of each respective countie within this dominion make it their perticular [*sic*] care, that this act be put in effectuall execution.[2]

It was not so much cohabitation or marriage across racial lines that inspired fear in the hearts of colonial lawmakers as the issue of these relationships. In the North American colonies, the terms *mulatto* and *free black* were practically synonymous: slave owners were much more likely to emancipate slaves with white blood (and lighter skin), especially those related to their own families. But this humane practice undermined the whole edifice of slavery by creating a class of people whose very existence attested to the blatant failure of the colonists' efforts to keep the races separate (and the whites "pure"). As slavery became a central, essential institution in Virginia, the presence of freed slaves could no longer be tolerated. From a political standpoint, these blacks posed a potential threat, their freedom serving as a dangerous example to their less fortunate fel-

---

1. Jordan, *White Man's Burden*, 222.
2. Quoted in Woodson, "Miscegenation," 342. In 1753, the law against interracial marriage was changed so as to punish any white settler who married a black or mulatto with a sentence of six months in prison and a fine of 10 pounds. A minister who performed such a marriage was subject to a fine of 10,000 pounds of tobacco. *Ibid.*, 344.

low Africans. Hence, the brunt of colonial law now fell heavily upon them. As their number increased, free blacks were stripped of several of their rights. This included the right to own white servants.[1] To push them out of the colony, law-makers first took away the right of newly manumitted slaves to own property and then, in 1691, ordered them to leave as soon as freed, at their former master's expense.[2] Blacks who were already manumitted were barred from residing in several Virginia counties. In addition, intensifying white hostility made it more difficult for them to own land.[3]

Further oppressing blacks and legally demarcating the races helped to make the slave system palatable. Dehumanizing slaves also brought whites of different social classes closer together. This tendency had already been developing for some time. As noted above, in the wake of Bacon's Rebellion, colonial authorities had sought to stop the coming of white servants with disorderly or revolutionary tendencies. Stricter immigration policies as well as a need for more highly skilled white labor (as slaves took over the lowly positions of field hands, and planter households became more affluent) had brought English men and women of a higher social standing to Virginia in the 1680s.[4] Their arrival had had the desired effect of defusing tensions between rich and poor and avoiding another civil uprising. Fear of slave revolts further deepened feelings of solidarity among white settlers. Also, as slaves filled the bottom rung of colonial society, the remaining indentured servants gained social mobility — and more enviable sta-tus.[5] They now looked down on blacks with derisiveness and contempt, regard-ing them not as fellow laborers but as merely chattel.[6] The days when the two races had toiled side-by-side in the tobacco fields — even escaped a loathed mas-ter together — were over. Former servants aspired to become landowners and

---

1. A law was passed in 1670 making such ownership unlawful. James H. Brewer, "Negro Property Owners in Seventeenth-Century Virginia," *William and Mary Quarterly* 12:4 (Oct. 1955), 576.
2. Morgan, *American Slavery*, 337.
3. Black freemen did not lose the right to own real estate and other forms of property, including slaves, but this right was exercised with much greater infrequency. For example, in 1693, more than one in ten landowners in Northampton county was black, but less than a quarter of one percent were in 1860. Allen, *Invention of White Race*, vol. 2, 185.
4. Breen, "Changing Labor Force," 26.
5. Morgan advanced the theory that the large-scale introduction of slavery into colonial Virginia had the unintended effect of liberating poor whites: "To a large degree it may be said that Americans bought their freedom with slave labor." By taking the place of class divisions, racial animosity allowed Revolutionary thinking to flourish in Virginia: "Racism made it possible for white Virginians to develop a devotion to the equality that English republicans had declared to be the soul of liberty." Morgan, *American Slavery*, 5, 386.
6. "The growth of the slave labor force displaced a nascent white proletariat. By 1750, nonslaveholding whites were for the most part tenant and yeoman farmers, not subject to the direct exploitation suffered by slaves." Deal, *Race and Class*, 189.

thus adopted the prejudices of that class. Thus, the large-scale introduction of slavery made race the chief element in Virginia's hierarchical social order.

But, while upwardly mobile whites distanced themselves from the slaves who were taking over most farming duties, they were also being hurt economically by this development. The spread of slavery strengthened the power of the planter elite, but weakened the position of independent, yeoman farmers. This group was already experiencing a major threat to its survival. Toward the turn of century, Tidewater tobacco planters faced challenging economic times, pitting them against each other. This competition for survival undermined the Europeans' race-based unity as large and small tobacco growers vied for increasingly costly and scarce resources. Several factors contributed to this trend. One was the decreasing supply of white servants: newly established yeoman farmers could not afford the going rate for this form of labor, let alone buy even more expensive slaves. Their shortage of field hands, in turn, prevented these farmers from cultivating larger tracts and becoming prosperous. Instead, they struggled to make ends meet, frequently without benefit of any help.[1] On the other hand, well-to-do planters purchased large numbers of slaves and relied upon them almost exclusively to extend their holdings. By the early 1700s, Virginia's whites were effectively divided into a small minority of wealthy slaveholders and a large majority of farmers with few or no slaves.[2] Importing more slaves only exacerbated these class divisions and created greater social and economic inequality among whites. As one historian has summed up: "The openness, opportunities, and freedom white men enjoyed during the middle decades of the [17th] century never returned, even in frontier areas, and the homogeneity of the population was forever severed after Africans poured into the region in the 1690s."[3] Ironically, poor whites tended to blame slaves, rather than the system that enslaved them, for this adverse turn of events. A significant consequence of this economic realignment was growing hostility among "plain folk" farmers toward blacks.

Another stratifying factor was a prolonged downturn in tobacco prices, which lasted from the 1620s up until the 1680s.[4] Planters with extensive acreage

---

1. Menard, "From Servants to Slaves," 381. Some small planters did manage to acquire one or two bondsmen. But attaining the status of a well-to-do slaveholder called for the acquisition of ten or more slaves. Rhys, *Transformation*, 21. In neighboring Maryland during the 1690s, some 90 percent of slaveholding households had only between one and five slaves. Audrey C. Land, "Economic Base and Social Structure: The Northern Chesapeake in the Eighteenth Century," *Journal of Economic History* 25:4 (Dec. 1965), 644.
2. 1704 records for 20 Virginia counties indicate that as many as 90 percent of landowners had fewer than three workers, including their sons, on their property. Phillips, *Life and Labor*, 34. By 1700, the top 10 percent of Virginia's white families owned between 50 and 75 percent of the colony's assets. Fischer, *Albion's Seed*, 374.
3. Kulikoff, *Tobacco and Slaves*, 38, 44.
4. Menard, "Tobacco Industry," 113.

under cultivation were better able to weather this drop in profits. For example, a large plantation owner could forego selling his tobacco for a year or so, storing it in warehouses until prices edged back up. Because of their wealth, these planters could also obtain loans more easily than could hard-strapped yeoman farmers. A subsequent development solidifying class lines was the higher cost of land. This increase stemmed from the colony's prosperity once tobacco prices started to rise again, around 1713. As production of the leaf surged, Virginia grew exponentially — both in population and in area — between 1700 and 1750. The number of white settlers tripled during this half century, from an estimated 42,170 to 129,581[1] — a rate of four percent annually. From a coastal enclave in 1700, colonial Virginia expanded toward the northwest, following the spreading, tapering fingers of its major rivers and creeks. Concomitantly, the amount of acreage in private hands increased from just over two to nearly seven million acres.[2] Ambitious Tidewater planters moved their families, slaves, and other possessions further upstream and established new plantations on rich bottomland with easy access to the sea and thus to English tobacco buyers on the other side of the Atlantic.

But not all took part in this expansion. There was, as it turned out, too little land to go around. The colonists' naively optimistic faith that cultivable land in the New World was boundless foundered on some inescapable topographical realities. For one thing, high-grade smoking tobacco required the richest of loams, and in the Tidewater region this was in relatively short supply and soon exhausted. For another, selling the crop at a profit required an inexpensive means of transporting it to markets — namely, navigable rivers — and so moving inland was unadvisable. On top of these restraining factors was the danger posed by Indians: although the tribes that had lived near the coast were driven out by 1705,[3] those living in the interior periodically mounted attacks on encroaching European settlers.

Hemmed in by these barriers, tobacco plantations grew steadily smaller. This trend had already started during the first half of the 17th century, when the average land patent had diminished from 709 acres to 405 within a span of just five years.[4] Early in the next century, as the number of landowners rose by 66 percent, the amount of land owned by each one declined further, down from 417 acres in 1704 to 336 in 1750.[5] With demand mounting for the remaining available

---

1. "Estimated Population of American Colonies," *Historical Statistics*, part 2, 1168.
2. Peter V. Bergstrom, *Markets and Merchants: Economic Diversification in Colonial Virginia, 1700-1775* (New York: Garland, 1985), 24, 35, 38. These figures are based on the quit-rents — fees levied when land was purchased — collected during these years.
3. Isaac, *Transformation*, 14.
4. Bruce, *Economic History*, vol. 1, 530. This was from 1635 to 1640.
5. Morgan, *American Slavery*, 341-2.

land, speculators stepped forward to buy up large tracts on the banks of the Potomac and turn a quick profit. Former servants hoping to strike out on their own could not pay these inflated prices and were thus unable to join the ranks of planters.[1] Once again, the choice opportunities fell largely to Virginia's landed aristocracy. They accumulated more and more virgin tracts, cleared them with more slave labor, and planted more tobacco. As a result, a few Tidewater grandees grew immensely wealthy. The richest of them all, Robert "King" Carter, had acquired 300,000 acres, 1,000 slaves, and 10,000 pounds in cash by the time he died in 1732.[2] The planter elite built impressive stone manor houses on their sprawling estates and graced them with fine furniture, china crockery, costly silverware, large libraries, paintings, and other luxury items shipped over from England. Colonial plantation life acquired a patina of Old World splendor. These were the golden years of the Tidewater colony.

Owning slaves made all the difference. Slaves were the key to success in the plantation South — a visible symbol of wealth as well as the instrument for attaining it. In neighboring Maryland, where a similar system of tobacco-based agriculture developed, the linkage was all too apparent. In the 1690s, only families with estates worth 100 pounds or more had sufficient surplus income to own slaves or employ servants; the remaining households lived year to year with practically no savings. The skewed nature of the Chesapeake class system is revealed in the unequal distribution of landholdings: only slightly more than a fourth of Maryland families could afford slaves, whereas the remaining three quarters — all non-slaveholding ones — occupied the lowest tier of the planter class.[3] In Maryland and Virginia, as well as much of the Deep South, the large-scale introduction of slavery proved to be a decidedly mixed blessing for the white population.

On the one hand, slave labor stimulated and sustained the plantation economy, bringing greater prosperity to the region as whole. Even small landowners and landless whites in Virginia, for example, benefited from the periodic upswings in tobacco prices.[4] Virtually all of these whites accepted slavery without question, and most wanted to become slaveholders themselves. But, on the other hand, slave ownership created an unmistakable fault line in colonial society, dividing rich from poor and thwarting the hopes for social mobility that had originally motivated thousands of settlers to cross the Atlantic as bonded servants. Slaves had first — of necessity — taken the place of these servants in the tobacco fields and then, by developing into a massive, static proletariat, pre-

1. Galenson, *White Servitude*, 154.
2. Marambaud, *Richard Byrd*, 5.
3. Land, "Economic Base," 643-4.
4. Cf. Morgan, *American Slavery*, 343.

vented subsequent lower-class white arrivals from lifting themselves out of poverty and building better lives in the Southern colonies. The predominance of blacks on the plantations effectively lowered the status of white agricultural day laborers and servants by — in the eyes of higher class whites — degrading the social value of their work, casting "a stigma on labor that was almost as harmful to the poor white man as to the black."[1] Resentment over this turn of events grew into a deep hatred toward slaves, which would fester and intensify for generations to come among the descendants of these poor white Southerners.

By the first quarter of the 18th century, Tidewater Virginia was losing much of its agricultural luster. Years of growing tobacco had worn out its rich soils, decreased their yields, and caused planters to diversify their production. After the turn of the century, tobacco gradually surrendered its economic preeminence in the Chesapeake. Having previously employed three out of four colonial workers, tobacco gave way to corn, wheat, and other crops, so that by 1755 only about a third of Tidewater laborers were still toiling in tobacco fields. After having accounted for 99 percent of Virginia's exports in 1701, tobacco dropped to 87% of that total in 1727, 77% in 1733, and 61% in 1774.[2] At the same time, the standard of living in the Tidewater declined during the second and third decades of the century, and anxious planters began to cast their eyes farther west. In the 1720s, cheaper, more abundant soils inland beckoned — in the rolling, forested plateau known as the Piedmont, which stretched across the Upland South, separating the Blue Ridge Mountains from the coastal plain. For the richest of plantation owners, this still largely uninhabited region offered the prospect of gaining more wealth — the chance to multiply their holdings two- or threefold and pass along sizeable estates to their heirs.

For neighboring whites of more modest means, the interior of Virginia promised to fulfill less grandiose but equally important aspirations — to secure land of their own, establish themselves as yeoman farmers, and live freely and securely, without worrying about one day having to abandon their livelihood. As would often be the case subsequently, settlers who were not well off looked to the frontier for economic salvation. With so many slaves now working the tobacco fields, small farmers in the Chesapeake region could not produce and sell their crops at competitive prices. Their economic and social mobility were blocked. Former servants seeking to buy land and establish an independent existence could not afford the prices now being demanded where they lived. If they could not move upward in Tidewater society, they would have to move west or to other colonies to fulfill their dreams of a better life. Away from the

---

1. Virginius Dabney, *Virginia: The New Dominion* (Garden City: Doubleday, 1971) 188.
2. Bergstrom, *Markets and Merchants*, 40, 49, 133, 151.

coast, land was far more affordable, going for one twentieth of what Tidewater real estate could command.[1]

Poverty was thus a major reason for Southern white migration. But economic hardship was closely associated with race: blacks were blamed for the decline of "plain folk" fortunes. Thus, early in the 18th century, the hills and valleys of the Piedmont attracted small, fiercely independent farmers for another reason: the region contained few slaves. Instead, it offered these whites a racial sanctuary. They opted to move into the upcountry as much for what it did lacked as for what it offered them. This decision by struggling white farmers to head west in order to escape economic competition from Chesapeake slaves would establish a pattern of migration that would be repeated, again and again, in the settlement of the frontier. As one historian has observed, "The great movement westward over the Appalachian range which followed the War of 1812, the pilgrimages of homesteaders to the northwest and the Pacific coast, find their precedent in the exodus of these poor families from the tobacco fields of Virginia."[2]

---

1. Land in the backcountry sold for only a few shillings per acre during the 18th century, compared to five pounds an acre in the Chesapeake. Fischer and Kelly, *Bound Away*, 77.
2. Wertenbaker, *Planters of Colonial Virginia*, 140. For an overview of the pivotal role played by "plain folk" farmers in settling the frontier, see John S. Otto, "The Migration of the Southern Plain Folk: An Interdisciplinary Synthesis," *Journal of Southern History* 51:2 (May 1985), 183ff. Otto concurs with other historians that these small farmers led the way west because they were adapt at transplanting their small-scale agricultural practices in the backcountry.

II. Running for the Virginia Hills

It was poor whites who first hacked a path through the underbrush and ventured into the undulating hills and valleys of Virginia's Piedmont, where the resounding thud of an axe had scarcely been heard before, and the thick, reddish soil never cleaved by a plow. They were former servants from the Tidewater, adventurers by habit, pioneers of necessity. Not grand dreams, but pressing economic need drove them west. Plainly put, they had no money and no better prospects. Land and jobs along the Chesapeake coast were no longer available to a settler of little means. The coming of slaves in large numbers had made such people superfluous; but the largely uninhabited Piedmont offered these indigent, hard-pressed Europeans a chance to make it on their own in the New World. So, during the late 1600s, they slipped free of the tenuous bonds of colonial civilization, followed muddy footpaths along the tidal estuaries, and trudged toward America's first inland frontier, where they knew the land was vacant. For a while, they could live on it without paying as much as a shilling for the privilege — as squatters, hunting, trapping, and growing a few rows of corn until the affluent owners many miles downstream got around to dispatching their minions, armed with stamped documents and maps, to lay claim to the tracts of sloping forest stretching in all directions and drove these makeshift homesteaders off.[1]

These first arrivals did not hold the land for long or leave much of a mark upon it. In the sweep of civilization westward, they were merely transients. By the turn of the century, other Virginians were looking west with bigger dreams and bigger purses to make these dreams come true. Tobacco growers were hun-

---

1. Fischer and Kelly, *Bound Away*, 95.

gering after large expanses of fertile land to replace what they had used up and to enlarge their domains. The colonial government in Jamestown encouraged this migratory interest by relaxing its land policies. The need for greater security was a motivating factor: settlement of this frontier would create a protective buffer against raids by hostile Indians. Anxious to so fortify the colony's perimeter, Virginia's General Assembly voted in 1701 to make royal holdings above the fall line enticing to potential buyers. More generous purchase terms were approved: a would-be owner could receive a headright to property in the Piedmont not only by importing another settler (or slave), but also by paying the colonial authorities the sum of five shillings for each holding of 50 acres. This policy opened up the interior to speculators, who could buy up tracts spanning tens of thousands of acres, survey them, divide them into smaller, affordable estates, and then resell these properties at a considerable profit to plantation owners and small farmers. The only proviso was that the speculators had to complete these sales within two years or lose their holdings.[1]

As a result of this new policy, the Piedmont attracted "gentlemen" venture capitalists living in comfortable homes in Jamestown and environs — men of means who had the sagacity to perceive the future value of this untapped wilderness, the vision to imagine how it might be developed, and the financial resources to capitalize upon the opportunity.[2] They dispatched their agents westward to reconnoiter, to hike up the James, Rappahannock, and Roanoke until those meandering rivers morphed into turbulent, rock-strewn waterfalls — streams racing down from the mountains — to form a natural barrier against the inroads of civilization.

Members of the planter elite watched this initial exploration of the Piedmont with keen interest. By and large, these tobacco growers had by now concluded that the Tidewater's heyday lay in the past. They realized that their plantations near the Chesapeake Bay could no longer meet Europe's insatiable demand for high quality Virginia tobacco. New virgin lands had to be cultivated, and inevitably the planters would have to relocate inland. From a financial standpoint, the time was ripe for such a move. Prices for tobacco took an upswing in the early decades of the 18th century, and the large planters consequently had considerably more cash left in their pockets at the end of each growing cycle. In addition, many of these planters had young sons, who one day would have families of their own and — because of the prevailing system of pri-

---

1. Otto, *Southern Frontiers*, 24. But this rule was rarely enforced. See Robert D. Mitchell, "The Shenandoah Valley Frontier," *Annals of the Association of American Geographers* 62:3 (Sept. 1972), 466-7.
2. Richard L. Morton, *Westward Expansion and Prelude to Revolution, 1710-1763* (Chapel Hill: University of North Carolina Press, 1960), 540.

mogeniture — would need acreage of similar size and value elsewhere to main-tain their prominent positions in the colony.[1] Newly surveyed estates in the Piedmont met that need well, and at a reasonable price, so these well-off planters began buying up as much land as they could afford — typically, twice as much as they owned in the Tidewater.[2]

Colonial authorities approved other measures to promote development in the Blue Ridge Mountains. This band of high ground running parallel to the Appalachians was strategically important not only for keeping the warriors of the Six Nations from attacking the colony but also for deterring French settlers from encroaching on English territory. Jamestown officials wanted this remote region settled as quickly as possible. Therefore, they offered tax abatements for the first ten years, deferral of payment for land purchases, funding for military supplies, and publicly financed shipments of arms and ammunition.[3] These inducements were designed to persuade the Tidewater elite, which enjoyed close ties to the land-issuing Virginia Council, to purchase lands on this fron-tier.[4] The unprecedented size of the tracts made available in or near the Blue Ridge Mountains reveals that this was the Council's intent.[5] The previous restriction of estates to 1,000 acres was lifted. Throughout the Piedmont, most of the grants made prior to 1735 were for estates ranging in size from 1,000 to 15,000 acres — far out of reach for all but the most affluent families.[6] For example, the planter William Beverley received a grant for 11,8,491 acres in the Shenandoah Valley, and an adjacent tract encompassing 92,100 acres was bought by a New Jersey land agent named Benjamin Borden.[7] Among those in the forefront of this movement into the region bounded by the confluence of the Appomattox and James rivers were eminent families with names like Randolph, Byrd, and Jeffer-son — families that would shape the history of Virginia and the nation as a whole. William Byrd, later the founder of Richmond, bought a plantation in Lunenburg County, not far from the North Carolina border, as early as 1729, and

---

1. Cf. Abernethy, *Three Virginia Frontiers*, 42. For more on inheritance patterns in colonial Virginia, see Philip D. Morgan and Michael L. Nicholls, "Slaves in Piedmont Virginia, 1720-1790," *William and Mary Quarterly* 46:2 (April 1989), 216.
2. Philip D. Morgan, *Slave Counterpoint: Black Culture in the Eighteenth-Century Chesapeake and Lowcountry* (Chapel Hill: University of North Carolina Press, 1998), 44.
3. Warren R. Hofstra, "'The Extension of His Majesties Dominions': The Virginia Back-country and the Reconfiguration of Imperial Frontiers," *Journal of American History* 84:4 (March 1998), 1289.
4. From 1680 to 1775, just 25 great planter families controlled two-thirds of the seats on the Royal Council. Fischer, *Albion's Seed*, 222.
5. Starting in 1720, the Council sold only tracts of 400 acres or larger in the Piedmont, thus discouraging the migration of small planters. Parent, *Foul Means*, 53.
6. Abernethy, *Three Virginia Frontiers*, 47.
7. Mitchell, "Shenandoah Valley Frontier," 467.

Peter Jefferson, father of Thomas, moved his family into the western part of Goochland County in 1742.

So it was members of Virginia's elite who now laid claim to the untapped resources of this hilly backcountry, taking full advantage of their wealth and social connections to buy up its choicest land before their less well-off neighbors had the chance to stake out their own share. But these purchases did not lead to a mass exodus westward. Not all of the colony's leading families wanted to uproot themselves abruptly and move west. Many of these planters were too content with their comfortable lives along the Chesapeake, too tied to a particular estate or to a particular set of friends, to pack up their belongings and venture into the rugged interior. They might have been eager to profit from this newly opened domain, but not so keen to tackle the trying tasks of clearing its lands and establishing new tobacco plantations there. Instead of moving to the estates they had obtained, a number of well-to-do planters (and land speculators) promptly turned around and sold off parcels of these lands to small farmers, making a windfall for themselves. Others remained absentee owners, particularly in the Shenandoah Valley.[1] Thus, this frontier was first settled largely by yeoman farmers from the Tidewater — men of "small fortune and crude steadings"[2] — who bought up tracts of several hundred acres carved out of much larger estates.[3]

However, while these "plain folk" farmers soon constituted the bulk of the upcountry's population, they did not create a different social order on the Virginia frontier. Instead, the westward movement of tobacco growers during the 1720s and 1730s essentially transplanted Tidewater society intact 100 miles or so inland from Jamestown. Large landowners and small farmers moved in tandem but settled in a dispersed manner, reflecting their differing socioeconomic positions. The same hierarchical structure was recreated, with the best land and the power that came with it accruing to the well-to-do, while poor and landless whites, former servants, aspiring planters, and small farmers struggled to make a living on less accessible and less desirable parcels.[4] And this pyramid was not wholly made up of whites. At the bottom were black slaves, brought west by plantation overseers to chop down trees, haul away rocks, and turn the untrod-

---

1. Barbara Rasmussen, *Absentee Landowning and Exploitation in West Virginia, 1760-1920* (Lexington: University Press of Kentucky, 1994), 1. This practice was also prevalent in several counties in present-day West Virginia.
2. Phillips, *Life and Labor*, 37.
3. Supporting this view of migration to the interior are colonial land records. In Spotsylvania County, the average amount of land for which deeds were issued during the 1720s was only 487 acres. Wertenbaker, *Planters of Colonial Virginia*, 154.
4. Kulikoff, *Tobacco and Slaves*, 96. Cf. John Majewski, *A House Dividing: Economic Development in Pennsylvania and Virginia Before the Civil War* (Cambridge: Cambridge University Press, 2000), 15.

den Piedmont into tobacco fields with their bare hands. Moving to this frontier thus did not — as Frederick Jackson Turner would later theorize — necessarily foster a more egalitarian way of life. Instead, the distribution of economic power and social status remained essentially the same. If anything, enlarging the colony's size only increased the disparities among classes: the rich grew richer while the rest fell farther behind.[1]

This intrusion of whites into the Piedmont sparked conflict with some neighboring Native Americans. Widely dispersed plantations remained vulnerable to attack, and so the colonial administration took additional steps in the early decades of the 18th century to increase settlement of the interior. Forts were also built on the fall line to protect new arrivals.[2] Organizing the Piedmont into counties also facilitated migration to the frontier, in addition to establishing colony authority there. In 1721, Alexander Spotswood, then near the end of his long term (1710-1722) as Virginia's governor, oversaw the establishment of the region's first county, the eponymously named Spotsylvania (destined, nearly a century-and-a-half later, to be the site of one of the Civil War's bloodiest battles). After having first explored the Appalachians in 1716, Spotswood and a group of settlers moved to the Blue Ridge Mountains in 1727 and built an outpost there.[3] One of his goals was to strengthen trade ties with friendly tribes in the area. After he left office, one of his successors, William Gooch, further championed expansion into the Piedmont and the Great Valley by creating Goochland County in March of 1728. Three more counties were organized within the span of six years, bringing this new upland region firmly into the colony's fold.

Economically, the Piedmont frontier closely resembled coastal Virginia. Tobacco was the driving force behind the backcountry's rapid growth. Abundant, fertile, and relatively cheap soil attracted planters of all income levels. Soon the region reverberated with the felling of trees and the building of log cabins. Tracts were cleared and the first seedlings planted. A new wave of farmers soon arrived, some bringing more slaves and more plantations took shape. Within a few decades, the Piedmont's tobacco culture was well established. Indeed, this part of Virginia quickly surpassed the Tidewater in economic importance. After 1748, when the first hogsheads were rolled overland over crude roads and loaded on waiting flatboats for the journey down the James River, the backcountry became the center of tobacco growing in the colony.[4] As the region thrived,

---

1. For comments on Turner's frontier thesis and settlement of the Piedmont, see, for example, Morton, *Westward Expansion*, 540, and Abernethy, *Three Virginia Frontiers*, 60.
2. Fischer and Kelly, *Bound Away*, 79.
3. Abernethy, *Three Virginia Frontiers*, 41.
4. Morton, *Westward Expansion*, 557.

impoverished farmers living near the coast came to regard moving there as their best hope for survival in increasingly difficult times.

Escaping untenable economic realities, landless whites and small farmers flocked to the central Piedmont in the second half of the century. They migrated there out of desperation, after agricultural conditions in the Tidewater worsened during the 1740s. Tobacco prices took another of their periodic plunges, following two decades of good profits, as the result of overproduction and unfavorable trading conditions in Europe.[1] Those farmers with the fewest acres under cultivation were once again hardest hit by this downturn. They scrambled to grow other crops to supplement their meager incomes, but these endeavors could not make up for the precipitous drop in tobacco revenues.[2] Even after prices started to improve, at mid-century, most small planters did not experience a return of their previous standard of living. Tidewater farmland was now priced out of their reach. Saddled by mounting debts, a number of small farmers had to abandon tobacco growing entirely, leaving this erratic but highly lucrative enterprise in the hands of the Chesapeake's remaining large plantation owners.[3] As yeoman farmers were eased out, members of the planter elite bought up whatever land came on the market, increasing their Tidewater holdings so that, by 1750, estates of 5,000 or more acres were not at all uncommon.[4] By then, power and wealth were more concentrated than ever.

This cornering of the coastal tobacco market coincided with the large-scale introduction of slaves into the Chesapeake. Land values continued to soar in this densely settled area, with the wealthy planters willing to pay top dollar. They employed more slaves to labor in these newly purchased fields. To keep up with the demand, the African slave trade grew exponentially. During the period 1700-1760, 59,000 slaves arrived by ship in the colony.[5] As a result of these imports and the natural increase in population, coastal Virginia was rapidly turning into

1. Menard, "Tobacco Industry," 124. Between 1739 and 1740, the amount of tobacco exported to England fell by 22 percent. It increased sharply the following year, but then declined by over 27 percent in 1742. Series Z 441-448, "Tobacco Imported by England, by Origin: 1697 to 1775," *Historical Statistics*, part 2, 1190.
2. Peter Bergstrom has analyzed shipping manifests and concluded that Virginia's economy was much more diversified, in terms of exports, than is generally believed. See Bergstrom, *Markets and Merchants*, 14, *passim*. For a similar view of the Tidewater's transformation, see Majewski, *House Dividing*, 14.
3. T.H. Breen points out that indebtedness was also a problem for wealthy plantation owners after 1750. A quarter of a century later, unwilling to curtail their gentlemanly lifestyle, at least ten of Virginia's elite planters owed five thousand pounds or more — an enormous sum in the 18th century. See Breen, *Tobacco Culture*, 25, 86, 91, 122, 128, *passim*.
4. Rouse, *Planters and Pioneers*, 121.
5. Fischer and Kelly, *Bound Away*, 63. The U.S. Census Bureau estimates 51,915 slaves entered Virginia during this period. Series Z 146-149, "Slave Trade in Virginia: 1619 to 1767," *Historical Statistics of the United States*, part 2, 1172.

an African colony on the North American seaboard. The same trend was evident throughout the South: the black proportion of the region's population grew from approximately 25 percent in 1720 to nearly 40 percent by 1770.[1] But these statistics are somewhat deceiving; in fact, more than half of the slaves employed in North America lived in just two colonies — Maryland and Virginia.[2] In the latter, as a result of a rapid infusion of slaves, the proportion of blacks in the population climbed from 31 percent in 1720 to 45 percent in 1750.[3] Whereas Maryland slaveholders gradually began to emancipate slaves they could no longer use during the second half of the century, those in Virginia continued to buy more.

More than any other American colony, Virginia was heavily dependent upon the slave system — socially as well as economically.[4] But slavery was a double-edged sword. Any swelling of the black population decreased the whites' numerical advantage and increased the chances of a violent slave uprising. Other changes in the Tidewater's demographics were equally worrisome. Large numbers of slaves were now housed on fewer plantations. In 1780, for example, the 100 leading planter families owned an average of 180 slaves each.[5] In the Chesapeake county of Gloucester, 57 of the 320 slaveholders in 1783 owned 16 or more slaves, and in Dinwiddie County, 60 of the 633 planters with slaves had 21 or more.[6] These concentrations made it easier for blacks to congregate in their free time, plot together, and rise up against their masters. Furthermore, due to natural increase, coastal Virginia now contained more slaves than the region needed or could use.[7] This excess of black field hands and domestic servants was deeply troubling, as idleness undermined discipline and endangered white control. But, risky as this was, keeping so many blacks subjugated in close quarters was preferable to the alternative — letting the slaves go free. Even if this course of action

---

1. Robert William Fogel and Stanley L. Engerman, *Time on the Cross: The Economics of American Negro Slavery* (Boston: Little, Brown: 1974), 21. Population growth due to natural increase rather than importation occurred after 1710. Kulikoff, "A 'Prolifick' People," 125. For data on the rate of natural increase in Virginia, see Philip D. Morgan, "Slave Life in Piedmont Virginia, 1720-1800," in *Colonial Chesapeake Society*, 435.
2. Fogel and Engerman, *Time on the Cross*, 47. This was the case in 1790.
3. Deal, *Race and Class*, 175. Virginia's population in 1750 was 231,033, and this included an estimated 105,000 slaves. See Morgan, *Slave Counterpart*, Table 10, "Africans in the Virginia and South Carolina Slave Populations, 1700-1800," 61, and Hughes and Cain, *Economic History*, 20.
4. Richard S. Dunn, "Black Society in the Chesapeake, 1776-1810," in *Slavery and Freedom in the Age of the American Revolution*, ed. Ira Berlin and Ronald Hoffman (Urbana: University of Illinois Press, 1986), 52.
5. Rouse, *Planters and Pioneers*, 137-8.
6. Wertenbaker, *Planters of Colonial Virginia*, 157-58.
7. In the decades leading up the Revolution, the average age at which a female slave first gave birth was 18.2. Subsequent births usually followed after an interval of 28 months. Morgan, "Slave Life," 445.

were economically feasible (which it was not), white Virginians were convinced this would lead to a horrendous racial bloodbath.

While the colony's transition to an overwhelming black labor force caused some concerns among the slaveholding class, it had a more direct and more decidedly negative impact on poor, landless whites. After 1750, flush with cheap slave labor, plantation owners had little need of white hired hands in their fields. Thousands of them lost their jobs. With their labor no longer highly valued, most former servants could not gain an economic foothold in the Chesapeake and afford to buy land in the counties where they had previously worked.[1] If they were going to start families and become economically independent, these colonists now had very little chance except by leaving the region, with hopes of making a living in the backcountry as yeoman farmers, tenants, craftsmen, or day laborers.[2] Starting in the mid-18th century, they would leave coastal Virginia (as well as Maryland) in massive numbers. Between 1790 and 1820 alone, approximately 250,000 whites would vacate the Chesapeake — almost all of them small or aspiring farmers.[3] Most of them headed first to the Piedmont. Albemarle County, for example, saw its population grow by more than 50 percent — from 12,585 to 19,751 — over these 30 years. But many settlers ended up relocating several times — within Virginia's interior counties as well as to other colonies and territories. The frequency with which a large percentage of newly arrived immigrants hop scotched from place to place during the first half of the 18th century suggests how difficult it proved for them to support themselves in slave-dominated Virginia.[4]

The proliferation of slave labor made the position of small Chesapeake planters with few or no slaves equally untenable. As one historian has succinctly put it, Virginia's wealthy plantation owners "forced out a generation of impoverished planters from the soil."[5] Owning slaves became the *sine qua non* for survival in the Tidewater. For example, in Northampton County, on Virginia's Eastern Shore peninsula, the percentage of landowners who owned at least one slave rose from 40 percent in 1744 to 58 percent a quarter century later.[6] Not able to afford what Tidewater land was still available for cultivation, economically hard pressed on all fronts, yeoman farmers, too, had no realistic strategy for survival other than to pack up their belongings and head to the frontier. As these largely

1. For example, less than 10 per cent of former servants living in Lancaster and nine percent of those in Northampton in the 1690s could afford to buy land in their respective counties. Fischer and Kelly, *Bound Away*, 74.
2. Abernethy, *Three Virginia Frontiers*, 48.
3. Kulikoff, *Tobacco and Slaves*, 77.
4. Wertenbaker, *Planters of Colonial Virginia*, 146.
5. Parent, *Foul Means*, 39.
6. Deal, *Race and Class*, 175.

non-slaveholding whites moved out, the proportion of slave owners among Tidewater farmers grew even higher: two of every three planters owned slaves by the 1780s.[1] (During the next few decades, a similar consolidation of power in the hands of large landowners and a subsequent "thinning out" of the ranks of small slave owners and non-slaveholding farmers would occur in the "black belts" of Georgia.[2]) Near the mouth of the York River, in Glouchester County, the tax rolls for early in that decade show that, of the 490 white families residing there, fully 65 percent owned slaves. Further to the west and south of the James River, in Dinwiddie County, only 210 white households out of 843 did not possess any slaves. As these figures indicate, Tidewater Virginia was turning into a land of "masters and slaves."[3] White farmers without chattel played at best a marginal role in its economy. Their future had to be found elsewhere.

Meanwhile, the Piedmont appeared welcoming to yeoman farmers, with bountiful acreage on which they could plant either commercial or subsistence crops — in case tobacco prices plummeted once again. The red clay prevalent above the fall line was well suited to growing the popular (and more profitable) variety of tobacco known as *oronoco*, but the thick grasslands and sloping forests of the upcountry would also support other, edible plants. Land there was widely available at a good price. Therefore, starting in the early 1740s, hundreds and then thousands of farmers began streaming into the backcountry, grabbing up whatever parcels had not already been claimed by wealthy planters. Invariably this was less desirable terrain, located on ridges between the upland rivers. But the going price of only a shilling per acre (compared to as much as five pounds for the same amount of land along the riverbanks) made these sites attractive to settlers with little cash at hand, even though a preponderance of rocky, uneven terrain made it more costly to clear for planting, and the greater distance from navigable rivers and creeks added to transportation expenses.

In general, these "plain folk" tended to settle in counties containing few large plantations.[4] There, they could hope to establish farms without having to worry about losing out in a price war over additional acreage. Meanwhile, the large planters were consolidating their holdings in more agriculturally favorable areas.[5] In this patch quilt manner, the central Piedmont was soon filled with settlers, rich and poor coexisting in relative peace and harmony. Between 1729 and

---

1. This development was partially due to the inheriting of slaves by children of slaveholders. Kulikoff, *Tobacco and Slaves*, 136.
2. These regions derived their name from the color of the soil. For a detailed examination of this pattern of population displacement in the Cotton South, see Ulrich B. Phillips, "The Origin and Growth of Southern Black Belts," *American Historical Review* (July 1906): 798-815.
3. Wertenbaker, *Planters of Colonial Virginia*, 151.
4. Fischer and Kelly, *Bound Away*, 77, 75.

1773, the number of taxable inhabitants (or tithables) in the region grew from eight percent of the colony's total to 44 percent.[1] By 1780, Virginia's upcountry was so thickly populated that almost all the tobacco-growing land was taken. Altogether, during the half a century prior to the American Revolution, some 200,000 whites "swarmed beyond the fall line" to start new lives there, increasing the Piedmont's population to a quarter of a million.[2]

Not all of these settlers were driven out of the Tidewater by its dominant slave system. Others came from farther afield, but they, too, were looking for more freedom to live as they pleased and greater economic opportunity. Many who made the trek into Virginia's interior were Scotch-Irish immigrants. Finding themselves unwelcome in the North,[3] and unable to afford land there, they had journeyed on foot south from Pennsylvania and New Jersey to the Southern fall line in Virginia and the Carolinas during the 1730s and 1740s.[4] Many had come at the urging of their fellow countryman, Col. James Patton, who had paved the way by buying up 30,000 acres in western Virginia in 1737.[5] They were also attracted by the relatively low land prices: acreage in the Shenandoah Valley was then selling for about one third the price of similar parcels in southeastern Pennsylvania.[6] These newcomers were a hardy, independent lot — toughened by harsh living conditions in their adopted Ireland, where they had settled after crossing over from Scotland early in the 17th century. Religious intolerance and persecution during the reign of the converted Catholic James II (1685-1688) and later under his Protestant daughter, Queen Anne (1702-1714), had convinced many of these "dissenting" Presbyterians to seek new homes across the Atlantic. Tens of thousands had boarded ships bound for Philadelphia in the 1710s and 1720s.[7] All told, some 80,000 Scotch-Irish crossed over to the British colonies

---

5. Governor Spotswood had hoped to see the planters develop the region in a more balanced way by requiring them to purchase tracts that included lands of varying soil quality, but these plans were thwarted by the planters' eagerness to occupy only the best parcels for growing tobacco. Price, *Dividing the Land*, 142.

1. Majewski, *House Dividing*, 15.

2. Morgan and Nicholls, "Slaves in Piedmont Virginia," 215. Otto, *Southern Frontiers*, 55.

3. E. Estyn Evans, "The Scotch-Irish: Their Cultural Adaptation and Heritage in the American Old West" in *Essays in Scotch-Irish History*, ed. E.R.R. Green (London: Routledge & Kegan Paul, 1969), 75. Among others, the secretary of the Pennsylvania colony, James Logan, objected to the influx of Scotch-Irish and German immigrants in the 1720s. See E. Douglas Branch, *Westward: The Romance of the American Frontier* (New York: Appleton, 1930), 49.

4. A small band of Scotch-Irish settlers arrived in the area near Little Roanoke and Briery Creek in early 1730s. Morton, *Westward Expansion*, 561.

5. Patricia Givens Johnson, *James Patton and the Appalachian Colonists* (Verona, Va: McClure Press, 1973), 9.

6. Mitchell, "Shenandoah Valley Frontier." 467.

7. For more details on this migration, see Charles Knowles Bolton, *Scotch Irish Pioneers in Ulster and America* (Baltimore: Genealogical Publishing Co., 1967), 35.

during the 18th century. They constituted one of the largest and historically most important of the European migratory streams to North America.

Arriving in the wild Virginia backcountry, these refugees from northern Ireland felt immediately at home. Primitive frontier conditions called for a good measure of self-reliance and self-sufficiency, and centuries of isolated living in rural Scotland and Ireland had instilled these traits in abundance. The social bonds these immigrants valued were the well-established kinship ties to their own people, and these tended to make them cool and standoffish toward other settlers.[1] Rather than adapt to colonial British ways and blend casually with their new neighbors from the Tidewater, the Scotch-Irish established their own way of life in the upland country. Many settled in Virginia's Great Valley and in the foothills of the Shenandoah Mountains. After paying hefty fees to speculators for parcels of land, they built simple log cabins in hills and valleys far removed from the sight of others, took up farming as practiced by the local Indians, grew tobacco, beans, and various gourds, hunted, and raised small numbers of pigs and other livestock.[2] In the decades preceding the American Revolution, so many Scotch-Irish migrated from the North to the Piedmont the region came to be known as "Greater Pennsylvania."[3] They soon made up the majority of settlers in the upland South, and, as a result of this numerical dominance, largely shaped the character of this inland region.[4]

Indeed, the sizeable presence of hardscrabble immigrants from Ireland, together with yeoman farmers and poor whites from the Tidewater as well as other new arrivals from the German Palatinate, brought a democratic ethos into parts of the Piedmont, suggestive of the frontier experience as Turner would later characterize it. Where these independent pioneers from generally humble backgrounds made up a majority of the population — as they did, for example, in Virginia's Great Valley[5] — an egalitarian, live-and-let live way of life took hold.[6]

---

1. Scotch-Irish settlers liked to keep a distance of five miles between them and their nearest neighbors. See Frederick Merk, *History of the Westward Movement* (New York: Knopf, 1978), 50. According to David Fischer, backcountry pioneers believed it was not right to build a homestead where one could hear the bark of a neighbor's dog. Fischer, *Albion's Seed*, 760. For a description of kinship ties among these immigrants on the frontier, see John Solomon Otto, "Upland South Folk Culture: The Oral Traditional History of a 'Plain Folk' Family," *Mid-America Folklore* 9:3 (Winter 1981), 74.
2. Evans, "Scotch-Irish," 78-86. Scotch-Irish purchasing land from spectators had to pay three pounds for 100 acres — six times the amount that public land then cost. Abernethy, *Three Virginia Frontiers*, 55.
3. Otto, "South Folk Culture," 45.
4. Roughly 75 percent of the population in western Augusta county was Scotch-Irish in the 1770s. Fischer and Kelly, *Bound Away*, 121.By 1775, the Scotch-Irish accounted for three quarters of settlers in Virginia's Great Valley. Russel L. Gerlach, *Settlement Patterns in Missouri: A Study of Population Origins With a Wall Map* (Columbia: University of Missouri Press, 1986), 15.
5. Mitchell, "Shenandoah Valley Frontier," 469.

Most landholdings were relatively small — between 100 and 400 acres.[1] The great majority of farmers lived at a subsistence level. Slave ownership was not common. (Recent migrants from Europe settled mainly in the upper Shenandoah Valley, while English planters took up residence, often with their slaves, further downstream, to the north.[2]) Families took care of their own needs and lived contentedly without much contact with coastal Virginia. While tolerating great disparities in household income between themselves and nearby planters,[3] these self-reliant backcountry farmers were less charitable in their attitude toward colonial authorities. The latter's imposition of unwanted rules, regulations, and — most annoyingly — taxes vexed these frontier folk considerably. (The fact that British officials of the Anglican faith governed them was particularly galling to the Scotch-Irish Presbyterians.)[4] They deeply resented such outside intervention and wanted to run their own affairs. As one Scotch-Irish pastor put it, "men are called to the magistracy by the suffrage of the people whom they govern, and for men to assume unto themselves power is mere tyranny and unjust usurpation."[5] Like other colonies along the Atlantic seaboard, Virginia came to split politically into eastern and western halves.[6] Residents of these two regions regarded each other with disdain: Tidewater "tuckahoes" — slaveholding planters of English extraction — were particularly disliked by "cohees" — Scotch-Irish and Germans — living in the backcountry. Settlers living beyond the fall line came to chafe at the greater political power wielded by the colony's aristocratic Council, which was dominated by wealthy easterners, and felt their own voices were not heard sufficiently in the popularly elected House of Burgesses.[7] Migrating yeoman farmers also disliked this planter elite for having pushed them out of the Tidewater. This hostility increased when more eastern plantation

---

6. By contrast, a more aristocratic lifestyle emerged in areas such as Roanoke County, where the planter elite had claimed the best land and dominated local affairs. Abernethy, *Three Virginia Frontiers*, 59, 49.
1. In the 1790s, only about three of ten farmers owned more than 400 acres. Mitchell, "Shenandoah Valley Frontier," 474, 483.
2. In 1790 there were 7,594 slaves living in the lower valley, compared to only 3,021 in the upper part. Mitchell, "Shenandoah Valley Frontier," 473.
3. According to 18th century tax lists, Appalachian counties had the highest discrepancies of income in colonial America. See Fischer and Kelly, *Bound Away*, 125
4. Otto, *Southern Frontiers*, 57.
5. Quoted in Constance Lindsay Skinner, *Pioneers of the Old Southwest: A Chronicle of the Dark and Bloody Ground* (New Haven: Yale University Press, 1921), 3.
6. For a discussion of these east-west colonial tensions, see Frederic L. Paxson, *History of the American Frontier, 1763-1893* (Boston: Houghton, Mifflin, 1924), 24-31.
7. Planters in eastern Virginia enjoyed greater political representation because of their slaveholdings: allocation of seats in the legislature was based not on the white population but on the total numbers of persons living in a particular county. Up until 1851, when a new constitution was drafted, the franchise in Virginia was also limited to freeholders — white males over 21 in possession of at least 25 acres of land.

owners relocated to the Piedmont starting in the mid-1740s.[1] Two decades later, Scotch-Irish anger over high taxes imposed by the colonial administration would lead to violent protest.[2]

For the most part, however, tensions between social classes — and parts of the colony — did not erupt into open clashes. Class delineation was a given in 18th-century English society, and the British colonists who had migrated up coastal rivers and streams from the highly stratified Tidewater accepted such a top-down arrangement as normal, even if they were not always treated fairly. Indeed, they tended to look up to those who occupied a higher station in society, out of — to borrow the words of Adam Smith — "admiration for the advantages of their situation."[3] But if downtrodden white farmers could live within a class-ordered system, they had far less tolerance for one that incorporated another race. The introduction of this polarizing element, brought about by the whole-sale importing of slaves to the Piedmont, would cause considerable consterna-tion, animosity, and dislocation. The "plain folk" farmers and white laborers who had fled the Tidewater in order to work freely, without fear of competition from slave labor, would soon find their hopes frustrated. The relentless spread of the Southern plantation system would once again make their way of live unsustain-able — and drive them further west.

Throughout the Upper South, tobacco and slavery were now inextricably bound together. Despite the chronic ups and downs of the marketplace, tobacco remained the region's indispensable cash crop. All of their economic eggs were placed in this agricultural basket. If the tobacco industry faltered, the income and standard of living for most whites would decline drastically. Large-scale growing of this plant continued to require a large, inexpensive workforce, and only slaves could now meet this need: the more slaves owned, the greater the amount of land that could be cultivated. In the late 18th century, the Atlantic slave trade was setting new records, with more than 75,000 slaves arriving annu-ally on North American shores.[4] As a consequence, during the years 1730-1765, blacks made up a greater percentage of the continent's population than at any other point in its history, past or future. In Virginia alone, the number of slaves more than doubled between 1760 and 1790 — soaring from 140,500 to 293,000.[5]

---

1. Ray Allen Billington, *Westward Expansion: A History of the American* Frontier, 4th ed., (New York: Macmillan, 1967), 99.
2. Carl Bridenbaugh, *Myths and Realities: Societies of the Colonial South* (Baton Rouge: Loui-siana State University Press, 1952), 159.
3. This disposition helped to explain a tolerance for "the distinction of ranks" in English society. See Adam Smith, *The Theory of Moral Sentiments*, Chap. 2, Section 3: www.adam-smith.org/smith/tms/tms-pl-s#-c2.htm
4. Breen and Innes, "*Myne Owne Ground*," 4.
5. Morgan, *Slave Counterpart*, 61.

But, if tobacco growing had come to rely upon slave labor, the slave system was now even more dependent on the tobacco industry.[1] Well-to-do planters had invested heavily in this human capital and now had to reap a substantial return on their expenditures by putting these slaves profitably to work. And, in 18th-century Virginia, there was nothing else for them to do but plant, cultivate, harvest, cure, and pack tobacco in hogsheads for shipment to Europe. Given the high price — and short supply — of land in the Tidewater, this goal could only be accomplished by expanding inland, where the costs of starting and running a plantation were appreciably lower. So the logic of economics made the wholesale introduction of slavery in the Piedmont inevitable.[2] This was tobacco's next frontier.

But there was another, equally compelling reason for putting slaves to work elsewhere. A high birth rate had created an abundance of chattel in the Tidewater. The existence of large numbers of blacks with time on their hands was a dangerous development. For Virginia's whites, the nightmare of a rebellion came alarmingly close to becoming a reality in 1730, when some 200 slaves gathered in secret and chose leaders for a revolt, only to have their plan exposed before it could be carried out.[3] Unsuccessful slave uprisings in Maryland and outside Charleston, South Carolina, during the following decade intensified white anxiety.[4] This fear was revealed in Virginia's 1757 militia statue, which denied "free mulattoes, negroes, and Indians" the right to bear arms.[5] The Piedmont served as a convenient "safety valve" for potential troublemakers. Bringing surplus chattel to frontier plantations would disperse the slave population and make conspiracy less likely. So for reasons of security as well as economics, landowners regarded the expansion of the slave system to the interior as essential.

Thus, after 1750, Virginia experienced a massive westward migration of slaves. Between 17,000 and 20,000 were transferred overland from the Tidewater to newly created Piedmont plantations.[6] Nearly 100,000 more left the Chesapeake region between 1790 and 1810.[7] Slaves arriving from Africa were now

---

1. Several historians have concluded that without tobacco, slavery would have died out in the South. See, for example, Bruce, *Economic History*, vol. 2, 573.
2. For evidence of how this logic applied to Southern cotton growers, see Gavin Wright, *The Political Economy of the Cotton South: Households, Markets, and Wealth in the Nineteenth Century* (New York: W.W. Norton, 1978), 11.
3. Morton, *Westward Expansion*, 524.
4. Herbert Aptheker, "The Quakers and Negro Slavery," *Journal of Negro History* 25:3 (July 1940), 343.
5. Rhys, *Transformation of Virginia*, 105. An earlier Virginia law, adopted in 1726, had established patrols to prevent slaves from gathering on holidays.
6. The figure of 17,000 is cited in Morgan and Nicholls, "Slaves in Piedmont Virginia," 222. However, in his more recent work on slavery in the Chesapeake, Morgan uses the higher estimate. Morgan, *Slave Counterpart*, 60. These numbers apply to the period 1755-1782.

taken by boat directly up the James River to be sold on wharves at various points along the way, where prospective backcountry buyers, alerted by newspaper ads, assembled to bid for them. The slaves then completed the last leg of their long journey on foot. This westward flow of black men, women, and children enlarged the territory in which slaves made up a substantial portion of the population. Augmented by births among young male and female slaves brought inland to work in freshly opened tobacco fields, the percentage of blacks grew quickly, so that, by 1755, fully one third of 120,000 Virginia's slaves were living in the Piedmont.[1] This transporting of slaves to the frontier accelerated when the colonists took up arms against their English homeland: one fifth of the total number originally located in the Tidewater were transported inland from 1775 to 1782.[2] By the end of the Revolution, nearly half of the former colony's 229,088 slaves would be residing in the upcountry. In many newly created interior counties, the increase in blacks outstripped the growth of the white population so that these areas gained a slave majority. In 1755, only three of the existing 14 Piedmont counties had reached this point. But a quarter of a century later, 10 of 24 counties had more black than white residents.[3]

Most slaves could be found in counties along the York River, up which the slave traders brought their human cargo for sale. There were also large concentrations in the southern Piedmont and Southside, where a great deal of Virginia's tobacco was now being grown.[4] For example, in prosperous Amelia County, which bordered the James River about 60 miles west of Jamestown, the number of slaves owned by a typical white household increased by almost two-fifths during the years 1736-1749.[5] Whites held a three-to-two numerical advantage over blacks a year after the county was established, in 1735, but within 30 years, the proportions were reversed. And, in the nearby Southside county of Lunenburg, the percentage of slaves among the county's tithables rose from 33 percent in 1750 to 60 percent over the next 20 years.[6]

Lunenburg provides a vivid example of how the coming of large tobacco plantations transformed the racial composition of Virginia's Piedmont. In the 1740s this county, located far from major coastal rivers, was relatively poor, having been first settled largely by yeoman farmers. Deprived of the help of slaves or hired hands, they could grow tobacco only on three or four acres of their land. (Slightly more than a fifth of Lunenburg's early settlers could afford slaves, and

7. Dunn, "Black Society," 59.
1. Morgan and Nicholls, "Slaves in Piedmont Virginia," 211, 215.
2. Morgan, "Slave Life in Piedmont Virginia," 437.
3. *Ibid.*, 454.
4. Dunn, "Black Society," 56, 58.
5. Kulikoff, *Tobacco and Slaves*, 75.
6. Morgan and Nicholls, "Slaves in Piedmont Virginia," 218, 217.

only two percent owned more than five.) The costs of shipping harvested tobacco downstream to market discouraged these small farmers from depending heavily on this one crop. But, by mid-century, after the arrival of more affluent planters, tobacco was being extensively cultivated in this southern Piedmont County. Meanwhile, the slave population rose to 44 percent in 1764 and became a majority just five years later. The arrival of large slaveholders drove the price of land up, creating greater economic disparity among whites living in Lunenburg.

Tobacco grew more and more dominant as the county's chief source of income and, concomitantly, the number of slaveholding families also increased; by 1760, this equaled 44 percent of all households. With slaves continuing to move in and reproduce at a rate of three percent annually, Lunenburg emerged by the last decade in the century as the county with the largest absolute number of slaves and the highest percentage of blacks in its population. Once largely free of slavery, this part of Virginia became its greatest bastion and one of the most vociferous defenders of the chattel system, for the well being of its dominant white group — the affluent slaveholders — hinged upon keeping the "peculiar institution" thriving.[1] The planter elite had also grown so accustomed to having slaves on hand to perform household chores and wait on them that they could not envisage life without such help. Although there was now some talk in the colonies of doing away with slavery, in light of the revolutionary fervor of the times, these arguments ran up against this kind of dependence in much of the South. As the wealthy planter Landon Carter noted in his diary, in 1776, "Much is said of the slavery of negroes, but how will servants be provided in these times? Those few servants that we have don't do as much as the poorest slaves we have. If you free the slaves, you must send them out of the country or they just steal for their support."[2]

The most agriculturally desirable sections of the Piedmont — namely, the bottomland abutting the James River and its tributaries — soon fell under the sway of the planter elite just as the Tidewater had done a century before. The great planters sought to cement their dominance through legal measures. In 1723, they successfully lobbied to have a duty on slave imports imposed by the colony's General Assembly. This 40-shilling tax made the cost of slave ownership prohibitively expensive for many small tobacco growers, particularly those in the Piedmont.[3] Would-be small slaveholders were similarly thwarted by the passage and enforcement of tobacco inspection acts during the 1730s: these mea-

---

1. Richard R. Beeman, *The Evolution of the Southern Backcountry: A Case Study of Lunenburg County, Virginia, 1746-1832* (Philadelphia: University of Pennsylvania Press, 1984), 31, 33, 40, 64, 163, 167.
2. Carter, Col. Landon, *The Diary of Colonel Landon Carter of Sabine Hall, 1752-1778*, ed. Jack P. Greene (Richmond: Virginia Historical Society, 1987), vol. 2, 1055.
3. This tax was rescinded by the Crown in 1729. Parent, *Foul Means*, 180.

sures resulted in the burning of substandard tobacco grown by "plain folk" farm-ers, greatly diminishing their incomes.[1] Meanwhile, the planters owning many slaves added to their holdings. Between 1700 and 1770, the proportion of planta-tions in inland and coastal counties with 21 or more slaves rose from 10 percent to 33 percent, whereas the percentage of estates with small slaveholdings (1-5) declined from 39 to 15.[2] The presence of so many slaves, in such concentrations, changed the character of the backcountry.

Whites on Virginia's frontier were becoming somewhat more divided over slavery. These differences of opinion reflected the greater diversity of settlers drawn there. Whereas most English colonists had come to accept chattel labor as the economic underpinning of the plantation way of life, other Europeans who moved to the southern Piedmont did not share this casual tolerance of such an oppressive system. Like the Scotch-Irish, these pioneers had been victims of per-secution in their home countries and had come to the New World seeking more religious freedom. Their personal experience with prejudice and subjugation made them critical of a system that enslaved others, even if the victims were blacks. Among these immigrant groups were Huguenots, forced out of France by Louis XIV's anti-Protestant Edict of Nantes in 1685, and given refuge in England by William and Mary. The first group of 800 Huguenots settled on a large tract along the James River.[3]

There was also a large contingent of Quakers who, starting in the mid-17th century, had begun to trickle down to the South through the Appalachian Val-ley, chiefly from Pennsylvania.[4] They had come looking for cheaper land as well as a more tolerant environment.[5] After originally having passed a law to keep them out, Virginia had adopted a more welcoming posture toward Quakers and

1. Rhys, *Transformation of Virginia*, 137. Small planters along the Chesapeake refused to comply with this act in March 1732 out of fear that doing so would result in the loss of their crops. Parent, *Foul Means*, 192.
2. Morgan, *Slave Counterpart*, Table 2, 41. The counties surveyed for these statistics were Amelia, Charlotte, Chesterfield, Essex, Goochland, Halifax, Isle of Wight, Lunenburg, Mecklenburg, Northampton, Orange, Pittsylvania, Prince Edward, Spotsylvania, and York. In the latter, located on the Chesapeake, the changeover from small to large slaveholdings was particularly striking. In the period 1711-1720, 29 percent of planta-tions had 1-5 slaves, but between 1736 and 1745 this had fallen to 14 percent. Over the same decades, the proportion of York estates with 21 or more slaves increased from 17 to 52 percent. Allan Kulikoff, "The Origins of Afro-American Society in Tidewater Maryland and Virginia, 1700 to 1790," *William and Mary Quarterly* 35:2 (April 1978), Table III, "Plantation Sizes in Tidewater Maryland and Virginia, 1658 to 1740," 241.
3. Rouse, *Planters and Pioneers*, 50.
4. Quaker records show that 76.9% of those emigrating to Virginia between 1711 and 1750 came from Pennsylvania. See Larry Dale Gragg, *Migration in Early America: The Virginia Quaker Experience* (Ann Arbor: UMI Research Press, 1978), 30.
5. Ibid., 47-49. Most Quakers leaving the North came from modest circumstances and could not afford to keep up with rising prices, which forced small farmers either to become tenants or move out.

other dissidents once the Protestant William of Orange and his wife Mary came to the throne in 1688, vowing to respect religious rights.[1] Back in England, members of the Society of Friends had condemned slavery and the slave trade, but in the New World they were initially more equivocal about these practices. Many, including William Penn, were reluctant to give up their slaves even when urged by fellow Quakers to do so, and anti-slavery positions were not immediately adopted by individual groups of Friends in the various colonies. In fact, Quakers did not begin emancipating their own slaves until the 1770s.[2] As might be expected, their opposition to slavery was voiced later in the South than in the North: fear over what might happen to whites if the slaves were abruptly freed deterred Quakers in these colonies from disavowing the chattel system.[3] But many individual Friends considered the existence of slavery in their midst — let alone personal ownership of slaves — morally reprehensible. Indeed, it was the prevalence of slavery in the Tidewater that convinced many of the early Quaker immigrants to make their homes in the then relatively slave-free Piedmont.[4] Over time, some Friends came to regret having left the more racially tolerant environment of Pennsylvania, and a small number did, in fact, reverse migrate back to the City of Brotherly Love.[5] Others began to quietly raise questions about slavery's future in Virginia.

Unhappiness with slavery for religious reasons was less marked than distress over its economic consequences. For the dominance of slave labor was highly divisive: wealthy planters literally reaped its harvest, while small farmers contended against it. As slave ownership became more widespread in the Piedmont, the efforts of these yeoman farmers to survive became more and more arduous. They continued to grow small quantities of tobacco and other crops for commercial sale, but the relentless expansion of the slaveholders kept these "plain folk" constantly at a competitive disadvantage. The large planters bought up most of the cultivable, highly fertile land and pushed up the prices of what remained to be sold. And there was little of this left. Like the Tidewater before it, upcountry Virginia had a limited supply of desirable farmland, and migrating settlers frequently ended up with holdings no larger than those they had previously owned along the Chesapeake coast. Even though considerable quantities of royal land were put up for private sale in the first half of the 18th century — a

---

1. Virginia's General Assembly voted to ban Quakers in 1660, but members of this religious group continued to come to the colony, nonetheless. See Rouse, *Planters and Pioneers*, 104
2. Not until 1772 did Philadelphia's Society of Friends vote to excommunicate any member who refused to free his slaves. See Rouse, *Planters and Pioneers*, 138.
3. See Aptheker, "Quakers and Negro Slavery," 334-43.
4. Gragg, *Migration in Early America*, 54.
5. Fischer and Kelly, *Bound Away*, 110.

total of nearly five million acres — growth in the number of white settlers offset this territorial gain. Virginia's overall population multiplied more than five times over in less than 60 years — from an estimated 57,596 at the start of the century to 293,472 by 1756. It rose even more after an economic downturn in England, reaching 447,008 in 1770. [1]

Consequently, as the colonial era was coming to a close, Virginia was too crowded to allow the vast majority of planters to stake out large tracts of land for themselves. Only a small elite — roughly the top five percent of white households[2] — had the necessary resources to purchase such acreage. The rest lagged far behind, with less land — particularly less fertile, productive soil — at their disposal. Throughout the colony, the average amount of acreage per laborer fell considerably — from 112.62 acres in 1700 to 82.58 in 1755, when the Piedmont was heavily settled. By 1783, the top ten percent of landowners in the Shenandoah Valley controlled 45 percent of the total acreage.[3] In the four counties within the valley, between 23 and 52 percent of tax-paying whites did not own any land at all.[4] Only on the far western frontier, beyond the colonial pale, where hostile Indians lurked, was more land available for those daring enough to relocate there.[5] As the well-off planters took over extensive swaths of interior Virginia and brought in slaves to work these fields, they also made commercial agriculture less viable for yeoman farmers. The latter's production of tobacco and other cash crops fell sharply.[6] What these figures clearly suggest is an increasingly inequitable distribution of land, and wealth, in pre-Revolutionary Virginia. As had happened less than half a century earlier, the coexistence of whites from different classes on the same land was becoming unsustainable. More and more poor whites were forced out. In the north central county of Orange, for example, nearly four dozen men — or six percent of all householders — abandoned their homes during a single year, 1738.[7] The era in which, as one historian has expressed it, "mansion house and small dwelling rose side by side" on the Piedmont frontier was rapidly coming to an end.[8] Confounding Thomas Jefferson's

1. Bergstrom, *Markets and Merchants*, 35, 38. Put in another perspective, nearly a quarter of a million Virginians were living on just over 42,000 square miles of land in 1735. This translates into an average of 5.5 persons per square mile. See Bridenbaugh, *Myths and Realities*, 2.
2. Between three and ten percent of the planters belonged to this elite. See Breen, *Tobacco Culture*, 32.
3. Mitchell, "Shenandoah Valley Frontier," 484.
4. Robert D. Mitchell, *Commercialism and Frontier: Perspectives on the Early Shenandoah Valley* (Charlottesville: University Press of Virginia, 1977), 88. The four counties were Augusta, Rockingham, Rockbridge, and Fredericksburg.
5. Bergstrom, *Markets and Merchants*, 40, 44.
6. Cf. Phillips, *Slave Economy*, 15.
7. Kulikoff, *Tobacco and Slaves*, 96-97.
8. Bridenbaugh, *Myths and Realities*, 5.

later expressed hopes that America would prosper as a land of small, independent farmers, the nation that was about to be born evoking his rhetoric as its rallying cry was clearly developing into a quite different kind of society.

Repeating the psychological pattern set in the Tidewater, anger and frustration over this widening gap between rich and poor focused largely on the slaves who were the instruments for creating the economic disparity. Although some frontier settlers, such as the Quakers, had expressed moral sympathy for the slaves' plight, the majority of these Virginia pioneers continued to hold blacks in contempt and believe that they deserved no better fate than to serve as the property of whites, to spend their entire lives in abject servitude, treated scarcely better than animals. Instead of doing away with slavery, these settlers aspired to become slaveholders themselves. What angered them was the slave system's negative impact on their own lives. And for this state of affairs, the yeoman farmers and landless whites blamed the victims — the slaves who were, in effect, taking away their chance to rise out of poverty and join the privileged classes. (The disinclination of small farmers to blame the plantation way of life for their woes exemplifies what social psychologists today call "system justification theory" — a form of cognitive dissonance that prevents the victims of a political, social, or economic system from acknowledging how they are harmed by it.)

Two other factors deepened hostility toward blacks in the Piedmont. First, among the colonists living in the Chesapeake, there still lived a small number of white servants.[1] Despite the switchover to slave labor, colonists had continued to bring over poor whites under contracts of indenture during the 18th century, in large part because they were cheaper, in the short run, than slaves.[2] Many of them had come from Ireland and, after 1750, from Germany.[3] (Servants from Germany came under a redemptioner system, which enabled would-be immigrants with little money to pay off the costs of their transatlantic passage by working for several years.[4]) When their contracts had expired, these aspiring yeoman farmers realized their best opportunities to purchase land lay in the Piedmont, and they eagerly joined the mass exodus of planters, small farmers, laborers, craftsmen, servants, and slaves heading upriver. Once in the backcountry, these former servants found to their dismay that slaves were already hard at work in the best tobacco-growing fields and that the land remaining for sale hardly mea-

---

1. However, white servants had all but disappeared from Tidewater counties such as York and Surry by the end of the 1690s. Menard, "From Servants to Slaves," 362.
2. According to recent estimates, 307,400 whites migrated to British colonies between 1700 and 1775. Approximately half of these new colonists came as servants. Morgan, *Slavery and Servitude*, 44.
3. Roughly one fourth of all immigrants to the Chesapeake prior to the American Revolution came from either Ireland or Germany. Bridenbaugh, *Myths and Realities*, 7.
4. Morgan, *Slavery and Servitude*, 47.

sured up to their expectations. Their hopes of succeeding as independent farm-ers were often dashed. In the Shenandoah Valley, for example, the number of white settlers who could not afford to own land climbed steadily, particularly where slaves were most prevalent.[1] Thwarted in their bid to enter the landown-ing class, many of these migrants had no choice but to seek employment as ser-vants in planter households. Often, this meant remaining in servitude for the rest of their lives. And, in their minds, slaves were responsible for this unhappy turn of events. In the words of one historian, "More than any other class, these people [white servants] hated the black slave and regarded him as a real competitor."[2] Similar feelings of racial resentment were common among the Piedmont's white tenant farmers, who had worked on estates for absentee landowners until these Tidewater planters imported slaves to take the tenants' place.[3]

Secondly, the human tide sweeping across the Piedmont also included a number of freed slaves. Most of these had been emancipated by planters who had elected, for a variety of reasons, to remain in the Tidewater, but — because of the decline in tobacco growing there — had less need for chattel labor. A few were the children of formerly emancipated slaves. The great majority had one distin-guishing feature — lighter skin color: they were mulattoes, products of liaisons between white male settlers and black female slaves.[4] The facts of their origin — namely, their blood ties — made planters more kindly disposed toward these slaves and more willing to manumit them. But, while these free blacks were few in number,[5] their presence made most white Virginians extremely uncomfort-able. Instinctively these colonists equated the words "black" and "slave" and regarded any breach in the colony's rigid racial barriers with consternation. Manumitted slaves could easily constitute a vanguard of black revolutionaries eager to turn on their masters. For this reason, whites preferred to see freed slaves depart the Tidewater for the frontier; the Piedmont functioned as a conve-nient dumping ground for these racially anomalous individuals, just as other states would in the early decades of the 19th century.[6]

---

1. By 1800, 40-50 percent of residents of the upper Shenandoah Valley were landless, and as many as 65 percent in the lower half of the valley, where most slaves were to be found. Mitchell, "Shenandoah Valley Frontier," 475.
2. Bridenbaugh, *Myths and Realities*, 7.
3. Dunn, "Black Society," 79.
4. Morgan, "Slave Life," 461.
5. In 1790, Virginia had a population of 12,866 free blacks, of which a large but indetermi-nate number were mulattoes. The frequency of newspaper ads seeking the return of missing mulattoes suggests the number was not insignificant, however. See Rouse, *Planters and Pioneers*, 133.
6. Virginia sought to reduce its surplus slave population by selling slaves outside the state after 1810. Dunn, "Black Society," 81.

On the other hand, emancipated slaves were not welcome in the backcountry. Not only did they arouse the same racial animosity as slaves, these in-migrating blacks also presented an economic threat to former indentured servants and other poor whites who were then attempting to eke out a living in Virginia's interior. These groups sought the same jobs, as laborers, tenant farmers, craftsmen, and household help. Landless whites had already suffered from this interracial competition in the Tidewater, just as slaves had disadvantaged small, independent farmers there. Indeed, many whites at the bottom of the economic ladder had moved west, in part, in order to escape these rivals. The westward trickle of former slaves rekindled this animus, with greater intensity.[1] Regardless of where they lived, or their economic status, practically all of Virginia's whites were alarmed by the growing presence of mulattoes. As war with England approached, they began to discuss ways of ridding themselves of this problem. Clearly, the migration of former slaves to the Piedmont had not solved it.

Despite unease among non-slaveholding whites, slaves continued to move inland in greater numbers. Between 1755 and 1782, the slave population in the Piedmont increased at an impressive annual rate of 7.1 percent (more than twice the rate of natural increase in the colony.) This growth would decrease by more than half in the decade following the Revolution, but by then backcountry Virginia had replicated — and even exceeded — the numerical parity between blacks and whites that had earlier existed along the Chesapeake.[2] As the plantation system enlarged its domain, slaves became a majority of the population as far away as Louisa County, a few miles north of the James River and roughly 30 miles north and west of Richmond. To the south, near the North Carolina border, the same pattern was evident. In Lunenburg, for example, the proportion of slaves reached 53 percent by 1769.[3] An area that had first attracted only small farmers because of its lack of access to coastal rivers was now so completely dominated by large plantations that less well-off families began to move out, adumbrating a mass exodus from all over the Piedmont in the decades ahead. These lower-class whites bore a "stigma of dependence" for their failure to make it on their own, chiefly as tobacco growers, and this psychological scar pushed them further west. County records from the 1760s and 1770s show that 50 white families moved out of Lunenburg for every 75 that moved in. Those who left were mostly small farmers. They headed further west, bringing with them a lasting hostility toward the slaves who — in their view — had prevented them from making a livelihood in Virginia's Southside. This displacement of economically

---

1. See, for example, Dabney, *Virginia*, 188.
2. Morgan, "Slave Life," 435.
3. Beeman, *Southern Backcountry*, 64.

dependent whites represented another negative consequence of slavery's coming to Virginia's Piedmont.[1]

Nor was this impact limited to backcountry Virginia. Further to the south, in the colony of South Carolina, slaves were increasingly being employed to perform a raft of jobs previously performed exclusively by whites. Working-class whites in Charleston and inland towns joined forces to vent their outrage at this development: shipwrights, chimney sweeps, carpenters, bricklayers, tailors, and other skilled workers took to the streets in one of America's first organized labor protests. In the Carolina countryside, blacks were also taking over such skilled and semiskilled jobs as blacksmith and creating more anti-slave animosity.[2] At the bottom of the Southern economic pyramid there was simply not enough work for both poor whites and slaves, and, more often than not, it was the wage-earning whites who lost out. Because of the investment already made in them, slaves were invariably the more economical choice. However, it appears that whites of little means were not forced out of colonies south of Virginia to the same extent that they were in the Old Dominion itself. For example, while competition from slaves did make survival very difficult for these whites in Georgia, a more diversified economy allowed them to find jobs and remain there. In and around Savannah, whites worked as cooks, household servants, shoemakers, tailors, tavern owners, overseers, and clothing makers. Even though the proportion of blacks in Georgia rose sharply from 20 percent in 1751 to 40 percent in 1773, there is little evidence that this influx led to a large out-migration of poor whites.[3]

In Virginia, the flip side of this economic coin was accumulating capital among the large planters. Despite a steep climb in land prices, their holdings continued to grow. This was as true for the Tidewater as it was for the Piedmont. In the northern Chesapeake, Maryland and Virginia, planters with estates worth 100 pounds or more consolidated their economic primacy by staying out of debt and setting aside enough money to provide for their heirs. Those at the very top of the pyramid — households owning land valued at over 1,000 pounds — supplemented their incomes by moving into other spheres of economic activity. This diversification protected them against future slides in tobacco prices. Some bought goods and sold them profitably to other planters. Others, like Vir-

---

1. *Ibid.*, 68-69, 79, 99. Beeman say that the large number of debt cases in the county support this conclusion that many whites could not make a living in Lunenburg during the second half of the 18th century.
2. Morgan, *Slave Counterpoint*, 311.
3. For a detailed account of the impact of large-scale slavery in Georgia's non-slaveholding whites, see Lockley, *Lines in the Sand*. He finds evidence that blacks and whites working together developed relations that were not "highly antagonistic." Instead, "biracial interaction sometimes blurred the strict boundaries of race." *Ibid.*, xvii.

ginia's William Byrd, became venture capitalists; they lent money or dabbled in land speculation, purchasing estates in the Piedmont and then encouraging small farmers to migrate there, either leasing or selling off small parcels of land to the newcomers. Some members of the planter elite opened rural stores, invested in iron making, or entered the highly lucrative professions.

By succeeding in these undertakings, the great planters added to their already considerable wealth. During the 1730s, for example, the proportion of estates bordering the northern Chesapeake Bay worth between 100 and 500 pounds increased from slightly more than one fifth to nearly one third of the total. But, while a handful of families were growing richer, the vast majority of settlers, with the least amount of land at their disposal, were not. Farmers who owned property valued at 100 pounds or less continued to constitute nearly three fourths of the landowning whites. Conversely, families with farms worth 500 pounds or more made up just 2.2 percent of the landed class. [1] This same skewed distribution of wealth could be found inland. The Southside's Lunenburg County typified the pattern. Whereas most farms there extended over some 600 acres, the average amount of land owned by a member of the county's planter elite in the 1760s was 1,481 acres.[2] Forty miles to the north, in Albemarle County, the richest 10 percent of planters, which included Thomas Jefferson, had accumulated 70 percent of the privately-held property and owned over 60 percent of all slaves by the time of the American Revolution.[3]

As the Piedmont evolved economically from a frontier backcountry into a heavily settled agricultural region, it came to look more and more like the Tidewater. The same hierarchy became well entrenched. Headed by the planter elite, it included yeoman farmers, tenant farmers, laborers and craftsmen, white servants, freed blacks, and slaves. For several decades, these various groups coexisted without much conflict — largely because they were widely dispersed and had little contact with one other. At the same time, a prosperous tobacco economy rewarded rich planters and small farmers alike. Thanks to their comparably affordable prices, massive tobacco exports from the Chesapeake colonies dominated the European market, averaging some 100 million pounds by the early 1770s. But this prosperity would be short lived. The coming of war with England would curtail the sale of tobacco overseas. Meanwhile, the intense cultivating of Piedmont lands quickly exhausted the rich soils. Within a few decades, the backcountry had lost its agricultural attractiveness. Good acreage became scarce, and what was still available grew more expensive, making it more diffi-

---

1. Land, "Economic Base and Social Structure," 645, 647, 649, 651, 654.
2. Beeman, *Southern Backcountry*, 71, 31.
3. Majewski, *House Dividing*, 15. Thomas Jefferson inherited 5,000 acres in Albemarle when his father died in 1757.

cult for small farmers to buy. The high cost of clearing backcountry tracts also disadvantaged them.

Even the planter elite was adversely affected by these agricultural changes. By the end of the century, Thomas Jefferson was bemoaning the fact that, in Albemarle and adjacent counties, "The unprofitable condition of Virginia estates in general leaves it now next to impossible for the holder of one to avoid ruin."[1] As had been the case in the Tidewater, it was this dire prospect that led many backcountry planters, as well as "plain folk" farmers, to contemplate moving further west, once again. In addition to facing unfavorable economic conditions, small farmers also sensed that the freedom and independence they had once enjoyed in the Piedmont were now slipping away. In their minds, this loss was due to several interrelated factors — greater political power being wielded by the eastern half of the colony, higher taxes and other farming-related costs, the establishment of a more stratified social order, the arrival of well-heeled Chesapeake planters, and their bringing of so many slaves. The latter posed an economic threat, but they also embodied the antithesis of the values held most dear by backcountry farmers: slaves were patently *unfree* and thus inimical to the flourishing of liberty and individual rights on Virginia's frontier.[2]

How negatively each of these developments was viewed by backcountry farmers and their families is difficult to ascertain. Most likely it was their cumulative impact that made remaining in the Piedmont increasingly unattractive. What held these farmers back was a lack of better options. Under the terms of the Treaty of Paris, which was signed in 1763, Great Britain had agreed to respect the territorial rights of the Six Nations to all land west of the Appalachians. Settlers living near the fall line were, by and large, kept from venturing further inland. Land speculators, such as the Virginia-based Ohio Company, did dispatch expeditionary parties across this mountain barrier to reconnoiter, but only a few intrepid trappers and hunters followed in their footsteps. Farmers and their families did not dare to venture beyond the reach of colonial authority,

---

1. Boynton Merrill, *Jefferson's Nephews: A Frontier Tragedy* (Princeton: Princeton University Press, 1976), 47. Quoted in Majewski, *House Dividing*, 18. The poor quality of soil in AlbemarleCounty had caused land prices to stagnate.

2. Edmund S. Morgan has argued to the contrary in *American Slavery/American Freedom*. Here he writes that the decrease in the number of freed indentured servants as a result of large-scale slavery in Virginia brought benefits to the remaining poor whites: "they were allowed not only to prosper but also to acquire social, psychological, and political advantages that turned the thrust of exploitation away from them and aligned them with the exploiters." Morgan, *American Slavery*, 344. The antipathy toward slavery felt by Virginians in the western half of the state is evident in the 1831-32 vote in the House of Delegates on abolishing slavery. Representatives from the inland half of the Old Dominion unanimously favored this proposal. For details on this vote, see Allan Nevins, *Ordeal of the Union*, vol. 1, *Fruits of Manifest Destiny* (New York: Scribner's, 1947), 148.

where troops could not be expected to help them ward off Indian attacks. Still, pressure to push into the interior continued to mount. So did resentment toward the British government for thwarting this desire. Being held back by an arbitrary barrier ran counter to the settlers' instincts and inclinations. They wanted to live their lives according to their own rules, not those imposed upon then. And now, above all else, frontier folk in Virginia and elsewhere craved open spaces, more land — what they referred to colloquially as "elbow room."[1]

Talk of freedom was very much in the air in the late 1760s and early 1770s, as the burdens of excessive taxes and other British policies weighed heavily on the North American colonies. The war they would soon fight to gain their independence was symptomatic of an even greater distrust of authority and external control — distrust that dated back as far as Bacon's Rebellion a century before. In the aftermath of the American Revolution, settlers spread from New England all the way south to Georgia would exercise their newfound freedom not only by taking charge of their own economic and political affairs, but also by heading west and laying claim to parts of the great unknown wilderness that lay on the far side of the mountains. By taking this momentous step, they would be simultaneously fulfilling their longing for more autonomy and escaping a slave system that manifested the same oppressiveness and injustice against which they had just rebelled.

If the economic consequences of slavery had pushed small, independent Virginia farmers into the Piedmont during the colonial period, it was a combination of economics and political ideology that prompted these same farmers and their offspring to undertake another trek westward in the years after the Revolution. The arrival of thousands of slaves in the backcountry had made tobacco growing unprofitable for planters of modest means, but, worse than that, it had destroyed the appeal of living on the frontier. The region's character was now shaped by a labor system these "plain folk" farmers now considered abhorrent. Poverty and hard times, they were prepared to endure. But the denial of freedom, they could not tolerate.

---

1. Cf. Dale Van Every, *Forth to the Wilderness: The First American Frontier, 1754-1774* (New York: Arno Press, 1977), 44.

III. BLUEGRASS, BLACK DOMINANCE

The Revolutionary War revealed a widening schism in American thinking about slavery. Influenced by Enlightenment views on human liberty and individual rights, many colonists, particularly in the North, had begun to argue for gradually abolishing the chattel system in the years leading up to the War for Independence. They recognized that owning slaves undermined their arguments in favor of breaking free of Britain.[1] At the same time, some religious groups, notably the Quakers, had openly condemned slavery as immoral and incompatible with Christianity. In the 1740s, the evangelical Great Awakening embraced blacks as fellow Christians and thus bestowed upon them a higher status. In this climate, Northern public opinion gradually began to turn against slavery: petitions calling for its abolition reached the colonial governments of New Jersey and Pennsylvania shortly before the start of the Revolutionary War.[2] Abolitionists in Massachusetts, Rhode Island, and Connecticut also attempted — although without success — to ban the slave system

But this admirable "compassion for afflicted humanity" had an economic basis as well.[3] In contrast to the South, slavery in the North was not essential to

---

1. For a full discussion of Northern attitudes toward slavery before the Revolution, see Leon Litwack, *North of Slavery: The Negro in the Free States, 1790-1860* (Chicago: University of Chicago Press, 1961), 3-13. For perceived parallels between the plight of the colonists and that of black slaves, see Gary B. Nash, "Red, White, and Black: The Origins of Racism in Colonial America," in *The Great Fear: Race in the Mind of America*, ed. Gary B. Nash and Richard Weiss (New York: Holt, Rinehart & Winston, 1970), 21.
2. Arthur Zilversmit, *The First Emancipation: The Abolition of Slavery in the North* (Chicago: University of Chicago Press, 1967), 91, 93. A number of Northern blacks also petitioned to be set free in the years leading up to the Revolution.
3. This phrase comes from David Brion Davis, *The Problem of Slavery in Western Culture* (Ithaca: Cornell University Press, 1966), 411.

economic growth. There was no counterpart to the plantation system above the Mason Dixon Line. While some of the farms in the Northern colonies employed slaves — and would continue to do so for decades after the Revolution — most were too small to utilize such a workforce. In New England, where the township system of land division prevailed, farms rarely exceeded 500 acres in size. During the 1750s, a family of five in western Massachusetts or Connecticut could live off what it produced by its own labor on just a dozen arable acres.[1] Since much of Northern agriculture remained at the subsistence level, the need for field hands was limited. Furthermore, those white workers who were employed on farms in states such as Massachusetts and New York were unhappy about having to compete for jobs with the slaves and wanted to see the chattel system disappear.[2] In addition, the merchants, craftsmen, and shopkeepers in Northern villages and cities did not have great use for slaves in this pre-industrial era. On top of these economic reasons, blacks (and other "outsiders") were not welcome in the North, especially in New England, because of racial bias.

Prior to the Revolution, anti-slavery sentiment had also made some inroads in the South. Quakers who migrated to Virginia spread abolitionist thinking there. So did Baptist and Methodist preachers, who first came to the Piedmont in the 1750s.[3] Scotch-Irish and German settlers in this region also brought religious-based objections to slavery. But those who dared to make the case against owning slaves faced an uphill fight. By now, the South's plantation economy was more dependent than ever upon chattel labor. The sheer number of slaves in the region — amounting to 40 percent of the population[4] — made whites leery of freeing them. A few Southern planters like Thomas Jefferson had concluded that slavery was wrong and should eventually end, but hesitated to call for immediate emancipation, fearing this would lead to racial bloodshed and chaos. Such concerns made it difficult for lofty philosophical arguments against inequality, such as those Jefferson crafted so eloquently in the Declaration of Independence, to be translated into concrete action to free the slaves. (At most, "enlightened" Southerners were willing to make slavery less harsh and more humane.[5]) Instead, well-

---

1. Mitchell, "Shenandoah Valley Frontier," 475.
2. Donald L. Robinson, *Slavery in the Structure of American Politics, 1765-1820* (New York: Harcourt Brace Jovanovich, 1971), 22. Cf. Jordan, *White Over Black*, 130, and Zilversmit, *First Emancipation*, 35, 46.
3. Morgan, "Slave Life in Piedmont Virginia," 475-77.
4. This was in 1770. Fogel and Engerman, *Time on the Cross*, 21.
5. James Brewer Stewart, *Holy Warriors: The Abolitionists and American Slavery* (New York: Hill and Wang, 1976), 23. But this was not always the case. Masters were particularly harsh with runaways. In one instance, a slaveholder named John Meaux advertised a reward of five pounds for the return of one of his bondsmen and ten pounds "for his head sever'd from his body, to be paid in cattle at cash price." *Kentucky Gazette*, 22 Jan. 1791.

intentioned slaveholders accepted a high degree of incongruity between their attitudes and their practices. Jefferson himself, in his *Notes on the State of Virginia*, would call slavery a "blot" on the new nation's character and urge that blacks be removed to another part of the country to live in freedom, but did not get around to manumitting any of his several hundred slaves until 1796 — fully two decades after he had affirmed that "All men are created equal."[1] Thus, while the newly independent Northern states debated freeing slaves residing within their bound-aries and gradually passed laws to this effect, the South remained stubbornly wedded to its chattel system.

Not only North and South were divided over slavery, however. Just as great a difference in attitude separated Southerners living on or near the Atlantic coast from many of those who had ventured into the backcountry. In the eastern part of colonies like Virginia resided a well-heeled gentry — English in manner, con-servative in politics, dedicated to maintaining a hierarchical order that would protect their wealth and power. This status quo depended largely on their slave-holdings. But slaves were also important to many more whites in the Tidewater: nearly half of all families now owned slaves.[2] The chattel system was central to the region's way of life. On Virginia's frontier, the situation was different. While large plantations had been established throughout the Piedmont and the Great Valley, they had not yet displaced small tobacco growers to the same extent as further east. The chimneys of small farms dotted the hills and rocky valleys, where "plain folk" farmers, including many from northern Ireland, stubbornly clung to their independent, democratic way of life in spite of the massive infu-sion of slaves from the coast. In addition to selling some tobacco, they survived by growing subsistence crops and raising livestock. Philosophically as well as economically, these backcountry settlers regarded slavery as harmful to their own existence and therefore favored proposals to limit or do away with it. For example, Jefferson's 1784 proposal to ban slave ownership from the newly acquired territory of the Old Northwest would be applauded on this frontier.[3] Although non-slaveholding property owners made up a majority of voters in western Virginia, a disproportionate awarding of legislative seats, first in the

---

1. Thomas Jefferson, *Notes on the State of Virginia*, ed. William Peden (Chapel Hill: University of North Carolina Press, 1955), 87, 137. Jefferson freed his chef, James Hemings, the brother of Sally Hemings, on 5 Feb. 1796, and another Hemings relative during his life-time. However, at the time of his death, Jefferson still owned over 120 slaves in Albe-marle County. See "Farm Book Listing Slaves, 1795-1796," *http://www.lib.virginia.edu/speccol/collections/tj/farm.html*. The only other slaves Jefferson freed, in his will, were five other members of the Hemings family, including two of Sally's sons, Eston and Madison.
2. By 1782, 46 percent of white households in the Chesapeake owned slaves. Dunn, "Black Society in the Chesapeake," 66.
3. Rouse, *Planters and Pioneers*, 139.

colonial House of Burgesses and then in the state assembly, gave the eastern planters and their supporters a numerical advantage, and they made full use of this power to block any plan for altering the slave system.[1] As long as this situation did not change, there would be no prospect of freedom for black slaves in the Old Dominion. Nonetheless, the continuation of the slave system struck many as disconcertingly out of step with the radical political direction the American colonies were now pursuing.

At the time of the Revolution, freedom was, of course, foremost in the minds and hearts of many North American colonists. To them, "freedom" meant many things. First and foremost, it meant bringing an end to oppressive British rule and gaining independence for the colonies. These objectives were grounded in economics — the burden of excessive taxes imposed by the Crown — but embraced as philosophical imperatives. "Freedom" was the innate, God-given right of all men. "The natural liberty of man is to be free from any superior power on earth, and not to be under the will or legislative authority of man, but to have only the law of Nature for his rule," John Locke had written in his *Second Treatise of Government* (1690). With these words he rejected the divine right of kings, defied oppressive governments, and helped to shape Revolutionary thought.[2] Locke also stressed the importance of land ownership in establishing one's independence and freedom — a theme that resonated well with many frontier families. Furthermore, by equating freedom with life itself, the English philosopher emphasized its fundamental incompatibility with slavery. This reasoning suggested two possible outcomes. Either slavery should be outlawed, as some followers of Locke believed,[3] or else blacks, because they had submitted to being enslaved, had to be considered *ipso facto* incapable of enjoying freedom. If one accepted the latter premise, then efforts to emancipate slaves were illogical and doomed to fail. Instead, whites should create a society that excluded blacks so that, in it, freedom could truly flourish. Since large numbers of slaves already existed in the South and were unlikely to suddenly vanish, the best way to attain this kind of freedom was for whites to move elsewhere — further west, into the wilderness.

On the frontier, "freedom" was associated with self-reliance and independence, values required for survival in the remote, isolated, and dangerous environment that existed beyond the Blue Ridge Mountains. The Scotch-Irish

1. This imbalance of power between east and west led to so-called "peasant revolts" in several colonies, with many frontiersmen deciding to move west to other territories in search of more independence. See Paxson, *History of the American Frontier*, 26.
2. John Locke, *Second Treatise of Government*, ed. C. B. MacPherson (Indianapolis: Hackett Publishing, 1980), 17.
3. For example, in 1783 a Massachusetts court ruled that slavery violated the doctrine of "natural rights." Zilversmit, *First Emancipation*, 114.

immigrants who settled in Virginia's Great Valley and western hills cherished these values and spread them widely. Others quickly learned their importance. Hunters, trappers, and subsistence farmers in the backcountry succeeded or failed on the strength of their own efforts, not because of any help they received from anyone else. Still other pioneers simply relished the chance to enter into a wholly untamed and uncivilized world and survive within it. In the words of one historian, "Their real impulse was so strong as to verge upon the irrational. They yearned to get to that wilderness while it was still totally wild. They were striving to escape the ordered world behind them and its clutter of such frustrations as quitrents, taxes, debts, wages, laws . . . They were reaching for precisely what the Indians were struggling to save — escape from routine, those peculiar satisfactions known only to the confirmed hunter, the comfort of intimacy with nature, the assurance of self-dependence, license to roam."[1] Either by wont or out of necessity, these frontier folk preferred to lead their lives as they saw fit and regarded any outside intervention in their affairs as unwanted and harmful meddling. So, in their minds, "freedom" also came to mean being left alone.

Accordingly, much of their ire was directed at the colonial — and later state — government, for the taxes, regulations, and other laws it sought to impose on them. (At the same time, western Virginians complained bitterly about their political under-representation and inadequate state funding for local roads, bridges, and canals — revealing ambivalence about government that would characterize most states in the West.) Outrage over such laws periodically led to protests and acts of defiance, echoing the actions of Nathaniel Bacon and his followers in the 1670s. After the Revolution, when western lands became more accessible, many frontier families were more than eager to wish organized society good riddance and strike out on their own into the uncharted interior.[2] Their "autonomous spirit"[3] embraced freedom in its fullest sense — freedom from economic want, freedom from encroaching neighbors, freedom from social dependence, freedom from intrusive government, freedom from tenancy and squatting — and freedom from an oppressive chattel system. Frontier settlers tended to equate slavery with the British tyranny they had only recently overthrown. Therefore, as one historian has written, they "hated the institution and endeavored more than ever to keep their section open to free labor."[4] In fact, the ill effects of slavery on poor, independent whites underlay desire for all of these freedoms and gave them their powerful driving force.

1. Van Every, *Forth to the Wilderness*, 43-4.
2. Many early explorers showed their disdain for government by overlooking laws barring them from settling west of the Appalachians. See Cardinal Goodwin, *The Trans-Mississippi West, 1803-1853: A History of Its Acquisition and Settlement* (New York: Russell & Russell, 1967), 19.
3. Paxson, *History of the American Republic*, 35.

The westward spread of slavery during the Revolutionary War weakened the cause of freedom. It also exacerbated the tensions between large slaveholders and small, non-slaveholding farmers. To avoid losing any slaves to the British Army, many Tidewater planters moved their black laborers to backcountry estates during this conflict. Others were relocated due to the continuing depletion of coastal soils as well as the economic depression brought about by a wartime cessation of trade with Great Britain. All told, 20,000 slaves were removed from the Chesapeake between 1755 and 1782, increasing by half the population of blacks living in the interior, bringing it up to 46 percent of the total.[1] By 1790, half of Virginia's slaves — the single largest concentration in the new nation — were to be found in this part of the state. This demographic shift increased the unhappiness of yeoman farmers and their interest in seeking out new homesteads further west. Uneasiness over slavery increased early in the war, when the deposed colonial governor appealed to slaves to run away and gain their freedom by going over to the British side.[2] In November 1775, the 4th Earl of Dunmore made this promise to any Virginia slave who managed to reach his garrisons. As a result, an estimated 4,000 ran away from the Tidewater during the war — the largest freeing of slaves at one time prior to the Civil War.[3] Among the colony's independent farmers there was some sympathy for these runaways: many backcountry settlers saw the parallels between the blacks' and their own struggle for freedom, while noting the irony in the fact that it was the British, not the American rebels, who had made this offer of emancipation. This challenge to the chattel system reinforced frontier hostility toward slavery and its backers and prompted many "plain folk" to move out of its sphere of dominance once the war was over.

After its victory in the Revolutionary War, the new government of the United States was anxious to see settled the lands it had gained from Great Britain. This vast area — bordered by the Appalachians in the east and the Mississippi River in the west and stretching north from the Ohio River to Canada —

4. "Actual abolition was never popular in western Virginia, but the love of the people of that section for freedom kept them estranged from the slaveholding districts of the State . . ." Carter G. Woodson, "Freedom and Slavery in Appalachian America," *Journal of Negro History* 1:2 (April 1916), 140, 142.

1. Morgan and Nicholls, "Slaves in Piedmont Virginia," 218. Morgan, *Slave Counterpoint*, 521.

2. Initially, some Northern colonies, facing manpower shortages, had accepted slaves in the ranks, and a few took part in early battles such as the one at Bunker Hill. So did a larger number of freed slaves. All told, an estimated 5,000 blacks served in the Continental Army. But the Southern colonies, fearing that putting weapons in the hands of blacks was dangerous, banned their recruitment, and several Northern colonies soon followed suit. For a full treatment of this topic, see Benjamin Quarles, *The Negro in the American Revolution* (Chapel Hill: University of North Carolina Press, 1961).

3. Morgan, "Slave Life," 480. Large numbers of slaves also ran away from their masters in Maryland and South Carolina. Rouse, *Planters and Pioneers*, 139.

nearly doubled the size of the original Thirteen Colonies and presented an unprecedented opportunity for economic growth and expansion. The Continental Congress had already promised veterans between 100 and 500 acres of land as payment for their military service, and this commitment put pressure on the federal government to organize the newly acquired territory quickly and open it to settlers. The Ohio Company, a group dominated by planters from the Tidewater's Northern Neck, was eagerly waiting to purchase large tracts in what was then known as the Northwest Territory — a 260,000 square-mile area that encompassed present-day Ohio, Indiana, Illinois, Michigan, and Wisconsin, as well as part of Minnesota. But there were a couple of sticking points. One had to do with slavery.

As chairman of the congressional committee charged with drawing up a government for this new acquisition, Jefferson had put forth a plan calling for its division into ten territories and stipulating that neither slavery nor involuntary servitude should be allowed in any of them after 1800. His motives for making this latter recommendation were complex and even contradictory. On the one hand, Jefferson wanted to see slavery abolished. He had drawn up a resolution to this effect while serving briefly as a delegate to the House of Burgesses, in 1769. In drafting the Declaration of Independence, Jefferson had originally written a section condemning George III for forcing slavery upon the colonies, but then deleted the passage after delegates from Georgia and South Carolina had strongly objected. Subsequently, he had helped to draw up a scheme for gradual emancipation for the Virginia Assembly to consider, but then, realizing that the Tidewater planters who controlled the legislature would vote against any form of emancipation, Jefferson and his mentor, George Wythe, had withdrawn their proposal. But, despite these compromises, Jefferson firmly believed the fate of the young nation lay in the hands of its yeoman farmers — the embodiment of the self-governing, independent-minded American spirit that he had come to admire while growing up on the Virginia frontier.[1]

Nothing was more inimical to this agrarian ideal of noble freemen than a system of bondage. Slavery was degrading to blacks, but also to whites who came into contact with it. The two races, Jefferson argued in *Notes on the State of Virginia*, were inherently different and unequal. Whites possessed superior intellect as well as physical qualities, and any mixing with blacks could only be to the former's detriment. Worse, he wrote, the bitter legacy of oppression and antago-

---

1. For example, in an August 23, 1785 letter to John Jay, Jefferson wrote: "Cultivators of the earth are the most valuable citizens. They are the most vigorous, the most independant [sic], the most virtuous, & they are tied to their country & wedded to it's [sic] liberty & interests by the most lasting bonds." Thomas Jefferson, *Writings* (New York: Library of America, 1984), 818.

nism could not be overcome, and if the two races were forced to live together, this circumstance would "produce convulsions which will probably never end but in the extermination of the one or the other race."[1] To forestall such deleterious racial contact in the future, when slavery would be abolished, blacks should first be removed to another part of the country where, Jefferson suggested, they could develop as a free and independent people. Segregation would supplant subjugation as a more humane and durable solution to the nation's race problem.

If one examines Jefferson's plan for organizing the Northwest Territory in light of what he had to say about race in his contemporaneous *Notes*, it appears that protecting the well being of white settlers was more important to the future president than striking a blow against black servitude. Certainly this was the prevailing attitude among political figures of his day, even those who did not care for slavery or want to see it continue.[2] Virtually none of them evinced any sympathy for the black man or any willingness to lift a finger in order to improve his lot. During the lengthy deliberations of the Constitutional Convention in Philadelphia, only one delegate, New York's Gouverneur Morris, ventured to speak out in favor of abolition. Most of the other framers were, in the words of one historian, "either unperturbed about slavery or else completely resigned to its presence in America." They were prepared to sidestep the issue in order to achieve national unity on other matters. In the halls of the various state legislatures, as among the white public, "No one but a few idealists . . . cared about slavery."[3] Jefferson may have distinguished himself from most Revolutionary leaders in calling for an eventual end to the slave system; nonetheless, he, too, looked at the nation's racial quandary first and foremost from a white man's perspective.

The question of whether or not to open the Western lands to slavery was actually not considered very important at the time.[4] Delegates to the Continental Congress spent little time debating Jefferson's proposal and, although it was voted down along North-South lines, the interests of both regions converged in wishing to see the Northwest developed as quickly as possible.[5] Thus, when a

---

1. Jefferson, *Notes*, 138.
2. In addition to Jefferson, support for the eventual abolition of slavery was voiced by such Revolutionary leaders as Patrick Henry, John Adams, James Otis, and Alexander Hamilton. See Woodson, "Freedom and Slavery," 138, note 16.
3. Robinson, *Structure of American Politics*, 233, 27.
4. One historian has observed that the article dealing with slavery was "not of the substance of the Ordinance." B.A. Hinsdale, *The Old Northwest* (New York: Townsend MacCoun, 1888), 346. A ban on the slave system was a pre-condition for the Ohio Associates, a major land company, to purchase tracts in the territory.
5. Jefferson was the only Southerner to vote in the affirmative. However, his proposed exclusion of slavery was defeated only because one of the New Jersey delegates, John Beatty, was ill and unable to cast his vote.

similar proposal was put forward in 1787 by Nathan Dane of Massachusetts, it was unanimously approved, again without much discussion, even though, ironically, a majority of states voting "yes" this time were slave-holding ones.[1] Since the Northwest Ordinance did not impose any ban on slavery south of the Ohio River, Southern delegates appeared content to accept this implied *quid pro quo*.[2] However, this vote would mark the last time that elected officials from the South would support any measure to restrict expansion of the slave system.

Indeed, this compromise reached by the Continental Congress was a harbinger of far more rancorous debate and upheaval over slavery in the coming decades. After glossing over their differences in order to ratify the Constitution and establish the Union, Northerners and Southerners would repeatedly lock horns over slavery's extension into western lands, as the economic, political, and territorial stakes increased, and each region felt increasingly threatened by any gains made by the other.[3] But while national attention would come to focus on this fierce and protracted inter-regional struggle, the less dramatic but equally consequential conflict over the slave system *within the South* was being decided on the ground. Wealthy slaveholders were moving west to stake out a new realm for their plantations. At the same time, "plain folk" families were voting against black bondage — and the white economic and social order that depended upon it — with their feet, by abandoning their Piedmont homes and following the routes recently laid out by Daniel Boone and other pioneers through the Appalachians into a new Land of Milk and Honey known as "Kentucky country."[4] By and large, those seeking to escape the influence of the slave system were not act-

1. The reporting committee only inserted the ban on slavery at the last minute. See *The Continental Congress*, ed. Edmund Cody Burnett (New York: Macmillan, 1941), 685. This modified version was made more palatable for the Southern delegates through inclusion of a provision for the capture and return of fugitive slaves from the Northwest Territory. For a full discussion of Article 6 of the Northwest Ordinance, see Peter S. Onuf, *Statehood and Union: A History of the Northwest Ordnance* (Bloomington: Indiana University Press, 1987), 109-12. Onuf cites various reasons why Southern delegates did not oppose the ban on slavery, namely, a belief that their economic interests in the Northwest Territory would be well served if a slave system were not introduced there, specifically since this would eliminate northern competition for the tobacco industry. Cf. *Continental Congress*, 683-84.
2. There is speculation that some Southern representatives went along with the provision because they were opposed to slavery. Others wanted to make sure that tobacco production did not take hold north of the Ohio and create competition. See, for example, Charles T. Hickok, *The Negro in Ohio, 1802-1870*. (1896; reprint, New York: AMS Press, 1975), 20-23.
3. Many delegates to the Constitutional Convention had anticipated that conflicts between small and large states would prove most divisive, but they discovered, instead, that slavery was far more contentious. Only by agreeing not to press the issue (or even use the word "slave" in the Constitution) were Northern delegates able to dissuade the Southern states from refusing to join the inchoate Union.
4. The word "Kentucky" came from *Kanta-ke* — the Iroquois term for the land west of the Blue Ridge Mountains. Landon Y. Jones, *William Clark and the Shaping of the West* (New York: Hill and Wang, 2004), 23. The term was first used in a 1753 issue of the *Pennsylvania Journal*. Hazel Dicken Garcia, *To Western Woods: The Breckenridge Family Moves to Kentucky in 1793* (Rutherford: Fairleigh Dickinson University Press, 1991), 29.

ing out of moral revulsion, but because of economic necessity. Both slave owners and non-slaveholding farmers trudged out of the Virginia backcountry hoping to perpetuate their distinctive ways of life on more accommodating land. But this next migration west would only bring these two groups into more conflict.

Initially, the allure of abundant and bountiful land drew whites from many different social classes — and with differing aspirations — toward this promising new frontier. Interest in the wilderness beyond the Appalachians had existed for several decades. As early as the late 1740s, British land companies had drawn up plans for exploring Virginia's interior. Thomas Lee organized the Ohio Company in 1748, receiving a grant of 200,000 acres in the Ohio Valley. The first of the company's emissaries, a surveyor and physician named Thomas Walker, discovered a way through the Appalachians — the famed Cumberland Gap — as early as 1750 and happened upon promising fertile land north of the Cumberland River. Two years later, John Finley followed this route across the mountains and then traveled downstream by canoe on the Ohio River to the site of present-day Louisville. Another group keenly eager to develop the frontier, the Loyal Company, was formed in the early 1750s and given a grant for 800,000 acres west of the Appalachians.

Under the Treaty of 1763, which ended the Seven Years War, England had acquired all of the territory east of the Mississippi that had formerly belonged to France — a huge swath stretching from the Gulf of Mexico northward to the Great Lakes region and eastern Canada. In order to avoid another costly war with Native American tribes living beyond the Appalachians, George III issued a proclamation that same year declaring these lands off limits to his countrymen, but Virginia fur traders ignored this royal decree and ventured across the mountains on several occasions during the 1760s. Growing pressure to open up more land for settlement led the British government to force the Iroquois to agree to another treaty, in 1768. This pushed the eastern boundary of Indian territory back to the banks of the Susquehanna and Ohio rivers. Some 200,000 adjacent acres were promised to veterans, and a survey of these lands undertaken. With the danger of hostilities now reduced, the legendary "long hunter" and explorer Daniel Boone blazed a trail into eastern Kentucky in 1769.[1] Like many of those who first entered this uncharted territory, he was looking for greater freedom and adventure — escape from the increasingly crowded farm communities of the eastern colonies. But, ironically, the reports of his journey, along with those of other early pioneers, had the effect of encouraging thousands more settlers to head west and establish homesteads there.

---

1. Boone first ventured into the Appalachians in 1767, inspired by the travels of John Baker and James Ward.

The colonial government now encouraged this migration by adopting more liberal land policies in the 1770s. Initially, these favored small farmers and landless whites. In 1773, authorities in Jamestown agreed to grant preemption rights (that is, the right to bid first on property) to squatters occupying tracts owned by one of the early land companies. The bargain price of three pounds per 100 acres — much less than what non-residents would have to pay — prompted a small stampede of would-be landowners across the Appalachians.[1] But their frontier hegemony would be short lived. Land speculators were also attracted by the opportunities Kentucky presented. In short order, some of them took a bold step to secure this territory for themselves. In March 1775, acting without any official sanction, Col. Richard Henderson and several other representatives of the newly created Transylvania Company signed an agreement with the Cherokees to purchase all the land north of Cumberland to the Ohio River (encompassing most of present-day Kentucky), for the sum of 10,000 pounds.[2] This 20-million acre domain was named the Transylvania Colony. With visions of developing an empire there, Henderson then hired Boone to forge the Wilderness Road, running over 200 miles through the mountains to Kentucky.

In the years after 1775, Boone guided several caravans of dozens and even hundreds of persons — men, women, children, and slaves — along this route. These pioneers braved disease and bitter cold in the mountain passes, traveling on foot or on horseback over narrow trails etched into the rocky face.[3] Emerging on the far side of the Cumberland Gap, they next followed a path westward across the Cumberland Plateau, and then turned northward toward the fertile Bluegrass region.[4] At the end of one of these trips, they came upon large herds of bison grazing upon long, billowing grasses in idyllic tranquility.[5] The glowing tales of Boone's followers prompted many more settlers, including Abraham Lincoln's grandfather, to move west into the Ohio Valley.[6] So did the reports of other adventurers. John Filson returned to declare that the Bluegrass contained "the best tract of land in North-America, and probably in the world." When Felix Walker arrived in the same region, he noted: "We felt ourselves as passengers through a wilderness just arrived at the fields of Elysium, or at a garden where there was no forbidden fruit."[7]

---

1. Hughes and Cain, *American Economic History*, 42.
2. The Cherokees and several other tribes complained that the Iroquois did not have the right to cede this territory to the British, as they had done in 1768.
3. For details of these early journeys through the Cumberland Gap, see Dick, *Dixie Frontier*, 15-6.
4. Lynch, "Westward Flow," 309.
5. Otis K. Rice, *Frontier Kentucky* (Lexington: University Press of Kentucky, 1975), 26.
6. For details on early movements of the Lincoln family, see Ira M. Tarbell, *In the Footsteps of the Lincolns* (New York: Harper & Row, 1924), 53-70.
7. Quoted in Otis K. Pike, *Frontier Kentucky* (Louisville: University Press of Kentucky, 1875), 71.

Not waiting for surveys to be conducted, speculators with deep pockets bought up the best lands available. By the beginning of 1776, over 900 claims were on the Transylvania books, encompassing more than half a million acres.[1] Most of these early purchases were made by speculators and well-to-do planters, and this land grab caused considerable resentment on the part of squatters shortly after the Revolutionary War broke out.[2] They gathered in Harrodsburg, Kentucky's first colonial outpost, in June 1776, and drew up a petition demanding that Virginia authorities take possession of this territory so that more equitable land policies would be enforced. Later that year, in response to this protest, the land bought from the Cherokees was officially made part of Virginia and designated Kentucky County.[3] But this partial victory for squatters and small homesteaders would not stand for long. As the colonies were wresting their independence from England, powerful interests reasserted their influence on this frontier.

The Land Act of 1779, written by George Mason with the help of Thomas Jefferson, put large tracts extending over 38 million acres in present-day Kentucky up for sale via treasury warrants. The smallest parcel available for sale consisted of 400 acres and cost 80 pounds. The size of this minimum purchase effectively shut most small farmers out of the land market[4] — an outcome starkly at odds with Jefferson's professed goal of establishing a western yeomanry. Within a year of enacting this policy, the Virginia government had issued grants totaling close to seven million acres.[5] But the greatest concentration of holdings went to just a handful of purchasers. Twenty-one individuals and partnerships secured properties of 100,000 acres or more. By virtue of these holdings, they became the dominant economic and political force in this part of Virginia. Indeed, when Kentucky entered the Union, in 1792, this small group of landowners owned over a quarter of its territory. [6]

---

1. For details on the early settlement of Kentucky, see Thomas D. Clark, *A History of Kentucky* (New York: Prentice-Hall, 1937), 29-86, *passim.*
2. Neal O. Hammon, *Early Kentucky Land Records, 1773-1780* (Louisville: Filson Club, 1992), xv.
3. Stephen Aron, "Pioneers and Profiteers: Land Speculation and the Homestead Ethic in Frontier Kentucky," *Western Historical Quarterly* 23:2 (May 1992), 189-90.
4. See Victor B. Howard, *The Evangelical War against Slavery and Caste: The Life and Times of John G. Fee* (Selinsgrove: Susquehanna University Press, 1996), 13. On the other hand, squatters who had arrived before 1778 were still able to purchase 400 acres for far less — only 40 shillings. Otto, *Southern Frontiers,* 71.
5. Hughes and Cain, *American Economic History,* 43. Land owned by the Transylvania Company was made available to men who had served in the French and Indian War. Military warrants held by Revolutionary War veterans were subsequently honored in the southwestern part of Kentucky. From 2 Nov. 1779 to 25 April 25 1780, claims for over 370,000 acres were registered. Hammon, *Kentucky Land Records,* xv-xvi.
6. Aron, "Pioneers and Profiteers," 190.

But by no means did they have this frontier all to themselves. When the American Revolution ended, the floodgates holding back settlers opened, and they poured through the Cumberland Gap into eastern Kentucky and Tennessee. In addition, some 1,000 flatboats were transporting settlers down the Ohio River from Pittsburgh each year.[1] By 1790 there were over 61,000 whites living in Kentucky alone; this population jumped to nearly 180,000 in the next ten years.[2] Between 1795 and 1810, an estimated 200-300,000 settlers traversed the Wilderness Road to this new frontier. While other pioneers were entering the northern Ohio Valley, responding to Congress's organizing of the Northwest Territory and putting up its lands for sale, migrants from the Upper South, particularly Virginia, set their sights on Kentucky. According to one estimate, as many as 375,000 people — whites, black freemen, and slaves — left Virginia during the years 1790-1840. This was far more than the number that moved out of the Northern free states.[3]

Indeed, the western part of the Old Dominion was the nation's single largest source of pioneers. Among its migrating native sons were some of the most prominent names in national exploration and politics — men like George Rogers Clark, his brother William Clark, Meriwether Lewis, Henry Clay, Richard Henderson, and Zachary Taylor.[4] By the middle of the 19th century, close to 400,000 white persons who had been born in Virginia were living on the Western frontier.[5] By another count, nearly a quarter of a million residents of Virginia and Maryland left their homes in the three decades after 1790 and resettled in Kentucky, the Northwest Territory, and the upland regions of the Carolinas, Georgia, Tennessee, and Alabama.[6] Nearly one of every eight Virginians headed

1. Jones, *William Clark*, 51.
2. According to other estimates, nearly 70,000 settlers crossed the Appalachians into Kentucky between 1775 and 1792. See, for example, Dicken Garcia, *Western Woods*, 15.
3. This estimate was made by the president of Washington College in 1847. The historian C.W. Thornwaite calculated that Virginia's net population loss was 335,000. See William L. Miller, "A Note on the Importance of the Interstate Slave Trade of the Ante Bellum South," *Journal of Political Economy* 73:2 (April 1965), 183. But no accurate figures exist on the Virginia exodus during this period. See Fischer and Kelly, *Bound Away*, 137. Cf. Dwight L. Dumond, *Antislavery: The Crusade for Freedom in America* (New York: W.W. Norton, 1961), 88.
4. Henderson formed the Louisa Company, which later became the Transylvania Company, to further settlement in Kentucky and Tennessee. George Rogers Clark, who had been living in Kentucky prior to the Revolution, led American troops in the West against the British. For his military triumphs he came to be known as the "Hannibal of the West." The Clark family came from Caroline County, Va. Taylor, member of a prominent Virginia family, moved to Kentucky shortly after he was born in 1784. See John H. Gwathmey, *Twelve Virginia Counties: Where the Western Migration Began* (Richmond: Dietz Press, 1937), 1-3.
5. William O. Lynch, "The Westward Flow of Southern Colonists before 1861," *Journal of Southern History* 9:3 (Aug. 1943), 303. According to the 1850 census, 387,893 native Virginians, including whites and free blacks, were then living in other states, territories, and the District of Columbia. See Fischer and Kelly, *Bound Away*, Table 6, "Native Virginians living in other states, 1850 and 1860," 325.
6. In all, more than a million persons — including 300,000 slaves — emigrated west and south from Virginia. Fischer and Kelly, *Bound Away*, 139, xiii.

west in the 1790s, and one in six during the early decades of the 19th century.[1] Not surprisingly, many moved to the adjacent territory of Kentucky. In fact, roughly half of the first settlers relocating there came from Virginia.[2] Most of them were from the Piedmont or Great Valley, particularly from Albemarle and Augusta counties. According to one historian, twelve counties in central Virginia, east and west of Richmond, supplied the great majority of trans-Appalachian emigrants, as well as their leadership.[3]

Why was this particular movement of settlers out of Virginia so disproportionately large?[4] One obvious reason is geography. Prior to entering the Union, Kentucky was part of the Old Dominion, separated from the rest of the state by only a mountain range. Virginia customs and laws extended over this frontier, and so it was only logical that it would attract large numbers of settlers from the neighboring Piedmont.

Another reason was population density. With 747,550 persons living within its borders in 1790, Virginia was more heavily settled than any other state in the Union; in fact, it had more residents than Massachusetts and New York combined. This many people could not thrive under a dominant plantation system, in which tobacco fields stretched across much of the arable land, and centers of commerce or manufacturing had not yet been established.

A third driving impulse was a hunger for open space and isolation. This desire motivated economically and socially marginal types — constitutionally restless backwoodsmen from Virginia, as well as from other parts of the colonial interior. Hunters, trappers, and traders envisioned Kentucky's untrammeled wilderness not as land to be conquered and turned into plantations, but as a kind of Garden of Eden. These pioneers imagined they could wander about this unmarked frontier, live off its pristine land, respecting its ways and enjoying a degree of freedom in the wild that was not possible where settlers had already cleared a path. Not interested in owning property or settling down, these peripatetic pioneers wanted to move unencumbered from place to place, hunting the abundant game, raising a few crops, and tending some livestock. They preferred to lead self-reliant, self-contained lives, and Kentucky appeared to accommodate

---

1. Kulikoff, *Tobacco and Slaves*, 77.
2. By 1850, seven percent of Kentucky's free population had been born in Virginia. Missouri was then the only other state with a slightly larger proportion of Virginia natives — eight percent. Fischer and Kelly, *Bound Away*, Table 6, 325.
3. These counties were Albemarle, Augusta, Caroline, Essex, Gloucester, Goochland, Hanover, King William, King and Queen, Louisa, New Kent, and Orange. Gwathmey, *Twelve Virginia Counties*, 1.
4. The greatest number of Virginians had migrated by the mid-19th century to the states of Ohio, Kentucky, Tennessee, Missouri, Indiana, and Illinois. They represented 80 percent of all those who had left the state.

this need well. Land was there for the taking, and so was the wild game — until they nearly wiped it out.[1]

Acquiring more fertile land for commercial agriculture was clearly another major reason for the movement of Virginians into Kentucky. Many of the early migrants were lowland planters who made a living from tobacco, and growing this crop was both labor- and land-intensive. Plantation agriculture required more land per farmer than in the North, where different crops could be commercially grown on smaller plots. Since fertilizer was not applied, tobacco fields were soon exhausted and their value declined.[2] By the last decades of the 18th century, Piedmont plantation owners were becoming desperate to cultivate new lands as their existing holdings were virtually used up. Furthermore, the sharp decline in prices as a result of the war with England had severely eroded the planters' profits, and they needed cheaper land to restore their good fortunes. The western frontier seemed to hold the solution. Early reports of explorers, hunters, and traders who had ventured into present-day Kentucky and Tennessee told not only of its vast, forested wilderness, but also of its rich and bountiful soils. Inspired by these accounts, well-to-do planters were more than willing to leave behind their Piedmont estates and head west.

Early on, the prospect of reaping large profits from selling Kentucky lands to these planters also attracted speculators, both in Virginia and back in England.[3] Using their greater financial leverage, they bought up choice tracts, displacing squatters and driving up prices beyond the reach of smaller farmers. Along with speculators, a number of planters purchased land as an investment, allowing tenant farmers to occupy and cultivate these tracts in their absence. Others dispatched agents to buy up contiguous parcels in Kentucky to create tobacco plantations. Once the land had been cleared and homes built, these Virginia planters brought their belongings and families west to settle on their new estates.[4] The coming of "gentry law makers" from Virginia inevitably led — particularly in the Bluegrass — to the demarcating of property boundaries, lengthy legal sparring over title, and, ultimately, the barring of access to hunters.[5] In the

---

1. In 1775, Daniel Boone introduced a bill in the House of Delegates of the Transylvania Colony to provide for better management of the rapidly disappearing game. Stephen Aron, "Pigs and Hunters: 'Rights in the Woods' on the Trans-Appalachian Frontier," in *Contact Points: American Frontiers from the Mohawk Valley to the Mississippi, 1750-1850,* ed. Andrew R. L. Cayton and Frederika J. Teute (Chapel Hill: University of North Carolina Press, 1998), 197.
2. Depletion of soils throughout the South resulted in a sharp decline in land values. By 1850, the average acre of land below the Mason Dixon Line was selling for only $5.34, compared to $28.07 in the North. See Albert B. Hart, *The American Nation: A History,* vol. 16, *Slavery and Abolition, 1831-1841* (New York: Harper & Brothers, 1906), 57.
3. Aron, "Pioneers and Profiteers," 182.
4. The planters themselves had no desire to "brave" the frontier. Clark, *History of Kentucky,* 91.
5. Aron, "Pigs and Hunters," 202.

process, much of the economic opportunity and independence first associated with Kentucky's wilds was lost. In just a few decades, the open spaces the backwoodsmen had sought in this wilderness would disappear.

Slaveholding Piedmont farmers also felt compelled to move inland because of the labor situation they faced. The war-related drop in tobacco production had left some slaves idle — a costly and potentially dangerous development. Thousands of untilled acres in Kentucky would provide ample work for these black workers. In addition, many younger planters wanted to establish estates further west because of a change in Virginia's inheritance law after the war: the demise of primogeniture meant that plantations now had to be divided up equally among a deceased's male offspring instead of passed on to the eldest.[1] Hence, younger planters, who also worried about another economic downturn in the Piedmont during their lifetime, were the most apt to migrate. Still others had fallen deeply into debt and wanted to start life anew on the frontier.[2] For all of these reasons, many members of the planter elite left Virginia beginning in the 1790s. More than 300 families from just one county — Albemarle, where Thomas Jefferson's home, Monticello, was located — left for Kentucky and Tennessee during the following two decades.[3] And with them came thousands of slaves.

Among the early slaveholders to undertake this westward journey was John Breckinridge, of Albemarle County, who sent ahead 18 of his slaves and an overseer to carve out a homestead in the wilderness.[4] Robert Johnson, father of Martin Van Buren's controversial running mate in 1836, brought a large contingent of slaves from Orange County, Virginia, to a site near Louisville in 1779.[5] Overall, blacks made up a significant portion of the early Kentucky migrants. At three settlements founded in 1775, including the outpost founded by Boone, fully ten percent of the estimated population of several hundred persons was black, according a census taken two years later.[6] After the land was cleared, most slaves worked in the fields, planting tobacco and a new commercial staple — hemp.[7]

1. Otto, *Southern Frontiers*, 73.
2. Everett Dick, *The Dixie Frontier: A Social History of the Southern Frontier from the First Transmontane Beginnings to the Civil War* (New York: Knopf, 1948), 53.
3. Cited in Majewski, *A House Dividing*, 17-20.
4. Fischer and Kelly, *Bound Away*, 158. Breckenridge first settled outside Lexington.
5. Richard Mentor Johnson, who was born in Beargrass, Kentucky, in 1780, never married but openly lived for many years with a mulatto slave named Julia Chinn and had two children by her. Even though she had died three years before Johnson sought election to the vice presidency, the relationship with his common-law wife created a sensation during the 1836 campaign.
6. The population of the Bluegrass is believed to have been 300 in 1775. See Pike, *Frontier Kentucky*, 71. The percentage of blacks living in the region is cited in Jack M. Sosin, *The Revolutionary Frontier 1763-1783* (New York: Holt, Rinehart & Winston, 1967), 174-5.
7. By 1800, Kentucky farmers were annually exporting more than 40,000 pounds of hemp to Cotton Belt states. Stephen Aron, *How the West Was Lost: The Transformation of Kentucky from Daniel Boone to Henry Clay* (Baltimore: Johns Hopkins University Press, 1996), 129.

Small, independent farmers and would-be landowners had some similar reasons for wanting to relocate west of the Appalachians. Many were pushed out by sharply rising land prices in the Piedmont. Small tobacco growers had been hit particularly hard by the war-related downturn in the market and needed to look elsewhere for large acreage. Some of these farmers even had hopes of turning a fast profit by dabbling in speculation — buying and selling property in Kentucky.[1] The absence of slavery on land to the west made it even more enticing to them, since this meant they would not have to worry about competition from the plantation system. In addition, landless whites saw a chance to achieve the elusive ambition of owning real estate in an area where prices were generally lower.

Both the need for more land and the desire for more "elbow room" were closely related to the changing demographics in the Piedmont and other parts of western Virginia — namely, the steady increase in slave labor since the middle of the 18th century. This trend looked likely to continue. It appeared that, in the South, slavery was a thriving, expanding system. While Revolutionary enthusiasm for the natural rights of man led the states in New England to abolish the slave system after the war, it remained well entrenched below the Mason Dixon Line. Economically, it was essential: plantation agriculture would collapse without slave labor. The laws of the new nation tolerated the existence of slavery. The Constitutional debates in 1787 gingerly steered away from confrontation over this volatile and highly divisive issue. Southern delegates managed to prevent any anti-slavery provisions from being adopted by threatening to leave Philadelphia and boycott the sessions if they did not get their way. This victory boded badly for non-slaveholding farmers in the South. Slavery was the greatest threat to their well being, and it did not look as if it was going to diminish in the near future. If anything, it was only growing stronger.

The arrival of large numbers of slaves in the Piedmont had coincided with the takeover of the best tobacco-growing land by the great planters. This consolidation of economic power squeezed small farmers out. In Albemarle, for example, the top ten percent of households controlled 70 percent of the real estate by the end of the century. They also owned 61 percent of Albemarle's slaves.[2] The more slaves a planter had, the more he could produce and the wealthier he became. The reverse was true for small slaveholders, or those who did not own any slaves. Inequality in holdings and incomes increased to the point where "plain folk" farmers could no longer sustain themselves and their families. They blamed their plight on the slaves, who were now thickly settled in their midst.

---

1. Aron, "Pioneers and Profiteers," 182.
2. Majewski, *House Dividing*, 15. In 1760, Thomas Jefferson was the second largest slaveholder in the county.

Indeed, the Piedmont was becoming as black as the Tidewater before it. Toward the end of the 18th century, only slightly more than half of the people residing in this part of the state were white, and most of them were either widely dispersed on large plantations or clustered in cities like Richmond, Lynchburg, and Charlottesville. Blacks constituted majorities in inland counties such as Amelia (62 percent), Chesterfield (53 percent), Cumberland (54 percent), Goochland (60 percent), Louisa (60 percent), and Spotsylvania (53 percent).[1] All told, by 1790, four of every ten slaves in the United States were living in Virginia.[2] This was to a great extent the result of large-scale imports earlier in the century and a high birth rate among blacks. But now, due to a drop in tobacco production caused by the war and the attendant disruption of trans-Atlantic trade, the Old Dominion had more slaves than it could use.[3] In order to keep its black population from continuing to soar (and to protect its own domestic slave trade), Virginia joined with Delaware and Maryland in instituting a ban on importing slaves.[4] At the same time, these states began exporting chattel. Between 1820 and 1860, approximately 800,000 slaves would be removed from states that bordered the Atlantic, either by owners taking them west or by traders looking for buyers in the interior.[5] However, despite these measures, natural increase continued to swell Virginia's slave population.

The presence of so many Africans was most immediately worrisome to non-slaveholders, who saw their livelihoods quickly disappearing in a chattel-dominated economy. Not surprisingly, a high black population density discouraged further white migration into the Piedmont. Largely as a result, by the early 19th century, growth of the Piedmont's white population virtually stopped. In fact, the number of whites in eight counties declined during the three decades after 1790.[6] Lunenburg, for example, lost 20 percent of its white residents between 1810 and 1820.[7] In Albemarle, the number of whites did not grow appreciably

1. In 1790, the Virginia counties with the highest proportion of slaves in their populations were Powhatan (63.4), King William (63.4), Amelia (62.5), Middlesex (61.8), Essex (59.6), New Kent (59.3) and James City (59.1).
2. At that time, the proportion of blacks in the overall U.S. population reached an historic high of 19.3 percent. George Henderson, *Migrants, Immigrants and Slaves: Racial and Ethnic Groups in America* (Lanham: University Press of America), 215.
3. Dabney, *Virginia*, 189.
4. In the 1770s, before imposing a ban, Virginia imported 3,900 slaves. Morgan, *Slave Counterpoint*, 59. Southern states cited "moral" reasons for ending the trade, but these concealed worries about not being able to control a larger slave population. Cf. Robinson, *Structure of American Politics*, 80.
5. It is estimated that between two-fifths and one half of the slaves moved west were sold to new owners there. Miller, "Interstate Slave Trade," 182.
6. This applies to Albemarle, Culpeper, Fauquier, Fluvanna, Loudoun, Louisa, Prince William, and Orange counties. The combined white population in these counties declined from 67,181 in 1790 to 66,746 in 1820.
7. Beeman, *Evolution of the Backcountry*, 171.

larger once the slave population surpassed 50 percent of the total, in 1810.[1] This demographic trend was worrisome to all white residents, regardless of whether or not they owned slaves. As Virginia grew more and more black, they could foresee the day when their own race would become a minority, highly vulnerable to slave revolts. The concentration of slaveholdings on large plantations added to this anxiety. So did a series of black uprisings — in neighboring Maryland in 1795, and the so-called Gabriel's rebellion, which involved 1,000 Richmond slaves, on August 30, 1800, as well as ones in Haiti and Santo Domingo.

A sharp increase in the number of freed slaves living in the South also made Virginia whites nervous, since such blacks could easily serve as an inspirational example to their enslaved brethren. This was a problem the whites had brought upon themselves. With demand for tobacco declining, some planters began releasing slaves in the early 1790s.[2] From 1800 to 1810, the percentage of free men and women within the state's black population rose from less than half a percent to more than seven percent. This increase followed in the wake of a 1782 law that made manumission possible while an owner was still alive[3]: over 11,000 slaves were emancipated in the decade after its adoption.[4] Throughout the Chesapeake, the number of freed slaves quadrupled during the three decades after the Revolutionary War. This development was most pronounced in Maryland.[5] Not all of these blacks gained their liberty by being manumitted, however. Others did so by serving in the military, fleeing their plantations, or by suing for their freedom in the courts. Emancipation in Virginia was part of a national trend as Northern states rejected slavery for a mixture of economic and humanitarian reasons.[6] There were only a hundred free blacks in the United States in the 1770s, but close to 50,000 by 1810.[7] In the two decades after 1790 alone, the proportion

---

1. For statistics on Albemarle's population changes, see Majewski, *House Dividing*, 18.
2. Some slaveholders also manumitted slaves after the Revolution who had attempted to escape to the British side, fearing they might incite other blacks to flee. This was the case with one of James Madison's slaves. See "Brief History of Indians in Virginia and Public Policy," http://www.majbill.vt.edu/history/shifflet/Notes.htm.
3. For statistics on Virginia's black population, see Morgan, *Slave Counterpoint*, 61. Up until 1782, masters could only grant slaves freedom in their wills.
4. For statistics on manumission, see Peter D. McClelland and Richard J. Zeckhauser, *Demographic Dimensions of the New Republic: American Interregional Migration, Vital Statistics, and Manumissions, 1800-1860* (Cambridge: Cambridge University Press, 1982), Table D-28, "Manumission Rates, 1800-60," 187.
5. Berlin, *Generations of Captivity*, 119. By 1810, one third of the blacks in Maryland had been freed, and emancipated slaves outnumbered those still enslaved by a ratio of 3:1. Jordan, *White Over Black*, 407. For statistics on slaves emancipated in Virginia after 1782, see Dabney, *Virginia*, 187.
6. The Northern states with the fewest slaves were the first to emancipate them, indicating that pragmatism, rather than humane concern, dictated these changes in policy.
7. Berlin, *Generations of Captivity*, 104.

of free blacks within the nation's African American population rose from nearly 8 to over 13 percent.[1]

The emergence of this hybrid, socially ambiguous group upset the strict racial dichotomy in American society. Whites had tended to equate the terms "black" and "slave," and the existence of so many free blacks confounded this way of thinking. What did it mean if a black gained his freedom? He was certainly not on a par with whites, but his status was not well defined. This fact alone caused some uneasiness. Free blacks were not subject to the harsh discipline and subjugation that kept slaves in their place, and what they might do with this newfound freedom was unclear. Because so many emancipated slaves were mulattoes, their "superior" white blood bestowed upon them greater intelligence, in the minds of Southern whites. They were also more likely to have learned to read and received some education, and this background gave them an elevated stature among their fellow blacks. Some might take advantage of this to stir up trouble. Even white farmers who had once favored emancipation now worried about their own safety.[2]

This disturbing development forced whites to reexamine their assumptions about blacks. It also gave rise to proposals for safeguarding their position in a more fluid racial environment. One way of limiting the impact of free blacks was to keep them at bay. Accordingly, all the slaveholding states — as well as two Northern ones — soon passed laws either barring free blacks from entering their territory or forcing those already in residence to leave.[3] In addition, fears of racial mingling gave rise to schemes for shipping freed slaves back to Africa, or — as Jefferson proposed in his *Notes on the State of Virginia* — to a colony of their own somewhere in the American West. Slave owners also joined forces to pressure lawmakers into overturning laws that had made manumission so common.[4] Another strategy was to tighten controls over enslaved blacks. Responding to local white concerns as well as recent black revolts, Virginia's General Assembly passed a slave code in 1792 that reduced slaves to the status of "personal property."[5]

---

1. Jordan, White over Black, 406.
2. See letter to the printer from a "cornplanter," *Kentucky Gazette*, 12 July 1788.
3. In March 1788, the Massachusetts General Court ruled that blacks could not stay in the state more than two months, despite the fact that Massachusetts had only recently voted to end slavery. Jordan, *White over Black*, 410-11. After 1806 Virginia required freed blacks to leave the state within on year or else be re-enslaved. By passing restrictive immigration laws, Southern states also sought to block the coming of rebellious blacks from the Caribbean.
4. For example, in Virginia's Lunenburg county, slaveholders signed petitions in 1785 protesting against the increase in freed blacks, even though they still made up scarcely one percent of the local population. See Beeman, *Evolution of the Backcountry*, 221.

One other way for whites to allay their misgivings about the presence of so many slaves was for them to move out of the slave states. After the Revolution, a number of Southerners chose this solution, many doing so out of moral antipathy toward the chattel system. Some slaveholders found themselves torn between the dictates of their faith and those of economic survival. Prosperous Quakers faced just such a dilemma. If they persisted in keeping slaves, they were liable be excommunicated from the Society of Friends, whereas if they freed their chattel they courted economic disaster. To escape from this quandary, Quakers in Virginia began migrating north and west to free states such as Ohio, notably in the late 1780s.[1] In these frontier states, they helped to establish communities that later became havens for slaves escaping the plantation system. For other Southerners, however, the decision to move away from enslaved blacks had little to do with revulsion at the latter's treatment. They were not interested in promoting the emancipation of the slaves. Rather, they were looking for places where *they* could live "in freedom."[2]

That the growing slave population contributed significantly to the exodus of non-slaveholding whites can be inferred from census data for Piedmont counties with the highest percentage of slaves in their populations during the 1790-1820 period. These show a correlation between a continuing increase in slaves and a decrease — or, at best, a smaller increase — in the number of whites. For instance, Albemarle County saw its black population nearly double between 1790 and 1820, whereas the number of whites only increased by 27 percent. In Chesterfield, the number of slaves increased from 7,487 to 9,513 during the same decades, but the white population only grew from 6,358 to 7,543. In Cumberland, the number of slaves rose 53 percent, from 4,434 to 6,813, but the tally of whites showed only a slight upswing, from 3,577 to 3,966. Culpeper had 13,809

---

5. Richard R. Beeman, *The Old Dominion and the New Nation, 1788-1801* (Louisville: University Press of Kentucky, 1972), 95. Cf. Dunn, "Black Society," 80. He argues this new slave code responded to the growing unhappiness with the large number of freed slaves in Virginia. This view is supported by other historians. See, for example, Dorothy Twohig, "'That Species of Property': Washington's Role in the Controversy over Slavery," *The Papers of George Washington*, http://gwpapers.virginia.edu/articles/slavery/.

1. Gragg, *Migration in Early America*, 75-6. He shows that more Quakers began to leave Virginia than migrate there starting in 1792. By 1800, out-migration accounted for 93.9 percent of Quaker movement in and out of the state. See Table 27, "Slavery's Effect on Out-Migration," 66. While conceding that other factors, such as the availability of cheaper land elsewhere, induced this Quaker exodus, Gragg concludes (65): "it is clear that many . . . left Virginia and other southern states because the institution of slavery in one way or another was destroying their vision of society."

2. John H. Gwathmey makes the case for this desire for freedom, not the depletion of tobacco-growing soil, being the main impetus behind migration from Virginia into Kentucky. He contends that the same reason prompted the previous generation of small farmers to head west out of the Tidewater. See his *Twelve Virginia Counties*, 1, 35, *passim*.

whites and 8,226 slaves in 1790; the number of whites dropped to 11,136 in 1820, while the slave population climbed to 9,468. Fauquier County experienced a doubling of its slave population over these decades — from 6,642 to 11,167 — but the white population remained essentially static, at just over 11,000. And, in Louisa County, as slaves increased 65 percent, the number of whites rose only 54 percent. Further to the west, near the Blue Ridge Mountains, there was less need for slave labor, as few plantations existed there. Thus, these population trends are not evident there. Instead, whites maintained a strong numerical dominance. For example, Augusta County, founded in 1738, had 1,567 slaves and 9,260 whites in 1790, compared to 3,512 slaves and 12,963 whites in 1820. Similarly, Shenandoah County had a population of 9,979 whites, but only 512 slaves in 1790; the figures in 1820 were 12,461 and 1,038, respectively.[1]

In Kentucky, whites with slaves were a small minority. The vast majority of early migrants were families of modest means, with few or no slaves, drawn further into the interior by the lure of cheap acreage — and freedom from inhospitable political and economic conditions.[2] In addition to those who took possession by squatting, many were Revolutionary War veterans, whose financial circumstances had worsened due to the conflict. They eagerly accepted frontier land in payment for their service.[3] Nearly half of these former soldiers who left Virginia in the years after independence headed straight for Kentucky.[4] The biggest influx of former soldiers occurred after the issuing of land warrants in 1784, when some 10,000 persons migrated across the Appalachians.[5] Other, more prosperous Virginians moved west at this time hoping to acquire larger landholdings. Some of them bought up land that originally had been granted to veterans. Representative of these non-slaveholding migrants was Abraham Lincoln, grandfather of the future president, who sold 250 acres of Shenandoah Valley property in 1780 and used part of the proceeds from this sale to buy 400 acres of farmland about twelve miles east of Louisville. A cousin of Daniel Boone's, Lincoln tripled

---

1. These and subsequent demographic figures cited in this book are derived from federal census data, as compiled by the Historical Census Browser of the University of Virginia Library: http://fisher.lib.virginia.edu/collections/stats/histcensus/
2. Cf. Asa E. Martin, *The Anti-Slavery Movement in Kentucky Prior to 1850* (Louisville: Standard Printing, 1918), 139. After 1790, the number of slaves in Kentucky's population increased more slowly than the white population did. Over the next two decades, as the total number of Kentuckians rose from 73,000 to 400,000, the percentage of slaves only increased from 17 to 23 percent. Robinson, *Structure of American Politics*, 44.
3. However, a number of Revolutionary War veterans found the offer of prairie land in the region of Kentucky known as "the Barrens" unattractive and declined it. See Aron, *How the West Was Lost*, 151.
4. Fischer and Kelly, *Bound Away*, 140, 324. This was by far the most popular destination. In fact, more Virginia veterans left for Kentucky than did to all other Western states and territories combined.
5. Lowell H. Harrison, *Kentucky's Road to Statehood* (Lexington: University Press of Kentucky, 1992), 8. This brought the total population up to 30,000.

his Kentucky holdings that same year when he purchased 800 acres in the southwestern part of the state. In 1782, he brought his family to live on this estate south of the Green River, in Jefferson County.[1] A few years later, the elder Abraham Lincoln owned a total of 5,544 acres of fertile farmland, making him one of the largest non-slaveholding farmers in the territory.[2]

Despite their small numbers, Virginia plantation owners with considerable wealth — and slaveholdings — capitalized upon their political connections to acquire larger tracts of prime Bluegrass property. Their influx started in 1780, when a planter named James Wade staked out a claim in this region, brought his slaves there, and began to grow tobacco as well as other crops.[3] Wade introduced hemp, which quickly became a major Kentucky export. Primarily used for making cloth and rope for baling cotton and for ship rigging, it grew readily in central Kentucky, where the temperatures were milder — and the growing season shorter — than in the Deep South. Hemp was also less labor-intensive than either tobacco or cotton, making it an attractive cash crop for farmers with small slaveholdings.[4] Soon, great planters like Wade controlled much of the agriculturally rich Bluegrass. As a consequence, this part of frontier Kentucky lost much of its casual, egalitarian social atmosphere.[5] One newly arrived settler lamented in a 1781 petition to Congress that "almost the whole of the lands . . . are Engrossed into the hands of a few Interested men, the greater part of which live at ease in the internal parts of Virginia."[6]

This trend would continue. By the turn of the century, just over one hundred men owned 10,000 or more acres in Kentucky.[7] While these exceedingly wealthy men constituted less than one percent of the state's population, they held a third of its total acreage.[8] The percentage of land owned by this elite had actually increased since 1790. Here, too, Frederick Jackson Turner's thesis about the frontier promoting a more democratic way of life appears to have had only a fleeting validity. Speculators soon drove the price of land up to as much as $100 per acre, putting highly desirable Kentucky farmlands out of reach for most settlers. "Plain folk" farmers had to move on to other, less productive soils. Indeed,

---

1. Tarbell, Footsteps of the Lincolns, 59.
2. David H. Donald, *Lincoln* (New York: Touchstone, 1996), 21.
3. Phillips, *Slave Economy of the Old South*, 15.
4. Otto, *Southern Frontiers*, 88.
5. In 1796, a planter fresh from the Tidewater was surprised to find "many opulent and some Genteel people" still living in log cabins in the Bourbon County, Ky. Quoted in Elizabeth Perkins, "Distinctions and Partitions amongst Us: Identity and Interaction in the Revolutionary Ohio Valley," in *Contact Points*, 225.
6. Fischer and Kelly, *Bound Away*, 158.
7. One of the largest landowners, Robert Morris, and several of his Philadelphia associates held rights to more than one million acres in Kentucky. Price, *Dividing the Land*, 190.
8. Lee Soltow, "Kentucky Wealth at the End of the Eighteenth Century," *Journal of American History* 43:3 (Sept. 1983), 624.

Bluegrass real estate became so expensive that even well heeled planters had to limit their purchases to 100 acres or less.[1] In the 1790s, because of this spike in prices, or because they had been bought out, or had lost land claims, a majority of Kentucky families owned no land whatsoever.[2] This percentage still held a decade later: a sample of tax records lists only 15,617 white adult males as property holders, out of a total of 31,662.[3] The rest were reduced to making a living as squatters or tenant farmers on the extensive holdings of absentee owners. Their dreams of achieving independence on their own land had been dashed.

Most of this displacement of the poor occurred in the Bluegrass, where Virginia's most eminent families settled down on large estates to live amid the great splendor to which they were accustomed. Crude log cabins were abandoned for brick "great houses," in which oil paintings, fine furniture, and locally made silverware created an aura of frontier opulence, emulating the Tidewater way of life. Estates owned by men like Henry Clay and Alexander Scott Bullitt sprang up on the most desirable sections of the Bluegrass and further west, near Louisville, with romantic names like "Oxmoor," "Farmington," "The Larches," "Cabell's Dale," "Ashland," "Runnymeade," and "Chaumier du Prairie."[4] Slaves clad in livery waited on the owners and their guests. Horse-drawn carriages traversed the dirt roads leading from one estate to the next, and the landed elite gathered to enjoy one another's company by hunting foxes, hosting dances, watching theatrical performances, and breeding racehorses.[5]

To enjoy such a lifestyle, affluent planter families imported large numbers of slaves. By 1790, slaves constituted nearly a quarter of the population in Woodford County, in the central Bluegrass, and 16.8 percent of all the people living in the territory.[6] But the vast majority of Kentucky pioneers needed only two or three pairs of helping hands to fell trees, move boulders, trap game, fend off Indian attacks, build a temporary shelter, plant a few crops, tend livestock, look after the household, and ready the fallow land for cultivation.[7] Under trying,

---

1. Abernethy, *Three Virginia Frontiers*, 65.
2. The displaced included Boone, who moved on to Missouri in search of land of his own.
3. L. Soltow, "Kentucky Wealth," 620.
4. J. Winston Coleman, Jr., *Slavery Times in Kentucky* (Chapel Hill: University of North Carolina Press, 1940), 22-3.
5. Horseracing took place in Kentucky as early as 1787. F. Garvin Davenport, *Ante-Bellum Kentucky: A Social History, 1800-1860* (Oxford, Ohio: Mississippi Valley Press, 1943), 16. The first racecourse opened in 1789. Clark, *History of Kentucky*, 104.
6. Federal census figures cited in *Kentucky Gazette*, 28 May 1791.
7. Only 12 percent of Kentucky slaveholders had 20 or more slaves. George Wright, "Afro-Americans," *Kentucky Encyclopedia*, ed. John E. Kleber, et al. (Lexington: University Press of Kentucky, 1992), 4. As late as 1850, one quarter of Kentucky's 38,385 slave owners had only one slave. Marion B. Lucas, *A History of Blacks in Kentucky*, vol. 1, *From Slavery to Segregation, 1760-1891* (Frankfort: Kentucky Historical Society, 1992), 2. The average number of slaves owned was five.

primitive conditions, slaves worked closely with their masters and thus developed a more casual relationship than could exist on the Virginia plantations, where stern overseers kept large gangs of blacks under strict control.[1] The slave system here tended to be more humane, less rigidly hierarchical. Whites came to regard their human chattel with a degree of kindness and compassion. Even though the number of slaves steadily increased during the first decades of settlement — up to 12,000, according to the first federal census in 1790, out of a total population of nearly 75,000[2] — Kentucky did not develop as high a density of slaves as existed in Virginia and throughout the Deep South.[3] One major factor was topography — the hilly terrain of eastern Kentucky and other parts of the territory was not suited to plantation agriculture. Nor were the climate and soils in many areas favorable to growing either tobacco or the Deep South's emerging cash crop, cotton.[4] The independent farmers who settled in the these regions had to resort to producing other crops, on small plots, and thus could not afford to own more than a few slaves, if any at all.[5] In addition, there was opposition to growing tobacco because of how it quickly depleted the land. Members of the territory's influential Political Club, meeting in Danville in April 1787, agreed that this crop would not be beneficial to the territory, taking to heart Thomas Jefferson's admonition that tobacco produced a culture of "infinite wretchedness."[6] For all these reason, small farms rather than large plantations became the norm throughout Kentucky. Large chattel concentrations were limited to the major hemp- and tobacco-producing regions — the Bluegrass and Pennyroyal.[7] (Toward the end of the century, slaves were also brought to the area south of the

---

1. Cf. Berlin, *Generations of Captivity*, 181. In the Deep South, some 25 percent of slaves lived together in concentrations of 50 or more, on large cotton or tobacco plantations. Lucas, *History of Blacks*, 2.
2. In 1784, there were an estimated 4,000 slaves in Kentucky. *Ibid.*, xv. By 1800, the number had increased to 40,000, while the overall population stood at 220,000. Figures are cited in Coleman, *Slavery Times*, 15, 17.
3. However, Kentucky's slave population increased at a faster rate than its white population during the period 1790-1810. While the number of whites rose by 194 percent between 1790 and 1800, and by 80.2 percent during the following ten years, the number of slaves rose by 241 percent and 99.7 percent during the same two decades. Miller, "Interstate Slave Trade," 182.
4. The invention of the cotton gin in 1793 gave a tremendous boost to cotton growing further south.
5. Suzanne Marshall, *Violence in the Black Patch of Kentucky and Tennessee* (Columbia: University of Missouri Press, 1994), 16. In the eastern mountains, the slave population did not exceed 10 percent of the total. Lucas, *History of Blacks*, xv.
6. Quoted in Thomas Speed, *The Political Club, Danville, Kentucky, 1786-1790: Being an Account of an Early Kentucky Society from the Original Papers Recently Found* (Louisville: John P. Morton, 1894), 230.
7. By 1850, more than half the people living in the Bluegrass were slaves. See Phillips, "Origin and Growth of Southern Black Belts," 810.

Green River, after the Kentucky legislature voted in 1795 to open up this part of the state.[1])

The other, closely related reason was the diversified nature of Kentucky's emerging economy. Expectations of supplanting their depleted tobacco holdings in Virginia had motivated the great planters to move west, and in their first years, they fared well. As early as 1790, a quarter million pounds of Kentucky tobacco were sold on the New Orleans market.[2] Lexington, the hub of the tobacco and hemp industries, experienced a commercial boom by the end of the century.[3] By 1809, its future looked so rosy that one observer, noting the prevalence of wealthy farmers and their well-appointed carriages on its streets, dared to predict Lexington would become "the great inland city in the western world."[4] But harsh economic realities soon dampened this initial optimism. The cost of transporting hogsheads of tobacco to market by flatboat were higher than it was in the east, mainly due to the greater distances involved. It took, for instance, an average of 28 days for boats laden with tobacco to reach New Orleans for export.[5] Furthermore, in the second decade of the 19th century, prices for the leaf took an abrupt dip.[6] Although tobacco did become Kentucky's leading export, its sales alone could not generate sufficient income to support most arriving farmers. They soon turned to raising livestock, growing wheat, fruits, and hemp, and mining salt.[7] These pursuits required fewer slaves than the tobacco industry.[8] Hence, the new territory became not so much a slave society, per se, as a white society with slaves.

---

1. Marshall, *Violence in the Black Patch*, 7.
2. Axton, *Tobacco and Kentucky*, 41.
3. Most of Kentucky's hemp factories were located in Fayette and neighboring counties. In 1810, there were nine such plants in Lexington alone, with each producing approximately 100 tons annually. See letter from unnamed Lexington correspondent to an unnamed friend in Charleston, S.C., 1 May 1810, reprinted in *Political Observatory & Fairfield Register* (Lancaster, Ohio) 15 Sept. 1810. These hemp factories employed a large number of slaves, and the population of Lexington was one-fourth black in 1800. The slave proportion of the city climbed to 41 percent four decades later. Lucas, *History of Blacks*, xvii.
4. Letter of Nathaniel Hart to James McDowell, 18 June 1809, quoted in Phillips, *Life and Labor*, 79. In 1817, another visitor noted that Lexington had 12 cotton manufacturers, as well as more than a dozen other plants producing wool, paper, gunpowder, lead, iron, leather goods, soap, candles, and furniture. Henry B. Fearon, *Sketches of America: A Narrative of a Journey of Five Thousand Miles through the Eastern and Western States* (London: Benjamin Blom, 1969), 245.
5. Fearon, *Sketches of America*, 246.
6. Prices as high as 15 cents per pound on the New Orleans market in 1816 encouraged tobacco growers to come to Kentucky, but then, in 1818, the price plummeted from nine to six cents. Otto, *Southern Frontiers*, 89-90.
7. In 1818, tobacco exports of 24,000 hogsheads were valued at $1.9 million. Martin, *Anti-Slavery Movement*, 7, and Otto, *Southern Frontiers*, 89.
8. It required only three slaves to grow over 50 acres of hemp, producing a total of 35,000 pounds. Coleman, *Slavery Times*, 44.

Socially, Kentucky evolved differently for its white population as well. Unlike colonial Tidewater, where tobacco was king, and all wealth, power, and social status flowed from the size of a planter's acreage and his slaveholdings, here there was no one dominant cash crop — or one, all-encompassing social order, but two distinct ways of life. To a great extent, transplanted Tidewater planters — the so-called "tuckahoes" — and in-migrating backcountry "plain folk" — or "cohees" — occupied separate worlds, eyeing one another with suspicion, disdain, and, occasionally, hostility.[1] As Kentucky matured, entering the Union as the 15th state in 1792, these two cultures persisted. In the agriculturally rich Bluegrass, tobacco barons from Virginia recreated the way of life they had enjoyed for generations, heavily dependent upon slave labor. In a space of two decades, these great planter families cemented their power by buying up the best pieces of property and importing large numbers of slaves to tend them. The coming of this elite drove out many less affluent planters. For example, in Woodford County, where 8 percent of all households had owned over 1,000 acres in the 1790s, only 2.4 percent held so much acreage by 1825.[2] Over this same period, the proportion of slaveholding families in this agriculturally rich county increased from 36.6 percent to 53.3 percent, and owners of 20 or more slaves increased from 1.9 percent of slaveholdings households to 5.8 percent.[3] Commenting on this trend, a recent historian has concluded: "The pyramid of land and slave ownership in the Bluegrass region eliminated all but a handful of aspirants [for status] . . ."[4]

At the same time, the coming of slaves forced tenant farmers off land they had originally tilled, repeating the scenario that had happened to many belonging to this social class in the Chesapeake and Piedmont regions of Virginia. Some moved on to other territories.[5] The transformation of the Bluegrass labor force was rapid and dramatic. While the slave proportion of those living in the inner counties of the Bluegrass rose from a quarter to fully a third by 1830, the white population grew until 1820, but then started to decline. For example, there were 6,929 whites living in Bourbon County — then the state's second most populous — in 1790; 10,627 in 1800; 13,650 in 1810; 12,369 in 1820; and 11,272 in 1830. Thereafter, the tally of whites continued to taper off, reaching a low of 7,155 at mid-century. (Three inner Bluegrass counties — Bourbon, Clark, and Fayette — experienced significant drops in their white population between 1810 and 1840.) However, over the same decades, the number of slaves in Bourbon rose as fol-

---

1. Perkins, "Distinctions and Partitions," 210. Dress, customs, and accent distinguished these two groups.
2. Aron, *How the West Was Lost*, 172, Table A.5, 203.
3. *Ibid.*, Table A.6, 204.
4. *Ibid.*, 128, 127.
5. Phillips, *Life and Labor*, 84. Many of these farmers moved on to Missouri.

lows: 908 (1790); 2,136 (1800); 4,169 (1810); 5,165 (1820); 6,868 (1830). In 1850, the county contained 7,066 slaves: by then, whites and blacks were numerically equal. To put it in another perspective, between 1790 and 1830, Bourbon's white population grew by 63 percent, but its slave population increased by *656 percent*.[1] These sharply contrasting trends remain, even if one allows for decreases in the area of this and other counties over these four decades. Clearly, there was a strong inverse relationship between the spreading of slavery throughout the Bluegrass and the disappearance of many poor whites.[2] This "plain folk" exodus reflected what had previously occurred in the Chesapeake, and then in the Piedmont, and what was simultaneously taking place in some parts of the Cotton South.[3]

Demographically as well as socially, the Bluegrass was another Tidewater. But its opulent lifestyle was not enjoyed by many Kentuckians. Big-tobacco country was a world unto itself, sealed off from the hardscrabble conditions elsewhere in this new territory. In the isolated mountains to the east, on the generally infertile and hilly lands ringing the inner Bluegrass, on the farmland located beyond this belt known as the outer Bluegrass, and to the southwest, another kind of Kentucky was taking shape. In these outlying regions, poor white farmers unable to purchase choice real estate and thus improve their status were forging a distinctive frontier society of their own.[4] These were people of Daniel Boone's ilk — rough-hewn, self-reliant, independent-minded, and adventurous. They wanted nothing to do with the plantation system that had spread west with them and regarded it with considerable suspicion as well as apprehension. Its way of life was the antithesis of theirs.[5] But they faced tremendous challenges in attempting to survive on the fringes of the wilderness. The land they could afford was not conducive to commercial farming. Without the benefit of slaves or other help, they cleared it dutifully and planted seeds they had brought with them, but little came of their efforts. Cut off from markets by a dearth of roads and waterways, farmers in the hill country could not profitably sell their produce, and so these migrants — mainly Scotch-Irish from Virginia — resorted to

---

1. Statewide, the white population of Kentucky rose by nearly 60 percent in the two decades leading up to 1830, while the slave population increased by 105 percent.
2. Kim Gruenwald makes this point, adding that conflicting land claims also discouraged migration to Kentucky. Kim M. Gruenwald, *River of Enterprise* (Bloomington: Indiana University Press, 2002), 83.
3. See Phillips, "Origin and Growth of Southern Black Belts," 810-13. He shows how, in three upland Georgia counties, the growth of the cotton industry resulted in large producers driving small ones out. More generally, the total white population declined after 1810 in those Southern counties in which plantation agriculture took hold and prospered.
4. Revolutionary War veterans settled on lands made available to them south of the Green River, in the southwestern part of Kentucky. Abernethy, *Three Virginia Frontiers*, 67.
5. Cf. Axton, *Tobacco and Kentucky*, 32.

scratching out a living by grazing cattle, planting a few subsistence crops, and felling trees for more well-to-do settlers. Some who lived near the Bluegrass or the Pennyroyal found work as day laborers on hemp and tobacco plantations. Others found menial jobs in the booming cities of Lexington and Louisville.[1] Their lives were defined by poverty and hardship. Half of Kentucky's counties were financially insolvent.[2] As tobacco- and hemp-producing areas prospered, these rural areas lagged further and further behind.[3] Those who lived in the mountains came to be looked down upon — even by neighboring slaves — as "po' white trash."[4]

Although Kentucky's poor whites found themselves decidedly at an economic disadvantage vis-à-vis the great planters, these "plain folk" were growing numerically stronger and had hopes of asserting their power politically. The first test of their clout came with the territory's first constitutional convention, which opened in April 1792. A desire to break off from Virginia had been growing for some time, largely as a result of a trade dispute. Authorities in eastern Virginia were unwilling to press Kentucky's demand that Spain grant the territory's tobacco and hemp exporters navigation rights down the Mississippi to the port of New Orleans. This conflict highlighted the vast economic and social differences that divided the two halves of the state and led first to a gathering of elected representatives in 1785, and then, after several years of contentious debate, to the drafting of a state constitution. This process gave Kentuckians a chance to create a frontier society more in tune with their interests and values. The delegates did so in several ways. For one thing, the convention affirmed the right to worship freely more forcefully than the early state constitutions, such as Virginia's, had done. (This embrace of religious freedom reflected the non-establishment clause in the U.S. Constitution.) Pressure from democratic-minded representatives also resulted in the convention's adopting a provision calling for universal white male suffrage — a major break with the property-owning or tax-paying qualifications for voting then common in other states, including Virginia. However, the landed elite managed to safeguard its prerogatives by insisting that state senators and the governor be chosen by an electoral college, instead of directly by the voters.

---

1. "Undesirable" freed slaves also sought work in these cities. See Davenport, *Ante-Bellum Kentucky*, 23.
2. Thomas D. Clark, *Agrarian Kentucky* (Lexington: University Press of Kentucky, 1977), 54.
3. By 1800, hemp had replaced tobacco as the leading Bluegrass export, with over 40,000 lbs. being sent to the Cotton South. Aron, *How the West Was Lost*, 129.
4. For a discussion of disparaging slave opinions of Kentucky's mountain people, see "Race Relations in the Mountain South," www.scholar.lib.vt.edu/faculty_archives/mountain_slavery/race.htm. This article quotes one former Bluegrass slave as expressing pleasure that "'dere was no po' white trash in [thei]r 'munity; dey was kep' back in de mountains.'"

A central issue to be resolved at that 1792 gathering was the status of slavery in Kentucky. This was the first time in the history of the United States that the people of a state could freely decide for themselves whether or not to allow the "peculiar institution" on their soil. This matter was highly controversial, reflecting a clash of interests and attitudes between the large slave owners in the Bluegrass and Pennyroyal and the much greater number of non-slaveholding whites.[1] In 1790, fully 83 percent of Kentucky's white families did not own slaves and did not derive any direct benefit from the chattel system.[2] Instead, it was harmful to their economic well being. The pro-slavery position was argued most forcefully by a man who would serve as the state's first attorney general — George Nicholas. He was a member of a prominent Virginia family, a colonel in the Revolutionary War, and the son of Robert Nicholas, a Williamsburg attorney and president of Virginia's 1775 Revolutionary Convention. As a recognized legal expert, he drafted Article IX of the 1792 state constitution, making emancipation of any slaves in Kentucky illegal unless approved by their masters. Nicholas and other pro-slavery delegates argued that the presence of slaves was essential to the new state's economic development. They also offered the rationale that blacks were better off under the control of whites, who would look after their welfare: slavery was thus a "positive good." During the lengthy and bitter debates held in a courthouse at Danville, supporters of the chattel system also cited biblical evidence supporting their cause — namely, the fact that Jews, the "chosen people," had once owned slaves.[3] Some slaveholding delegates also spoke of slavery as a "necessary evil," hinting of the dire consequences for whites that would result from granting blacks their freedom. Because the landed elite controlled the committees that oversaw drafting of the constitution, their views gained ascendancy.[4]

The fight to bar slavery in Kentucky was led by a group of ministers who attended this historic convention. As one might expect, they expressed their strong opposition chiefly on moral and religious grounds. Their most articulate and compelling spokesperson was the Rev. David Rice. A Presbyterian minister

---

1. After 1790, the number of small farmers grew appreciably, and they thus came to pose a political challenge to the slave system. Howard, *Evangelical War*, 14.
2. This statistic is found in Lynch, "Westward Flow," 507. According to another estimate, one of four Kentucky households owned slaves between 1790 and 1800. Lucas, *History of Blacks*, xv.
3. For this characterization of the debates, see George Lee Willis, *Kentucky Democracy: A History of the Party and Its Representative Members — Past and Present* (Louisville: Democratic Historical Society, 1935), vol. 1, 57.
4. Populists complained bitterly about the undue influence exercised by the wealthy landowners in shaping Kentucky's constitution. See, for example, "A.B.C.," "An Address to the Good People of Kentucky," *Kentucky Gazette*, 3 Dec. 1791. The author objected to the "impropriety" that "these committees should obstruct the free deliberations of our representatives . . ."

and graduate of Princeton, he had come to Kentucky from his native Virginia with his family in 1783 and taken over congregations in Danville and two other towns located on the fringe of the Bluegrass. For his subsequent efforts to bring his religion to the state's mountain people, Rice is generally regarded as "the father of western Presbyterianism."[1] Shortly before the constitutional convention was to convene, he had written an anti-slavery pamphlet — the first to appear in Kentucky — under the pseudonym of "Philanthropos," and this had led to his being elected to defend this point of view.[2] On the rough-hewn courthouse floor, he made an impassioned speech to the delegates, condemning slavery as "in a high degree unjust and cruel" for reducing fellow human beings to an "abject wretched state" contrary to the laws of God and Nature. The tall, slender Rice spoke with deep compassion about the plight of the slaves:

> I have lived free, and in many respects happy for near sixty years; but my happiness has been greatly diminished, for much of the time, by hearing a great part of the human species groaning under the galling yoke of bondage. In this time I lost a venerable father, a tender mother, two affectionate sisters, and a beloved first-born son; but all these together have not cost me half the anxiety as has been occasioned by this wretched situation of my fellow-men, whom without a blush I call my brethren.[3]

Rice and the other frontier clergymen in attendance proposed that Kentucky's slaves be gradually set free; this would minimize the threat both to whites' safety and to the state's economy. But, although it consisted of a majority of the attending delegates,[4] the antislavery faction lacked the political organizing skills — and active public backing — necessary for their position to prevail.[5] When a proposal to strike the pro-slavery article of the constitution was introduced on April 18, 1792, it was defeated by a vote of 26-16.[6] Although Kentucky would thus become a slave state, with a subsequent constitutional convention in 1799 enshrining this status, the vote at Danville clearly demonstrated there was a

---

1. Rice, *Frontier Kentucky*, 114.
2. Martin, *Anti-Slavery Movement*, 13.
3. David Rice, "Slavery Inconsistent with Justice and Good Policy, Proved by a Speech Delivery in the Convention Held at Danbury, Kentucky," http://memory.loc.gov/cgi-bin/query/r?ammem/faw:@field(DOCID+icufawcbc0007).
4. John D. Barnhart, *Valley of Democracy: The Frontier versus the Plantation in the Ohio Valley, 1775-1818* (Bloomington: Indiana University Press, 1953), 94. Conservatives won over moderates to their position and thus defeated those opposed to the introduction of slavery.
5. Asa E. Martin argues that, since the vast majority of Kentucky voters at that time were from Virginia, they would have voted to continue the slave system. See Martin, *Anti-Slavery Movement*, 17. Pro-slave forces also had critical power at the convention. For example, the president, Alexander Scott Bullitt, was a major slaveholder from Jefferson County. Furthermore, as Howard points out, the antislavery group was not well organized. Howard, *Evangelical War*, 13.
6. Martin, *Anti-Slavery Movement*, 16.

deep split in public attitudes on this issue.[1] (Some opponents of slavery — namely, poor farmers who owned no slaves — had difficulty finding an opportunity to express their views. The need for them to remain on the land prevented many of these farmers from participating in the public debate.[2]) The fact that members of clergy led the antislavery movement would suggest that opposition was chiefly rooted in religious conviction, but this remains in doubt. For one thing, the evangelical revivalist movement known as the Second Great Awakening did not spread down from New England to the hills of Kentucky until the late 1790s — several years after the first convention.[3] Membership in the Baptist Church was relatively insignificant when the first constitutional vote on slavery took place.[4] One of the first (and most influential) Presbyterian ministers in Kentucky, James McGready, did not address a camp meeting in the state prior to 1796.[5] The first massive, interdenominational revivalist gathering — which drew an impressive throng of 10,000-20,000 people — occurred five years later at Cane Ridge, in rural Bourbon County.[6] (This event gave a tremendous boost to both the Methodist and Baptist churches in Kentucky.[7]) Furthermore, all of this evidence, plus the fact that delegates at the 1792 convention not associated with the evangelical Christianity also voted against slavery, indicates that non-religious reasons also lay behind this position.

The revivalists were certainly sympathetic toward the plight of slaves and the black race in general. The version of Christianity they brought to the frontier embraced all of God's creatures as equals, and white and black preachers frequently spoke at the same frontier camp meetings.[8] After the failure to bar slavery under the state constitution, leaders of the Protestant churches in Kentucky

1. Changes adopted in the constitution in 1799 made it virtually impossible for slavery to be abolished in Kentucky.
2. In 1799, Henry Clay noted that 600 wealthy landowners were able to attend a political meeting in Fayette County, while work demands kept more than twice that number of poor farmers away. See Soltow, "Kentucky Wealth," 617.
3. Howard, *Evangelical War*, 15. For a brief discussion of the impact of Presbyterianism in Kentucky, see Ralph E. Morrow, "The Great Revival, the West, and the Crisis of the Church," in *The Frontier Re-Examined*, ed. John Francis McDermott (Urbana: University of Illinois Press, 1967), 69-71.
4. In 1790, only 3,105 of the 73,677 Kentuckians were Baptists. http://library.sebts.edu/sprescott/Spring%202003%20HIS%20302/4.05.01%20-%20The%20Second%20Great%20Awakening.htm
5. "Old Gasper River Meeting-House: The Birth Place of Cumberland Presbyterianism," *The Cumberland Presbyterian*, 10 Feb. 1876. http://www.cumberland.org/hfcpc/churches/GasRivKY.htm.
6. To put this figure in perspective, the largest city in Kentucky at that time, Lexington, had a population of only 1,795.
7. Davenport, *Ante-Bellum Kentucky*, 129.
8. For an illustration of these integrated gatherings, see P.S. Duval, "Sacramental Scene in a Western Forest," lithograph (1801), General Collections, Library of Congress, http://www.loc.gov/exhibits/religion/rel07.html.

continued to play a leading role in advocating for emancipation. But opposition to the slave system in Kentucky also had an economic basis — namely, the state's unequal opportunities for farmers. As was pointed out above, the fabled "Land of Milk and Honey" west of the Appalachians had failed to live up to its billing. The Bluegrass and Pennyroyal regions, where the state's major cash crops, tobacco and hemp, could be grown and harvested in abundance, were thriving, but other areas of Kentucky were mired in stubborn poverty. The guaranteeing of slave ownership under the state's second constitution, in 1799, induced more wealthy planters to move westward to Kentucky and start plantations there.[1] This influx accounts for the doubling of the slave population over the next decade.[2] But, while these wealthy landowners reaped a good return on their investments, the promise of prosperity for other whites was not realized.

Instead, many of these small farmers were forced out of the Bluegrass into rural valleys and mountains, where agriculture was scarcely profitable, and poverty abounded. Non-slaveholding whites were also displaced from the Green River Country to the south and west, as the tobacco grandees expanded their domain, driving up land prices in the process.[3] As a result, fewer whites could afford to own land. For example, by 1795, in Logan County (south of the Green River and west of Bowling Green), eight of ten white families did not own the land on which they were living.[4] During the early decades of the 19th century, the lot of Kentucky's poor farmers continued to worsen as speculators grabbed up acreage for which title was in doubt.[5] The antislavery sentiments expressed at the 1792 convention bespeak this unhappiness with how the plantation system was harming these "plain folk." Clear evidence of this sentiment can be found in the backgrounds of the delegates to the Danville convention. All but one of the nine opponents of slavery who was not a minister owned only small tracts of land. Among them there happened to be a slaveholding farmer from Virginia.

1. Article VII, Section 1 of the 1799 constitution stated that "The legislature shall have no power to pass laws for the emancipation of slaves without the consent of their owners, or without paying their owners previous to such emancipation, a full equivalent in money, for the slaves so emancipated."
2. In the inner Bluegrass, slaves increased from one fourth to one third of the population between 1800 and 1830. Aron, *How the West Was Lost*, 143.
3. *Ibid.*, 150.
4. *Ibid.*, 152.
5. See letter of "Plough Boy" to "Citizens of Kentucky," *The Mirror* (Russellville, Ky.), 22 Aug. 1807, warning about the "insidious gripe [sic] of thousands of speculators" who were organizing themselves to purchase properties with disputed ownership in the Green River region, forcing small farmers into poverty: 'you will soon find, that many of you, like an old frail and tattered bark, who at length has received a dry dock for the faithful tour of service performed, will again be wasted; upon the barren deserts of poverty with your little tender progeny, at your feet, emploring [sic] you as their father for bread, to alleviate the horrid pains of hunger, and you only tears to give . . .'"

Another anti-slavery delegate came from western Pennsylvania, and at least three others had migrated from Europe, where there was little support for enslaving blacks.[1]

Concern about the negative consequences of slavery had existed for some time. It could be found among some slave owners as well as non-slaveholding farmers. Planters arriving from Virginia had quickly sensed that the newly opened territory was not as widely suited to producing tobacco as was their native state. This realization made them question the wisdom of transplanting slave-based, plantation agriculture west of the Appalachians. But the planters' concern was not just economic. Some prominent Kentuckians had come around to questioning the moral justification for slavery. Those who belonged to Danville's Political Club, which included many judges, army officers, lawyers, and other professionals, urged Congress not to wait until 1808 to end the slave trade but instead to take steps sooner to end this "odious business."[2] But some Kentucky whites were also worried about their own safety. Since tobacco was the only agricultural product (other than cotton) requiring slave labor to grow and harvest it profitably, it was unclear how blacks could be kept busy — and under control — if farming in Kentucky developed in another direction. This problem was compounded by the continuing increase in the slave population largely due to a high birth rate. This fecundity helped to increase the proportion of slaves in Kentucky's population from 16.87 percent in 1790 to nearly 20 percent two decades later.[3] Fears of slave uprisings were thus easily aroused.[4] Such anxiety was fueled by rumors and alarming reports from afar.

For example, in the summer of 1792, a month and a half after Kentucky had entered the Union, word arrived from Richmond of a recent revolt on Virginia's Eastern Shore. According to one published report, as many as 900 slaves "armed with muskets, spears, clubs, &" had gathered at different locales and "committed several outrages upon the inhabitants."[5] This kind of news heightened feelings of white vulnerability on the frontier.

Furthermore, many wealthy Virginians migrating to Kentucky had read and taken to heart Jefferson's cautionary words in his *Notes on the State of Virginia* about the ill-effects of "racial mixing" and accordingly wanted to reduce, if not

---

1. Barnhart, *Valley of Democracy*, 93-4.
2. Quoted in Speed, *Political Club*, 151.
3. Some 12,544 blacks lived in Kentucky in 1790, out of a total population of 73,677. By 1810, the black population had reached 82,274, and the overall number of people living in the state was 406,511.
4. Kentucky slaveholders had "an almost paranoiac fear of slave rebellion." But a large uprising never occurred in the state. Lucas, *History of Blacks*, 59. There were, however, two revolts of slaves being transported to the Deep South in 1820s caused considerable alarm in Kentucky. See Howard, *Evangelical War*, 15.
5. *Kentucky Gazette*, 14 July 1792.

end, their dependence on slave labor.[1] Other newly arrived settlers of more modest origins were uncomfortable with the idea of slavery. An immigrant farmer from Ireland named Philip Philips, then living in the outer Bluegrass, voiced that view in a letter published in November 1791. He took umbrage at the opinion held by Colonel Nicholas and other pro-slavery spokesmen that blacks deserved no better fate than to toil in bondage for whites. "I am a friend to the liberties of the pepel [*sic*]," Philips wrote, "and I do not see why the black Deels [*sic*] should not have thare [*sic*] liberties too."[2]

All of these concerns convinced many delegates to reject sanctioning the slave system within Kentucky's borders. This opposition was strong even where slavery was well entrenched. In several counties where the percentage of blacks in the population was among the highest in the state, more votes were cast *against* slavery than for it.[3] Once the new state's constitution was adopted over these objections, non-slaveholding white farmers saw that their economic future was imperiled. Many of them began to contemplate moving to another part of the country. Significantly, they entertained these thoughts not because agriculture in the Bluegrass State was facing a decline but because the dominance of slave labor was making the outlook for them — farmers with few or no slaves — increasingly gloomy.

At the same time, many would-be migrants from Virginia and neighboring states reconsidered their plans to come to Kentucky. This ebbing of the new state's appeal — exacerbated by disputes over land claims — can be seen in the subsequent slowing of the growth of the state's white population. After having tripled between 1790 and 1800, and then nearly doubled the following decade, the number of free whites grew only by 83,151 — or 16 percent — in the 1820s and only by 12 percent in the 1830s. In some counties that had experienced an influx of slave labor, the white population fell substantially. In Logan, for instance, it dropped by over 13 percent in just one decade (1820-1830). Increasingly, with the state's economic growth and progress inextricably tied to slavery, it was becoming apparent that Thomas Jefferson's vision of an agrarian democracy in the west was not going to be fulfilled in Kentucky. Small farmers who had believed in this future would have to look for it somewhere else.[4]

---

1. For details on doubts about introducing slavery in Kentucky, see Martin *Anti-Slavery Movement*, 9-10.
2. Letter of Philip Philips to the printer, *Kentucky Gazette*, 26 Nov. 1791, and 3 Dec. 1791.
3. Fayette County, with a 25 percent slave population, voted 3-2 against slavery; Mercer, with a 23 percent slave population, also voted 3-2 against; Lincoln, with 18 percent slaves, similarly voted 3-2 against. However, the three other counties with slave proportions of at least 18 percent — Jefferson, Lincoln, and Woodford — voted for slavery, by 2-0, 3-2, and 5-0, respectively. See Martin, *Anti-Slavery Movement*, 16, note 25.
4. For a thorough treatment of frontier Kentucky's transformation into a bastion of slavery, see Aron, *How the West Was Lost*, 198-9, *passim*.

In particular, this lack of economic opportunity caused many poor white Kentuckians to consider moving north, across the Ohio, to territories where slavery was banned under the Ordinance of 1787.[1] Partially for this reason, this new addition to the United States had attracted settlers as soon as it had been organized into the Northwest Territory. How many Southerners left their native region because of the slave system is difficult to gauge. No data on reasons for interstate migration exist. However, the political and social views held by these migrants provide some insight into their motives — and racial outlook. These will be discussed in the following chapter. It is clear that residents of the Upper South who migrated to free states in the Old Northwest were *ipso facto* rejecting life under a slave-dominated economy. While a number of slaveholders would circumnavigate the Ordinance of 1787 prohibition by importing slaves as indentured servants, the overwhelming majority of Southern migrants did not own slaves. They gained no material advantage from the presence of slaves and, indeed, suffered economically wherever the "peculiar institution" was firmly entrenched. From a social standpoint, these relocating Southerners, like nearly all whites north or south of the Mason Dixon Line, harbored a deep disdain for black people and had no desire to live among them, certainly not on anything approaching equal terms. By crossing the Ohio, they were opting to leave a biracial society for one that was virtually all white. (In 1810, for example, there were only 1,899 blacks in Ohio, out of a total population of 230,760. This equaled 0.8 percent of the state's inhabitants. By contrast, 20 percent of the people in Kentucky were African Americans.) By heading north these frontier settlers were taking a radical step — abandoning a culture, traditions, and values held dear by their families, in many cases for generations. That so many thousands were willing to follow this unprecedented migratory path from South to North suggests that reasons other than a desire for more land and better opportunities were at play.

For a mixture of economic and racial reasons, many small farmers, skilled and semiskilled workers, and other laborers began to move to the Old Northwest. Large numbers of settlers had recently arrived there from other parts of the country looking for affordable land and a better life. In 1788, the Ohio Company had established a permanent outpost at Marietta, on the eastern border of what would become the state of Ohio, and soon thereafter migrating pioneers had started other settlements further west along the northern bank of the Ohio

1. While the single largest contingent of Kentucky emigrants (69,694) was living in a slave state — Missouri — in 1850, 127,233 free white and black natives of Kentucky were then living in the free states of Illinois, Indiana, Iowa, and Ohio. This accounted for nearly half of all émigrés from the Bluegrass State. Table XX, "Place of Birth of the White and Free Colored Population of the United States, 1850," *Mortality Statistics of the Seventh Census of the United States, 1850* (Washington: A.O.P. Nicholson, 1855), 38-9.

River. The new American government put pressure on resident Native American tribes to cede these lands because they had sided with the British during the Revolutionary War.[1] The United States considered these Indians to be defeated nations, subject to any conditions the victor might impose. But the Indians did not see the situation this way and fought back.[2] Warriors of the Miami Nation ambushed U.S. troops near Fort Washington (Maryland) in November 1791, killing 623 soldiers. It was not until after several tribes were defeated by forces led by Gen. Anthony Wayne, at the Battle of Fallen Timbers (Ohio) in 1794, that they reluctantly signed a peace treaty the following year, granting much of the Northwest Territory to the U.S. government. As a consequence, settlers swarmed northward across the Ohio River, and these littoral settlements grew rapidly in size and number. Because of ready access to a major water route connecting it to the New Orleans market and an abundance of rich alluvial soil, the local economy boomed, with cattle, hogs, and grain being the principal exports. Because of its geographical proximity and comparable method of agriculture, the southern tier of the so-called "butternut" states (Ohio, Indiana, and Illinois) attracted impoverished backcountry Southern farmers, chiefly from Virginia and Kentucky. Early in the 19th century, these "plain folk" began an exodus to the north — the first phase of a massive relocation of Kentuckians during the antebellum era. Their migration was spurred by Congress's passage of a land act in 1800, reducing the minimum size of tracts available for sale in the Northwest Territory.[3] By 1860, 331,904 natives of the Bluegrass State — or 31.5 percent of the total — would be living elsewhere in the United States and its territories.[4]

North of the Ohio, relations between whites and blacks were not clearly delineated by an oppressive, legally sanctioned slave system, but were more

---

1. The war's outcome was a "disaster" for these Native Americans, who no longer could count on British help in staving off the American advance. See Reginald Horsman, *Expansion and American Indian Policy, 1783-1812* (East Lansing: Michigan State University Press, 1967), 3.
2. R. Douglas Hurt, *The Indian Frontier, 1763-1846* (Albuquerque: University of New Mexico Press, 2002), 104.
3. Up until then, only parcels of 4,000 acres or more were for sale, effectively pricing the territory out of the reach of small farmers. As territorial representative from Indiana, William Henry Harrison was instrumental in enacting this law.
4. The proportion of native-born residents who had left the state was greater than that of any other Southern state except for South Carolina. In 1860, 41 percent of native South Carolinians and 34.2 percent of Tennesseans were living outside their birth states. Other states with a rate of exodus greater than Kentucky's were Vermont (42), New Hampshire (32.8), and Connecticut (32). Table 0 0 — "Nativity of Americans residing in each State and Territory," *Statistics of the United States in 1860; compiled from the Original Returns of the Eighth Census* (Washington: Government Printing Office, 1866), lxi-lxii. A decade earlier, nearly 30 percent of white Kentucky natives were living outside this state. Tables XIV and XV, "Nativities of White and Free Colored Population," *Mortality Statistics of the Seventh Census*, 36.

complex and fluid. Just how this evolving situation would affect the well being of migrating non-slaveholders from the South was not at all clear. On the one hand, poor white farmers would not have to worry about being reduced once again to poverty and flight by sprawling slave plantations. But, on the other hand, on the "free" soil of the Old Northwest there were no guarantees that blacks would not pose another kind of threat. As laborers not bound to any master, with the right to work and live wherever they chose, emancipated Northern blacks could compete against these Southerners on another level — not as pawns in a dominant agricultural system, but as individuals. Only after crossing the Ohio and trying their luck on the other side would these "plain folk" farmers discover which situation was better — and which worse — for them.

IV. White Flight Across the Ohio

The nation's first real battle over slavery was fought in the Ohio Valley. It was fought there not with rifles or cannon or charging brigades, but with bushels of corn and cold cash. In the newly settled Midwest, for the first time in American history, two vastly different economic systems — one free, the other slave — collided head-on. In open competition, the merits of one were tested against the other. The outcome of this clash not only shaped the political and social outlook of the Midwest for decades to come, but also gave new direction and impetus to the subsequent flow of settlers across the continent.

This momentous confrontation between North and South took place in the Ohio Valley for two reasons. The first was geographic. In a part of the country not otherwise well fed by rivers, the westward flowing Ohio served as a major conduit for goods and travelers, carrying them some 980 miles from Pittsburgh to Cincinnati to Louisville and on to the farthest point in Kentucky, on the Illinois border, where it merged with the mighty Mississippi. This river bore barges and steamboats another 1,100 miles southward past cotton plantations, sand bars, and bayous to the port of New Orleans and the Gulf of Mexico. In the decades before the coming of the railroad, rivers and creeks bound the United States together and made commerce between its coasts and interior feasible. Thus, it was along the Ohio that the first pioneers established trading outposts, pushing back hostile Indian tribes to do so. The river and its rich banks also beckoned farmers from both the North and the South. Squatters took up residence north of the Ohio as early as the late 1770s, ignoring a government ban on settlement there. Veterans of the Revolutionary War living in the New England states entered the valley in the 1790s, under the auspices of the Ohio Company.[1] Other settlers bought public lands put on the market for the affordable minimum price of $1 per acre. Many more swept into the region after a treaty was signed with Indian tribes in 1795. These new arrivals cleared fields on the northern side of the Ohio, planting wheat and other crops for export back east. At the same time, farmers from the Upper South settled along the other bank of river for similar reasons. Having crossed over the Appalachians by an arduous and hazardous land route, they welcomed having ready access to eastern markets via the Ohio. Hence, several major outposts in Kentucky — most notably, Louisville — sprang up along the southern bank. Like its northern counterpart, Cincinnati, Louisville quickly developed into a center for manufacturing and commerce, attracting thousands of workers eager for well-paying jobs on this frontier. Thus, opportunities afforded by the Ohio River brought settlers from slave and free states into close proximity and contact with one another.

Inevitably, this geographical closeness bred familiarity. In the Ohio Valley, the terms "North" and "South" were not abstractions; they denoted two neighboring communities with many common interests. Living only a few miles apart, separated only by the natural boundary of the river, farmers, craftsmen, laborers, shop owners, and factory workers on both sides shared many of the same ambitions and faced similar frontier challenges, despite belonging to rival sections of the country. In going about their trade and business, Northern and Southern settlers came to know each other. This familiarity bred some contempt, but much curiosity as well. Pioneers on opposing banks of the Ohio observed one another with keen interest. In particular, those living in slaveholding Kentucky peered north to learn how well whites fared in an economy that excluded slaves. A dawning awareness that Northerners were not just doing well, but in fact doing much better under a system of free labor soon turned this curiosity into envy. The perceived advantages of making a living outside the slave system made the territory north of the Ohio increasingly appealing to many non-slaveholding Southern whites. Rather than see slavery spread further north, they began to dream of building a more secure and prosperous existence for themselves by leaving this system behind and resettling across the river, where few blacks lived. These Southerners came to conclude that a thriving economy and the absence of blacks were closely linked. By moving in large numbers to free territories and states in the Ohio Valley early in the 19th century, "plain folk" whites were acknowledging that living in a slave society had served them poorly. Their movement out of Kentucky into Ohio, Indiana, and Illinois amounted to a tacit endorsement of the North's way of life over the South's.

---

1. The Ohio Company bought up one million acres north and west of the Ohio River. Malcolm J. Rohrbaugh, *The Land Office Business: The Settlement and Administration of American Public Lands, 1789-1837* (New York: Oxford University Press, 1968), 11.

This northward migration of Kentuckians — many of them natives of Virginia — and others from the Upper South was historically distinctive for both in its size and its direction. Tens of thousands crossed the Ohio in just a few years. Their ranks far exceeded the number of persons moving elsewhere during the first decades of the 19th century. An article published in a Danville, Kentucky, newspaper painted a vivid picture of this human tide: "Emigrants — the number of movers passing daily through this place westward, is astonishing. They are generally poor, having their plunder packed on horses, or in carts drawn by calves, cows, and horses, or in some instances by oxen and horses. Several days during the last week the road was literally filled with movers. Nine-tenths of these movers are from North Carolina, South Carolina, Georgia, Virginia and other southern and eastern slaveholding states; the remainder are all our citizens, all pressing to the free states on the western frontier."[1] This massive relocation also defied the prevailing thrust of American migration — namely, westward along the same latitudinal lines, within which climate and soil were familiar to arriving settlers.[2]

Overall, Southerners were more apt than Northerners to relocate out-of-state during the period 1800-1830.[3] One analysis of War of 1812 veterans, for example, found that 45 percent of those who had been living south of the Mason Dixon Line moved after this conflict to another state or territory, while less than one third of former soldiers who had previously resided in the New England or mid-Atlantic states did so.[4] By mid-century, the states of Virginia, North and South Carolina, Georgia, Tennessee, and Kentucky had experienced a net loss of nearly one million persons.[5] However, almost all Southern migration remained *within* that region. Specifically, most of this movement was into the adjacent Old

---

1. Quoted in Richard L. Power, *Planting Corn Belt Culture: The Impress of the Upland Southerner and Yankee in the Old Northwest* (Indianapolis: Indiana Historical Society, 1953), 26.

2. For an analysis of the dominant migratory pattern in American history, see Richard H. Steckel, "The Economic Foundations of East-West Migration during the 19th Century," *Explorations in Economic History* 20:1 (Jan. 1983), 14-36. Soils and climate in southern Illinois were found to be comparable to what existed in the Upland South, and these conditions made the former region appealing to farmers in Kentucky and Virginia. Cf. Douglas K. Meyer, *Making the Heartland Quilt: A Geographical History of Settlement and Migration in Early-Nineteenth-Century Illinois* (Carbondale: Southern Illinois University Press, 2000), 17. One demographic analysis of the movement of farmers from the South has shown that the northerly route they took in the decades prior to the Civil War stands at variance with the prevailing migratory path westward. See McClelland and Zeckhauser, *Demographic Dimensions*, 7.

3. To a large extent, Northerners were deterred from moving west by the prospect of Indian attacks.

4. James W. Oberly, "Westward Who? Estimates of Native White Interstate Migration After the War of 1812," *Journal of Economic History* 46:2 (June 1986), Table 1, "Migration of War of 1812 Veterans," 434.

5. This figure is derived from subtracting the number of persons from out-of-state living in those states in 1850 from the number of natives of Virginia, the Carolinas, Georgia, Tennessee, and Kentucky who were residing in other states in that year. See Miller, "Interstate Slave Trade," 183.

Southwest — comprising Alabama, Mississippi, Louisiana, and Arkansas — where the cotton industry was flourishing, and rich soils were plentiful. This pattern held most true in the Deep South. In 1850, one of five natives of Georgia and South Carolina were living in other Southern (or border) states or territories, but only 1.6 percent of them were residing in non-Southern states or territories. Likewise, of the 1,434,055 whites born in Georgia and South Carolina who were alive in 1880, 317,389, or 22 percent, were then living in other Southern or border states, versus 26,898, or less than two percent, in states or territories outside the South.[1] For these Southern migrants, the benefits of remaining within a slave economy — namely, familiar climate, crops, and agricultural methods, family ties, longstanding cultural traditions, proximity to their native states, and adequate economic opportunity — apparently outweighed any inherent drawbacks.

But, for residents of the Upper South — chiefly, those in Kentucky (and, to a lesser extent, Tennessee) — the attractiveness of free states was much greater.[2] Because they lived close to the Northern states, they could more easily move in that direction, but proximity alone does not account for their migration. If it did, one would expect to find an equally large flow of Northerners crossing over to the southern side of the Ohio, but this was not the case. In 1850, only 9,985 white and free black natives of Ohio were living in Kentucky, whereas 13,829 persons born in the Bluegrass State had migrated the other way. This one-way trend was even more pronounced between Kentucky and the free states of Indiana and Illinois.[3] At mid-century, there were 68,651 white and free black Kentucky natives living in Indiana, and 49,588 in Illinois, while only 5,898 Hoosiers and 1,649 Illinois natives had moved to this neighboring Southern state.[4] How can one explain this greater appeal of the free states?

As in earlier westward migrations, most migrating families were poor, in search of a better life. Numerous contemporary observers commented upon this fact. For instance, a German visitor in the 1820s watched some 200 wagons loaded with Southerners cross the Ohio into eastern Indiana "in flight from the

1. Table XI, "Native White Population of the United States," *Statistics of the United States at the Tenth Census,* 484-6. States outside the South here include Missouri, Kansas, Iowa, Colorado, and California.
2. Whereas 58 percent of non-slave Kentucky natives were living in free states in 1850, only 23 percent of Tennesseans living elsewhere at that point resided in free states. The single largest northern concentration of whites and free blacks born in Tennessee was in Illinois (32,303). "Place of Birth," *Mortality Statistics of the Seventh Census,* 39.
3. Nationally, the same pattern was evident. By 1860, twice as many slave-state residents had moved to free states as had migrated in the other direction. Bruce Levine, *Half Slave and Half Free: The Roots of the Civil War* (New York: Hill and Wang, 1992), 37.
4. *Ibid.,* 38. There were more adult white male immigrants originally from Kentucky living in Illinois than from any other state except for New York. See Meyer, *Heartland Quilt,* 138. Meyer reproduces data from the *Seventh Census Population Schedules, 1850.*

insolent behavior of their more wealthy neighbors." Poverty was reported to be widespread in the southern counties of Indiana and Illinois, where farmers from Kentucky and Virginia had clustered.[1] One can, therefore, deduce that economic necessity played a major role in the decision to move north. For farmers who had no stake in the slave system, the so-called "butternut" states offered many inducements. (Most Kentucky slaveholders, naturally, found western territories that tolerated the owning of chattel — especially ones in the Cotton Belt — more enticing.) First and foremost was the profitability of their agriculture. When data on farm products were first collected by the Bureau of the Census, in 1850, they revealed a stark contrast between the amount and value of what was then being grown in the free and slave states. These figures provide some, albeit limited (since considerable economic growth occurred during the subsequent decades), basis for assessing the relative attractiveness of these states to farmers earlier in the century. In brief, these agricultural data reveal decidedly lower rates of productivity and profit in the Southern states.

All told, farms in these states yielded a value of $155,223,415, compared to $214,422,523 in the free states — a 16 percent difference. (Ohio alone produced more corn than any other state in the Union, and this crop was nationally as valuable as all wheat, cotton, and hay combined. Ohio also ranked first in the production of wool and whisky, and second in wheat and cheese.[2]) Measured by weight, the North overall outperformed the South even more dramatically, growing more than *six times* the amount of foodstuffs, animal feed, and other agricultural products. Furthermore, the value of Northern non-manufactured goods sold to the South exceeded what the free states imported from below the Mason Dixon Line — mainly cotton, tobacco, and wheat — by a considerable margin.[3] In analyzing these regional figures in 1857, the North Carolina-born writer Hinton Helper (the son of a poor farmer from that state) reached the inescapable conclusion that "the profits arising to the North from the sale of provender and provisions to the South, are far greater than those arising to the South from the sale of cotton, tobacco and breadstuffs to the North." The greater appeal of a Northern state like Ohio over a slave one like Kentucky is evident in their diverging rates of population growth after 1800: in Ohio, the population rose from

---

1. Power, *Corn Belt Culture*, 26. An 1818 survey of 700 Illinois settlers found that 53 percent came from Southern states. E. Douglas Branch, *Westward: The Romance of the American Frontier* (New York: Appleton, 1930), 289.
2. Thomas S. Berry, *Harvard Economic Studies*, vol. 74, *Western Prices Before 1861: A Study of the Cincinnati Market* (New York: Johnson Reprint, 1966), 4.
3. These figures are cited in Hinton Rowan Helper, *The Impending Crisis of the South: How to Meet It* (New York: Burdick Bros., 1857), 66. See http://docsouth.unc.edu/nc/helper/helper.html.

45,356 to 937,903 in 1830, but Kentucky's only increased from 220,955 to 687,917 over these three decades.[1]

Rising land prices in the Northern states provided a second powerful motive for moving to the free states. There is some statistical evidence suggesting that the value of property north of the Ohio River was increasing significantly during the early decades of the 19th century, while it was stagnating on the other side. For example, newspaper advertisements in Kentucky newspapers *circa* 1805 carried asking prices in the $1-2.50 per acre range for properties located in the southwestern part of the state, while prices in desirable sections of Ohio were at least twice as much at the time.[2] (In a letter written in 1795, George Washington confided that he fully expected to sell river bottomlands he owned near Marietta in what was known as "Ohio Country" — present-day western Pennsylvania, West Virginia, and most of Ohio — for a minimum of $4 per acre, or 50 percent more than what they had been worth two years before.[3] In 1787, the Ohio Company had originally sold acreage in the Northwest Territory for only eight cents an acre.[4]) Thirty years later, improved farming land some 70 miles from Cincinnati was reported to be going for between $4 and $25 per acre.[5] More reliable comparable figures are available, however, starting in the middle of the century. Then it was determined that the average price for an acre of land in the free states was $28.07, compared to $5.34 in the slave states. More specifically, a visitor to the Ohio Valley in the 1850s reported that the greatest price land commanded in Kentucky was $8 an acre, versus a *minimum* of $16 across the river in Ohio.[6] While acreage was more expensive in Ohio, Illinois, and Indiana than in the slave states, the return on such an investment was appreciably greater. This

1. In just one decade, 1800-1810, Ohio experienced a net in-migration of 161,697 persons. See Richard K Vedder and Lowell E. Gallaway, "Migration and the Old Northwest," in *Essays in Nineteenth Century Economic History: The Old Northwest*, ed. David. C. Klingaman and Richard K. Vedder (Athens: Ohio University Press, 1975), Table 2, "The Components of Population Change, Ohio, 1800-1860," 162.

2. In 1815, unimproved lots located more than 12 miles from Cincinnati were selling for between four and eight dollars in 1805, whereas fertile, cultivated land in Miami County, in northwestern Ohio, cost an average of $12 per acre. Berry, *Western Prices*, 11.

3. Letter of George Washington to Charles Morgan, 17 Jan. 1795, George Washington Papers at the Library of Congress, 1741-1799, http://memory.loc.gov/cgi-bin/query/r?ammem/mgw:@field(DOCID+@lit(gw340057))

4. Stewart Holbrook, *The Yankee Exodus: An Account of Migration from New England* (New York: Macmillan, 1950), 21. However, other source put this initial price at 10 cents per acre. See, for example, Hughes and Cain, *American Economic History*, 91.

5. Letter of Gershom Flagg to Artemis Flagg, 1 June 1817, *The Flagg Correspondence: Selected Letters, 1816-1854*, ed. Barbara Lawrence and Nedra Branz (Carbondale: Southern Illinois University Press, 1986), 7.

6. Helper, *Impending Crisis*, 136. This informant claimed that all along the Ohio prices on the northern side were between 100-200 percent greater than those on the opposite bank. The conclusion that low land prices correlated with the presence of slave labor was not supported by what happened in the South after the Civil War — namely, a decline in land values. See Foger and Engerman, *Time on the Cross*, 169.

fact made the free states of the Old Northwest highly attractive to small farmers — particularly younger ones — who could afford to buy land there and then wait to reap a sizeable return on these investments.[1] Furthermore, with most good farmland having been bought by slaveholders in Kentucky, the availability of fertile acreage in states above the Ohio was enticing, even if the prices were higher. The percentage of Kentuckians migrating north who did not then own land but who intended to acquire some on the other side of the river is not known, but, given the fact that half of all heads of households in the state fell into this landless category, one can reasonably surmise that it was significant.

The desirability of Northern land is evident in descriptions of these free states and territories published in the early 1800s. An article that was reprinted in a Kentucky newspaper, for example, hailed the rapid growth that had occurred in Wayne County, Ohio, (southwest of Akron), and lauded its enticing natural resources: "There are however in the county several prairies of considerable extent, and two or three small but beautiful lakes. It is abundantly watered with good springs, and mill streams; the soil is excellent and is equally adapted to grain and grass, both which it yields in abundance."[2] The same newspaper also published a letter from the Missouri Territory's representative in Congress, praising the western lands north of the Ohio as free of poverty, rich in fertile soil, and full of promise: "Every person, however poor, may with moderate industry, become in a very short time a landholder; his substance increases from year to year; his barns are filled with abundant harvests; his cattle multiply . . . Truly may it be said of that fortunate and highly favored country, A *paradise of pleasure is open'd in the wild.*"[3] When the English Quaker Morris Birkbeck first laid eye on Illinois lands west of the Wabash River, he jotted down in his journal that they were "so beautiful with their surrounding woods, as to seem like the creation of fancy; gardens of delight in a dreary wilderness..."[4] Such hyperbolic first-hand accounts no doubt fueled interest in relocating from Kentucky to the Old Northwest.

The economic rationale behind poor Southern farmers moving north across the Ohio can also be gleaned from contemporary books on frontier life in the Old Northwest. These works reveal local attitudes toward the slave system and how its absence benefited whites in this region, socially as well as economically. For

---

1. Younger farmers would have more years to recoup their initial investment. Hence, they were more apt to move northward than older farmers. Cf. Steckel, "Economic Foundations," 31.
2. "Topography," *The Eagle* (Maysville, Ky.), 14 Nov. 1817, reprinted from Ohio *Spectator.*
3. Letter of Rep. Rufus Easton to Sen. William Hunter, 30 April 1816, published in *The Eagle,* 13 Sept. 1816.
4. Morris Birkbeck, "Notes on a Journey" in *Prairie State: Impressions of Illinois, 1673-1967, by Travelers and Other Observers,* comp. Paul M. Angle (Chicago: University of Chicago Press, 1968), 64.

instance, in 1817, Richard Clough Anderson, Jr. — member of a distinguished slaveholding Louisville family, graduate of William and Mary, attorney, and newly-elected state legislator — traveled east by way of Ohio. Passing through Rushville, west of Zanesville in the southeastern part of the state, Anderson was struck by the differences he observed in Northern agriculture: "The rapid improvement of this Country shews [*sic*] the good policy of excluding slaves & of the high benefit of dividing land into small parcels into congress manner."[1]

Shortly after arriving from England, Birkbeck had purchased 16,000 acres in Illinois and then founded the town of New Albion in the 1810s. He enthusiastically assumed the role of gentleman farmer and for doing so came to be derisively known as the "Emperor of the Prairies."[2] Birkbeck also became a fervent opponent of slavery, arguing that it drove down land values and "degraded" whites who came into contact with it. In seeking to keep the "peculiar institution" out of Illinois, this English immigrant appealed to the self interest of white workers: "To labour for his living among slaves, or to labour at all where the idea of slavery is so blended with labour as to communicate to it something of disgrace, would be a sad exchange to a very large portion of the citizens of this State, where labour is, as it ought to be, in high and honourable estimation, and the sure road to independence." By contrast, in the South, Birkbeck claimed, "There is a contempt of labour, encouraging indolence and its companions, dissipation and profligacy . . ."[3]

When the British naval officer Basil Hall traveled through the South more than a decade later, he came away with a favorable impression of how the slave system operated, even while conceding it was inherently "evil." However, after crossing the Ohio at the end of May, 1830, and observing free laborers in Cincinnati, Hall immediately perceived the superior value of their approach to work: "There is probably something in its being placed in a non-slave-holding State," he noted, "which contributes to give it so spirited and agreeable a character."[4] Touring the United States a year later, ostensibly to learn about its prison system, Alexis de Tocqueville keenly took in much more about the American way of life, including the affect of slavery on its people and economy. In Louisville, he interviewed a wealthy merchant who admitted that his state lagged far behind Ohio — because of a chattel system that was "even more prejudicial to the mas-

1. Richard Clough Anderson, Jr., *Diary Journal of Richard Clough Anderson, Jr., 1814-1826*, ed. Alfred Tischendorf and E. Taylor Parks (Durham, Duke University Press, 1964), entry for 26 Aug. 1817, 68.
2. Simon A. Ferrall, *A Ramble of Six Thousand Miles Through the United States of America* (London: Effingham Wilson, 1832), 165.
3. Morris Birkbeck, *An Appeal to the People of Illinois on the Question of a Convention* (Shawnee-town, Ill.: C. Jones, 1823), 11-12.
4. Basil Hall, *Travels in North America in the Years 1827 and 1828* (Edinburgh: Cadell, 1830), vol. 3, 389.

ters than to the slaves . . . slavery prevents emigrants from coming to us. It deprives us of the energy and spirit of enterprise that characterize the States that have no slaves."[1] After having glimpsed life on both sides of the river, de Tocqueville concluded: "On the right [i.e., northern] bank of the Ohio everything is activity, industry, labor is honored; there are no slaves. Pass to the left bank and the scene changes so suddenly that you think yourself on the other side of the world; the enterprising spirit is gone. There, work is not painful; it's shameful, and you degrade yourself in submitting yourself to it."[2] A similar observation was made about this time by another English visitor, George Featherstonhaugh, when he toured Indiana by stagecoach:

> The change from a state where slavery exists, which it does in Kentucky, though in somewhat a mitigated form, to a State with a free population, is obvious here. In Indiana you see neat white women and their children, with here and there a free negro; and every thing is cleaner and tidier than in Tennessee and Kentucky. The mistress of the house and her daughters wait upon you at table, instead of the huge, fat, frowsy negresses that, in the slave States, poison you with the effluvium of their skins, when they reach over to set anything on the table.[3]

On the eve of the Civil War, this economic imbalance had not changed. Whites in the South remained mired in a two-tiered caste system, made up of "rich planters and poverty-stricken peasants," according to another English visitor of that time. While growth and vitality were apparent in the Northern states, the slaves states had ground to a halt: "Here things seem all at a stand-still; there is no go-aheadness; you never come across a new 'city' rising in the wilderness."[4]

The North's economic superiority appeared to stem largely from its racial homogeneity. Six river counties in Kentucky contained 13,326 slaves in 1820 — equal to 42 percent of their total population — but adjacent counties on the northern side were almost exclusively white.[5] The region was "free" in many senses of the word, but what mattered most to prospective migrants from the Upper South was the absence of slave labor: they could move north without fear of being driven off later by encroaching plantations, as had happened to so many of them in Kentucky. The Northwest Ordinance thus gave those who "were flying from the economic evils of slavery" a green light to cross the Ohio.[6] On the

---

1. Alexis de Tocqueville, *Journey to America*, trans. George Lawrence, ed. J. P. Mayer (Westport: Greenwood Press, 1981), journal entry for 9 Dec. 1831, 92.
2. Journal entry for 20 Dec. 1831, quoted in George W. Pierson, *Tocqueville in America* (Baltimore: Johns Hopkins University Press, 1996), 581.
3. George W. Featherstonhaugh, *Excursion through the Slave States* (New York: Harper & Brothers, 1844), 62. Featherstonhaugh toured the region in late 1834.
4. James Stirling, *Letters from the Slave States* (New York: Kraus Reprint Co., 1969), 43.
5. More than half of these slaves were living in Jefferson County, which included the city of Louisville.
6. Charles Jay Wilson, "The Negro in Early Ohio," *Ohio Archaeological and Historical Quarterly* 39:4 (Oct. 1930), 728.

other side, they could finally escape its pernicious influence.[1] This argument was advanced, decades later, by Helper in his influential book *The Impending Crisis of the South*. Although here he condemned the chattel system in moral terms, writing that "the difference between freedom and slavery is simply the difference between sense and nonsense, wisdom and folly, good and evil, right and wrong,"[2] — his rejection of the "peculiar institution" had a pragmatic basis: it was simply not materially beneficial to the South, particularly its small farmers. Thus, he looked to these "plain folk" whites to rise up and overthrow an institution that worked against their best interests:

> Non-slaveholders of the South! farmers, mechanics and workingmen, we take this occasion to assure you that the slaveholders, the arrogant demagogues whom you have elected to office of honor and profit, have hoodwinked you, trifled with you, and used you as mere tools for the consummation of their wicked designs. They have purposely kept you in ignorance, and have, by moulding your passions and prejudices to suit themselves, induced you to act in direct opposition to your dearest rights and interests. By a system of the grossest subterfuge and misrepresentation, and in order to avert, for a season, the vengeance that will most assuredly overtake them here long, they have taught you to hate the abolitionists, who are your best and only true friends. Now, as one of your own number, we appeal to you to join us in our patriotic endeavors to rescue the generous soil of the South from the usurped and desolating control of those political vampires.[3]

Significantly, a few years later, during the 1860 presidential campaign, the Republican Party would distribute 100,000 copies of Helper's book to buttress its own case against slavery on similar grounds.

Other ammunition used at that time to attack the economic weaknesses of the "peculiar institution" came from the celebrated landscape architect (and designer of New York's Central Park) Frederick Law Olmstead. As a correspondent for *The New York Times*, Olmstead toured the Southern states in the mid-1850s, producing two books that assailed the slave system's ill effects on agricultural income and on white laborers. In Virginia, he discovered that land prices were a third of what they were in Pennsylvania, and that these values declined within the Old Dominion as the proportion of slaves increased. Furthermore, slaves cost their owners more than did hired labor. Because they were not motivated, slaves farmed inefficiently and — through their bad example — undermined the work ethic of white hired hands: "A man forced to labor under their system is morally driven to indolence, carelessness, indifference to the results of skill, heedlessness, incon-

---

1. One early 20th-century historian noted that many white farmers pushed out of Kentucky and neighboring states crossed the Ohio "carrying with them a dislike of the negro . . ." Hart, *Slavery and Abolition*, 76.
2. Helper, *Impending Crisis*, 48. Helper found that the value of all Southern agricultural products amounted to $155,223,415, compared to $214,422,523 for Northern products (mainly hay, butter and cheese, and wool).
3. *Ibid.*, 120-1.

stancy of purpose, improvidence, and extravagance."[1] Olmstead gained a similar impression from visiting the Southwestern backcountry. There the journalist talked to a Mississippi slave owner who — strangely enough — favored abolition: slavery was morally wrong, the man told Olmstead, but, worse than that, it was debasing to whites. Mechanics who lived nearby "felt slavery to be a great curse to them and . . . wanted to see it brought to an end in some way. The competition in which they were constantly made to feel themselves engaged with slave-labor was degrading to them, and they felt it to be so."[2]

That the coming of large-scale slavery and the ensuing economic displacement of small, independent farmers and landless whites largely account for their migration into the Old Northwest is further indicated by demographic data collected as part of the federal census starting in 1850. In Indiana, for example, where native Kentuckians made up nearly 18 percent of white residents born out-of-state in 1850,[3] the great preponderance of *all* Southern migrants came from within or near the Bluegrass, where slaves dominated the working force and plantation owners held much of the land.[4] Similarly, in 1850, among the non-slave population of Ohio, the single largest group from the South consisted of persons born in Kentucky — 13,829 out of 452,338 non-native residents. And in Illinois, there were 49,588 natives of Kentucky out of 393,297 white and free black residents born in other states.[5] Indeed, there were more persons born in Kentucky living in Illinois at mid-century than natives of any state except for New York and Ohio.[6] (The Southern state providing Illinois with the second largest out-of-state contingent was North Carolina, with 13,851.[7]) These figures do not include persons born in Virginia who had resided in Kentucky before moving north across the Ohio — a considerable number. All told, 152,278 Virginia-born whites and free blacks were

1. Frederick Law Olmstead, *A Journey in the Seaboard Slave States in the Years 1853-1854* (New York: G.P. Putnam's Sons, 1904), vol. 1, 90, 237, 164.
2. Olmstead, *A Journey in the Back Country in the Winter of 1853-4* (New York: G.P. Putnam's Sons, 1907), vol. 1, 198.
3. The precise figure is 17.3 percent. Gregory S. Rose, "Hoosier Origins: The Nativity of Indiana's United States-Born Population in 1850," *Indiana Magazine of History* 81:3 (Sept. 1985), 215.
4. *Ibid.*, 206-7, and Rose, "Upland Southerners: The County Origins of Southern Migrants to Indiana by 1850," *Indiana Magazine of History* 82:3 (Sept. 1986), 254-7. Rose shows that, by far, the greatest number of these settlers had previously lived in the part of Kentucky bordered by Lexington in the east and Louisville in the west. See Fig. 4, "Previous Residences of Southern Migrants to Indiana Who Purchased Land from the General Land Office," 254.
5. "Place of Birth," *Mortality Statistics*, 38.
6. By 1880, the three states with the most native-born Kentuckians were Illinois (55,965), Indiana (60,963), and Missouri (93,431). Table XI, "Native White Population of the United States, Distributed According to State or Territory of Birth: 1880," *Statistics of the Population of the United States at the Tenth Census* (Washington: Government Printing Office, 1883), 484-5.
7. "Place of Birth," *Mortality Statistics*, 38-9.

living in the "butternut" states in 1850.[1] Most of these newcomers from the Old Dominion and Kentucky were clustered in the southern counties of these states.[2] Because of this concentration, these transplanted Southerners had a major impact on the way of life in Ohio, Illinois, and Indiana.

These "plain folk" from the Upper South could have moved elsewhere. Indeed, early in the 19th century, rich soils and good farming prospects could also be found *south* of Kentucky — in the valleys of eastern Tennessee. There, in fact, yeoman farmers had already transplanted their distinctive way of life. But for others of their ilk, Tennessee had one decided disadvantage. It had entered the Union on June 1, 1796 as a slave state. In its central and western lowlands, large landowners were employing slaves to produce tobacco and cotton for commercial export, much as was being done on the best farmland throughout the Upper and Deep South.

In these slave economies, independent white farmers faced stiff competition. Skyrocketing cotton prices did help to sustain them during the antebellum period, but producing this cash crop with only a few or no slaves prevented these farmers from significantly improving their economic status and moving up the social ladder. Because of these limiting conditions, a sizeable number of them were more inclined to strike out north rather than move somewhere else in the Cotton Belt.[3]

Among these migrating families were the Lincolns. They decided to leave Hardin (now LaRue) County, located on the western fringe of the Bluegrass, for southern Indiana in 1816, when Abraham, the only surviving son, was seven years old. While a dispute over land ownership was a major contributing factor, so was slavery.[4]

---

1. *Ibid.*
2. This was truer for Ohio and Illinois than for Indiana, where both Kentuckians and Virginians settled throughout the central and southern regions. According to the 1850 federal census, the single largest group of migrants from Kentucky then living in Indiana was to be found in the central county of Putnam. Other major concentrations existed in the central counties of Hendricks and Montgomery, with large numbers of Kentuckians in such southern counties as Jefferson and Decatur. In terms of percentage of the population, migrants from the Bluegrass State were most evident in southeastern Monroe and Orange counties, where they made up over 90 percent of the residents. Rose, "Hoosier Origins," 214.
3. Kentucky natives showed a preference for Northern states when moving elsewhere. For instance, only 12,609 persons born in Kentucky were living in Tennessee in 1850, compared to 13,829 in Ohio. All told, 107,738 Kentuckians were then residing in slave states, and 148,696 — or nearly 58 percent — in free states. "Place of Birth," 39-9.
4. Abraham Lincoln once noted that his father's decision to move north was "partly on account of slavery, but chiefly on account of the difficulty in land titles in Ky." (Significantly, Lincoln did *not* contend that his father was opposed to slavery on moral or religious grounds.) Quoted in Donald, *Lincoln*, 24. Virginia's 1786 law abolishing primogeniture had not yet taken effect. When he decided to relocate to Indiana, Thomas Lincoln had already lost three farms due to conflicting land titles. For a more detailed discussion of these circumstances, see Gerald R. McMurtry, "The Lincoln Migration from Kentucky to Indiana," *Indiana Magazine of History* 33:4 (Dec. 1937), 385-421. Many other small farmers encountered similar problems with their claims. For example, members of the Finley family, which had been living in Bourbon County in the early 1790s, lost their title to land speculators and moved across the river, with several hundred members of their congregation, to a site near Scioto, Ohio, in 1794. See James B. Finley, *Autobiography of Rev. James B. Finley*, ed. W. P. Strickland, D.D. (New York: Hunt & Easton, 1853), 100.

This part of Kentucky was rapidly being taken over by the great planters, and it contained more than six slaves for every ten white males over the age of 16.[1] The community near where the Lincolns had settled, on Knob Creek, was bitterly divided over the slavery issue, but the trend was clearly toward more reliance on black labor.[2] In such a climate, the future for a struggling independent farmer like Thomas Lincoln, with only 238 acres to his name, was decidedly bleak.[3] His displacement by the planter class and its slaves was a common occurrence among Kentucky's small farmers.[4] The chattel system's negative economic impact on non-slaveholding landowners would not be forgotten by his young son.

Revulsion at working among blacks was particularly strong among Scotch-Irish immigrants who were living in Virginia and Kentucky at the close of the 18th century. They considered slavery anathema. The chattel system had also cost many of them of their livelihood as farmers. Some of these settlers may have decided to relocate north of the Ohio because of a philosophical abhorrence of slavery, but others did so, in the words of one historian, "because they did not particularly relish an environment which was marred by the presence of a shiftless, ignorant, and irresponsible race."[5] Their antipathy was directed equally at both slaves and free blacks. Indeed, fear that runaway or emancipated slaves would migrate north to the Old Northwest added a new dimension to white racial bias. In the free states, it was not only slaves that posed a threat to whites of limited means, but free blacks as well. Non-slaveholding whites banded together to keep both groups at bay. Most of these Scotch-Irish farmers who left the Upland South settled initially

1. Hardin County had a population of 940 slaves, equal to 14.2 percent of the total of 6,603, according to the 1810 federal census.
2. The church in Knob Creek, where the Lincoln family lived, finally came out against slavery in 1812. Louis A. Warren, *Lincoln's Parentage and Childhood: A History of the Kentucky Lincolns Supported by Documentary Evidence* (New York: Century, 1926), 288.
3. When Lincoln's grandfather, Abraham, was killed by Indians in 1786, all of his property passed to his oldest son, Mordecai. Thomas Lincoln then had to work as a carpenter and manual laborer in order to save up enough money to make this land purchase, in Hardin County. Donald, *Lincoln*, 22. The older Lincoln's objections to slavery were based upon both religious scruples and material self-interest. One historian has summarized his situation thusly: "As a sometime common laborer, he [Thomas Lincoln] had to compete for wages with slaves who were rented out by their masters, and as a member of the local Baptist church, he was a parishioner in a religious body formed by persons who had seceded from other churches out of opposition to slavery." Mark J. Neely, *The Last Best Hope of Earth: Abraham Lincoln and the Promise of America* (Cambridge: Harvard University Press, 1993), 3.
4. For example, the family of Peter Cartwright, a Methodist preacher, left Kentucky for many of the same reasons. They had owned a small farm of 150 acres in the Cumberland District, but then decided to relocate to Ohio in the spring of 1823, partially due to a religiously based abhorrence of slavery and the need for more land for their six children, but also because the father wanted to "raise my children to work where work was not thought a degradation." Peter Cartwright, *Autobiography of Peter Cartwright, the Backwoods Preacher* (New York: Carlton & Porter, 1857), 245.
5. Wilson, "Negro in Early Ohio," 720.

in what was then designated as the Virginia Military District — a 6,527-square-mile region of south-central Ohio bordered by the Little Miami and Scioto rivers. Their strong opposition to living among blacks helped defeat a petition, introduced at the first meeting of the territorial legislature in 1799, which would have allowed veterans to bring slaves into this part of Ohio.[1]

In Indiana, most white settlers were just as strongly opposed to having blacks as neighbors, whether slave or free. Only a minority of Southern migrants, wealthy native Virginians residing in far western Knox County, pushed for slavery to be tolerated in the territory (thus circumventing Article 6 of the Northwest Ordinance) and managed to pass a law in 1805 making it legal to bring in blacks over the age of 15 as contracted laborers.[2] This measure was broadened by the territorial legislature two years later to encourage the migration of well-to-do Southerners, whose presence some whites deemed vital to rapid economic development. The new bill made it legal for all blacks performing "voluntary servitude" to take up residence.[3] Many who entered Indiana under these terms came with white families from Kentucky, which settled in nearby counties such as Knox and Clark.[4]

But the antislavery determination of the majority of residents intensified after Indiana entered the Union in 1816, when delegates approved a measure making it impossible for the state's constitutional ban on slavery ever to be altered. Support for this bill was strongest among Upland Southerners who had been previously displaced by the advance of slavery.[5] (Under its territorial governor and future president, William Henry Harrison, Indiana had taken a more laissez-faire approach to enforcing the Northwest Ordinance's prohibition on importing slaves.[6])

In upholding this position, state representatives were not at all moved by compassion or moral indignation. Rather, they were expressing "a desire to preserve the soil of Indiana for white men."[7] This goal was largely achieved: according to the 1820 census, only 1,420 blacks were then living in the state, out of a popula-

1. *Ibid.*, 722, 733.
2. Emma Lou Thornbrough, *The Negro in Indiana: A Study of a Minority* (Indianapolis: Indiana Historical Review, 1957), 9. Cf. John D. Barnhart, "The Southern Influence in the Formation of Indiana," *Indiana Magazine of History* 33:3 (Sept. 1937), 262-3
3. James Simeone, *Democracy and Slavery in Frontier Illinois: The Bottomland Republic* (DeKalb: Northern Illinois University Press, 2000), 29.
4. Thornbrough, *Negro in Indiana*, 10.
5. Barnhart, *Valley of Democracy*, 265-8. He points out that four of the Virginia-born delegates came from the Piedmont and speculates that they and other antislavery leaders in the Indiana Territory were farmers "who emigrated [to Indiana] as the plantation system spread to the westward."
6. Cf. Onuf, *Statehood and Union*, 118.
7. Thornbrough, *Negro in Indiana*, viii.

tion of nearly over 145,000.[1] Practically the only transplanted Southerners in Indiana who cared about the welfare of blacks were Quakers who had moved northward, mainly from North Carolina, as the chattel system had tightened its economic grip in the Upper South. They subsequently sought to honor the dictates of their faith by providing sanctuary to runaways from the slave states. For the most part, these Quakers settled in Wayne County, on the Ohio border — an area which would subsequently attract many escaped slaves and free blacks.[2]

Poor Southern whites who entered Illinois in large numbers after the War of 1812 similarly objected to having enslaved blacks as neighbors.[3] Up until then, a large number of slaves had been living in this territory, mainly in counties bordering the Ohio, having been brought in as "servants."[4] Other black bondsmen — so-called "French slaves" owned by settlers from that country living in places like Kaskaskia and St. Mary's — were exempt from the 1787 exclusionary clause.[5]

So, under the territorial legislature's interpretation of this provision, were all other slaves already residing in Illinois as of that date: they were considered legally protected "private property."[6] During the early territorial period, blacks were relatively numerous. An informal census conducted in 1726 found that they made up nearly a quarter of the territory's population. This proportion rose to a third by the middle of the 18th century.[7] Because of their reliance on this sizeable black workforce, wealthy landowners attempted as early as 1796 to overturn Article 6 of the Northwest Ordinance and make slavery fully legal in Illinois.[8] After this proposal was defeated, territorial legislators adopted a law in Septem-

---

1. In the decade between 1810 and 1820, the white population of Indiana increased by more than 121,000 while the number of blacks — slaves and freemen combined — grew by only 790.
2. Chelsea L. Lawlis, "Migration to the Whitewater Valley, 1820-1830," *Indiana Magazine of History* 33:3 (Sept. 1937), 229, 234.
3. One scholar has estimated that 71 percent of those who migrated to Illinois between 1815 and 1818 came from the states of Kentucky, Tennessee, Virginia, North Carolina, South Carolina, Georgia, and Maryland. Cited in Simeone, *Democracy and Slavery*, 33.
4. As late as 1830, there were still some 746 black "servants" employed in the state. R. Carlyle Buley, *The Old Northwest: Pioneer Period, 1815-1840* (Indianapolis: Indiana Historical Society, 1950), vol. 2, 622.
5. Andrew R.L. Cayton and Peter S. Onuf, *The Midwest and the Nation: Rethinking the History of an American Region* (Bloomington: Indiana University Press, 1990), 14. One historian states that French settlers brought as many as 1,000 black and Native American slaves into southern Illinois in 1752. Simeone, *Democracy and Slavery*, 19, 29. The right to keep these slaves was protected under the 1784 Act of Cession foregoing Virginia's claims to Western lands.
6. When a bill was brought before Congress in 1800, stating that "after the year 1800 there shall be neither slavery nor involuntary servitude in any of the said States [to be formed from the Northwest Territory]," it was soundly defeated. Randall Parrish, *Historic Illinois: The Romance of the Earlier Days* (Chicago: A.C. McClurg, 1905), 319.
7. James E. Davis, *Frontier Illinois* (Bloomington: Indiana University Press, 1998), 54.
8. The first effort to bring about this change originated in Kaskaskia. Onuf, *Statehood and Union*, 117.

ber 1807 permitting slaveholders to keep their indentured servants until the latter reached the age of 30 (for males) or 28 (females).[1] Children of these "servants" could take over their parents' "voluntary" responsibilities.

But settlers who arrived after 1815 — largely yeoman farmers pushed out of the Upland South by expanding plantations — were determined "to settle where slaves would not follow."[2] They wanted to live where white labor was valued and protected, where a more egalitarian way of life could flourish, and where economic opportunities were available for all members of their race. Despite the attempts by Illinois' *de facto* slaveholders to enlist the backing of these poor Southern migrants by appealing to their racial bond — and by exploiting the new arrivals' precarious social status — this effort failed. Support for slavery was too geographically confined: in an 1822 vote, majorities in only two of the state's 19 counties favored its legalization. And, two years later, voters decisively — 6,640 to 4,972 — rejected a proposal to convene a new constitutional convention for the purpose of making slavery lawful in Illinois. The argument advanced by Morris Birkbeck was most persuasive: the chattel system harmed independent Southern farmers, he said. They had fled north precisely because they could not "thrive by honest labor among slaveholders and slaves."[3]

Generally speaking, the negative consequences of slavery *for whites* figured prominently in Midwestern abolitionist thinking. How much of this was merely political tactics and how much fundamental conviction is difficult to say.[4] But, unlike New England, where opposition to this grossly inhumane system was largely driven by moral repugnance and religious principle, views in the Old Northwest were distinctly tinged with concern for the welfare of white farmers and wage earners. This concern is evident in the writings and speeches of prominent antislavery figures throughout the antebellum period. For instance, James G. Birney, a native of Kentucky who was persuaded to free his own slaves in 1832 and then moved to Cincinnati three years later to promote the abolitionist cause (and who subsequently ran twice for President as the candidate of the antislavery Liberty party), once conceded in a letter that those who wanted to free the

---

1. For a discussion of these pro-slavery measures, see Parrish, *Historic Illinois*, 321-2.
2. In 1818, over a third of Illinois residents were natives of the southeastern states, and another 37 percent had been born in either Tennessee or Kentucky. Davis, *Frontier Illinois*, 159.
3. Quoted in Theodore Calvin Pease, *The Frontier State: 1818-1848* (Urbana: University of Illinois Press, 1987), 89.
4. Some historians have made the case that moral opposition to slavery was the primary reason why many settlers, particularly well-to-do ones, moved north of the Mason Dixon Line around 1800. For example, Dwight Dumond states: "There were hundreds who came North to escape slavery and worked quietly for emancipation in local antislavery societies and at the ballot box." Dumond, *Antislavery*, 93. Yet he concedes that the Kentucky Abolition Society, founded in 1808, never had more than 200 members and dissolved in the 1820s. The weight of historical evidence suggests that moral or religious objections to slavery were, for the most part, secondary to economic ambitions.

slaves "believed from the first, that the tendency of slavery is to produce, on the part of the whites, looseness of morals, disdain of the wholesome restraints of law, and a ferocity of temper, found, only in solitary instances, in those countries where slavery is unknown."[1]

Another leading representative of this viewpoint is Cassius Marcellus Clay. A cousin of Henry Clay and a slaveholder, he was educated at Yale, where he came under the irresistible influence of the abolitionist leader William Lloyd Garrison and embraced the latter's cause of black emancipation. Returning to Kentucky, Clay was elected to the state legislature in 1835 and soon declared his desire to see slavery abolished. He branded it an unmitigated evil — "morally, economically, physically, intellectually, socially, religiously, politically . . ." But, as a shrewd and ambitious politician, Clay chose not to stress those aspects of slavery, but rather articulated the more popular view that the presence of slaves on Kentucky soil harmed non-slaveholding whites: in the absence of a truly free economy, they lagged behind their counterparts in the free states. (Even this approach did not make Clay well liked. In 1845, a hostile mob destroyed the printing press for his antislavery weekly newspaper, the *True American*.) Even worse, he argued, slavery either forced out free white laborers or reduced them to the level of chattel. In one of his writings, Clay noted that Southern mechanics were losing work "because the local market was continually evaporating through the process of engrossing the land, driving out the small farmers, and replacing them with slaves, who were not very good customers."[2]

Understandably, some Southern slave owners looked across the Ohio River through different eyes. Early in the 19th century, the "butternut" states beckoned them as a promising new frontier. Like their forebears, these well-to-do farmers faced a Hobson's choice: either expand their holdings to new, fertile lands where their increasing number of slaves could be put to work, or else watch their wealth evaporate and have idle blacks grow restless and turn upon their masters. The way west was uncertain. The United States had acquired vast lands beyond the Mississippi as a result of the 1803 Louisiana Purchase, but the danger of attacks by hostile Indians or Spanish colonists made migration in that direction relatively uninviting.[3] These inhospitable circumstances, as well as the ensuing war with England, kept large numbers of settlers from moving to Missouri until after 1815.

---

1. Letter of James G. Birney to F.H. Elmore, 8 March 1838, quoted in James G. Birney and F.H. Elmore, *The Anti-Slavery Examiner No. 8: Correspondence Between the Hon. F.H. Elmore and James G. Birney* (New York: American Anti-Slavery Society, 1838), 26.
2. Quoted in Bernard Mandel, *Labor: Free and Slave, Workingmen and the Anti-Slavery Movement in the United States* (New York: Associated Authors, 1955), 28-9.
3. The pledge by President Jefferson, in his 3 Dec. 1805 Annual Message to Congress, to dispatch troops to protect settlers west of the Mississippi eased these fears somewhat. The threat from Indians decreased greatly by 1818.

The route northward held fewer obstacles and more discernible rewards, especially for farmers. As was pointed out above, many Southern slaveholders had already traversed the Ohio River and purchased tracts on the other side. They had found a way around the antislavery provision of the Northwest Ordinance and brought their black laborers north with them to cultivate these new farms.

As early as 1794, following the defeat of nearby Indians, planters and small farmers from Virginia — many of them Revolutionary War veterans claiming land promised them for their military service — had crossed over to the south central part of present-day Ohio. There, in the Virginia Military District, they had rapidly asserted their political clout, forming what was called the "Chillicothe Junto" to defeat a local group opposed to slavery and create a climate more favorable its introduction. (Many of these Virginians, like Col. Thomas Worthington — Ohio's first U.S. senator and fourth governor — had first freed their slaves and then brought them along as servants.[1] According to one account, "whole colonies" of blacks were given their freedom so that they could be moved to Ohio.[2] These blacks were most heavily concentrated in Ross County — the area around Chillicothe traversed by the Scioto River.) When a visitor from England named Henry Fearon traveled down the Ohio River to Cincinnati and then ventured inland in 1818, he made note of the fact that "Many persons in this State have coloured people, which they call their property." In Middletown, along the banks of the Great Miami River, Fearon witnessed an unapologetic white man whipping a teenage black boy, making vividly apparent that such abusive measures were not confined to the slave states.[3]

Enlarging this foothold for black labor on Northern soil grew more urgent as land prices in Virginia plummeted a few decades later — the total value of Old Dominion real estate dropped from $203 million in 1817 to $90 million in 1829. A stagnation in Kentucky property sales made slave owners in that state also inclined to seek their fortunes on the far side of the river. They were drawn to Ohio's rich bottomlands, keenly aware of the substantial agricultural profits that were being realized there. Slaveholders in the Bluegrass State were equally cognizant of the fact that they possessed more black chattel than they could profitably put to use, now that the labor-intensive tasks of clearing land and building homes were finished. Tobacco growing had not absorbed as many slaves as had

---

1. Worthington took 60 of his former slaves with him when he moved to Ohio in 1793. Wilson, "Negro in Early Ohio," 727.
2. Henry Noble Sherwood, "Movement in Ohio to Deport the Negro," *Quarterly Publication of the Historical and Philosophical Society of Ohio* 7:2-3 (June/Sept. 1912), 54.
3. Henry B. Fearon, *Sketches of America: A Narrative of a Journey of Five Thousand Miles through the Eastern and Western States* (London: Benjamin Blom, 1969), 224, 240-1. Fearon reported that blacks were purchased and kept as "apprentices," and then, when their usefulness was exhausted, they were sold "down the river" in New Orleans.

been hoped. Their masters now needed to push on, and, paradoxically, the "free" states to the north seemed to be the best destination for them.

To go there, many wealthy Southern farmers nominally emancipated their slaves and imported them as servants. This partially accounted for the sharp rise in "free non-whites" living in Ohio after 1800, when only 337 had resided there. This number multiplied six times in the first decade, more than doubled in the second, and doubled twice between 1820 and 1840. However, not all of the blacks so designated were, in fact, slaves; some were truly free individuals who had willingly opted to accompany their former owners northward.[1] And others were former slaves who had escaped across the Ohio to freedom. Just how many blacks came to Ohio as "servants" and how many as "free non-whites" is difficult to ascertain. It is likely that white settlers who brought blacks with them as quasi slaves underreported these workers to census takers because importing enslaved blacks was illegal. The actual number of "servants" was doubtless much higher than the official figures suggest.[2] In nearby Illinois, the most reliable population survey for 1818 showed that 284 free blacks and 612 classified as "servants" or "slaves" were living in the eleven counties tallied.[3] Two years later, the federal census listed 917 slaves and 457 free blacks in the state. But in Ohio, the situation was quite different. Most blacks there were concentrated along the Ohio River. According to the 1830 census, the overwhelming majority of blacks were then residing inside the Virginia Military District; three of the four counties with the greatest black populations — Hamilton, Ross, Belmont, and Gallia — bordered slave states.[4] The single largest grouping of black Ohioans — nearly 700 in the mid-1820s — was in Cincinnati. This city attracted both black and

---

1. So, for example, did 12 of the 14 slaves belonging to the Finley family in Kentucky, after a deed of emancipation had been issued for them in the fall of 1796. See Finley, *Autobiography*, 110. The Quaker family of William Dean Howells also brought along, as "apprenticed servants," two children of a black family that had worked for them when they moved from Loudoun County, Virginia, to Steubenville, Ohio, in 1819. William Cooper Howells, *Recollections of Life in Ohio, from 1813 to 1840* (Cincinnati: Robert Clarke, 1895), 21.

2. Cf. Clayton E. Cramer, *Black Demographic Data, 1790-1860: A Sourcebook* (Westport: Greenwood Press, 1997), 15.

3. Solon J. Buck, *Illinois in 1818*, rev. ed. (Urbana: University of Illinois Press, 1967), 65, 70, 71, 75, 76, 77, 79, 86, and 91. These figures based upon the population schedules for that year. The overall population of Illinois in 1818 was 23,618.

4. Cincinnati, Hamilton's county seat, had by far the state's largest black population — approximately one third of the state's total. This was estimated to have been 690 in 1826 and officially enumerated as 2,240 in 1840. See *Race and the City: Work, Community, and Protest in Cincinnati, 1820-1970*, ed. Henry Louis Taylor (Urbana: University of Illinois Press, 1993), 32. Many blacks moved into cities like Cincinnati to escape hostility from whites in rural areas. However, by 1860, nearly three quarters of all blacks in the Old Northwest were living in the countryside or in small villages. See Stephen A. Vincent, *Southern Seed, Northern Soil: African-American Farm Communities in the Midwest, 1765-1900* (Bloomington: Indiana University Press, 1999), xii.

white workers because it was a booming trading center — the "emporium of the West." Since it would have been nearly impossible for escaped slaves to secure jobs in white-owned businesses and factories, it is reasonable to conclude that most of the blacks who migrated northward to Ohio and settled there were free men.[1] Runaways were more likely to continue their journeys to Canada via the Underground Railroad.

On the issue of slavery, whites in the Old Northwest were somewhat divided, depending largely on where they came from and how well off they were. Many prosperous migrants from the South, who had settled in counties on or near the Ohio River, favored the slave system and wanted to circumvent federal restrictions on it so that their large-scale farming enterprises could flourish. On the other hand, new arrivals from New England, New York, New Jersey, and Pennsylvania by way of the Erie Canal and the Great Lakes were just as adamantly opposed to any introduction of slavery. By and large, they stood squarely for free labor and against any form of black servitude that might adversely affect the welfare of white workers. Joining them in opposition to slavery were men and women of principle — from the South as well as the North — who rejected the system as antithetical to Christian teaching and natural law. Some of them had, in fact, migrated to the Old Northwest with hopes of building public support there for emancipation. But while religion and morality played some part in the slavery debate, the overriding question that had to be resolved by these Midwestern states was purely economic: would the legalization of slavery help or hinder their growth and development? On this question, white residents were split along social and economic lines.

On one side of this debate were those who stood to benefit directly from the presence of a black labor force. Chiefly, these were the sons and grandsons of Virginia's great planters, who had already moved north and found the rich soils in the lower counties of Ohio, Indiana, and Illinois suitable for Southern-style agriculture. This included the commercial production of tobacco and corn. During their first years in the Old Northwest, particularly in present-day Indiana and Illinois, farmers employing slaves in their fields had prospered, and now they wanted to increase their landholdings. But doing so would require additional slaves. Relying on their wealth and political clout, these Southerners began to lobby for loosening, if not removing, the existing restrictions on these black farmhands. They were joined in these efforts by local land speculators, who

---

1. So conclude William Cheek and Aimee Lee Cheek, "John Mercer Langston and the Cincinnati Riot of 1841," in *Race and the City: Work, Community, and Protest in Cincinnati, 1820-1970*, ed. Henry Louis Taylor (Urbana: University of Illinois Press, 1993), 33. The authors note that 80 percent of blacks living in Cincinnati in 1840 were under the age of 36. Many had come to the city after more jobs became available following the Panic of 1837.

believed that legalizing the slave system would attract other well-to-do Southern farmers, cause land prices to soar, and create a windfall in profits. To argue their case, the speculators enlisted some powerful political allies.

Perhaps the most influential was the first territorial governor of Indiana, William Henry Harrison. On several occasions, he took advantage of his position to petition Congress to lift the ban on importing slaves.[1] The son of a Virginia plantation owner who had signed the Declaration of Independence and a former slaveholder himself, Harrison had first come to the Northwest Territory as an ensign in the U.S. infantry in 1791. There he distinguished himself in combat against the Indians in the Battle of Fallen Timbers, under Gen. Anthony Wayne. Later, Harrison married the daughter of one of the largest land speculators in the Indiana Territory. As a representative of the territorial government in Washington, he was deeply committed to promoting western settlement. Harrison wanted to make lands north of the Ohio affordable to small farmers. Thanks in considerable part to his efforts, Congress voted to divide up public holdings in the Old Northwest into tracts as small as 320 acres, which could be bought on credit.[2] Previously, only land speculators and wealthy farmers could afford the 4,000-acre minimum purchase. But, despite this populist bent, "Old Tippecanoe" (as he would later come to be known for defeating Tecumseh's Shawnee warriors at a creek with this name in November 1811) remained true to his planter origins.

On slavery, Harrison was a moderate. Although he had belonged to a society in Virginia that favored gradual emancipation, he had brought west with him at least one former slave, employed as his personal servant.[3] In 1801, he was appointed territorial governor of Indiana, and, in this capacity, Harrison sought to bolster the rights of slave owners. Many of them were neighbors of his in the two far western counties that surrounded the territorial capital of Vincennes. He apparently accepted the logic that an influx of slaves was essential for Indiana to grow rapidly and become economically strong. Accordingly, Harrison summoned a convention in December 1802 to consider the repeal of Article 6 of the Northwest Ordinance. At this gathering, John Randolph was appointed to chair a committee on the slavery question. He delivered a report in March 1803, which concluded that the development of neighboring Ohio had demonstrated that "the labor of slaves is not necessary to promote the growth and settlement of colonies in that region."[4] But this was not to be the convention's final word on the

---

1. William W. Freehling, *The Reintegration of American History: Slavery and the Civil War* (New York: Oxford University Press, 1994), 22.
2. Land prices were set at a minimum of two dollars per acre under this act.
3. According to one source, this servant, Jackson Butler, had been freed by Harrison after his term of service had ended. Together with his wife and six children, Butler was kidnapped from his home near Vincennes and taken to Illinois in May, 1823. Parrish, *Historic Illinois*, 323.

subject. Ignoring Randolph's recommendation, the delegates in Vincennes passed a resolution asking Congress to suspend the federal antislavery provision: a majority of them felt that westward bound farmers were not settling down in Indiana, but only passing through on their way to Missouri, because of the latter's more welcoming attitude regarding slavery, and that this state of affairs was hurting the local economy.[1] But Congress declined to act on this 1803 petition.[2] Undeterred, Harrison and his allies adopted the strategy of tolerating the "voluntary servitude" of blacks within the territory. They shrewdly calculated that the federal government would not take any steps to block slave ownership in Indiana as long as the 1787 ordinance was not flagrantly violated.[3]

Subsequently, Harrison devoted much of his time to impeding the rise of a popular party whose victory at the polls would have spelled the end of indentured service.[4] Nonetheless, this party gained strength as more settlers entered the eastern part of Indiana from New England and the mid-Atlantic states and became politically active. Excluding the chattel system was high on their agenda. Within a few years' time, several anti-slavery petitions were submitted to the territorial legislature. In 1808, a report prepared by Gen. Washington Johnston presented an economic rationale for *not* allowing slavery: blacks would devalue white labor in the territory. Johnston further declared that continuing to tolerate indentured servitude in Indiana would represent a "retrograde step into barbarism."[5] But support for this practice remained strong, and Johnston's motion to end it was defeated on a second reading. However, by 1809, antislavery sentiment had gained sufficient ground in the territory so that candidates for seats in the General Assembly were forced to reveal their positions on the chattel system, and this led to a major defeat for Harrison and his allies.[6] The struggle between pro- and anti-slavery forces came to a head at the 1816 constitutional convention,

---

4. Quoted in Hinsdale, *Old Northwest*, 352.
1. A minority of delegates argued against slavery on the same grounds. Thomas Randolph, while the owner of more than 300 slaves, opposed this petition, noting that Ohio was attracting many settlers because it had banned slavery, which he considered a "curse to any community." Logan Esarey, *A History of Indiana: From its Exploration to 1850* (Indianapolis, B.F. Bowen, 1918), vol. 1, 197. Randolph, a native Virginian and an ally of William Henry Harrison, had originally backed the introduction of slavery in Indiana.
2. Congress responded that "it is inexpedient to suspend the operation of the Sixth Article of the compact between the original states and the people and states west of the river Ohio." Quoted in Stephen Middleton, "Freedom's Early Ring: Ending Slavery in the Illinois Country, 1787-1818," *Illinois History Teacher* 5:1 (1998), 4. http://www.lib.niu.edu/ipo/iht519802.html.
3. Onuf, *Statehood and Union*, 119. Congress's reluctance to enforce the antislavery provision of the 1787 ordinance reflects the dominance of property owners in the legislative branch. See Freehling, *Reintegration of American History*, 22.
4. Barnhart, *Valley of Democracy*, 264.
5. Quoted in John D. Barnhart and Dorothy L. Riker, *Indiana to 1816: The Colonial Period* (Indianapolis: Indiana Historical Society, 1994), 354.
6. The pro-Harrison forces lost in all counties but Knox.

held at Corydon. Here, a fateful decision had to be made. No longer restrained by the Northwest Ordinance (which applied to Indiana only as long as it had territorial status), delegates could now vote to make the nascent state "free" or "slave." The upstart "popular" party, led by a lawyer from New Jersey named Jonathan Jennings, opposed any form of slavery in Indiana. Whereas wealthy landowners saw the slave system as a boon to the state's economy, the populists feared it would spell disaster for small farmers. They would either be driven out of business by large plantations, or dissuaded from coming to Indiana because of an antipathy toward blacks in general, and slaves in particular.

The "Jennings Party" represented the interests of whites who had not fared well elsewhere under the slave system. Most of its delegates came from Virginia's Piedmont, with several others from Kentucky. A few, including some Quakers, hailed from the New England and mid-Atlantic states and probably opposed slavery on religious or moral grounds, but this was clearly a minority position. The party had its strongest base in the eastern and southeastern parts of the state, where natives of the South had settled in large numbers. In the main, they were yeoman farmers pushed out of other states by the inexorable advance of the plantation system. An examination of voting records in counties where many "plain folk" farmers settled provides some supporting evidence for this contention. For example, Gibson County, located in the southwestern corner of Indiana, had a decidedly Southern orientation: in 1850, 60 percent of its residents had been born below the Mason Dixon Line (with 26.8 percent being natives of Kentucky alone).[1] Some of these Southerners were slaveholders: the federal census for 1820 lists 38 slaves in the county, out of a total population of 3,884, including 45 free blacks. But the vast majority were small, non-slaveholding farmers. When choosing four delegates to the 1816 constitutional convention, voters in this county elected candidates — two Southerners and at least one immigrant from Europe — who did not have any ties to the "peculiar institution."

One was a Baptist minister, Alexander Devlin, who had come originally from the Virginia backcountry. A second was Frederick Rapp, adopted son of George Rapp, a German religious leader who had founded the non-conformist Harmonist Society before emigrating to the United States in 1803. Another delegate was David Robb, an Irish immigrant unlikely to have supported slavery.[2] A more general antislavery attitude among Gibson County residents can be gleaned from letters published prior to the constitutional convention. One which appeared in the March 2, 1816, issue of *The Western Sun* (Vincennes) urged

1. Rose, Table 1, "Nativity, by County, of Indiana's United-States Born Inhabitants according to Most Frequent Source of Origin in 1850" in "Hoosier Origins," 206-7.
2. The fourth delegate, James Smith, had migrated from Orange County, Va., to Indiana in 1808. This biographical information is derived from "Members of the Convention of the Indiana Territory, 1816," http://www.statelib.lib.in.us/www/ihb/resources/convmembers1816.html.

the election of delegates who would vote to prohibit the slave system, toward which "the soul of every freeman must naturally revolt" in spite of the economic advantages it likely would bring to the new state.[1] A second letter contended that bringing slavery to Indiana would not constitute "good policy" because it would not make white settlers happier or wealthier. He implored his fellow voters to reject the "poisoned bribe."[2]

While the Harrison group was equally Southern in its orientation, it was more closely allied with the planter elite. During the convention's heated deliberations, Harrison and his associates argued that the decision concerning slavery should be left to the individual counties to decide. Taking this tack would have safeguarded the right of slaveholders in areas where they were concentrated.[3] But Jennings, who had spearheaded Indiana's bid for statehood, carried the day, and a majority of delegates voted to bar slavery throughout the state. When Jennings ran for governor in the fall of 1816 and handily defeated his Whig opponent, Thomas Posey (then the territory's governor), this victory cemented the control of antislavery forces in Indiana.[4] Not content to keep only slaves out, the delegates gathered in Corydon made the new state inhospitable to free blacks by soundly rejecting (with only one dissenting vote, out of 123 cast) a proposal that would have given the latter the right to vote.[5]

In Illinois, the battle over slavery likewise pitted large and small farmers against each other. During its first earliest pioneer days, Illinois' rich southern bottomlands had attracted a number of Southern planters who owned slaves. When Congress adopted the 1787 Ordinance, these farmers found themselves in a dilemma. Unlike their counterparts in Indiana, they accepted that the ordinance's antislavery provision was legally binding on them. Consequently, they faced two undesirable options: either release their slaves (and suffer economically) or move to more slave-friendly territory, such as Kentucky. Most wealthy Illinois farmers reluctantly chose one or the other course of action, but a few decided to challenge the slavery ban as Indiana slaveholders did. One of them, Bartholomew Tardiveau, lobbied the first governor of the Northwest Territory,

---

1. Letter of "A Citizen of Gibson," *Western Sun* (Vincennes), 2 Mar. 1816.
2. The writer pointed out that economic productivity declined where slavery was introduced: "Produce for exportation is always in proportion to the industry of its inhabitants . . . and slavery is the bane of industry amongst the white inhabitants — so true is this, that where there are many of them, very few of the whites are seen to labor, and where they do, it is a reproach to them, and they are held in contempt by those that own slaves." "Letter of Another Citizen of Gibson," *Western Sun*, 30 Mar. 1816.
3. In 1816, residents of St. Clair and Randolph counties sent a petition to Congress arguing that a ban on slavery would unjustly deprive slave owners of their property.
4. "The [electoral] contest was therefore largely between two groups of southerners, one holding to the democratic ideas of the Upland South, the other to parts of the philosophy of the Lowland South." Barnhart, "Formation of Indiana," 275.
5. Andrew R. L. Cayton, *Frontier Indiana* (Bloomington: Indiana Univ. Press, 1996), 296.

Arthur St. Clair, predicting that slave owners would continue to leave for points west and south unless Congress reversed its position on slavery in the region. St. Clair was easily persuaded. He had openly defied Article 6 by purchasing slaves after he had arrived in the Northwest to assume his post and by registering them as such on the federal census. So he did not hesitate to send off a letter to Congress in which he reasoned that strict enforcement of the 1787 ordinance would unjustly deprive citizens of their property. St. Clair also contended that Article 6 should only apply to persons who entered the territory after 1787. Those already in Illinois should be permitted to keep their slaves.

In Washington, many Northern lawmakers were willing to let such an interpretation of the law stand. They understood that forcing Southerners to free their chattel in order to comply with the ordinance would create considerable animosity. To appease these slaveholders, Congress agreed to let the territorial governor resolve this question. This meant that slavery would continue to be tolerated in the Northwest Territory. Following Indiana's example, Illinois' territorial legislature voted that blacks could be imported as servants as long as they "willingly" agreed to their work contracts. When Illinois sought to join the Union, in 1818, Congress chose to turn a blind eye on its practice of black indenture and grant statehood anyway. A legislature partial to slavery was elected the following year, and this led to further discrimination against blacks in the new state, as well as the erection of higher barriers against the migration of former or runaway slaves.[1] The constitutional convention that was held in Kaskaskia in August 1818, several months after Illinois was admitted to the Union, reaffirmed the new state's pro-slavery leanings. The campaign to choose delegates was fought almost exclusively over whether or not to legalize the chattel system, and passions ran high in both camps. On one side were Southern migrants who believed Illinois would be better off with the help of slave labor. They were led by Shadrach Bond — the son of a Maryland planter and the owner of 20 slaves, who was soon to be elected the state's first governor — and an ambitious young attorney from North Carolina named John McLean. Landowners who could afford to buy slaves stood to increase their wealth through such a workforce. Others predicted that legalizing slavery would bring to Illinois legions of well-to-do settlers otherwise bound for Missouri. This in-migration would rapidly populate the new state and spur its development. It would also benefit speculators who had already purchased large tracts in Illinois and now needed to attract well-to-do buyers to make a good return on this investment.[2] The rally-

---

1. Any white person who imported slaves to flee them was subject to a fine of $200. Thomas Ford, *History of Illinois* (Chicago: S.C. Griggs, 1854), 33. These new laws revealed a growing concern about the number of runaways in Illinois. See Davis, *Frontier Illinois*, 166.

ing cry of the pro-chattel camp was, "admit slavery and the forests will immediately be converted into the cultivated habitations of men."[1] A few proponents even argued — somewhat circuitously — that introducing slaves into Northern states like Illinois would ameliorate their condition and better prepare them for eventual emancipation.[2] Appealing to individuals who were opposed to slavery on principled grounds, these advocates claimed that spreading slaves thinly over a greater part of the nation would actually hasten the system's demise.[3]

On the other side of this heated debate stood Illinoisans who wanted no part of slavery. They were dismayed by the growing presence of slaves in the southern part of the state. Throughout Illinois, their number increased from 129 in 1810 to nearly 1,000 in 1820.[4] The most prominent antislavery spokesmen were the English Quaker Morris Birkbeck, a Baptist minister named John Peck, and Daniel P. Cook, a native of Kentucky who was then the editor of the leading newspaper, *The Illinois Intelligencer.* Some on the anti-slavery side railed against the cruelty, injustice, and inhumanity of the "peculiar institution." Others worried more about the long-term impact of bringing the two races together. First and foremost in their minds was concern that whites would be weakened morally and economically by contact with slaves: they corrosively sapped the former's energy and vitality, and "all the train of vices which idleness produces are visited upon the people."[5] Sexual congress between the races was the most "abominable" of these vices. Furthermore, a "landed aristocracy" of slaveholders would dominate Illinois' economy, while most small farmers would be reduced to the status of impoverished tenants.[6] But those opposed to the coming of slavery also grimly foresaw blacks one day rising up *en masse* and lashing out at their masters. If slavery took root on both sides of the Ohio, then the dreaded "evil hour of rebellion" would eventually toll in Northern states as well.[7] Finally, opponents argued that owning slaves really did not make good eco-

---

2. Greg Reinhart, "Illinois: Land of the Free and Home of the Slave" (unpublished undergraduate thesis, 1992), http://216.125.204.247/Cahokia_Beginnings/Historical%20Journals/Histor_1992.htm.
1. Unsigned editorial "Slavery," written presumably by Daniel Cook, *The Western Intelligencer* (Kaskaskia, Ill.), 1 April 1818.
2. Letter of "A Friend to Enquiry," *Illinois Intelligencer,* 22 July 1818. Cf. Letter of "Pacificus" to Members of the Illinois Constitutional Convention, *Illinois Intelligencer* (Kaskaskia, Ill.), 12 Aug. 1818. This writer proposed that slaves should be freed after reaching a certain age, after having learned to read and having had instruction in "the general principles of the christian [sic] religion."
3. Pease, *Frontier State,* 87.
4. Federal census figures for 1820 show a total of 997 slaves (or "servants") in Illinois.
5. "Slavery," *The Western Intelligencer,* 1 April 1818.
6. One correspondent felt that a slave-based economy would ruin Illinois' bountiful agriculture: "it is wrong in the extreme to subject the soil of such a country to the hands of monopolists, who will either hold it too high to enable many who are poor, and yet deserving, to acquire lands of their own, or who will permit it to lie in large uncultivated tracts, yielding nothing to the comfort of man, nor to the wealth of the country." Letter of D. P. Cook to the editor, *Illinois Intelligencer,* 29 July 1818.

nomic sense: over the long haul, hiring white laborers on a daily or monthly basis cost less.[1] Cook himself believed that affirming Illinois' antislavery posture would encourage migration into the state.[2]

When the votes were counted, in July 1818, the pro-slavery forces had elected a majority of the delegates to the state constitutional convention. More than a third of the 35 men chosen to attend had either owned or hired slaves at some point, and only a few had ever gone on record expressing anti-slavery views. Southern natives made up the largest single contingent.[3] But their political strength was tempered by realism. While a slaveholder, Elias Kane, wrote most of the constitution, he wisely crafted its language dealing with slavery so as to not cause Congress to reject Illinois' bid for statehood. Mirroring the Ordinance of 1787, the introduction of slaves was banned "hereafter," but the continued ownership of *de facto* slaves was permitted. The pro-slavery camp further solidified its hold over state politics by winning the governorship in October (Bond ran without any opposition), as well as the lieutenant governor's office, and electing Illinois' first representative to Congress. (McLean defeated Cook, for whom Cook County would later be named, if only by 14 votes.[4])

The issue of slavery re-emerged, with even greater intensity, during the years 1823-1824. During a December 1822 session of the state legislature, the son of a German immigrant named Conrad Will proposed that Illinois allow slaves to be brought in to extract salt from wells at Shawneetown — a potentially major source of income for his (southern) part of the state. Will's plan resonated with slave owners who had recently moved onto Illinois' lower bottomlands as well as with some yeoman farmers who saw a chance to boost their social status (and gain more economic freedom) at the expense of enslaved blacks. But farmers in the north and central part of the state, led by the new governor, Edward Coles, strongly objected to any further loosening of the restrictions on slavery — a system he considered morally pernicious.[5]

Coles, member of a socially prominent Virginia family, had inherited his family's slaves as a young man of 23, when he was serving as private secretary to

---

7. "Slavery," *Western Intelligencer*, 1 April 1818. Another contributor, thought to be Edward Coles, reminded his readers of recent slave uprisings, most notably in Santo Domingo, in which "the aged parent and the feeble stripling, the tender mother and her helpless infant, alike fell victims to the indiscriminating rage, the ungovernable fury, of a people bursting the bands of slavery, and thirsting for revenge." Letter of "Agis" to "the People of Illinois," *Illinois Intelligencer* (Kaskaskia), 1 July 1818.

1. Letter of "Agis," 1 July 1818.

2. Barnhart, *Valley of Democracy*, 203-4.

3. Of the 33 delegates who attended the convention, twelve came from the South, nine from other Western states, six from the mid-Atlantic region, two from New England, and one from Europe. See James A. Edstrom, "The Constitutional Convention of 1818: A Biographical Profile," *Illinois History* 47:1 (Dec. 1993), 2.

4. Cook defeated McLean in an 1819 rematch of this campaign for Illinois' sole congressional seat.

Pres. James Madison. But Coles had vowed to set them free because he felt that slavery was incompatible with American values of freedom and republicanism. When he relocated to Illinois in 1819, he surprised the slaves who were traveling down river on a flatboat with him by announcing that he intended to release them and give each family 160 acres of land.[1] In the summer of 1823, Coles was elected governor on an antislavery platform, by a slim margin of 59 votes out of more than 8,000 cast. (Indeed, he would have lost, had the pro-slavery vote not been split between two of the three other candidates.[2]) He immediately proposed that Illinois unequivocally abolish slavery, do away with its "black code," and prohibit the kidnapping of free blacks by slave dealers.[3]

The battle over slavery in Illinois finally came to a head the following year. Elements in favor of it wanted to convene a constitutional convention to loosen restrictions on slave ownership, while Cole and supporters such as Morris Birkbeck vehemently opposed constituting such a body. Coles warned that voting for such a convention would "write the epitaph of free government" in Illinois. The introduction of slavery would only make whites vulnerable to revolt, undermine morals, and dissuade "free labor" from settling in the state.[4] Birkbeck denounced the slave system as a "monster" and denied that its coming would boost the state's economy. Instead, it would deter European immigrants and Northerners from coming to Illinois. Birkbeck also argued that poor whites would suffer should a slave system be permitted: "Its introduction would always be felt by a very large part of the community as an invasion of their rights; they would view it as it stalked through the land, with a horror and impatient loathing as they would the intrusion of an armed foe."[5]

With the backing of antislavery groups both in and outside the state, and further helped by growing popular support for "free labor" and the departure of many slaveholders to the booming Cotton Belt, the "anti-Convention" forces came out on top, 6,640 to 4,972.[6] This result averted a major clash between Illinois and

---

5. Eugene H. Berwanger, The *Frontier Against Slavery: Western Anti-Negro Prejudice and the Slavery Extension Controversy* (Urbana: University of Illinois Press, 1967), 24. Coles is believed to have published several anti-slavery articles in the *Illinois Intelligencer* under the pseudonym "Agis." See, for example, the "Letter to the People of Illinois" in the issue of 17 June 1818. Here it is argued that Illinois' tolerance of indentured servitude violated the Ordinance of 1787. However, the authorship of these letters remains somewhat in doubt: Coles did not migrate to the Illinois Territory until 1819 and had been serving on a diplomatic mission in Russia prior to moving west from Virginia.

1. For manumitting his slaves in violation of Illinois' "black code," Coles was sued in 1823. He lost this case in a lower court, but the State Supreme Court later reversed this decision.

2. Davis, *Frontier Illinois*, 167.

3. Pease, *Frontier State*, 77.

4. Buck, *Illinois in 1818*, 244.

5. Morris Birkbeck, *An Appeal to the People of Illinois on the Question of a Convention* (Shawneetown, Ill.: C. Jones, 1823), 6, 8.

other Northern states, coming as it did in the wake of the highly charged Missouri Compromise of 1820. As one might expect, pro-slavery forces achieved their best showing in the state's more established, southern-tier counties.[1] Nonetheless, the strong turnout in favor of the convention reveals that a surprising percentage of Illinoisans, including many who did not own slaves, wanted the "peculiar institution" made legal north of the Ohio. On the surface, this appears illogical: why would white farmers whose way of life was perennially endangered by a slave economy, who had left states like Kentucky and Virginia in part to escape from its negative impact, abruptly turn around and vote *for* slavery?

One possible explanation for this puzzling behavior can be found in the contemporary observations of an English visitor to Illinois, William Blane. Traveling inland from the Ohio River to meet his countryman Birkbeck and other antislavery leaders, Blane was appalled to discover that many other English settlers at Albion, the town Birkbeck and his friend George Flower had founded, intended to vote in favor of slavery. After talking with some of them, Blane noted in his diary: "So powerful is avarice, and so weak is patriotism, that many inhabitants to whom I spoke upon the subject, acknowledged that it would ultimately be a great curse to the State; this was indifferent to them, as they intended going away. These wretches think, that if their State can be made a slave state, many of the wealthy southern planters will emigrate to it, and that thus the price of land will be increased. As they wish to sell theirs, many will on that account vote for slavery."[2] If true, Blane's analysis would explain how small Illinois farmers could cast votes seemingly in direct opposition to their self-interest.

And, in fact, there are some statistical data that substantiate this anecdotal testimony. If one looks at Illinois voting records for elections held during 1818 and 1824, it becomes apparent that many counties that showed a clear preference for making the slavery lawful contained few slaves and slaveholders. Majorities in these counties voted not to legalize a system that already existed there, but rather to *pave the way for its introduction*. Of course, areas where the slave population was already large also voted heavily in favor of slavery.[3] In 1820, Gallatin

6. Paul Finkelman, "The Northwest Ordinance: A Constitution for an Empire of Liberty," in *Pathways to the Old Northwest: An Observance of the Northwest Ordinance* (Indianapolis: Indiana Historical Society, 1988), 14. See also William P. Howard, *Illinois: A History of the Prairie State* (Grand Rapids: William E. Eerdsmans, 1972), 136-7, and Syla J. Saphir, "Governor Edward Coles," *Illinois History* 47:3 (April 1994), 63.

1. The counties giving the convention proposal at least a two-thirds majority were Gallatin, (82%); Jefferson, (70%); Pope, (69%); Hamilton, (67%); and Jackson, (66%). Pease, *Frontier State*, 89.

2. William N. Blane, *An Excursion Through the United States and Canada during the Years 1822-23 by an English Gentleman* (New York: Negro Universities Press, 1969), 170.

3. Conversely, several Illinois counties with fewer than 20 slaves — namely, Franklin, Johnson, Madison, and Monroe — voted strongly against the pro-slavery candidate for Congress in 1818.

County, with its salt wells at Shawneetown, contained the largest number of slaves in Illinois — 267. Over 90 percent of its votes went for the pro-slavery candidate for Congress in 1818, and 82 percent for the 1824 constitutional convention. The same holds for Randolph County, in western Illinois. Its slave population was estimated at 233 in 1820.[1] (Together these two counties then accounted for 54.5 percent of the state's slaves.) It, too, voted heavily for Pierre Menard, the slaveholder elected as lieutenant governor in 1818. Two thirds of county voters also backed another slave owner, John McLean, that same year.

But one finds the same preference expressed in Edwards County (which included Birkbeck's town of Albion). While only seven slaves lived there in 1820, nearly 60 percent of its votes went for Menard in the 1818 state election, and one third of the county's residents supported a constitutional convention to legalize slavery. In Jefferson County, 70 percent voted for the convention, as did 69 percent in Pope County, even though these areas together contained only *one slave* in 1820.[2] South central Washington County had just 26 slaves out of a population of 1,705 in 1818, but 89.4 percent of its votes were cast for Menard, and 74 percent for the pro-slavery McLean. A well-respected French Canadian immigrant, Menard enjoyed strong support around the state, and this may account for his faring so well at the polls, even among voters who did not want to see slavery allowed under Illinois' constitution.[3] But strong backing for other pro-slavery candidates and measures in counties with small black populations suggests this support was based upon policy issues, not personalities.[4] Without question, a large percentage of Illinoisans wanted to see the slave system take hold in their state because of the economic gain they felt this would bring them. Since very few of those who voted for slavery owned — or could afford — slaves, it seems apparent that they hoped to profit in other ways, such as by selling their land at a higher price.

---

1. There were believed to be about the same number a decade earlier. See John Melish, "Travels in the United States of America, in the years 1806, 1807, 1809, 1810 and 1811," in *Indiana as Seen by Early Travelers: A Collection of Reprints from Books of Travel, Letters and Diaries Prior to 1830*, ed. Harlow Lindley (Indianapolis: Indiana Historical Commission, 1916), 34.
2. This figure appeared in the federal census for 1820. However, the population schedule for Pope County recorded that 21 slaves were then living in that part of Illinois. See *Collections of the Illinois State Historical Library*, vol. 26, *Illinois Census Returns, 1820*, ed. Margaret Cross Norton (Springfield: Ill. State Historical Library, 1934), 228.
3. A change was made in Illinois' constitution specifically to allow Menard to hold state office. This reduced the years of U.S. residence required for office holders from 20 to two.
4. This analysis of voting trends in Illinois draws upon population data from the U.S. census for 1820, as well as figures published in the *Illinois Intelligencer*, 17 June 1818. Countywide population schedules are found in *Illinois Census Returns, 1820*. Returns from the 1818 election can be found in the *Illinois Intelligencer*, 7 Oct. 1818. County voting trends for the 1824 convention are taken from Pease, *Frontier State*, 89; Davis, *Frontier Illinois*, 167; and Darrel E. Bigham, *Towns and Villages of the Lower Ohio* (Lexington: University Press of Kentucky, 1998), 52.

Although the issue of slavery was effectively laid to rest by the 1824 rejection of a constitutional convention, the subjugation of blacks did not end. The system of "voluntary" indenture continued to exist in Illinois as late as 1848, and belief in white supremacy remained firmly entrenched not only there and in Indiana, but throughout much of the former Northwest Territory.[1] These facts belie the notion that states north of the Ohio offered former slaves a bona fide haven from oppression. A line clearly separating "free" from slave states did not really exist. On the contrary, slaves were very much present on Northern soil — and a desire to increase their number was widespread. In Indiana and Illinois, where Southerners remained a powerful political force, it was not inconceivable that another constitutional convention might one day open the doors more widely to the chattel system. Concern about this prospect would later help induce many non-slaveholding families living in these states to move further west, across the Mississippi.

In Ohio, pro-slavery sentiment was less of a factor. Unlike their counterparts in Indiana and Illinois, white residents of Ohio had never evinced much interest in introducing the chattel system. There are several reasons for this. For one thing, Ohio initially attracted more Northerners than did its neighbors to the west. As early as 1800, settlers from New York and Pennsylvania had started to come down the Ohio on flatboats, establishing modest homesteads near the river or else moving into the uncharted interior. In addition, northern Ohio's Western Reserve had ties to Connecticut dating back to 1786, when this region had been ceded to the Nutmeg State in lieu of other land claims. This New England connection produced communities in northern Ohio such as Cleveland. Because of their heritage, these towns later became centers of abolitionist sentiment. (The Underground Railroad was particularly active in the Buckeye State, thanks to a strong Quaker presence. As many as 30,000 slaves are believed to have crossed the Ohio at Cincinnati and found refuge there with the help of free blacks and sympathetic whites.) By mid-century, Ohio had more than twice as many white natives of Pennsylvania as Virginians living within its borders. While the majority of Indiana and Illinois populations had Southern roots, only a third of Ohio residents in 1850 came from slave states.[2] Because they lay further west and were less accessible from the northern states, Indiana and Illinois developed their lower counties first. According to the 1810 census, virtually all of the latter's residents were confined to just two southwestern counties — Randolph and St. Clair. By contrast,

1. Jacque Voegeli, "The Northwest and the Race Issue, 1861-1862," *Mississippi Valley Historical Review* 50:2 (Sept. 1963), 236. Voegeli argues that anti-black prejudice remained strong up until the Civil War not only in Illinois, but also in Indiana, Iowa, Michigan, Minnesota, Ohio, and Wisconsin

2. There were 85,762 white and "free colored" natives of Virginia living in Ohio in 1850, compared to 200,634 persons from Pennsylvania and 83,979 from New York. "Place of Birth," *Mortality Statistics*, 37-8.

Chicago only had about a dozen settlers by 1812.[1] Likewise, fully 80 percent of Indiana's 24,520 inhabitants in 1810 lived within 75 miles of the Ohio River.[2]

Second, Ohio was settled before both Indiana and Illinois. The first wave of migration there took place at a time when Kentucky, on the other side of the Ohio River, was also opening up to frontier families. Westward bound farmers thus had a choice of destinations. Both territories promised abundant, rich soil at affordable prices, but only Kentucky attracted slaveholders — in part because of its proximity (Ohio was somewhat further away from Virginia), and in part because of its climate and soils: the Bluegrass region was more suited to tobacco growing than the fields of southern Ohio. Thus, the planter elite and their slaves settled in that part of Kentucky. Planters opposed to the chattel system — or previously displaced by it — were more inclined to head to the other side of the river. Many of these were Scotch-Irish who had not previously managed to establish themselves as farmers in slave states. For these two streams of settlers, the antislavery clause in the Northwest Ordinance acted as a signpost, pointing one to the north and the other due west.

Nonetheless, as the territory comprising present-day Ohio prepared to enter the Union in 1802, some Southerners joined forces to fight for the introduction of slavery. This much smaller group hoped to cast aside the restrictions imposed by the Northwest Ordinance and open Ohio to the "peculiar institution." This pro-slavery element was based in the Virginia Military Tract — the area in south-western Ohio originally set aside for veterans of the Revolutionary War. In 1800, most of its residents hailed from the Virginia Piedmont. The overwhelmingly majority were small, non-slaveholding farmers. But some had forsaken their slaves in order to stake out claims to Ohio's rich soils and now had hopes of regaining the higher status (and standard of living) they had formerly enjoyed by making the chattel system legal in the Buckeye State. In this desire they were joined by settlers who felt that the coming of wealthy slave owners would spur economic growth in this part of the Old Northwest. As had occurred a decade earlier in Kentucky, forces for and against slavery first clashed at the convention tasked with writing Ohio's constitution, held in the territorial capital of Chilli-cothe during November 1802. Determining the future status of blacks was a major concern at this gathering. Over one hundred propositions on this subject were presented — far more than on any other issue — despite the fact that fewer than 400 blacks were then residing in Ohio.[3] Antislavery delegates dominated the convention: candidates who had run on a pro-slavery position had suffered

---

1. Parrish, *Historic Illinois*, 289.
2. Benjamin Moulton, "Changing Patterns of Population," in *Natural Features of Indiana*, ed. Alton A. Lindsey (Indianapolis: Indiana Academy of Science, 1966), 533.

lopsided defeats at the county level.[1] Consequently, a proposal to legalize slavery never made it out of committee.[2] The convention's disavowal of slavery — on both economic and moral grounds — represented a victory for Jeffersonian democracy on the frontier.[3] Delegates had been allotted to Ohio's existing nine counties strictly on the basis of population, and this assured that slaveholders could not impose their will upon the proceedings.[4] Instead, 26 of the 35 representatives belonged to the anti-slavery Democratic-Republican Party. Even those counties comprising the Virginia Military District did not support the slave system — chiefly because they could not abide living among blacks and wanted to gain a firm economic foothold for white labor. A number of leading business figures worried that the existence of slavery would deter both the settlement of Northerners and European immigrants and economic growth.[5]

Furthermore, from an agricultural perspective, Ohio was not well suited for the slave system, so even large landowners — the group that profited most from the chattel system in the South — did not advocate its introduction. For instance, 38-year-old Nathaniel Massie — who, together with the English-born physician, Edward Tiffin, the latter's brother-in-law, Thomas Worthington, and two other men, represented Ross County at the convention — did not support

---

3. Wilson, "Negro in Early Ohio," 739. Wilson's sources for this are Hickok, *The Negro in Ohio*, 33, and Robert E. Chaddock, *Ohio Before 1850: A Study in the Early Influence of Pennsylvania and Southern Populations on Ohio* (New York: Columbia University, 1908), 78. For the number of blacks living in Ohio in 1802, see Helen M. Thurston, "The 1802 Constitutional Convention and Status of the Negro," *Ohio Archaeological and Historical Quarterly* 81:1 (Winter 1972), 17.

1. John D. Barnhart, "The Southern Influence in the Formation of Ohio," *Journal of Southern History* 3:1 (Feb. 1937), 31.

2. According to some accounts, the convention's committee on the bill of rights considered an amendment to permit a limited form of slavery in Ohio. The committee was possibly influenced by Thomas Jefferson, who wanted thus to end the sectional divide over the slavery question and hoped that the presence of slaves in Ohio would hasten emancipation. A Federalist delegate, Ephraim Cutler, claimed that he cast the deciding vote defeating a proposal to allow a restricted form of slavery in Ohio. See Julia P. Cutler, *Life and Times of Ephraim Cutler* (New York: Arno Press & New York Times, 1971), 74, and William T. Utter, *The State of Ohio*, vol. 2, *The Frontier State, 1803-1825* (Columbus: Ohio State Archaeological and Historical Society, 1942), 19-20. But others dispute this account. One historian points out that the delegate alleged to have introduced the pro-slavery provision, John W. Browne, voted at the convention to give blacks the vote. See William E. Gilmore, *Life of Edward Tiffin* (Chillicothe: Horney & Son, 1897), 76. For more on Jefferson's desire to see slavery in Ohio, see Daniel J. Ryan, *History of Ohio*, vol. 3, *The Rise and Progress of an American State* (New York: Century History, 1912), 126-28.

3. "They [those opposed to slavery] thought that it would lower free labor; that it would create a life unfriendly to simplicity and industry, and establish a condition from which many of them sought to escape in the selection of their new home." Ryan, *History of Ohio*, 50.

4. There was to be one delegate chosen for each 1,200 white residents.

5. This argument was advanced chiefly by Jacob Burnet, an early legislative leader and investor in Ohio. See Stephen Middleton, *Black Laws in the Old Northwest: A Documentary History* (Westport: Greenwood Press, 1993), 3.

"involuntary servitude" in Ohio. Massie, the founder of Chillicothe, was one of the largest property owners in the state, primarily due to his having helped to survey the Virginia Military District in 1790.[1] Shortly thereafter, he had brought several blacks with him to Ohio as "servants" and still had several in his possession at the time of the convention. Massie coaxed a number of other Virginians, as well as Kentuckians, to migrate to Ohio, but made his case on the basis of its abundance of cheap land, not of cheap slave labor. And, at the convention, Massie declined to vote for legalizing slavery.[2]

The 1802 convention's summary rejection of the slave system, in effect, laid the issue permanently to rest in Ohio. The lawmakers had made it difficult for the constitution to be revised in the future — by requiring that a two-thirds majority of elected representatives vote to undertake this process. Largely for this reason, the state's constitution remained in effect as originally written for nearly half a century, until 1850.

***

By the 1820s, in spite of their differing political circumstances, the "butternut" states of Ohio, Illinois, and Indiana had reached a similar consensus on slavery. Reflecting the wishes of yeoman farmers from the South (and, especially in Ohio, of more recently arrived Northerners), all three states had banned any future enslavement of blacks. Thus, the "peculiar institution" soon died out in the Old Northwest.[3] Economically and philosophically, these states had cast their lot with the "free" North. At the same time, whites in Ohio, Illinois, and Indiana accommodated their Southern neighbors (and their own racist outlook) by honoring the federal Fugitive Slave Law of 1793, which permitted slave owners to retrieve runaways and made it a crime to assist any black fugitives in escaping. In eschewing the slave system, these states were motivated mainly by economic considerations: they were abandoning a stagnating, less profitable form of agriculture for a more dynamic, diverse, and demonstrably superior way of life. This combined farming with manufacturing, commerce, and entrepreneurship. If there was a moral dimension to this choice, it focused on the welfare

---

1. Worthington had also surveyed these lands and used this position to acquire a large holding for himself. Rohrbaugh, *Land Office Business*, 21.
2. Massie abstained when this vote was taken on legalizing involuntary servitude. County records show that Massie still had at least two black servants with him in 1811. See *Records of Court of Common Pleas*, Clerk's Office, Ross County, "Records of Negroes," vol. 2, cited in "A Preliminary Report on the Ohio Archives," *American Historical Association* (Washington: American Historical Association, 1908), 193-4: http://www.seorf.ohiou.edu/~xx057/ross.htm.
3. In 1820, 190 Indiana slaves were included in the federal census, but this count dropped to three in 1830. By 1850, no slaves were listed. Similarly, in Illinois, the number declined sharply from 917 (1820) to 747 (1830) and then to 331 in 1840 — the last decennial federal census to cite slaves in the state's population.

of *white* workers, not that of slaves. In the free states, white manual labor retained worth and dignity. Relatively poor whites could earn a decent income, provide adequately for their families, and attain a secure, if modest, social status. None of these goals was as achievable for them in the South.

By casting slavery aside, the "butternut" states prospered. The production and export of agricultural and manufactured goods, population, and infrastructure all increased more rapidly in Ohio, Illinois, and Indiana than they did below the Ohio River. This economic success disproved the argument that only an official sanctioning of slavery would make these new states wealthy. The absence of slaves had attracted migrants not only from Northern and Southern states, but also from Germany and Ireland — who had no desire to live where other human beings were enslaved. These new arrivals from Europe made significant contributions to economic growth in the Northern states, including in the Midwest.[1]

The lure of material success led to a population boom in the "butternut" states. During the second decade of the 19th century, Ohio's population rose by over 150 percent, and in just eight years (1810-1818) Illinois' climbed by more than 228 percent. One historian has termed this influx of humanity into the Ohio Valley "one of the great immigrations in the history of the western world."[2] Cheap, fertile land was the major draw, coupled with the chance to thrive in a time of burgeoning regional growth. But the fact that slavery did not exist certainly contributed to the Old Northwest's appeal during the antebellum period. The greater economic opportunities available north of the Ohio River also attracted a considerable number of blacks — largely those freed by their Southern masters.[3] As residual *de facto* slavery disappeared in this part of the country, even more blacks moved in. Ohio was their destination of choice: six times as many black freemen lived there in 1810 as had ten years before. Ironically, the very barriers put up to keep out an unwanted slave population were now encouraging an equally "undesirable" black migration.

Even though miniscule in terms of absolute numbers and percentage of the overall population, the presence of blacks unfettered by the slave system was

1. According to the 1850 federal census, 12.9 percent of Illinois' 846,034 residents had been born abroad; in Ohio, immigrants made up 10.9 percent of the population, and in Indiana, they accounted for 5.6 percent. By contrast, only 4.1 percent of those persons living in Kentucky were foreign born, as were 2.5 percent of Virginia residents in 1850. However, nearly 13 percent of Missouri residents had been born outside the United States. Table XIV and XV, "Nativities of White and Free Colored Population," *Mortality Statistics of the Seventh Census*, 36.
2. Malcolm J. Rohrbough, *The Trans-Appalachian Frontier: People, Society, and Institutions, 1775-1850* (New York: Oxford University Press, 1978), 158.
3. According to 1850 census figures, 8,384 of the 11,262 free blacks then living in Indiana were born in other states, making clear that migration, not natural increase, accounted for the surge in this population. See "Nativities of White and Free Colored Population," *Seventh Census*, 36.

especially disconcerting to transplanted Southerners. (One can draw a rough analogy with anti-Semitism in Nazi Germany, where the percentage of Jews in 1933 was equally small — less than one percent of the total.) Having moved north in part to escape the negative effects of slavery and slaves on their lives, these yeoman farmers now faced another kind of black threat. In their eyes, the future for whites like them was thus uncertain — and unsettling. Racial trends in the Old Northwest did not appear to be in their favor. Since Illinois and Indiana still unofficially tolerated slavery in the 1820s, these states might one day reverse their positions and vote to make the chattel system fully legal.[1] An infusion of slave labor would undermine the status of small white farmers, as it had done previously in Virginia and Kentucky. But, if slavery continued to be officially prohibited, the "butternut" states would draw more free blacks northward in quest of a better life. Either way, the impact on small farmers and landless whites would not be beneficial.

As they considered these scenarios, whites began to contemplate ways of protecting themselves against a dreaded black "invasion." This could be thwarted by two strategies: strictly enforcing laws that would discourage black in-migration and encourage black residents of the Old Northwest to leave; or devising a plan for removing freed blacks *en masse* from the region. Efforts to create a "whites-only" domain in the northern Ohio Valley by pursuing these courses of action would consume much of the time and energy of policy makers during the early decades of the 19th century. Their failure to achieve this exclusionary goal would result in another white exodus to the western frontier.

---

1. Rev. Peter Cartwright, who successfully ran for the Illinois state legislature as an anti-slavery candidate, feared that forces seeking to bring the slave system into the state would try again after their defeat in 1824. See Cartwright, *Autobiography*, 262.

V. HOLDING THE COLOR LINE IN THE OLD NORTHWEST

Jeffersonian-minded Scotch-Irish from the backcountry of Virginia and Kentucky migrating north of the Ohio River had taken legal steps to make sure that no slaves followed them to this new frontier and contended against them for economic survival.[1] But, early in the 19th century, other blacks sought to head in the same direction. This development threatened to confound white hopes of keeping this part of the United States racially homogeneous. To preserve this territory for themselves, racially intolerant and economically marginal whites could not simply rely upon anti-slavery laws. For, ironically, the banning of slavery in the Old Northwest made the region attractive to blacks who had either been recently manumitted in the border states or who were seeking to escape to freedom in the North or Canada. Much like white farmers and laborers, these blacks came to the northern Ohio Valley in order to build better lives there. They were particularly drawn to Ohio, where white hostility was less pronounced. As that state prospered, the rate of Southern black in-migration steadily accelerated.[2]

This development perturbed many white Ohioans, especially those who had moved above the Mason Dixon Line to escape "degrading" contact with blacks. But strong prejudice against migrating blacks would also characterize white attitudes throughout much of the western free states and territories. As the

---

1. Some Revolutionary War veterans living in Kentucky had petitioned the legislature of the Northwest Territory in 1799 to bring slaves with them to the Virginia Military District, but this request never made it out of committee. Wilson, "Negro in Early Ohio," 733.
2. In 1870, 31,378 Ohio blacks (out of 63,213) were natives of Southern states. This number represented nearly half of all Southern-born blacks then living in states formerly part of the Old Northwest Territory. "Migration of Blacks Out of and Into the South by States, 1870-1910," *Historical Statistics of Black America* (New York: Gale Research, 1995), vol. 2, 1633.

expansion of "peculiar institution" came to be limited by climate and geography, racially intolerant whites would focus their efforts on limiting the movement of blacks not controlled by the slave system. To some extent, the animus against this group stemmed from a dread of racial mixing — a more likely eventuality when blacks were not enslaved. Such fear would persist in southern Ohio for several decades and inspire efforts to rid the state of its black population. But animosity toward arriving blacks had an economic basis as well: their willingness to work for low wages took away jobs from whites and kept the latter's pay levels from rising. This explains why anti-black feeling became strong among some whites in a city like Cincinnati. For it was there, in a district known as Bucktown, that many ex-slaves from nearby Kentucky took up residence, finding jobs in local slaughterhouses and factories.[1] This particularly angered Irish immigrants who, in the decades preceding the Civil War, occupied roughly the same socioeconomic level. While many whites tolerated the presence of black freemen socially,[2] others strenuously objected to having members of this group living anywhere near them. These Ohioans considered the presence of freed slaves — despised as "the very drones and pests of society[3] — distasteful and "contaminating." Even Southern planters who had manumitted their slaves before moving to Ohio were not willing to open the state's borders to blacks seeking a new life in "freedom."[4]

Escaped slaves from Kentucky and other Southern states posed the most worrisome concern.[5] The abolition of slavery in Upper Canada (present-day Ontario) in 1793 had turned that part of Canada into a safe haven for slaves seeking freedom and made Ohio a major way station on the Underground Railroad. There are no statistics on blacks fleeing north across the Ohio, but anecdotal evidence points to a sharp upswing in the number of runaways who found temporary refuge there after 1800.[6] Newspapers of the time frequently carried notices

---

1. In 1800, 2,200 of Ohio's 7,500 free blacks were living in Cincinnati, and many others lived in towns where they were not as subject to racial harassment and discrimination as in the countryside. Albert B. Hart, *Salmon Portland Chase* (Boston: Houghton Mifflin, 1899), 29. Blacks also settled in Northern cities because they lacked the financial resources to purchase land and pursue farming.
2. According to one historian, blacks were unwanted in Cincinnati but did not become a "cause of much trouble" there until 1826. See Carter G. Woodson, "The Negroes of Cincinnati Prior to the Civil War," *Journal of Negro History* 1:1 (Jan. 1916), 3.
3. Quoted in Hart, *Chase*, 87.
4. Charles Worthington and his brother-in-law Edward Tiffin were prominent examples of Virginia slaveholders who freed their slaves and then became leading backers of anti-black legislation in Ohio. They also served as the state's first two governors. Wilson, "Negro in Early Ohio," 727.
5. As early as November 1799, the Legislature of the Northwest Territory had taken up the matter of persons "escaping into this territory from whom labor or service is lawfully claimed by any other persons." Quoted in Wilson, "Negro in Early Ohio," 734-5.
6. Not until 1817, however, did the Kentucky legislature submit an official complaint to Ohio about slaves who had escaped northward and then not been captured and returned to their owners. See Leo Alilunas, "Fugitive Slave Cases in Ohio Prior to 1850," *Ohio Archaeological and Historical Quarterly* 49:2 (April 1940), 169.

about fugitive slaves, such as one that appeared in 1810, offering a $20-reward for the capture of a 27-year-old male who had fled from nearby Newport, Kentucky.[1] Local officials cooperated with requests for help in apprehending these blacks, as the Fugitive Slave Law of 1793 required.[2] Ohio businessmen were particularly eager to see runaways caught and returned to their owners in order to protect their commercial interests in the neighboring slave states.[3]

Worry about becoming a conduit for escaped slaves led Ohio's General Assembly to consider a series of patently discriminatory measures when it first convened in Chillicothe in 1803. By now, the racial climate in the new state had changed. The bicameral state legislature — consisting of 30 representatives and 14 senators — had a more conservative cast than the preceding constitutional convention.[4] Natives of Virginia and Kentucky with an intense dislike of blacks had formed a solid bloc and held the balance of power.[5] They were bent upon closing the door on black migration. They were backed by representatives closely aligned with Ohio business interests. This latter group feared that Ohio would suffer economically if it allowed runaway slaves to find refuge within its borders: slave states like Kentucky might take retaliatory steps to limit trade across the Ohio. To maintain good ties with their southern neighbors, these legislators were fully prepared to deny runaways sanctuary and help return them to their masters.

After having dealt with tax matters, the creation of counties, and state appropriations, the elected representatives gathered in Chillicothe took up the pressing question of how to discourage this unwelcome in-migration. Sentiment voiced at the 1802 constitutional convention against legalizing slavery in Ohio was now mobilized to keep runaway slaves out. This shift strongly suggests that it was racial bias — not sympathy for the blacks' plight — that motivated this previous convention's decision to prohibit the "peculiar institution." In January, the two chambers comprising the General Assembly voted overwhelming in favor of several so-called "black laws" to deter escaped slaves from coming to the Buckeye State. The state's House of Representatives endorsed this legislation by a 19-8 vote, and it cleared the Senate by a 9-5 margin. Support for these black laws was strongest in the lower counties, where Southerners predominated,[6]

---

1. *The Whig* (Cincinnati), 21 Mar. 1810. A similar notice appeared in the same newspaper, dealing with two fugitive female slaves, on 25 April 1810.
2. The first runaway in Ohio was returned to Virginia in May 1810, in compliance with a request from that state's governor.
3. Woodson, "Negroes of Cincinnati," 4.
4. Middleton, *Black Laws*, 4.
5. Wilson, "Negro in Early Ohio," 753. At the 1802 constitutional convention, delegates from Southern states had outnumbered those from the North by only 18-17.
6. "The 'black code' of 1804 was the product of southern men from the river counties of Ohio who wished to render conditions in the state so uncomfortable for the negro that he would be discouraged so far as immigration was concerned. Furthermore, they wished to persuade those free negroes living in Ohio to go elsewhere." Wilson, "Negro in Early Ohio," 754.

but even senators representing the New England bastion of Marietta voted to make it extremely difficult for fugitive slaves to enter Ohio.[1] Modeled on Virginia's slave code, these laws prohibited any black or mulatto from being employed "unless he or she shall first produce a fair certificate from some court within the United States, of his or her actual freedom . . ."[2] All non-whites were also required to register with county officials. Ohio's black laws upheld all "lawful claim" to runaway slaves. Slave owners could enlist the help of local law-enforcement officials in reclaiming their chattel. (However, blacks could not be seized and taken out of Ohio without their identity as slaves first having been established.) Finally, the legislature voted to impose a fine of between $10 and $50 on any person who harbored an escaped slave or abetted his or her flight. Overall, these laws demonstrated that, largely out of economic self-interest, Ohio was siding with the slave states and against the slaves themselves. While nominally "free," the first state formed in the Old Northwest was not prepared to offer true freedom to oppressed Southern blacks.

Passage of these "black laws" made Ohio exceedingly inhospitable to would-be runaways in states such as Kentucky. Since they would not be able to produce the required documentation, they would face the constant threat of betrayal, arrest, and return. What is most revealing about these new laws is that they were both *pro-slavery* and *anti-black*. The right of slaveholders to repossess their human property was clearly upheld. And this happened frequently. Ohio newspapers regularly ran ads seeking help in recovering escaped Southern slaves, and these notices generated considerable local interest. Half the fine levied for assisting a runaway slave went to the person who reported the crime. Whites eager to claim the reward would sometimes overlook the fine points of the law, abduct black freemen, and transport them back to the slave states, to their purported masters. Such kidnappings were often better organized than efforts to help runaway slaves escape to freedom in Canada.[3] (As mentioned above, fines were levied to discourage people from helping escapees.)

But these harsh measures did not entirely stop escaping slaves from coming to Ohio.[4] Although many may have been dissuaded from taking this route out of bondage, others, particularly from nearby Kentucky and Virginia, were still will-

---

1. In the House, counties populated largely by New Englanders — Washington and Trumbull — voted against these laws. However, in Ohio's Senate, representatives of Marietta — a New England bastion — supported these anti-black restrictions. *Ibid.*, 755. Wilson contends that New Englanders originally sympathetic to the plight of blacks changed their minds after exposure to them in Ohio.
2. "Ohio Black Laws," http://www.usconstitution.com/BlackLawsofOhio1804.htm.
3. Buley, *Old Northwest*, vol. 2, 622.
4. A study of advertisements for runaway slaves in one Cincinnati newspaper shows a decrease in their number after the passage of the black laws. See Wilson, "Negro in Early Ohio," 753.

ing to take their chances on the northern bank of the river.[1] Aided by friends and relatives living in Ohio's lower counties, or by sympathetic white Quakers, they crossed the Ohio River by boat or walked across its frozen surface in winter and found transient hiding places while waiting to complete the journey to freedom. Since the numbers arriving were relatively small (and inconspicuous), and because they did not strain Ohio's relations with adjacent slave states, this trickle of fugitives into the state was generally tolerated.

Soon Ohio's whites faced what they considered a more serious racial threat. This came from a different quarter — free blacks migrating north from Kentucky. This was a largely unforeseen and unexpected development. When Ohio legislators drafted the state's constitution and its first black laws, the prospect of free blacks entering from the South seemed highly unlikely since so few of them lived nearby. When Kentucky became a state in 1792, only slightly more than one hundred blacks enjoyed freedom within its borders. But this population abruptly began to rise. It more than doubled over the next decade and increased another 61 percent by 1820. What accounted for this freeing of so many Kentucky slaves? While humanitarian impulses may have played some part, economics was the major driving force. Most manumitted slaves lived in or near the Bluegrass region, where the production of tobacco and hemp had turned out to be less lucrative than migrating slaveholders from Virginia and other slave states had originally hoped.[2] With profits not rising, costs had to be contained, and reducing the amount of money spent on housing, feeding, and clothing slaves was one obvious way to achieve that goal. Along with their counterparts in Virginia, Kentucky's slave masters were experiencing an increase in their chattel holdings due to a high black birth rate, and this population growth was adding to the labor surplus. Selling slaves to owners of cotton plantations in the Lower South enabled owners to deplete these holdings by approximately 3,000 a year, but many slaves were simply too old or ill to fetch a good price on the New Orleans slave market, and so the problem persisted. The only remaining recourse for Kentucky's planters was to grant these slaves their freedom. But doing so created another problem.

---

1. Henry Noble Sherwood, "Movement in Ohio to Deport the Negro," *Quarterly Publication of the Historical and Philosophical Society of Ohio* 7:2-3 (June/Sept. 1912), 54.
2. See Wilbur Zelinsky, "The Population Geography of the Free Negro in Ante-Bellum America," *Population Studies* 3:4 (March 1950), Fig. 1, "Free Negro Population, 1810 and 1830," 390. Few free blacks lived in Kentucky's rural southeastern counties. In 1830, the six counties of Adair, Cumberland, Monroe, Pulaski, Russell, and Wayne were 95 percent white, with only 105 blacks out of a total population of 37,997. Figures cited in Wali Kharif, "To Be Free and Black in the Upper Cumberland" (Paper presented at the Ohio Valley History Conference, Cookeville, Tenn., 22 Oct. 1999), Appendix 1, "Free Blacks in the Upper Cumberland in 1830."

Like most of their fellow Southerners (as well as Northerners), white Kentuckians found the presence of free blacks at best unsettling and at worst dangerous. In their minds, blacks who were granted rights otherwise enjoyed exclusively by whites set a bad example for their still enslaved fellows: the incendiary words of a few black freemen, exercising their freedom of speech, might incite a mass revolt. Increasingly worried by such a prospect, Kentucky legislators took several steps to make the Bluegrass State unwelcoming to non-whites. First, in 1798, the General Assembly took away blacks' equal legal status and reduced them to second-class citizens under a law dealing with "Slaves, Free Negroes, Mulattos, and Indians." Then, in rewriting the state constitution the following year, lawmakers explicitly limited the franchise to *white* males (while, at the same time, making the political process more democratic, giving qualified voters the right to elect the governor and state senators).[1] They also rescinded the right of free blacks to bear arms, serve in the militia, or hold public office. Finally, in February 1808, with the population of free blacks rising sharply despite these other discriminatory laws, the legislature passed an act prohibiting blacks and mulattoes from migrating to Kentucky. Black freemen already in the state were required to carry at all times a certificate vouching for their freedom. They were legally prevented from organizing or striking a white person, even in self-defense.

While no corroborating documentary evidence exists, one can surmise that these new laws convinced a number of Kentucky's free blacks to move north to Ohio. For them, it was the nearest and most unambiguously "free" part of the Old Northwest, as the legal status of slavery in Indiana and Illinois was still unresolved. Such migration from neighboring Kentucky would account for much of the sharp upswing in the Ohio's population of ex-slaves in the decade after 1800 — an increase of 463 percent.[2] But in-migration from Virginia was also significant, especially after 1808. For example, some 13 families moved from the Old Dominion to Pike County in the early 1820s, establishing one of the first black settlements in that southern central region of the state.[3] Brown County, along

---

1. Article II, Section 8 of Kentucky's 1799 constitution stated: "In all elections for representatives every free male citizen (negroes, mulattoes, and Indians excepted) who at the time being, hath attained to the age of twenty-one years, and resided in the state two years . . . shall enjoy the right of an elector." *Constitution or Form of Government for the State of Kentucky* (Frankfort: Hunter & Beaumont, 1799), http://memory.loc.gov/cgi-bin/ampage.
2. While no data exist on the birth place of free blacks living in Ohio early in the 19th century, one can infer that a large number came from Kentucky by the fact that, in 1810, 42 percent of Ohio's free blacks were living in eight southern tier counties close to the Bluegrass State. Sherwood, "Movement in Ohio," 54. This pattern persisted during the antebellum period: in 1850, approximately 20,000 of Ohio's 25,279 blacks lived in the lower half of the state.
3. Federal census records show that Pike County had 122 resident free blacks in 1820, after having none in 1810. These blacks from Virginia subsequently spread into neighboring Ross County. Another large group of former slaves from the Richmond area came to several southern counties in Ohio after 1815, when their English owner died, leaving money for them to purchase land elsewhere. One settlement in Highland County, at a place called Dark Town, grew to have a population of 900. See "African American Settlements in Ohio," http://www.angelfire.com/oh/chillicothe/Settlements.html.

the Ohio, also had two large communities of black freemen, largely from Virginia, which numbered about 500 each.[1] And, by 1860, more than a fifth of all blacks over the age of 16 then living in Cincinnati were natives of Virginia.[2] Overall, 70 percent of the Queen City's black population hailed from the slave states.[3] Most free blacks had moved there starting in the mid-1820s.[4]

This surge in the number of free blacks caused considerable consternation on the northern side of the Ohio River. Animosity toward free blacks was already expressed during the constitutional deliberations held at Chillicothe in 1802. While delegates readily agreed to prohibit slavery, they also voted not to grant free blacks many basic rights in Ohio. But, this was a much more hotly contested issue than the ban on slavery. In fact, there was considerable support at the convention for giving blacks additional rights. Initially, a motion to extend the suffrage to *resident* black and mulatto males over the age of 21 was adopted by a vote of 19-15.[5] Six of the Federalist delegates allied with Republicans, enabling the motion to pass. If this vote had been sustained, and blacks' right to the franchise had been written into Ohio's constitution, it would have been a truly historic occasion. In 1800, only a few New England states, in addition to New York, Pennsylvania, and the slave states of Maryland and Tennessee, did not limit voting rights to white males.[6] In fact, since the colonies had gained their independence, many states had stripped black freemen of this right— at a time when the number of such potential voters was beginning to climb.[7] For the first state carved out of the Old Northwest Territory to give black males the vote would

1. "Documents: Transplanting Free Negroes to Ohio from 1815 to 1858," *Journal of Negro History* 1:3 (June 1916), 302. One of these, Eagle Township, was formed in 1818.
2. Philip J. Schwarz, *Migrants Against Slavery: Virginians and the Nation* (Charlottesville: University Press of Virginia, 2001), Table 1: "Virginia-born African Americans in Northern Cities, 1850 and 1860," 6.
3. Gruenwald, *River of Enterprise*, 143. This percentage was reached in 1850.
4. Woodson, "Negroes of Cincinnati," 4.
5. Some initial support for black suffrage came from delegates representing all but two of Ohio's nine counties at that time. These included all those bordering slave states. However, only Hamilton County's delegation voted overwhelming to grant blacks the right to vote, with nine in favor and only one opposed. For this tally and other votes cast at the Chillicothe convention, see "First Constitutional Convention, Convened November 1, 1802," *Ohio Archaeological and Historical Quarterly* 5 (1897), 80-131: http://publications.ohiohistory.org/ohstemplate.cfm?action=toc&vol=5.
6. Free blacks in Connecticut could vote until the state's 1818 constitution explicitly limited the franchise to white males. Rhode Island did not deny blacks *per se* the right to vote, but its restricting the franchise to freeholders prevented most of them from going to the polls. Maine did not include any race-based suffrage qualification when it became a state in 1820. It was the only state entering the Union between 1800 and 1860 that did *not* deny blacks the right to vote. Free blacks in Kentucky and Tennessee enjoyed this right for short periods, from 1792 to 1799, and from 1796 to 1834, respectively.
7. For example, in New Jersey, free blacks were denied the vote in 1807, while in New York they effectively lost this right in 1821, when a property ownership requirement was added.

have set a potent precedent for subsequent constitutional proceedings in the West.

But proponents of enfranchising blacks pushed too hard, seeking (unsuccessfully) to extend the right to vote to male *descendants* of resident blacks and mulattoes. This broader amendment unified those hostile to non-whites, and in a second vote, the delegates reversed themselves and rejected a limited form of black suffrage, by a single vote.[1] The president of the convention, Edward Tiffin, cast the tie-breaking vote against this amendment, even though he happened to be a staunch opponent of slavery.[2] It is revealing that not only natives of the South voted against giving black freemen the right to vote. Opposition to this proposal was just as strong — indeed, somewhat stronger — among delegates from counties settled predominantly by Northerners.[3] Their eagerness to discourage free black migration by denying this group equal rights signaled that an aversion to slavery was by no means synonymous with racial liberalism. If Ohio was any indication, most whites in the North regarded blacks as their inferiors and preferred to treat them accordingly.[4] They also did not want to lose jobs to black workers.

Anti-black prejudice influenced the outcome of other constitutional proposals brought before the Chillicothe convention. One dealt with making involuntary servitude legal. While support for this form of *quasi* slavery was strong in Hamilton County, possibly due to the desire of business interests there to

---

1. In order to vote, blacks had to be already resident in Ohio at the time the constitution was adopted.
2. In fact, the delegates did *not* legally reject black suffrage because the votes required to do so were lacking. While the convention journal notes that Tiffin broke the tie with his vote to strike a provision giving blacks the vote, this was not factually correct. The number of votes against black suffrage only totaled 17, *including* Tiffin's, and a majority of 18 was needed to adopt any amendment. For a discussion of this long-overlooked miscounting of votes, see www.geocities.com/ohioconvention1802/blacksuffrage.html.publications.ohiohistory.org/ohstemplate.cfm?action=toc&vol=5. Tiffin explained that he voted against giving blacks the vote out of consideration for the neighboring slave states of Virginia and Kentucky, which did not want to see Ohio become more attractive to would-be runaway slaves. Utter, *State of Ohio*, 118.
3. In the decisive vote on striking the sentence giving all black and mulatto males then residing in Ohio the franchise, one of the two delegates from Trumbull County (formerly the Western Reserve) sided with the affirmative, as did three of five delegates from eastern central Jefferson County, both from adjacent Belmont County, and the two delegates representing central Fairfield County. Along with the outspokenly antislavery Tiffin, his brother-in-law, Thomas Worthington, and Nathaniel Massie also voted not to give black males the right to vote. Conversely, one of the two delegates from Clermont County (opposite Kentucky) and nine of 10 from neighboring Hamilton (which included Cincinnati) supported black suffrage. One could infer that the strong backing for this amendment in this county derived, at least in part, from a desire to make Ohio enticing to free black workers.
4. After carefully analyzing the votes at the 1802 convention, one researcher concluded that "no significant difference of voting based on region of origin or political party is indicated." Thurston, "1802 Convention," 33.

employ such labor in Cincinnati's new factories, this idea was unpopular with delegates from other parts of the state, and was thus not adopted.[1] Six of ten representatives from the other counties with large Southern populations voted against involuntary servitude, revealing their wish to keep blacks of any sort out of Ohio.[2] It appears that unwillingness to allow black "servants" into the state was rooted more in racial bias than economics, since Ohio's free black population was quite small, and any enlargement of it would have been confined to just a few counties.[3] In particular, several counties whose representatives emphatically opposed black indentured servitude had negligible non-white populations.[4] Apparently, they did not want this situation to change.

Another constitutional provision, first approved by a 19-16 vote, barred blacks from holding civil or military office, serving in the state militia, testifying in court against whites, and paying a poll tax. However, during the final debate over amendments on November 20, 1802, this "black code" was removed — by another one-vote margin, 17-16. While no documentary record of the delegates' comments at the convention has survived, one can gain some insight into their racial attitudes from the votes taken on various proposals relating to blacks and mulattoes. On how to treat blacks there was a broad range of opinion. Some representatives sought to make non-whites equal citizens, while others wanted to codify their subservient, second-class status. A few delegates were willing to strike a compromise for the greater good of completing the convention's business, adopting a constitution, and paving the way for statehood.[5] The reversal of

---

1. The amendment to allow *involuntary* indentured servitude in Ohio was voted down, 21-12. Seven delegates (out of 10) from Hamilton voted for this form of *de facto* slavery. Furthermore, a motion made immediately thereafter to prohibit slavery or "involuntary servitude" in any state "to be erected on the northwest side of the river Ohio" was soundly defeated, by 31-2. This lopsided result attests to a respect for the right of individual states to decide for themselves whether or not they wanted to allow slavery. This vote also suggests a wish not to offend neighboring slave states by categorically rejecting the chattel system.
2. All three delegates from Adams County, one of two from Belmont, and all but one from Ross (with Nathaniel Massie abstaining) voted to prohibit involuntary servitude.
3. In 1800, free blacks accounted for only 0.3 percent of Ohio's population. James Curtis, Table 5c: "Midwestern and Southwestern Population of Free Blacks, 1790-1860," *Institutional and Agency Effects on the Status of Free Blacks: Synthesizing Asymmetrical Laws and Social Conditions with Asymmetrical Economic Outcomes* (Feb. 2002), 38.
4. For instance, the central county of Fairfield had only 35 black residents in 1810 (out of a total population of 11,326), yet both of its two delegates to the 1802 convention opposed indentured servitude. On the other hand, counties with somewhat larger free black populations also opposed legalizing this practice. All but one of the five delegates from Jefferson County, on the West Virginia border, voted against black servitude. According to the 1810 federal census, it had a population of 124 blacks out of a total of 17,136. This was at that time the third largest number in a single county. Ross, with 370 blacks in a population of 15,144, had the highest. None of its five convention delegates in 1802 voted for indentured servitude.
5. The delegates' inner conflicts over how to treat blacks can be seen in a largely symbolic rejection of an amendment proposing that: "Nor shall there be either slavery or involuntary servitude ever admitted in any State to be erected on the northwest side of the river Ohio." This categorical ban was defeated, 31-2. This vote can only be seen as a way of affirming each state's right to decide such matters for itself.

positions on various motions clearly suggests a desire to find a mutually palatable middle ground on race questions.[1] Indeed, what makes the outcome of the Chillicothe deliberations so significant from a political perspective is that they marked the emergence of a powerful alliance between *antislavery* and *anti-black* (or white supremacist) forces in the Midwest.[2]

While some delegates considered slavery morally or religiously objectionable, others opposed it out of a general disdain for blacks and concern about the system's negative impact on whites. It was the latter group which joined forces with more overtly prejudiced whites to legislate Ohio's posture toward African Americans. For example, in the 19-16 vote to deny blacks certain civic rights (other than the franchise), five representatives identified with a distinctly anti-black bias sided with three who also opposed slavery (and two "swing" delegates) to pass the measure. Similarly, reversing the convention's earlier decision to grant blacks the vote depended upon the combined support of eight representatives opposed to slavery, five who were anti-black, and three delegates, including the tie-breaking Tiffin, who had mixed feelings about non-whites. Significantly, four of the delegates who cast their votes against black suffrage were natives of free states.[3] Unlike a Southern state like Kentucky, where whites could tolerate living among blacks under a slave system, north of the Mason Dixon Line race relations were less clearly delineated. This fact made many migrants from the South who had formerly owned slaves uncomfortable and anxious to avoid any contact with blacks.[4] By allying themselves with yeoman farmers from the Upland South and racially biased settlers from other regions, these whites could build a wall against black migration. In the coming decades,

---

1. On two amendments dealing with suffrage, four delegates switched sides, giving resident blacks the right to vote. These were Charles W. Byrd (Hamilton), Joseph Darlinton (Adams), John Reily (Hamilton), and John Smith (Hamilton). Restrictions on other rights for blacks were removed when John Milligan (Jefferson) changed his position, and both John McIntire (Washington) and Tiffin (Ross) abstained from opposing such a step. For a detailed analysis of the shifts in individual positions at the convention, see Thurston, "1802 Convention," 22-36.

    According to one observer, the convention had expressed a "warmth of feeling" on questions relating to blacks and realized that compromises had to be struck for the body to complete its work of drafting a constitution. Jacob Burnet, *Notes on the Early Settlement of the North-western Territory* (New York: D. Appleton, 1847), 354-5.
2. "Outrage over slavery and belief in white supremacy were two seemingly discordant strains of thought that were often harmonized in the antislavery intellect." Jacque Voegeli, "The Northwest and the Race Issue," 235. Voegeli notes that this conflation of positions was most evident in the Old Northwest.
3. Nine of the 13 delegates who came originally from Northern states, along with one immigrant from Europe, voted for black suffrage. But Southern natives voted 12-8 against this measure.
4. For the most complete treatment of how non-slave holding Southerners who moved north of the Ohio used their political power to keep slaves *and* free blacks out of the Old Northwest, see Berwanger, *Frontier Against Slavery*, 18-23, *passim*.

this collusion would shape the political landscape in other states and territories as fears of racial "mingling" mounted there, too.

Political expediency may also have influenced how delegates to the 1802 convention voted on race-related questions. They were also mindful that Congress still had to approve Ohio's constitution before granting statehood, and that they had to make certain compromises on the status of blacks in order to produce a document that did not directly contradict federal law. The delegates' awareness of the limitations under which they were operating is apparent in the preamble, which acknowledges Ohio's need to comply not only with the Constitution, but also with the Ordinance of 1787 and the 1802 Enabling Act, which had established the state's borders.[1]

Regardless of how the delegates at Chillicothe arrived at their final positions on the treatment of blacks, the new constitution gave the impression that Ohio intended to be racially relatively tolerant— at least according to its laws. True, blacks were denied the right to vote, but otherwise no explicit restrictions were placed on their rights. They could not be enslaved, or bound into servitude against their will. They enjoyed the same freedoms of religion, the press, judicial process, and against unwarranted searches and seizures afforded white citizens. Indeed, with the exception of suffrage, blacks were indistinguishable from whites under Ohio law. The constitution employed the word "negro" only once, in prohibiting blacks and mulattoes from being kept as servants for more than one year.[2] For any blacks contemplating moving north to Ohio, the document crafted at Chillicothe would have come as welcoming news. From their perspective, enslaved on farms in Virginia or Kentucky, or scratching out a meager existence in these states as freemen, prospects for them certainly looked more attractive on the other side of the river once Congress approved Ohio's constitution and the Buckeye State entered the Union on February 19, 1803.

Racially prejudiced and economically insecure whites did not anticipate that Ohio would attract large numbers of blacks even with such a relatively liberal constitution. Two years before the delegates had convened in Chillicothe, only 741 free blacks were living in nearby Kentucky, and they did not pose much of an economic or social danger. Virginia had far more emancipated slaves residing within its borders — over 20,000 in 1800 — but the chances of many of them migrating to Ohio seemed remote, given the overland distance separating these two states. For black families in the Piedmont to reach the Buckeye State by tak-

---

1. For the complete text, see "Constitution of the State of Ohio, 1802," http://www.ohio-history.org/onlinedoc/ohgovernment/constitution/cnst1802.html.
2. Section 2 of Article VIII (Bill of Rights) contained this statement: "Nor shall any indenture of any negro or mulatto, hereafter made and executed out of the State, or if made in the State, where the term of service exceeds one year, be of the least validity, except those given in the case of apprenticeships."

ing the alternative route down the Ohio also seemed improbable, since anti-black hostility was strong along this river. So, at the start of the 19th century, "plain folk" farmers who had resettled in Ohio had little reason to worry about free blacks sweeping northward into their backyards.

But this sanguine outlook would soon change. Around the time Ohio joined the Union, the free black population in nearby slave states began to increase sharply. In neighboring Kentucky, more surplus slaves were being given their freedom by hard-strapped masters no longer able to pay for their upkeep. Consequently, by 1810, enclaves of 100 or more free blacks could be found in four Kentucky counties — Fayette, Bourbon, Logan, and Jefferson — and the state's total number had reached 1,713. Indeed, Kentucky's free black population was multiplying at a faster rate than either its slave or free white populations. Between 1800 and 1810, the number of free blacks rose by over 131 percent, to 2,759, while the comparable figures for whites and slaves were approximately 80 and 100 percent, respectively. Over the next decade, there was a 61 percent increase in the free black population, versus 55.6 percent for slaves and 34 percent for whites. During the 1820s, the free black population grew by 120 percent, while the number of slaves rose by 31.7 percent, and that of whites by only 19 percent.[1] Still, as a proportion of the Bluegrass State's overall population, free blacks remained an exceedingly small minority: at its peak, in 1850, these blacks accounted for only 2.3 percent of the total.[2]

And this phenomenon was not limited to Kentucky. Unwanted slaves were being given their freedom in many of the older slave states, as the need for their labor decreased. The number of free blacks was growing in Delaware, Maryland, Tennessee, North Carolina, South Carolina, and, most of all, Virginia, where emancipated slaves made up six percent of the state's black population in 1800. Thirty years later, nearly one in ten blacks living in the South was free.[3] Concerned about their security, white Southerners put pressure on manumitted slaves to leave their states. Black freemen were subjected to various discriminatory laws designed to restrict their rights and push them out. As early as 1783, Virginia had prohibited the entry of free blacks, and in 1806, the state required all newly freed slaves to leave within a year or else face re-enslavement. At the same time, legal barriers erected in other slave states compelled these newly emancipated blacks to seek new homes outside the South.[4] Delaware also

---

1. These census data are found in Cramer, *Black Demographic Data*, 131.
2. Stabilization of the free black population after 1850 suggests that many were leaving the state. Between 1850 and 1860, the number of free blacks in Kentucky rose by only 573.
3. Hart, *Slavery and Abolition*, 91. Nationally, the population of free blacks surpassed 300,000 during the 1820s and reached an antebellum peak of 487,970 in 1860.
4. In addition to Kentucky and Virginia, Delaware also banned the entry of free blacks, in 1811. Those who violated this law were subject to a fine of $10 per week.

banned the in-migration of free blacks, in 1811. Those who violated this law were subject to a fine of $10 per week. The following year Maryland prohibited free blacks from growing or selling crops. Such discriminatory measures had the intended effect. Many of these manumitted slaves opted to migrate north and west out of the slave states.

This relocation, coupled with natural increase, caused the black population in the Old Northwest to shoot upward. In Illinois, the number of free blacks nearly quadrupled between 1820 and 1830. It tripled in Indiana, reaching 3,629, or over one percent of the population. And, in Ohio, where the existence of Quaker communities, a more racially humane state constitution, and a higher proportion of Northerners indicated a greater white receptivity, the free black population practically doubled every ten years between 1810 and 1840, when it reached 17,342. As this flow across its borders continued to swell, white Ohioans began to worry that their state was becoming a "dumping ground" for discarded Southern slaves.[1] This problem was most acute in the southern half of the state, where virtually all of the incoming blacks took up residence. (The northern counties — including the Western Reserve, which favored emancipation and which contained such abolitionist strongholds as Oberlin — had negligible black populations.[2]) The same demographic pattern was apparent in the other "butternut" states as well. In the Ohio Valley, most of this one-way movement took place between northern counties in Southern border states and adjacent free ones. Census data reveal a much steeper decline in slave and free black populations in counties along the Ohio River than in other parts of the Upper South.[3]

Ironically, former slaves from the South seeking a more hospitable locale ended up living in counties dominated by Southern "plain folk" migrants. For example, in 1830, 64.2 percent of Indiana's free blacks resided in just 12 of the state's 52 counties. All but three of these were located in the southernmost part of the state.[4] And here the numerical superiority of Upland Southerners was the

1. Wilson, "Negro in Early Ohio," 720, 754. Cf. Berwanger, *Frontier Against Slavery*, 21.
2. Lorain County, which included Oberlin, had only three free blacks in 1830 out of a population of 5,696, according to federal census figures. A decade later, this number had only risen to 62.
3. See Table 2, "Discrepancies in Negro population changes in border counties of border states as compared with other counties, 1850-60," Zelinsky, "Population Geography of the Free Negro," 399.
4. The exceptions were Wayne and Randolph counties on Indiana's eastern border, and Vigo, adjacent to Illinois in the west. Wayne County contained the largest concentration of Quakers in the state, based largely in the city of Richmond. Their presence accounts for the settlement of so many free blacks in this county. By 1820 there were also a number of Quaker families in Randolph County. Among these Quakers was Levi Coffin, a well-to-do banker from North Carolina who helped one thousand blacks escape to Canada and came to be known as the "father" of the Underground Railroad. See Levi Coffin, *The Reminiscences of Levi Coffin* (New York: Arno Press, 1968), 10-12.

greatest: in 1830, 61.9 percent of the population in Knox County, which had the largest number of free blacks (447), came from the Upper South; so did 58.3 percent of the residents of Floyd County, the southern tier county with the second highest number of black freemen (265); fully 81 percent of the people living in southern central Washington County, which included 206 free blacks in 1830, had roots in the states of Kentucky (30.6), North Carolina (25.9), Virginia (16.3), Tennessee (6.2), and Maryland 2.0).[1] Thus, while the absolute number of inmigrating blacks was small, their impact was disproportionately large precisely where they were most unwelcome. This coincidence greatly inflamed racial tensions in Ohio, Illinois, and Indiana. Even a slight increase in the free black population was disconcerting to Southern whites accustomed to subjugating blacks through the strictures of the slave system.

Economically, the arrival of close to a thousand black freemen in Ohio's lower counties endangered the well being of local working class whites, particularly in Cincinnati.[2] White workers in that city also considered it debasing to have to labor alongside blacks. Elsewhere in the Buckeye State, whites met arriving blacks with intimidation and threats of violence. The presence of *any* nonwhites imperiled Ohio's racial exclusivity, even if the actual proportion of blacks in the state's population did not increase dramatically.[3] Thus, when the state's General Assembly reconvened in Chillicothe in December 1806, erecting a high, impermeable barrier to black migration took on much greater urgency, especially for those living in the counties being populated by blacks.[4] More was at stake, now, than accommodating the wishes of slave states. Given the hatred that some

---

1. Southern population statistics can be found in Table 2, "Nativity Percentage, by County, of Indiana's United States-Born Inhabitants according to Most Frequent Source of Origin in 1850," Rose, "Hoosier Origins," 208-9. However, blacks tended to avoid southern counties with the highest proportion of Kentucky natives, perhaps because racial animosity and discrimination were more severe there. For example, in 1830 only 13 free blacks lived in Perry County, which had the greatest percentage of Kentuckians (58.7) in its population. Sullivan County, in which natives of the Bluegrass State made up 46.7 percent of the population, had only 39 free blacks and 1830, while Crawford County, with the same percentage of Kentucky-born residents, did not have a single black resident until after 1830.
2. Blacks in Cincinnati suffered severely under Ohio's black laws, as even residents who objected to slavery did not "relish the prospect of competing against cheap black labor in the free states." Daniel Aron, *Cincinnati: Queen City of the West, 1819-1838* (Columbus: Ohio State University Press, 1992), 302.
3. The proportion of free blacks in Ohio's population rose steadily but slowly — to 1.0 percent in 1810, 2.0 percent in 1820, and 3.0 percent in 1830. This reached its highest point before the Civil War in 1860, when blacks comprised 7.5 percent of the state's population.
4. "[T]here was almost unanimous agreement on the part of all the delegates from the southern part of the state that something had to be done to protect themselves against the black menace, and they voted practically in a block against the northern representatives." Wilson, "Negro in Early Ohio," 761.

whites felt toward all non-whites, it is not surprising that this session of the state legislature enacted even tougher measures to keep blacks out of Ohio. More than twice as many representatives backed these laws as opposed them. Support for the new restrictions placed on blacks was particularly strong in the eastern county of Washington, which was heavily populated by New England settlers. This suggests that it was not only Southern migrants who wanted to keep Ohio "free" for whites only.[1]

The new black laws adopted in January 1807 required any newly arrived black or mulatto to appear in court within 20 days of taking up residence, accompanied by two white men willing to vouch for his or her good behavior, and to produce a bond of $500 as financial support in case the black could not find a job. Any person who employed a black or mulatto without complying with this provision was subject to a fine of up to $100. The new laws also denied blacks the right to testify in court cases when one or more of the parties were white.[2] Although the 1807 legislation did not explicitly refer to "free blacks," it is clear from the restrictions imposed that they were the intended target. Runaway slaves were not going to show up in court, as the new laws mandated. While emancipated slaves might possess a certificate of freedom (and thus circumvent the 1804 restrictions), they had virtually no chance of obtaining the mandatory financial sponsorship. The vast majority of their fellow blacks already living in Ohio did not have much money, and even sympathetic whites could not be expected to help out. (They were more intent on aiding fugitive slaves.) By raising the bar in this way, legislators made it all but impossible for either fugitive slaves or free blacks to settle in Ohio legally.

Much of this officially sanctioned discrimination would dissipate over the ensuing decades as natives of New England, Pennsylvania, New York, and New Jersey populated Ohio's northern counties and came to dominate its politics,[3] and as the power of transplanted Southerners to impose their racial agenda diminished. (However, as late as 1831, state legislators would vote to bar free blacks and mulattoes from attending public schools in Ohio.) The black laws themselves would remain on the books, but would be rarely enforced. Increasingly, they came to been seen as an historical anomaly in a genuinely "free" state. The rise of abolitionist groups in Ohio and their prominence in the national

---

1. This time, the House of Representatives backed anti-black measures by a margin of 20-9, while the laws passed the Ohio Senate without a record of the vote. *Ibid.,* 760.
2. This provision left blacks at the mercy of racially biased white juries.
3. By 1850, slightly over 70 percent of Ohio residents born out of state came from the New England or mid-Atlantic states. Pennsylvania supplied by far the greatest number — 200,634 — of these Northern settlers. See "Nativities of White and Free Colored Population" and "Place of Birth of the White and Free Colored Population of the United States, 1850," *Mortality Statistics of the Seventh Census,* 36, 38-9.

movement to emancipate the slaves attest to the Buckeye State's more progressive attitude toward blacks prior to the Civil War. But, despite this broad shift in outlook statewide, anti-black feelings would remain strong — and even intensify — in certain quarters, particularly in the southernmost counties. This hostility would not be confined to Southern migrants in Ohio but would be found among natives of New England and the mid-Atlantic states as well.

One can discern the depth of this antipathy toward blacks in remarks made by delegates at Ohio's second constitutional convention, which was held in 1850-1851.[1] During its opening session, Benjamin Stanton, an Ohio-born lawyer representing rural Logan County (located northwest of Columbus and partially within the original Virginia Military District), introduced a measure, or a memorial, from his constituents requesting that all blacks be "extradited" from the state so that it could become exclusively white.[2] His proposal was seconded by James Loudon, a farmer from Kentucky then living in Brown County, along the Ohio. Loudon told his fellow delegates that both Whigs and Democrats in his county favored such a plan: the majority believed "with the fathers of this State . . . that this should be a State for the white man, and the white man only." However, the proposal was dropped. A few days later, a petition from voters in Clinton County was introduced, asking that blacks in Ohio be granted the same rights as whites. A blacksmith from St. Mary's, in western Auglaize County, called this idea "revolting" since the United States had been "designed by the God of Heaven to be governed and inhabited by the Anglo-Saxon race and by them alone." Echoing the fears of their predecessors half a century before, some of the legislators meeting in Cincinnati raised the specter of states like Kentucky dumping their "worn out and degraded" slaves north of the Ohio and called for more strictly enforcing laws designed to prevent this from happening. In addition to other unsuccessful petitions asking that Ohio bar black in-migration, the convention received more than two dozen memorials (some from blacks) seeking to elevate non-whites to equal stature with whites under the revised constitution, but all of these were voted down. When a motion was brought to the floor to strike the word "white" from that section of the document describing the

---

1. Anti-black amendments to the state's constitution were introduced by three natives of Pennsylvania, one from Massachusetts, and three delegates born in Ohio. Only two came from Southern-born representatives. Most of these delegates represented the lower counties, but several resided in central Ohio.
2. Stanton represented Logan County. A Republican, he later served as a member of Congress and, during the Civil War, as Ohio's lieutenant governor. Stanton's 1850 proposal was tabled, but it apparently enjoyed strong support among both Whig and Democratic voters in southern Ohio, specifically, in Brown County. For details of this proposal and other anti-black bills discussed at this gathering, see *Report of the Debates and Proceedings of the Convention for the Revision of the Constitution of the State of Ohio, 1850-51* (Columbus: S. Medary, 1851), vol. 1, session of 8 May 1850, 28-9, *passim.*

right of franchise, it was overwhelmingly defeated, 66-12 — far more decisively than a similar proposal had been back in 1802.[1]

Just as its infamous black laws of 1804 and 1807 set the tone for race relations in Ohio — even though they were rarely enforced — for nearly 50 years, they also established a legal model that would be emulated by other states wishing to force free blacks out or keep them from entering. The desire to do so became a paramount political concern as the free black population in the United States continued to grow at a rapid rate. This increase occurred for several reasons. First of all, slavery was gradually (but not completely) abolished in all states above the Mason Dixon Line by 1804.[2] The number of free blacks in the Northern states increased some 70 percent between 1790 and 1820, when it reached 92,723. This population growth occurred mainly in the mid-Atlantic states of New York, New Jersey, and Pennsylvania. Secondly, a natural increase of more than two percent annually added to the ranks of free blacks in all parts of the country.[3] Thirdly, many slaves were freed in the coastal South, particularly in Virginia, Maryland, and Delaware. These numbers increased after state manumission laws were relaxed in the 1790s, making it possible for owners to leave instructions in their wills that their slaves be granted freedom.[4]

Because of laws discouraging ex-slaves from seeking freedom or a better life within the slave states, the territories and newly formed states in the Old Northwest feared they would become the destinations of choice (or necessity) for would-be migrants. The 940-mile long border they shared with the slave states — nearly three-quarters the length of the Texas-Mexico frontier on the Rio Grande — made this highly likely. Accordingly, Illinois and Indiana — politically dominated by Upland Southerners during the early statehood period — quickly followed Ohio's lead in making themselves inhospitable to non-whites, particularly black freemen. As early as 1803, legislators in the Indiana Territory reduced the rights of free blacks (and left them legally vulnerable) by preventing them from testifying in court cases involving whites. A decade later, whites living in lower Indiana petitioned the territorial government to block the in-migration of either slaves or free blacks. That same year, the recently created territory of Illinois

---

1. Commenting on this outcome, one of the delegates caustically noted that members of Ohio's first constitutional convention had denied blacks the franchise by only five votes. (In fact, as pointed out above, this issue was decided in 1802 by only one vote.) For details of the convention's debates on black migration and other rights, see *Report of the Debates*, vol. 1, 28-31, 56, 59, 75, 107-8, 167, 237, 298, 313, 354, 374, 693, 726; vol. 2: 2, 5, 8, 34, 140, 159, 191-2, 231, 339, 552-5, 599-603.
2. New Jersey was the last state in the Northeast to free its slaves.
3. Between 1800 and 1850, the annual rate of natural increase for blacks ranged between 2.0 and 2.4 percent. See McClelland and Zeckhauser, *Demographic Dimensions*, 81.
4. The number of slaves manumitted exceeded 20,000 every decade after 1790 except during the 1810-20 period. According to one estimate, 34,493 slaves were given their freedom between 1800 and 1810, but only 8,666 in the following decade. (This decline is largely due to the tightening of manumission laws in states like Virginia.) 32,127 received their freedom during the period 1820-30, and another 20,759 in the ten years after 1830. *Ibid.*, Table D-28, "Estimated Manumissions, 1800-60," 187.

adopted the Southern strategy of expulsion, passing a law that required all newly arrived free blacks to leave. In 1819, the Illinois legislature emulated Ohio's first black laws by making it a crime for either former or runaway slaves to settle within the state without producing a certificate of freedom. During most of the antebellum period, blacks were further deterred from settling in Illinois by the stipulation that they post a prohibitively high bond of $1,000. The state's 1848 constitution went further, prohibiting non-white immigration outright. Indiana's constitution of 1851 did the same, while also voiding any contracts with whites and imposing fines on whites who employed blacks or encouraged them to stay.

But, as it turned out, none of these measures worked. As noted above, Ohio continued to experience an influx of free blacks, mainly in its southern counties. To cite just one example: some 400 former slaves from northeastern Virginia came to western Ohio in the 1820s, hoping to escape white animosity and establish themselves as independent farmers.[1] But all too often, the arrival of these blacks on "free" soil provoked a strongly negative response. When several hundred slaves manumitted in the will of a Virginia planter named Samuel Gist attempted to settle in southern Ohio after the War of 1812, local whites denounced the arrival of this "depraved and ignorant...set of people."[2] This unremitting prejudice forced these blacks to retrace their steps back to the Old Dominion.[3]

The number of black freemen in Illinois and Indiana also rose despite the fact that these states enacted similarly discriminatory legislation. The rate of increase in these states was much less, largely because of the existence of slavery there, but this did not lessen the disdain and hatred that black freemen aroused in whites of Southern origin. According to the federal census, Illinois had a population of nearly 2,000 "free colored persons" in 1820, but almost all of them worked at the salt springs in Shawneetown: although the state's 1818 constitution had declared slavery illegal, it had also made a temporary exception for "indentured" black labor at these salines.[4] In Indiana, the number of free blacks

---

1. For a detailed account of the settlement of two extended black families in the Old Northwest, see Vincent, *Southern Seed, Northern Soil.*
2. Donald D. Ratcliffe, "James Riley and Antislavery Sentiment in Ohio, 1819-1824," *Ohio Archaeological and Historical Quarterly* 81:2 (Spring 1972), 86.
3. They had originally settled in Brown and Highland counties. After returning to Virginia for ten years, these former slaves were forced to make a second trek to Ohio. Schwarz, *Migrants Against Slavery*, 16.
4. In fact, there were still some 746 black indentured servants in Illinois in 1830. Buley, *Old Northwest*, vol. 1, 622. Most of these were actually slaves. They were blacks contracted from out of state for only a year in order to prevent their being emancipated. Courts had ruled this was what the Northwest Ordinance required. After this period, "indentured servants" were supposed to return to their state of origin (Kentucky), but employers got around this by taking these blacks to the Ohio River and having them wade out a few feet. (At that time, the Kentucky border reached to the north bank of the river.) After making this journey, the workers could have their contracts renewed. Jacob W. Myers, "History of the Gallatin Salines," *Journal of the Illinois State Historical Society* 14:3-4 (Oct. 1921-Jan. 1922), 148. http://www.illinoishistory.com/1922-gallatin-salines.html.

rose from 1,230 in 1820 to 7,165 in 1840, but over half could be found in just eight counties.[1] Six of these counties happened to be ones in which the percentage of native Kentuckians was significantly higher than the state average, suggesting a likely cause of strong anti-black sentiment there.[2]

What mattered more than demographic statistics was a deeply seated, deeply irrational fear that, because the black population was both increasing in size and evolving in nature, it threatened the very survival of the white race. Up until the start of the 19th century, the slave system had restricted blacks geographically as well as socially, but it now appeared this containment was not going to last indefinitely. The wholesale freeing of slaves in the North, together with individual manumissions in the South, had created a new, anomalous black population — "neither fish nor fowl," neither wholly free (and equal) nor wholly subjugated. The consequences stemming from excess slaves being let go were only becoming worse. In the South, many of these unwanted workers could be profitably exported to cotton plantations further west, but doing so had not significantly slowed the increase in the free black population. Virginia planters, for example, sold 30,000 slaves out-of-state in 1790-1800, 44,000 during the next decade, 72,000 between 1810-1820, 75,000 over the next ten years, and 120,000 from 1830 to 1840, but the Old Dominion's free black population, nevertheless, kept on growing — to 12,866 (1790), 20,493 (1800), 30,575 (1810), 36,883 (1820), 47,348 (1830), and 49,852 (1840).[3] Whereas the number of free blacks had amounted to only 2.8 percent of the state's white population in 1790, it had reached 6.7 percent by 1840.

---

1. The counties were Jefferson, Clark, and Floyd on the southern border, Vigo and Knox in the west, and Randolph, Wayne, and Rush on or near the border with Ohio.
2. In the eight counties cited, Kentucky natives made up 23.8 percent of the total population in 1850, compared to a statewide average of 17.3. In two counties with large free black populations — Randolph and Wayne — the proportion of migrants from the Bluegrass State was considerably lower, namely, 3.7 and 4.3 percent, respectively. If these two are excluded, the percentage of Kentuckians in the remaining six counties rises to 30.5. However, Indiana counties with the highest proportion of Kentucky-born whites had relatively small free black populations, suggesting that, when a certain density of whites from this state was reached, blacks tended not to settle in these counties. More than 46 percent of the populations of Crawford, Perry, Putnam, and Sullivan had come from Kentucky, but these counties contained only 58 free blacks in 1830, compared to a total white population of 19,441. (According to the census conducted that year, Crawford had no free black residents.) This amounted to only 0.2 percent of the white population. Statewide in 1830, the free black population equaled 2.0 percent of the white population. For these figures, see Rose, "Hoosier Origins," Table 2, 208-9.
3. Figures on slave exports are taken from Philip D. Troutman, "Mapping the Migration of Enslaved Virginians," *Geographies of Family and Market: Virginia's Domestic Slave Trade in the 19th Century*, Geostat Center: Collections, University of Virginia Library: http://fisher.lib.virginia.edu/collections/stats/slavetrade/. Statistics on Virginia's free black population are derived from federal census data.

Nationally, the proportion of free blacks also appeared likely to rise, as the slave system could no longer absorb all non-white labor. The growth of the Cotton Belt and the extension of slavery there would continue to siphon off large numbers of bondsmen, but other areas of the country, like the Old Northwest, were not suited to slave-based agriculture. The profitable use of slaves would continue to be confined to states where cotton and tobacco could be grown commercially on large plantations. These apparent limitations on the spread of the "peculiar institution" presented a grave dilemma to racist whites in both the North and the South. If the "Slave Power" could not absorb new territory, the number of blacks living in existing or prospective slave states would increasingly outstrip the number whose labor was needed. For economic reasons, pressure to free these costly, superfluous blacks would inevitably mount. The manumitting of slaves that had already happened in Virginia would eventually take place in Kentucky, Tennessee, Alabama, Mississippi, Arkansas, and Louisiana. If other free states would not let these black freemen in, the two races would be forced to coexist in an "unnatural" way that would lead to the "amalgamation" of blacks and whites — that is, sexual relations.[1] Racial barriers upheld by slavery would fall, and whites would be "degraded" morally as well as physically by close contact with an innately "inferior" people. If emancipated slaves did leave for Northern states, they provoked even more intense hostility. "Free" states like Ohio, Illinois, and Indiana had discovered that they, too, were vulnerable to this kind of racial "mingling." In the absence of slavery, whites in such states had little institutional protection against in-migrating blacks, and this made them especially hostile and defensive. In the North, Alexis de Tocqueville observed, "the white no longer distinctly perceives the barrier that separates him from the degraded race, and he shuns the Negro with the more pertinacity since he fears lest they should some day be confounded together."[2] As

---

1. Fear of miscegenation lay at the root of much hostility toward blacks. Anxiety over interracial sexual relations was expressed in anti-abolitionist cartoons such as one titled "Practical Amalgamation," which appeared in 1839. Drawn by Edward W. Clay, it depicted a white woman kissing a black man on a couch, while, sitting beside this couple, a black woman was having her hand kissed by a kneeling white man. See Henry Mayer, *All on Fire: William Lloyd Garrison and the Abolition of Slavery* (New York: St. Martin's, 1998), illustrations following p. 232.

   After having spent a couple of years touring the United States around 1830, an English visitor concluded: "The white people, in the greater part of the country, have invincible prejudices to the intermarriage of persons of different colours, and to any intermixture between them. Nothing is more repugnant to the feelings of an American, than the mere idea that a female relation should be connected with a man of colour. The mere emancipation of the slaves, therefore, would still leave them a totally separate, and, of course, an unhappy set of beings." James Stuart, *Three Years in North America*, 2nd ed., rev. (Edinburgh: Robert Cadell, 1833), vol. 2, 61.

2. De Tocqueville, *Democracy in America*, trans. Arthur Goldhammer (New York: Library of America, 2004), vol. 1, part 2, 395.

pointed out earlier, white workers in the Northern states also worried that relocating blacks would secure low-paying jobs and jeopardize the whites' economic status.

It is no exaggeration to state that, by 1800, the growing free black population had superseded slavery as the most explosive racial issue the nation faced. The vast majority of white Americans were simply not prepared to countenance a future in which blacks were an integral, let alone equal, component of society. Dismay over this prospect spanned regional boundaries and the political spectrum. It encompassed the nation's leaders. Thomas Jefferson had been one of the first nationally prominent figures to warn about the inherent incompatibility of the two races and the need to keep them apart. In his *Notes on Virginia*, he had insisted that integration was impossible: "Deep rooted prejudices entertained by the whites; ten thousand recollections, by the blacks, of the injuries they have sustained; new provocations; the real distinctions which nature has made; and many other circumstances, will divide us into parties, and produce convulsions which will probably never end but in the extermination of the one or the other race."[1] After Gabriel Prosser — aided by black freemen — organized a slave revolt in Richmond in 1800, many whites came to dread that what Jefferson had warned about might soon become a reality. Henry Clay shared Jefferson's doubts about racial coexistence, declaring that, "because of unconquerable prejudice resulting from their color, [free blacks] could never amalgamate with the free whites of this country." At a meeting held in the nation's capital in December 1816 to discuss a scheme for sending the free black population to Africa, Clay confessed that he was a slave owner "without chagrin" and believed that "of all classes of our population the most vicious is that of the free colored."[2]

Even a leader of the antislavery movement like Benjamin Lundy — born to a Quaker family in New Jersey — accepted that the white and black races could not live together on American soil. He called for the latter's removal, just as Clay and many other Southern slaveholders did. White belief in racial separation would remain deeply entrenched throughout the antebellum period and beyond. Abraham Lincoln embraced this credo early in his career and continued to profess it as late as 1862, when he told a group of 500 black leaders gathered at the

---

1. Jefferson, *Notes on Virginia*, 138.
2. Clay's remarks at the first session of the American Colonization Society, quoted in http://beatl.barnard.columbia.edu/students/his3487/lembrich/seminar62.html. Speaking at the society's first annual meeting, in January 1818, Clay expressed sympathy for the plight of free blacks in the United States, while describing their presence as a "great moral evil threatening to contaminate all parts of society." See remarks of Clay, "First Annual Report of the Society for Colonizing the Free People of Color in the United States & the Proceedings of the Society at Their Annual Meeting, in the City of Washington, January, 1818," (Washington: D. Rapine, 1818), 18: http://memory.loc.gov/cgi-bin/query/r?ammem/murray:@field(DOCID+@lit(lcrbmrpt1503divl))

White House that: "You and we are different races. We have between us a broader physical difference than exists between any other two races ... Your race suffers very greatly, many of them, by living among us, while ours suffers from your presence. In a word, we suffer on each other ... But for your race among us there would be no war, although many men engaged on either side do not care for you one way or another. It is better for us both therefore to be separated."[1] A supposed progressive such as Horace Greeley also warned against bringing the races together. Blacks, he wrote in a letter written a few years after the Civil War, "are an easy, worthless race, taking no thought for the morrow, and liking to lean on those who befriend them. Your course [encouraging blacks to come to Washington] aggravates their weaknesses ... Unless you change your course speedily and signaly [sic], the swarming of blacks to the District will increase, and the argument that Slavery is their natural condition will be immeasurably strengthened."[2]

***

If blatantly discriminatory laws could not stop blacks from settling in predominantly white territories and states, then other ways of keeping the two races separate had to be explored. One alternative policy was *colonization* — the voluntary removal of freed slaves *en masse* to some uninhabited part of the United States or to a foreign country. Thus depopulating the nation of blacks not only would "restore" the continent to its racially homogenous state (ignoring the prior and continuing presence of Native American and Hispanic peoples), but also would do so in a relatively benign manner. Transported to some remote location, out of the reach of whites, blacks could establish their own free and just society (emulating white America's), without having to confront white hatred and oppression. Instead, thus segregated, blacks could develop more fully — individually and as a people — and fulfill their (albeit somewhat limited) human potential. Whites could feel good about allowing blacks to flourish on their own, without having to besmirch their consciences with remorse over inflicting any additional physical or psychological harm upon this "unfortunate" race.

While colonization was wreathed in such benevolent sentiments, it had its origins in more pragmatic self-concerns — namely, dismay over the growing free black population in the United States, most notably in the South. Among others, Thomas Jefferson had advocated a policy of gradual emancipation of the slaves in accord with the spirit of the American Revolution, but he had realized that such

---

1. Abraham Lincoln, speech delivered at the White House, 14 August 1862. For a summary of Lincoln's remarks, see *The Collected Works of Abraham Lincoln*, ed. Roy C. Basler (New Brunswick: Rutgers University Press, 1954), vol. 5, 370-5.
2. Letter of Horace Greeley to Josephine Griffing, 7 Sept. 1870, *History of Woman Suffrage* (New York: Source Book Press, 1970), vol. 1, 36-7.

a step would have to be combined with the removal of these freed blacks in order to forestall an otherwise unavoidable mixing of the races. So separating blacks from whites would restore "moral purity" on the North American continent.[1] In his *Notes on Virginia*, Jefferson had specifically recommended relocating manumitted slaves on the Western frontier. In addition, he had suggested that slaves convicted of serious crimes be transported back to Africa.[2] A few years later, the Virginia House of Delegates had considered setting up a penal colony for such undesirable blacks, but nothing ever came of this proposal.[3] In 1811, the former president had affirmed his backing for returning all blacks to Africa, stating in a letter that such action was "the most desirable measure which could be adopted for gradually drawing off" the nation's non-white population.[4]

Support coming from such an illustrious figure gave the colonization movement considerable clout. Other Southern slaveholders embraced Jefferson's goal of removing blacks to Africa once they were no longer enslaved, but the logistical and financial hurdles of repatriation proved insurmountable. Schemes to set up a black colony were thwarted by the steady, inexorable growth of the country's slave and free black populations. Jefferson himself would confide in an 1824 letter to the historian Jared Sparks that he had calculated it would cost the astronomical sum of $36 million, spent over a 25-year period, to export the one-and-a-half million slaves then residing in the United States.[5] In addition, many Southern whites were not enthusiastic about freeing the slaves, even if this step were linked to the blacks being taken back to Africa.[6]

After languishing for several years, the colonization movement was revitalized in the aftermath of the Great Awakening by a Congregationalist minister in Rhode Island named Samuel D. Hopkins. The evangelical spirit then coursing through American Protestant churches had led to the formation of numerous "benevolent societies," which sought to save souls and eradicate social ills like drinking and gambling. Hopkins, a Yale-educated disciple of Jonathan Edwards, was looking for a cause of his own to embrace and came up with an ingenious plan for simultaneously improving the lot of blacks, spreading the Gospel, and

---

1. Ronald T. Takaki, *Iron Cages: Race and Culture in Nineteenth-Century America* (New York: Knopf, 1979), 37.
2. Jefferson, *Notes on Virginia*, 138, 143, 146.
3. P.J. Staudenraus, *The African Colonization Movement, 1816-1865* (New York: Columbia University Press, 1961), 4.
4. Quoted in Henry Noble Sherwood, "The Formation of the American Colonization Society," *Journal of Negro History* 2:3 (July 1917), 210. http://docsouth.unc.edu/church/sherwood/sherwood.html.
5. Letter of Jefferson to Jared Sparks, 4 Feb. 1824, in Thomas Jefferson, *Writings* (New York: Library of America, 1984), 1485.
6. Henry Noble Sherwood, "Early Negro Deportation Schemes," *Mississippi Valley Historical Review* 2:4 (March 1916), 493.

solving the nation's racial dilemma. In 1793, he proposed that freed slaves, once they had been properly educated and steeped in Christian doctrine, be sent across the Atlantic to serve as missionaries in Africa. Hopkins' untimely death in 1803 took much of the momentum out of this plan, however. It required the efforts of a more politically savvy clergyman, the Rev. Robert Finley, to make colonization a viable national cause. Finley, a Presbyterian of Scotch-Irish heritage, was serving the New Jersey community of Basking Ridge, in a northern part of that state in which the population of free blacks happened to be exceptionally large.[1] Convinced that educating blacks would never overcome white antipathy toward them and enable them to become assimilated in American society, he decided to build support for the more efficacious strategy of repatriating former slaves on the other side of the Atlantic.[2]

On November 6, 1816, the 44-year-old minister convened a group of students, professors, and townspeople in Princeton, site of his alma mater, and announced his intention of establishing a national society made up of influential citizens to lobby the Congress for funds to ship blacks back to Africa and establish a colony for them there. Those attending the meeting agreed that blacks could only find true freedom and "rise to that condition to which they are entitled by the laws of God and nature" outside the United States, in a country of their own making.[3] Finley conceded their removal would also benefit whites, since free blacks were "unfavorable to our industry and morals." Seeking financial backing, he traveled to Washington in December. There, his brother-in-law, Elias Caldwell, an attorney who held the post of clerk of the Supreme Court, put Finley in touch with Francis Scott Key. Another well-to-do lawyer and former slave owner, Key had recently gained fame for penning the words to "The Star-Spangled Banner" after observing the ineffectual British bombardment of Baltimore's Fort McHenry. Key was also deeply committed to the evangelical cause, and he embraced Finley's scheme wholeheartedly. He also helped to spread word about black colonization among the capital's movers and shakers. When Finley arrived at Washington's Dana Hotel shortly before Christmas, on the evening of December 21, he found a formidable gathering of would-be allies waiting for him around the table.

---

1. In 1810, Somerset County, which included Basking Ridge, had more free blacks — 1,500 — than any other county in the state. Staudenraus, *Colonization Movement*, 15.
2. One historian has pointed out that a Virginia slave owner, Charles Fenton Mercer, who feared the rise of a free black working class also figured prominently in promoting colonization, both in Washington and in his native state. See Douglas R. Egerton, "'Its Origin Is not a Little Curious': A New Look at the American Colonization Society," *Journal of the Early Republic* 5:4 (Winter 1985), 463-80.
3. Quoted in Sherwood, "American Colonization Society," 214.

This included several figures of national stature, from different parts of the country and with varying views on the question of slavery. Representing Northern interests, along with Finley, was a New Hampshire congressman, Daniel Webster. But, the South's more pressing need to deal with a growing free black population was evident in the number and stature of political leaders from that region attending this meeting.[1] Along with Key, a Maryland native, was James Monroe's secretary of the treasury, William H. Crawford, who had previously represented Georgia in the U.S. Senate. Another Virginian present, John Randolph, was a member of one of that state's wealthiest and most distinguished families — and the owner of several hundred slaves.[2] Another slaveholder in attendance was Richard Bland Lee, brother of the famed Revolutionary War hero, "Lighthorse Harry" Lee, and a former member of Virginia's congressional delegation. Bushrod Washington, a Supreme Court Justice and slaveholding nephew of George Washington, was also present.[3] And the person who dominated this wintry Washington meeting and set its tone was one of the South's most gifted politicians — an ambitious and highly talented Kentucky lawmaker by the name of Henry Clay.

Since having been first elected to the House in 1811, Clay had served as Speaker for six subsequent sessions of Congress. As an articulate "War Hawk," he had helped rally public opinion behind the conflict with Great Britain and subsequently been dispatched to Europe as one of the U.S. negotiators to draft the Treaty of Ghent ending the War of 1812. A native of Virginia, Clay had risen to prominence and wealth in Kentucky by dint of his courtroom successes as a trial lawyer and his marriage to Lucretia Hart, member of a prosperous and socially prominent Lexington family. After leaving the House in 1815, Clay had returned to his 600-acre Ashland estate in that city, but had not abandoned his fervent hopes of someday rising much higher in the political firmament. Although, as one of Kentucky's largest landholders, he owned some 50 slaves, Clay harbored no great love for the "peculiar institution" and was inclined to support gradual emancipation. Interest in colonization had already surfaced in Kentucky as the number of free blacks seeking to settle in the state had soared after the War of 1812, and additional public lands had been put up for sale. In

---

1. In 1819, the president and nine of the 14 vice presidents of the American Colonization Society hailed from Southern states and the District of Columbia.
2. Upon Randolph's death, in 1833, all 400 of his slaves were freed.
3. Bushrod Washington was chosen to be the first president of the African Colonization Society at the group's first annual meeting, on 1 Jan. 1817. He had recommended that his aunt, Martha Washington, free the slaves she had inherited after her husband's death. However, Bushrod Washington had kept slaves of his own at Mt. Vernon and, in 1821, he was severely criticized for transporting 54 slaves to Louisiana, thus separating them from their families. See article on Bushrod Washington, *Dictionary of American Biography*, ed. Dumas Malone (New York: Charles Scribner's Sons, 1964), vol. 10, 509.

October, 1815, a newly formed Kentucky Colonization Society sent a petition to Congress, asking that territory further west "be laid off as an asylum for all those negroes and mulattoes who have been, and those who may hereafter be, emancipated within the United States . . ."[1] Clay liked Finley's plan to return blacks to Africa, but he saw this mainly as a way of solving the "problem" of an unwelcome racial minority in a white-dominated society, rather than offering greater freedom and hope to oppressed slaves.[2] In an address delivered in 1827, Clay would call free people of color a "common evil" afflicting states both north and south of the Mason Dixon Line.[3]

Indeed, it became apparent that Rev. Finley's original desire to rescue enslaved blacks from an intolerable plight was going to be given short shrift in the nation's capital. During this December meeting, discussion focused on ridding the country of a morally "contaminating" free black population. Former slaves were regarded as a socially undesirable element, like drunkards or thieves.[4] John Randolph spoke for many of those present when he declared that free blacks represented "a great evil," "a nuisance," and "a bugbear to every man who feels an inclination to emancipate his slaves."[5] He added that his fellow slaveholders considered free blacks "one of the greatest sources of insecurity" in the country.[6] (Largely for this reason, Randolph would require the 383 slaves he owned to leave Virginia after they were manumitted under the terms of his will in 1833.[7]) The danger of future slave revolts weighed heavily on the minds of the Southerners gathered at the Dana Hotel.[8] Less than two years before, in March 1815, a white storekeeper in Virginia named George Boxley had hatched a scheme calling for armed slaves to seize the cities of Richmond and Fredericksburg.[9] (A

1. American State Papers, Misc., II, 278, 279. Quoted in Sherwood, "Colonization Society," 211.
2. Clay had dismissed the alternative plans of transporting blacks further west or to Haiti as too expensive. See Stuart, *Three Years in America*, 60.
3. Henry Clay, "Speech of the Hon. Henry Clay Before the American Colonization Society in the Hall of the House of Representatives," January 20, 1827 (Washington: Columbian Office, 1827), 12.
4. George M. Frederickson, *The Black Image in the White Mind: The Debate on Afro-American Character and Destiny, 1817-1914* (New York: Harper & Row, 1971), 8.
5. Quoted in Sherwood, "Colonization Society," 222.
6. Quoted in Staudenraus, *Colonization Movement*, 29. George Tucker, a professor of law at the College of William and Mary, predicted that free blacks would become "caterpillars of the earth, and the tigers of the human race" if they were not removed from the country. *Ibid.*, 3.
7. Schwarz, *Migrants Against Slavery*, 78. Randolph left $8,000 in his will to pay for relocating these former slaves.
8. "The opinion was widespread in the whole South that if the time ever came when two races, as distinct as the white and the black, occupied the same territory, and were numerically not greatly unequal, a war of extermination was almost inevitable." Early Lee Fox, *The American Colonization Society, 1817-1840* (Baltimore: Johns Hopkins Press, 1919), 27.
9. Boxley was inspired by his "egalitarian" Christian beliefs. For more details on his efforts to organize a slave revolt, see Schwarz, *Migrants Against Slavery*, 88-100.

few years after this meeting in Washington, white anxiety would intensify when Denmark Vesey, a self-educated free black from the West Indies, organized the largest slave uprising in American history. As many as 9,000 blacks are believed to have been involved in this Charleston, South Carolina, plot, which was only foiled because a black domestic servant tipped off his master.[1]) It was agreed from the outset that colonization should not be designed to free the slaves, only to dispose of those who had gained their liberty. Acknowledging the motives that had brought so many Southerners to the hotel, Clay emphasized that he had no wish "to touch or agitate in the slightest degree, a delicate question, connected with another portion of the colored population of this country" — namely, emancipation.[2] Upholding the rights of white property owners mattered more than advancing those of blacks.

That animus toward blacks motivated this gathering can be gleaned from remarks delivered a decade later by Eliphalet Nott, Presbyterian minister and longtime president of Union College, to a group favoring black repatriation. After denouncing slavery as "repugnant," the Connecticut-born Nott declared:

> Here there can be no amalgamation. Our manumitted bondsmen have remained already to the third and fourth, as they will to the thousandth, generation — a distinct, a degraded, and a wretched race. When therefore, the fetters, whether gradually or suddenly, shall be stricken off — and stricken off they will be — from those accumulating millions yet to be born in bondage, it is evident, that this land, unless some outlet be provided, will be flooded with a population as useless as it will be wretched; — a population which with every increase, will detract from our strength, and only add to our numbers, our pauperism, and our crimes. Whether bond or free, this will be forever a calamity. When then in the name of God, should we hesitate to encourage their departure?"[3]

The colonization plan soon attracted considerable support, both in the halls of Congress and among the public at large, indicating how worried many white

---

1. For the impact of Vesey's uprising, see Phillips, *Slave Economy*, 206ff. An even more disquieting insurrection was led by Nat Turner, in Southampton County, Virginia, during late August of 1831. Turner and his fellow slaves massacred close to 60 whites before they were apprehended, tried, and executed. This revolt sent shock waves through the South for decades. At the time, a local newspaper reacted with these words: "What strikes us as the most remarkable thing in this matter is the horrible ferocity of these monsters. They remind one of a parcel of blood-thirsty wolves rushing down from the Alps; or rather like a former incursion of the Indians upon the white settlements. Nothing is spared; neither age nor sex is respected — the helplessness of women and children pleads in vain for mercy." "The Banditti," Richmond *Enquirer*, 30 Aug. 1831. www.pbs.org/wgbh/aia/part3/3h499t.html.
2. Quoted in Sherwood, "Colonization Society," 223. However, in 1820, the group's annual report stated that "hope of the gradual and utter abolition of slavery, in a manner consistent with the rights, interests, and happiness of society, ought never to be abandoned." See "The Third Annual Report of the American Society for Colonizing the Free People of Color of the United States," (Washington: Davis and Force, 1820), 29. http://memory.loc.gov/cgi-bin/query/r?ammem/murray:@field(DOCID+@lit(lcrbmrpt1506))
3. Quoted in Stuart, *Three Years in America*, 61-2.

Americans were about having to coexist with an increasing black population.[1] When John Randolph delivered a memorial on behalf of the group, originally designated "The American Society for Colonizing the Free People of Color of the United States," before Congress in January, 1817, it spurred prompt action. President Monroe, with whom Rev. Finley had spoken shortly after his arrival in the District, gave the proposal his tacit blessing, despite doubts about whether he had the authority to purchase land in Africa for a black colony.[2] Monroe had been convinced since the days of Gabriel's rebellion that the future safety of Southern whites hinged upon removing the threat posed by free blacks. (At that time, the rebels had planned to kidnap Monroe, who was then governor of Virginia. Monroe and then-President Jefferson had secretly corresponded in 1801 about promoting black colonization.) In Virginia, where sentiment among whites to get rid of unwanted and potentially dangerous ex-slaves was strongest, the House of Delegates and Senate gave colonization a ringing endorsement.[3] So, during the next few years, did the legislatures of Maryland and Tennessee, as well as church groups in those two states and North Carolina.[4] By 1827, lawmakers in Ohio, New Jersey, Rhode Island, Connecticut, Vermont, Kentucky, and Indiana had also gone on record in support of removing free blacks from the country.[5]

Congress was more equivocal. A House committee debated the merits of colonizing free blacks and issued a positive report in February 1817. This affirmed that separating former slaves from whites was essential, due to their "distinct character and relative condition." If a black colony were to be established on the North American continent, this would only lead to "quarrels and destructive wars" between it and the United States, so a site on the coast of Africa — preferably in Sierra Leone — was much more desirable. The committee advised the Congress to urge that President Monroe start negotiations with the British government leading to the absorption of freed slaves into that West African colony.[6] However, the full House did not get around to considering this report during its winter session. Many representatives, particularly those from the South, stood squarely behind the committee's recommendations, but others

---

1. This was the issue raised in the American Colonization Society's memorial to the Congress, dated 1 Feb. 1820.
2. Staudenraus, *Colonization* Movement, 51. However, Monroe did not publicly endorse the scheme until 12 Mar. 1819.
3. The lower chamber of the Virginia legislature voted for colonization by a margin of 135-9.
4. In June 1818 the General Assembly of the Presbyterian Church also urged its members to support the efforts of the ACS.
5. Fox, *American Colonization Society*, 79.
6. See *Annals of Congress*, House of Representatives, 14th Congress, Second Session, 11 February 1817, 939-40. The Committee on African Slave Trade also called for the President to urge other governments to end the trans-Atlantic trafficking in slaves.

prevaricated. They worried about the costs involved. Northern politicians also understood that repatriating the nation's free blacks was not a pressing issue in their overwhelmingly white half of the country. Congress asked for more information about the prospects for establishing an African colony before voting any funds for that purpose. It was not until 1819 that the House and Senate agreed to make a financial commitment — allocating $100,000 to help return a group of Africans who had been discovered on board a ship bound for American shores in violation of the nation's slave trade ban.[1]

Across the country, enthusiasm for colonization tended to be strongest where the free black population was either large or growing fast; those states contributed the most financially to this effort.[2] Indeed, the number of freed slaves in a given state – Northern or Southern — corresponded closely with the level of white support for black removal. To spread the word about its repatriation scheme and solicit the private donations needed to carry it out, the American Colonization Society (or ACS, as it was then known) set up auxiliary societies in various states. By the end of 1817, these were operating in Baltimore, Philadelphia, Ohio, Virginia, and New York.[3] Not coincidentally, the states with the largest free black populations were — in order of size — Virginia, Maryland, Pennsylvania, New York, and North Carolina. Other local chapters were subsequently established in Georgia and the Carolinas. But some Southern slave owners feared that freeing blacks, even if this were combined with sending them out of the country, would undermine the "peculiar institution."[4]

In Ohio, where the free black population more than doubled between 1810 and 1820, and where fear of being inundated with discarded slaves from other states was great, the antislavery Union Humane Society — founded in 1815 by the New Jersey-born Quaker, Benjamin Lundy — endorsed the plan.[5] Several Ohio counties sent off petitions in favor of colonization to Congress in 1817, and the following year the state legislature duly voted to urge Ohio's representatives in Washington to push for adoption.[6] But local interest in transporting ex-slaves out of the United States did not really grow until free blacks began "flocking"

---

1. J. H. Mower, "The Republic of Liberia," *Journal of Negro History* 32:3 (July 1947), 266.
2. Of the $14,031.05 raised to send the first shipload of black colonists to Africa, $8466.58 came from Maryland and the District of Columbia, while another $2,900.05 from the Southern states. Fox, *American Colonization Society*, 65.
3. In the latter, a desire to rid the state of its 30,000 free blacks was largely instrumental in building support for colonization. But donations remained sparse. Staudenraus, *Colonization Movement*, 76.
4. Frederickson, *Black Image in the White Mind*, 27.
5. Some whites foresaw the day when blacks would outnumber them in Ohio. Sherwood, "Movement in Ohio," 57.
6. Ratcliffe, "James Riley," 80. He notes that the resolutions adopted by both houses of the Ohio legislature were "cursory."

into the Ohio Valley in the mid-1820s.[1] This linkage is evident in the state legislature's voting, in 1824, to support gradual emancipation as long as it was coupled with repatriation.[2] Three years later, the state's governor, Jeremiah Morrow, told Ohio's lawmakers they had to approve funds for this purpose.[3] To popularize this goal, an Ohio branch of the Colonization Society was established in November of 1827. As it turned out, no black from the Buckeye State actually made the voyage across the Atlantic to Africa until 1833.[4]

In neighboring Indiana, support for resettling blacks overseas arose not out of any wish to free them, but out of a similar distaste for their presence.[5] Overt white hostility made black Indianans receptive to the idea of colonization. As early as 1817, one prominent white resident wrote to the ACS saying free blacks living near Vincennes were "desirous of going to Africa."[6] The state's auxiliary of the Colonization Society first convened in January 1820, in Corydon, in southern Indiana.[7] In Illinois, whites also responded positively to the notion of removing the state's blacks. The gathering convened by Rev. Finley in Princeton received favorable front-page coverage in the territory's chief newspaper, *The Western Intelligencer*, then edited by 24-year-old Daniel Cook, a leading foe of slavery. [8]

---

1. Staudenraus, *Colonization Movement*, 136-7. In 1819, fears were aroused in Ohio that a group of several hundred slaves freed in Virginia were going to be brought to settle in the southwestern corner of the state. One correspondent to the society reported that these blacks were "perhaps as depraved and ignorant a set of people as any of their kind, and that their departure is hailed with joy by all those who had lived in their neighbourhoods." See letter to the editor, *Hillsborough Gazette* (Ohio), dated May 1819, in "The Second Annual Report of the American Society for Colonizing the Free People of Color, of the United States," 119-20; http://memory.loc.gov/cgi-bin/query/r?ammem/murray:@field(FLD001+91898199+).
2. Two of these counties — Delaware and Harrison — were outside southern Ohio, indicating that opposition to blacks was not confined to migrants from the slave states.
3. Sherwood, "Movement in Ohio," 59. Morrow, a Pennsylvania native of Scotch-Irish heritage, had served in Ohio's territorial legislature, as well as the 1802 constitutional convention.
4. *Ibid.*, 66.
5. See, for example, Levi, *Reminiscences*, 223.
6. Letter of a "respectable gentleman" to Bushrod Washington, 15 October 1817, in "The First Annual Report of the American Society for Colonizing the Free People of Color, of the United States," 1 Jan. 1818, 26. http://memory.loc.gov/cgi-bin/query/r?ammem/murray:@field(FLD001+91898198+).
7. The first statewide organization was established in November 1829. Esarey, *History of Indiana,*, 326.
8. "Colony of Free Blacks," *Western Intelligencer*, 15 January 1817. In an editorial comment the following week, it was noted that the proposal to colonize blacks had been "taken up by a large number of the most influential men in the union, with Mr. Clay at their head." The writer — presumably Cook — went on to endorse the plan of exporting blacks to Africa: "By this means, it is expected to christianize and civilize the heathens and idoleters [*sic*] of that quarter of the globe. Thus the sum of humanity appears to have begun to beat upon our land, with an expansion of its rays to foreign climes. This subject we expect will become a national one — and with the aid of *American* omnipotence, it will certainly succeed."

On the other hand, the movement did not gain much ground in New England, where free blacks were largely invisible.[1] Some Northern ministers, mainly Quakers, did agree with Finley that colonization would help end black "degradation" in this country.[2] However, most Northerners wanted the Southern states to shoulder the financial burden for getting rid of former slaves. Some, particularly in the Midwest, welcomed this plan, hoping that deportation would keep blacks from migrating northward if larger numbers of slaves were manumitted in the South or the chattel system was abolished. But many whites felt colonization was wildly "utopian" and could never be pulled off. And, in some circles, the motives of the ACS were suspect. Observed one visitor from England: "Most of the people of the Northern States look upon this society with the contempt which its hypocrisy deserves."[3] At first supportive of gradually freeing the slaves and returning them to their native continent, abolitionist leaders like William Lloyd Garrison would eventually denounce the scheme as "proslavery" — designed to perpetuate the system by eliminating a threat to it.[4] He and others in the antislavery movement felt the best elements in the free black population were being shipped overseas. Other sympathetic whites regarded the sending of former slaves thousands of miles away to live on the coast of a faraway and uncivilized continent as "cruel" and "inhumane."[5]

Somewhat unexpectedly, most black leaders also looked upon this opportunity to live in "freedom" with a jaundiced eye. Although prominent free blacks in Richmond applauded the plan in principle, they admitted that they personally had no desire to go back to Africa. They preferred to resettle somewhere in the American West.[6] Black opponents in the North were more outspoken. In Philadelphia, a group of 3,000 freemen protested over being asked to leave the "luxuriant soil" of the only home they had ever known because they were considered a

---

1. Connecticut had the largest free black population in New England in 1820. But most of its 7,870 former slaves were concentrated in large cities, particularly in the southeastern part of the state. Emancipated slaves had moved into urban areas as their number throughout the state had increased. The four counties of New London, Fairfield, New Haven, and Hartford accounted for over 69 percent of these black residents.
2. Frederickson, *White Image in the Black Mind*, 7, 18. Many ministers felt that it was God's will that blacks return to Africa and bring Christianity to these "heathen" shores. For a detailed discussion of their motives, see Philip C. Wander, "Salvation through Separation: The Image of the Negro in the American Colonization Society," *Quarterly Journal of Speech* 57:1 (Feb. 1971), 57-67.
3. Blane, *An Excursion Through the United States*, 227.
4. After denouncing slavery and coming out in support of gradual emancipation and colonization during a speech before the Colonization Society at Boston's Park Street Church on 4 July 1829, Garrison joined the group in 1830, naively believing it sought to promote black freedom. After less than a year, however, he resigned from the Society, realizing it had no interest in emancipating slaves. For the text of Garrison's remarks, see http://teachingamericanhistory.org/library/index.asp?document=562.
5. Dumond, *Antislavery*, 128.
6. Staudenraus, *Colonization Movement*, 32, 34. Cf. Louis R. Mehlinger, "The Attitude of the Free Negro Toward African Colonization," *Journal of Negro History* 1:3 (June 1916), 276.

"dangerous and useless part of the community."[1] Black assemblies in places like New York, Trenton, Harrisburg, and Nantucket denounced colonization as a veiled attempt to drive them out of the country. They, too, had no hankering for Africa. The ACS sought to overcome such "repugnance" by convincing blacks that "the land of their fathers is not cursed by a perpetual and unvarying sterility, nor inhabited by the most sanguinary and ferocious savages."[2] But these efforts were largely unsuccessful, although a small number of blacks did elect to move to the colony of Liberia — a locale chosen after an initial attempt to settle in Sierra Leone failed. Over the next three decades, most organizations representing free blacks remained firmly opposed to any plans for repatriation:[3] one survey found that twice as many of these groups rejected colonization as favored it.[4] American blacks simply did not think of Africa as their homeland.[5] If anything, white attempts to coax them into leaving only unified blacks against this idea.[6] Since neither the government nor the Society was prepared to force blacks to leave the country against their will, this negative attitude greatly hampered the colonization movement.

But it was the expense involved, more than either black reluctance or white skepticism, which stymied the Colonization Society's grandiose scheme. Using Jefferson's estimate of $36 million a year for fully a quarter century, one can readily see why this was the case. The entire federal budget for 1817 was less than $26 million. Jefferson had hoped to finance the transporting of blacks outside the United States through the sale of public lands,[7] but his projection of expenditures did not include the costs of purchasing territory on the West African coast or building up a colonial infrastructure. Furthermore, the former president had based his estimate on the then-existing population of 1.5 million blacks. By 1830, this figure had surpassed 2.3 million, making the undertaking that much more expensive.[8] Even if resettlement were limited to the nation's 225,000 black freemen, the costs would have been prohibitive under economic circumstances of that day. The recently ended War of 1812 had drained the nation's coffers, siphoning off some $1.1 billion dollars, or 13 percent of the gross domestic prod-

---

1. Quoted in Mehlinger, "Attitude of the Free Negro," 277.
2. "First Annual Report," 10.
3. See, for example, Nevins, *Fruits of Manifest Destiny*, 515.
4. See Curtis, *Status of Free Blacks*, Table A1, "Free Black Organizations for and Against the African Colonization Movement," A-8. He lists 28 groups opposed and 14 in favor of colonization.
5. Cf. Litwack, *North of Slavery*, 25.
6. Free blacks who rejected colonization held their first national convention in Philadelphia in September 1830. See Thornbrough, *Negro in Indiana*, 78.
7. William W. Freehling, "The Misnamed Purchase, the Diffusion Prayer, and the Coming of the Civil War" (Paper delivered at the University of Texas's Bicentennial Conference on the Louisiana Purchase, 21 Feb. 2003), 6.
8. The Board of the Colonization Society tried to downplay costs by suggesting that "thousands" of blacks would pay their own way. See "First Annual Report," 12.

uct. This amounted to $120 per person.[1] A more modest and affordable proposal put forth by the colonization group called for merely *stabilizing* the black population — repatriating only the same number of free blacks (or, alternatively, slaves and freemen) that was added annually to the total. Figuring that each black colonist would cost $50 to take to Africa, the Society's board calculated these funds could be raised through a poll tax of between 2.5 and 25 cents per person.[2]

Given the political costs associated with imposing even such a small tax, leaders of the American Colonization Society had no choice but to turn to private individuals for help. But they, too, were short on cash. War had curtailed trade with Europe, mainly with England and France, and slowed the nation's economy. The export of farm products essentially stagnated during the decade after the conflict ended.[3] A protective tariff imposed on cheap British imports resulted in a sharp decline in sales of U.S. cotton abroad. After 1815, the reopening of European markets initially enabled American agriculture to expand, but then overproduction caused prices to collapse. Unable to repay bank loans, many farmers lost their assets. The Bank of the United States imposed a tight money policy. This financial contraction led to the Panic of 1819. Due to its impact, westward expansion of the U.S. economy virtually ground to a halt. As a result, most Southern planters were in no position to open their checkbooks to underwrite the costs of sending hundreds of thousands of blacks back across the Atlantic.[4] The Colonization Society did successfully solicit donations from its growing list of members in the 1820s, but a lack of resources continued to plague its efforts, which focused on purchasing slaves for the purpose of repatriating them.

Because of all of these problems, settlement of Liberia proceeded slowly and with many setbacks. Within weeks after the arrival of the first ship bringing colonists to Africa in 1820, 22 of the 88 blacks and all three whites accompanying them succumbed to yellow fever. Other vessels brought additional settlers to a healthier coastal site, and a colony was established on this 80-million acre loca-

---

1. The amount spent on the war is calculated in terms of current dollars. For these figures, see William D. Nordhaus, "The Economic Consequences of War with Iraq," 29 October 2002, Table 2, 7. www.econ.yale.edu/-nordhaus/iraq.doc. By contrast, costs for the Vietnam War equaled 12 percent of GDP.
2. The Society concluded that it would require the smaller tax to relocate the 5,000 free blacks annually being added to the U.S. population. "Third Annual Report," 33. Some years later Henry Clay used similar figures in defending the group's goal as attainable. See Clay, *Speech*, 7-9.
3. From a value of $40 million in the years 1810-1820, agricultural exports only rose $2 million during the following decade.
4. By the end of 1819, the Colonization Society acknowledged that its undertaking remained "precarious and unsteady, unless it be nourished by the resources, as well as countenanced by the authority of the Federal Government." See "Second Annual Report," 11.

tion, but neighboring Africans resented this intrusion into their territory and mounted a series of attacks. Meanwhile, barely a trickle of American blacks arrived on African shores. After a decade of existence, only 1,420 colonists had made the voyage to Liberia.[1] To put this figure in perspective, it was roughly equivalent to the increase in the free black population of just one state — Kentucky — during the same period.[2] Despite the fact that whites there strongly backed the repatriation of former slaves because of recent violent uprisings, fewer than 300 free blacks had left the Bluegrass State for Africa by 1850.[3] Black unwillingness to leave the United States accounts for these low numbers, as does waning white interest in freeing slaves in the South: the booming of King Cotton following widespread introduction of the cotton gin created a need for more slaves, and the market prices which they could command rose accordingly.[4] With the exodus of former slaves proceeding so slowly, it was obvious that the ACS could not possibly accomplish even its more modest goal of staying abreast of the steady increase in the nation's black population. Assailed by both pro- and antislavery groups, the Colonization Society saw its contributions decline until the 1850s, when the expansion of slavery further west re-ignited interest among Negrophobic whites.[5]

Meanwhile, the slave system was advancing across the South. In the years between 1812 and 1819, three more slave states — Louisiana (1812), Mississippi (1817), and Alabama (1819) — entered the Union, extending the political and demographic base of the "peculiar institution" into the lower Mississippi Valley. To enlarge and sustain cotton production, large numbers of slaves were brought into this part of the country. By 1820, the combined black population in these newest additions to the "Slave Power" exceeded that of any other state except

---

1. Records of the ACS show that 1,420 persons had made the trip to Liberia between 1820 and 1830. See Fox, *Colonization Society*, 89. Fox draws on statistics contained in the "African Repository," 292. According to another sources, 2,885 persons had been sent to Liberia by 1833. Over the next two decades, 7,836 American blacks made the journey to Liberia. Of these, nearly half — 3,868 — had been freed on condition that they emigrate. See Mehlinger, "Attitude of the Free Negro," 301.
2. Kentucky had 2,759 free blacks in 1820 and 4,917 a decade later.
3. Coleman, *Slave Times in Kentucky*, 287. In one 1826 incident, 77 slaves on a boat bound for New Orleans murdered five white men and then fled north to Indiana. In August 1829, a group of slaves on another vessel killed two whites and wounded a third in an unsuccessful bid for freedom. Howard, *Evangelical War*, 15.
4. Prices for slaves rose after 1808, when the slave trade was abolished. They remained high until the 1840s, when prices for cotton declined.
5. For example, between 1848 and 1851, the legislatures of Ohio, Indiana, and Illinois either reaffirmed or raised their barriers against black migration. Desire to get rid of blacks already residing in this part of the country was widespread. A leading figure in this effort was Dr. Daniel Drake of Cincinnati. In the words of one historian, "Drake spoke for many in his region in expressing the fear that, unless something were done, the Midwestern states might at some point be inundated by a flood of Negroes pouring across the Ohio River." Frederickson, *Black Image in the White Mind*, 134.

Virginia and the Carolinas. The proportion of slaves in the regional population had reached 40 percent, surpassing what it was at that time in such an Old South bastion of slavery as Virginia.[1] A band of land heavily populated by blacks now stretched all the way down both sides of the Mississippi River from the Illinois-Missouri border to the delta at New Orleans and across almost all of present-day Louisiana.[2] Furthermore, except for some largely unsettled parts of northern Mississippi, eastern and western Alabama, western Georgia, and Spanish-held Florida, slaves thickly populated the entire southeastern quadrant of the United States.

At the same time, free blacks were growing in number and moving west as well. Whereas a map of the country in 1810 shows former slaves residing mainly along the Atlantic seaboard, two decades later Southern states like Kentucky, Tennessee, and Louisiana had considerable numbers of them, as did Ohio and Indiana in the North.[3] Out of the U.S. total of 312,603 free blacks in 1830, 44,078 — or 14 percent — lived in states that did not border the Atlantic. In those states, they made up 1.4 percent of the population, versus 2.8 percent nationwide. From the point of view of racially xenophobic whites, it was not this demographic statistic per se that was disconcerting, but the fact that so many free blacks were being forced to migrate north and west, toward them, as a result of black codes that had been adopted in several Southern states with large concentrations of emancipated slaves.[4] Virginia, Kentucky, Delaware, Ohio, Indiana, Illinois, and — when it joined the Union in 1821 — Missouri all either prohibited the entry of free blacks or required those already in residence to move out or face stiff punishment. These race-based laws channeled many freemen into the Ohio Valley, despite blacks laws on the books there.

Along with the inexorable advance of the slave system into the nation's interior, the failure of both the black laws and the colonization movement to halt the northward migration of free blacks or to reduce their number made whites living in the Old Northwest anxious about their future. Some reacted by taking matters into their own hands, responding to the coming of blacks into their communities with intimidation and violence.[5] As had occurred among earlier generations, this growing disquietude over black encroachment induced many

1. In 1820, 39 percent of Virginia's population were slaves, whereas the comparable figures in Georgia and South Carolina were 43 percent and 51 percent, respectively
2. See Map 142, "Proportion of Slaves to Total Population, 1820," *Historical Atlas of the United States*, ed. Clifford Lord and Elizabeth H. Lord (New York: Holt, 1953), 90.
3. The 1830 federal census lists the free population of these states as follows: Kentucky, 4,917; Louisiana, 16,710; Tennessee, 4,555; Ohio, 9,568; and Indiana, 3,629.
4. Virginia had a free black population of 36,889 in 1820, second only to Maryland, with 39,730.
5. D.W. Meinig, *The Shaping of America: A Geographical Perspective on 500 Years of History*, vol. 2, *Continental America, 1800-1867* (New Haven: Yale University Press, 1993), 300.

non-slaveholding whites to contemplate pulling up stakes and heading toward the newest promised land on the American frontier — Missouri. In that newly opened territory, the perennial struggle for land and survival between whites who could not abide blacks and those who could not make a good living without them would be renewed. The outcome of the conflict there would, in turn, set in motion the final push of racially threatened pioneers across the Great Plains, by way of the Oregon Trail, to the Pacific.

VI. RACIAL STRIFE CROSSES THE MISSISSIPPI

While Americans and European immigrants were streaming into the Old Northwest from the East and Upper South, looking for better economic opportunities in a part of the country that was racially "free," settlers below the Mason Dixon Line were also considering a move further west. They, too, wanted affordable land and a better future. But different needs fueled their eagerness to migrate. And different destinations seemed to meet these needs. For the Southern slaveholding class, large expanses of rich, virgin soil were a perennial necessity — both to sustain the large-scale production of crops like tobacco, hemp, and wheat and to provide employment for the slave laborers in whom they had invested so heavily. For the majority of less well-off, non-slave-owning farmers, the overriding concern was economic survival. These "plain folk" had formed the vanguard of settlers heading inland from the Atlantic coast,[1] but had been displaced as the plantation system had followed in their wake, acquired vast landholdings, and become the dominant force in Kentucky, Tennessee, Alabama, and Mississippi. In the most fertile parts of these states, wealthy slaveholders had pushed up land prices, made it increasingly difficult for yeoman farmers to sell their produce at a profit, and forced many of them to move on to agriculturally less desirable areas. Slaves had also taken away the jobs of many skilled and semi-skilled white laborers. Increasingly, as in colonial Virginia, power and wealth came to be concentrated in the hands of those who owned the rich, alluvial soils in these Southern states — and large numbers of slaves.[2]

This displacement of frontier homesteaders by large landowners was most pronounced in Kentucky's Bluegrass, where slaves became the primary work-

---

1. This was especially so in the Cotton Belt. See, for example, Gavin Wright, *The Political Economy of the Cotton South: Households, Markets, and Wealth in the Nineteenth Century* (New York: W.W. Norton, 1978), 15.

force.[1] For these varying reasons, many Southern whites at either end of the region's economic and social hierarchies were ready to break new ground in the early decades of the 19th century.

But where would they go? The Ordinance of 1787 and the constitutions subsequently adopted by Ohio, Indiana, and Illinois had effectively put the Old Northwest off limits to slavery and thus made it unattractive to Southern planters. Small, independent farmers and laborers in Kentucky, Virginia, and Tennessee looked north with more ambivalence. As was pointed out earlier, thousands of them did decide to quit the South and move across the Ohio River in order to take advantage of the greater growth and prosperity the "butternut" states offered — as well as to escape the presence of slaves. But moving to the North was not an easy choice. In many ways, the territory beyond the Ohio was alien and unappealing. From an agricultural perspective, the Old Northwest did not suit Southern methods. With the exception of fertile bottomlands, soils there did not yield the crops that these yeomen had cultivated for generations. Nor were the climate or terrain north of the Ohio similar to those found in the slave states. To most Kentuckians and Tennesseans, this northern region was culturally unfamiliar as well; bound to the South by family and community ties, they were loath to rend these asunder.[2]

As a result, Southern farmers, rich and poor alike, turned their attention to the inviting, apparently unsettled territory that lay to the west — lands newly acquired by the United States on the far side of the Mississippi River.[3] Obtained by the administration of Thomas Jefferson from a cash-poor Napoleon for $15 million in 1803, the 800,000 square-mile Louisiana Purchase was the single largest addition to the nation's domain. Overnight it doubled the size of the United States. Stretching from the Canadian border in the north to the Gulf of Mexico in the south, and all the way to the foothills of the Rockies in the West, this immense wilderness — nearly four times the size of present-day France — promised to fulfill the pent-up appetite of settlers for new, unoccupied land.[4]

---

2. In his analysis of the economic transition in the Deep South, Ulrich Phillips pointed out that the concentration of slaveholdings changed dramatically between 1820 and 1860. For example, in Crawford County, Georgia, the proportion of white families owning slaves increased by only 8.5 percent during this period, but the average number of slaves owned more than doubled. Phillips, "Southern Black Belts," 801.

1. By 1830, slaves made up one third of that region's population.

2. Many historians have noted how important these human ties were in determining migratory decisions. For Southern farmers, such factors often mattered more than the appeal of fertile land in other parts of the country. See, for example, Meyer, *Making the Heartland Quilt*, 17.

3. In fact, an estimated 5,000 Native Americans were then living in the territory. Walter A. Schroeder, "Populating Missouri, 1804-1821," *Missouri Historical Review* 97:4 (Nov. 2003), 266.

4. One 1803 estimate put the total number of persons living within the bounds of the Louisiana Purchase at 49,473. This meant that there was a population density of one person for every 16 square miles. Goodwin, *Trans-Mississippi West*, 74.

For several years they had besieged Jefferson with petitions asking that the federal government buy these Western lands, and, shortly after this occurred, several hundred would-be migrants — mainly Scotch-Irish recently priced out of choice lands in the Ohio Valley[1] — gathered on the banks of the Cumberland River to await the go-ahead signal from Washington.[2] But, frustratingly, this did not come for over a decade. Some impatient pioneers from Kentucky, Tennessee, Virginia, and North Carolina did venture across the Mississippi, but several impediments kept a major migration from taking place.[3] For one thing, not all Americans had embraced Jefferson's vision of an agrarian "empire of liberty" in the West.[4] New Englanders were especially reluctant to see the nation grow so dramatically and their region thus lose its preeminent position. Indeed, only a bare majority of congressmen from the North voted to ratify the treaty awarding the Louisiana Territory to the United States.[5] This lack of enthusiasm for peopling lands west of the Mississippi then thwarted federal efforts to organize that expanse into smaller units and put parcels of public land up for sale.

A second major deterrent was the war against England, which commenced on June 18, 1812 — just two weeks after Congress had finally voted to create the Missouri Territory (covering roughly the same area as the future state) out of the land purchased from France and to promote settlement there. This conflict diverted Americans' attention away from the frontier and reduced the resources available for developing it. Indian hostility during the war also slowed settlement of Missouri. Even though the Osage tribe had ceded its holdings north of the Missouri River in 1808, violence against intruding white settlers did not end. The Shawnee chief Tecumseh aligned his forces with the British and stepped up raids on American outposts in the west, further discouraging any advances into the Missouri Territory until after the Native American leader was slain, at the Battle of the Thames, in October 1813.[6] In the territory itself, the coming of war all but ended the burgeoning fur trade, depriving frontiersmen of their chief livelihood. The prevalence of diseases along Missouri's rivers and the devastating New Madrid earthquake of 1811-12 also gave would-be migrants reason to hang back. In addition, the government's decision not to offer public lands for sale helped to keep this new frontier largely uninhabited until after the

---

1. Gerlach, *Settlement Patterns in Missouri*, 16. Cf. Milton D. Rafferty, *The Ozarks: Land and Life* (Fayetteville: University of Arkansas Press, 2001), 55.
2. Ellen Churchill Semple, *American History and its Geographic Conditions* (Boston: Houghton Mifflin, 1904), 103.
3. Most of the earliest American settlers traveled from these states down the Ohio River to the Mississippi. See Gerlach, *Settlement Patterns*, 13.
4. Richard White, *"It's Your Misfortune and None of My Own": A History of the American West* (Norman: University of Oklahoma Press, 1991), 62-3.
5. Robinson, *Slavery in the Structure of American Politics*, 395.
6. A peace treaty was signed with the Shawnees and several other tribes on 29 Sept. 1817.

war ended.[1] Farmers from Kentucky who had previously been entangled in land disputes there were reluctant to move to privately held acreage in Missouri where ownership was also unresolved.[2]

This delay built up pressure to push westward, much as had occurred along the Virginia fall line prior to 1763. When peace finally came, after the U.S. Senate ratified the Treaty of Ghent in February 1815, there was a surge of settlers across the muddy Mississippi. Over the next four years, as many as 50 wagons a day crossed the river at the major jumping-off point of St. Louis.[3] By and large, this was a Southern exodus: the states of Kentucky, Tennessee, and Virginia accounted for the vast majority of trans-Mississippian pioneers.[4] In the words of one observer of this human tide, "a stranger to witness the scene would imagine that Virginia, Kentucky, Tennessee and the Carolina's [sic] had made an agreement to introduce us as soon as possible to the bosom of the American family. Every ferry on the river is daily occupied in passing families, carriages, Negroes, carts & & — respectable people apparently able to purchase large tracts of land."[5] An upturn in agricultural prices following the War of 1812 gave them impetus. So did the exhaustion of tobacco-growing land in their home states. This movement west was further spurred by the issuing of "bounty land" warrants to Revolutionary War veterans, under a bill passed by Congress in May of 1812. This federal act opened up a total of two-and-a-half million acres in the

---

1. An official census undertaken in 1817 recorded a population of 19,218. *Memorial and Resolutions of the Legislature of the Missouri Territory and A Copy of the Census of the Fall of 1817* (Washington: Gales & Seaton, 1819), 6.
2. Schroeder, "Populating Missouri," 269. A Board of Land Commissioners was established to resolve these questions, but this legal process took a number of years.
3. Billington, *Westward Expansion*, 468.
4. In 1850 there were 69,694 free white and black natives of Kentucky living in Missouri; this number equaled more than 28 percent of all the white and free black Missouri residents born elsewhere in the United States. Tennesseans numbered 44,970, and Virginians 40,777. "Place of Birth," *Mortality Statistics of the Seventh Census*, 38-9. All told, migrants from these three states accounted for nearly 64 percent of all whites and free blacks born outside the state. However, in some counties the proportion of Upper South natives was much higher. According to one survey, fully 80 percent of the earliest settlers in Randolph County, north of the Missouri River, hailed from Kentucky alone. Walter H. Ryle, "A Study of Early Days in Randolph County, 1818-1860," *Missouri Historical Review* 24:2 (Jan. 1930), 220. In 1870, 49.4 percent of Boone County residents came from the Bluegrass State. James W. McGettingan, Jr., "Boone County Slaves: Sales, Estate Divisions, and Families, 1820-1865," *Missouri Historical Review* 72:2 (Jan. 1978), part 1, 176. Up until 1870, more Missourians came originally from Kentucky than from any other state; thereafter, Illinois became the largest supplier of migrants to the Show-Me State. See Table P-3, "Native Whites Born in Missouri by Selected States of Residence and Native Whites Resident in Missouri by Selected States of Birth, 1870-1950," *Population Redistribution and Economic Growth: United States, 1870-1950*, ed. Simon S. Kuznets (Philadelphia: American Philosophical Society, 1957), vol. 1, 272.
5. Quoted from the *Missouri Gazette* (St. Louis), 26 Oct. 1816, in Rohrbaugh, *Land Office Business*, 90.

Missouri Territory, although much of this land was not considered highly desirable for farming.[1]

The allure of bountiful acreage and easy money to be made on it proved irresistible. Visions of a Western "promised land" were instilled by glowing accounts written by early pioneers, government officials, and other travellers eager to promote settlement west of the Mississippi. About a year before the Missouri Territory was created, the lawyer and author Henry Marie Brackenridge spent several months sailing up the Missouri and then published an account of his adventures — one of the first detailed descriptions of this great wilderness. Brackenridge marveled at what he saw in its interior, near the French outpost of *Cole sans Dessein*: "The beauty and fertility of the surrounding country cannot be surpassed." Further up the river, he declared: "The Missouri is now, what the Ohio was once, the PARADISE OF HUNTERS." Animals like bison "exist in numbers almost incredible." After leaving the last white settlement behind, Brackenridge and his companions reached hauntingly deserted stretches of the river which inspired this poetic rhapsody:

> . . . there is a pleasure in giving wing to fancy, which anticipated the cheerful day when this virgin soil will give birth to millions of my countrymen. Too happy, if my after fame might survive on the plains of the Missouri. If the vast expanse of ocean is considered as a sublime spectacle, this is even more so; for the eye has still greater scope, and, instead of its monotony, now reposes upon the velvet green, or feeds on the endless variety of hill and dale . . . The mind naturally expands, or contracts, to suit the sphere in which it exists — the immeasurable immensity of the scene, the intellectual faculties are endued with an energy, a vigor, a spring, not to be described.[2]

Writing in 1818, a former clerk in the U.S. General Land Office depicted the Missouri Territory in equally enticing, if more prosaic language. He lauded the "first rate soil," ample "springs of excellent water," and "abundance" of timber to be found in eastern Missouri, as well as the equally desirable bottomlands along the Missouri River and the adjacent "inexhaustible" expanse of prairie for grazing cattle and other livestock. There were also large deposits of minerals, chiefly lead, waiting to be mined. Farmers could expect to produce 30 bushels of wheat or 60 bushels of corn per acre, and cotton could be grown commercially in the southern part of the territory.[3] The very same year, William Darby brought out a popular *Emigrant's Guide to the Western and Southwestern States and Territories*, also

---

1. Much of this land ended up being purchased by non-veterans. Schroeder, "Populating Missouri," 273-4.
2. Henry Marie Brackenridge, *Journal of a Voyage up the River Missouri, Performed in Eighteen Hundred and Eleven*, 2nd ed. (Baltimore: Coale & Maxwell, 1815), 29, 57, 105.
3. Nicholas Biddle van Zandt, *A Full Description of the Soil, Water, Timber, and Prairies of Each Lot, or Quarter Section of the Military Lands Between the Mississippi and Illinois Rivers* (Washington: P. Force, 1818), 98, 100.

lauding southern Missouri for its "extremely productive soil and moderate climate." Here, Darby wrote, "is a place of great, and we anticipate, not delusive promise."[1] Within just a few years, these early hopes were being fulfilled. A newspaper reported that planters from Virginia and Maryland were harvesting tobacco of the same high quality as was grown in their home states, and that "No part of the world produces better wheat." Furthermore, Missouri's miners had already located enough lead to meet the entire world's need for this ore.[2] In the Ozark Mountains, there was an abundance of pine needed for construction and other purposes.

Descriptions like these, the widespread availability of virgin land, the return of peace, and easy access down the Ohio convinced many settlers living south of that river to head west. But now, unlike before the war, these included families of means. Repeating the migratory sequence in colonial Virginia and Kentucky, the first wave of squatters, small farmers, and backwoodsmen was quickly supplanted by members of the planter elite looking to increase their wealth in the new territory. Here, too, Frederick Jackson Turner's thesis that settlement of the frontier reinforced democratic values and practices does not hold up. Once again, land policies favored the well to do. When the federal government first put public lands in Missouri — some five million acres — up for sale in 1818, it required a minimum purchase of a quarter section — or 160 acres — at two dollars per acre or more.[3] Since Washington was not extending any credit, would-be buyers had to come up with $320 in hard cash. This was a considerable sum, given the fact that per capita income in the United States was then only $1,287.[4] Many farmers with modest incomes were thus shut out of this initial offering.

In the main, only speculators and prosperous planters could afford these large tracts.[5] The former bought and sold land for considerable profit as the frenzy over Missouri real estate intensified. Slaveholders saw the rich, relatively inexpensive bottomlands of central Missouri as ideally suited to growing cotton and tobacco for commercial sale.[6] The soaring demand for cotton after the War of 1812 gave them added incentive to secure new holdings across the Missis-

---

1. William Darby, *The Emigrant's Guide to the Western and Southwestern States and Territories* (New York: Kirk & Mercein, 1818), 139.
2. *Arkansas Gazette*, 3 Dec. 1822, quoted in "Missouri in 1822: Reprint from *The Arkansas Gazette*," *Missouri Historical Review* 16:3 (April 1922), 337.
3. David D. March, *The History of Missouri* (New York: Lewis Historical Publishing Co., 1967), vol. 1, 247.
4. For this figure, see James McGuire, "Development Database: Income," http://woodstock.wesleyan.edu/acsocsci/jmcguire/table/income.htm.
5. Newspapers in 1818 typically advertised tracts for sale in the 320-1,500-acre range. Buying up large acreage by speculators was quite common. This practice drove up prices and caused anger among less affluent settlers. See, for example, letter of "A Missouri Farmer" to the Printer, *Missouri Gazette & Public Advertiser*, 1 Jan. 1819.

sippi.[1] In no time, almost all choice land on both sides of the Missouri River was grabbed up by the well-to-do. A local newspaper reported that, as of March 1819, a total of 107,000 acres had been sold.[2] Less affluent farmers continued to face major financial obstacles in moving to Missouri. Spiraling prices put more farmland out of their reach.[3] Squatters fumed while their right under the Preemption Act of 1814 to purchase the public lands they had occupied at the minimum price was withheld for five long years.[4] And numerous settlers in the part of Missouri devastated by the 1812 New Madrid earthquake had their claims bought up by unscrupulous speculators. Then a sudden drop in agricultural prices following the Panic of 1819 left small farmers with less cash to buy what was left. Many with too little money at hand had to resort to becoming squatters in order to establish homesteads across the Mississippi.

Hence, one saw large numbers of well-to-do, "respectable" families heading west. As one territorial newspaper somewhat hyperbolically reported in the spring of 1819, caravans from Kentucky and Tennessee were "flowing through St. Charles [on the Missouri west of St. Louis] with men servants and maid servants, their flocks and their herds, remind[ing] the citizens of the patriarchal ages . . . some turn to Boon's Lick, some to Salt River — lands of promise. The tinkling bells, the cloud of dust, the throng of hogs and cattle, the white headed children, the curly headed Africans, smiling infancy, blooming virgins, athletic manhood, and decrepit age, altogether form groups too interesting to be painted by the pencil of Teniers."[5] In October alone, some 3,000 persons swarmed through St. Charles on their way to Boon's Lick, in central Missouri.[6] Soon the tide of migrants into Missouri assumed truly epic proportions. After nearly dou-

---

6. By 1850, 43 percent of whites owning slaves in central Callaway County had migrated from Virginia, and 39 percent from Kentucky. Philip V. Scarpino, "Slavery in Callaway County, Missouri: 1845-1855," *Missouri Historical Review* 71:1 (Oct. 1976), part 1, 22.

1. From a low of just over 10 cents a pound in 1811, cotton prices on the New York market soared to a high of nearly 35 cents in 1817. See "Prices of Slaves in Four Markets and of Cotton Prices at New York, 1795-1860," Phillips, *Life and Labor in the Old South,* 177.

2. *Missouri Gazette,* 9 June 1819, cited in Harrison A. Trexler, "Slavery in Missouri Territory," *Missouri Historical Review* 3:3 (April 1901), 181.

3. Fertile tracts along the Missouri River was selling for as much as six dollars an acre in the spring of 1819 — three times the minimum amount originally set for public lands. R. Douglas Hurt, "Planters and Slavery in Little Dixie," *Missouri Historical Review* 88:4 (July 1994), 397. Speculators bought up much of the highly desirable bottomland and then sold this at a considerable profit. See James Flint, *Early Western Travels, 1748- 1846,* vol. 9, *Flint's Letters from America,* ed. Reuben Gold Thwaites (Cleveland: Arthur H. Clark, 1905), 129-30. Flint noted that as a result, "much of the best land, mill-seats, and other local advantages are withdrawn form the market at the first public sales."

4. Rohrbaugh, *Land Office Business,* 103-4.

5. *Missouri Gazette,* 9 June 1819, quoted in Hattie M. Anderson, "Missouri, 1804-1828: Peopling a Frontier State," *Missouri Historical Review* 31:2 (Jan. 1937), 169.

6. Article in *Franklin Intelligencer,* cited in E. M. Violette, "Early Settlements in Missouri," *Missouri Historical Review* 1:1 (1906), 51.

bling between 1804 and 1810, the territory's population more than tripled over the next decade, reaching 66,586.[1] This rate of growth was comparable to what had occurred in the Old Northwest during its early pioneer period. In the fall of 1810 alone, an estimated 12,000 people passed through St. Charles during one ten-week stretch. The Harvard-educated minister (and prolific writer) Timothy Flint observed a hundred persons trek through this Missouri River settlement in a single day, in a caravan made up of nine wagons, accompanied by scores of horses, cattle, pigs, and sheep, as well as an equally large number of slaves.[2]

The early settlement of Missouri and the introduction of slavery there were closely related. Original hopes — expressed by Thomas Jefferson in 1784 — that all land acquired by the United States west of the Appalachians would remain forever "free" were not realized. Ironically, Jefferson himself played a key role in dashing these hopes, when, as president in 1804, he declined to support prohibition of the "peculiar institution" throughout the Louisiana Territory.[3] This newly opened frontier appealed to well-to-do Southerners precisely because the chattel system of labor could thrive there. Slavery was not unknown in Missouri. Black bondsmen had existed on these lands since the days when the French had established their first permanent outposts early in the 18th century.[4] By 1800, some 883 slaves were living in eastern Missouri, and when the American government took possession of the Louisiana Territory in 1803, the number of blacks was estimated at 1,320. By 1810, it was close to 3,000, out of a total of 19,783.[5] To slaveholding Southerners contemplating a move to Missouri, the fact that slave labor had already proven its worth there was encouraging.[6] So was Congress's

1. For Missouri population figures during the territorial period see Schroeder, "Populating Missouri," 265.
2. Anderson, "Missouri, 1804-1828," 169.
3. This was proposed in a bill introduced by Connecticut congressman James Hillhouse. William E. Miller, *Arguing About Slavery: The Great Battle in the United States Congress* (New York: Knopf, 1996), 181. On the contrary, Jefferson recommended that a "rigorous slave code" be enacted in this new territory. See Don E. Fehrenbacher, "The Missouri Controversy and the Sources of Southern Sectionalism," in *The South and Three Sectional Crises* (Baton Rouge: Louisiana State University Press, 1980), 12.
4. The French used black labor in their mining operations. The number of slaves in Missouri had risen significantly after the founding of Ste. Genevieve, in the mid-18th century. Lorenzo J., Greene, Gary R. Kremer, and Antonio F. Holland, *Missouri's Black Heritage*, rev. ed. (Columbia: University of Missouri Press, 1993), 8-9.
5. Census records put the 1810 slave population at 2,875. See Schroeder, "Populating Missouri," 266. For a similar figure see Harrison Trexler, *Slavery in Missouri, 1804-1865* (Baltimore: Johns Hopkins Press, 1914), 9. Another historian estimates the black population of Upper Louisiana to have been 1,552 in 1804. See William E. Foley, *A History of Missouri* (Columbia: University of Missouri Press, 1971), vol. 1, 50.
6. Some historians have argued that Missourians were initially opposed to slavery, but the early introduction of slaves in the territory, coupled with pro-slavery statements made shortly after the Louisiana Purchase, refute this claim. For a discussion of these assertions, see Trexler, *Slavery in Missouri*, 100-1.

interpretation of the terms under which France had sold this territory to the United States. Federal lawmakers decided that here, unlike in the Old Northwest, the right to keep slaves would be honored.

Jefferson's dream of a western domain reserved for self-reliant, democratic-minded yeoman farmers would thus come to naught. He expressed his regrets over this development in a letter to his Secretary of the Treasury Albert Gallatin: "How much better to have every 160 acres settled by an able-bodied militia man, than by purchasers with their hordes of Negroes, to add weakness instead of strength."[1] Of course, Jefferson bore some responsibility for this turn of events. But, in any case, slaveholding planters were not to be denied access to this agricultural bounty. With few settlers arriving from the free states of Ohio, Indiana, and Illinois until 1820, these newcomers from the South rapidly introduced the chattel system onto their Missouri estates. This massive infusion of blacks made a strong *de facto* case for the continuation of slavery in this territory.[2] Future prosperity from large-scale farming also seemed to depend upon it. One could scarcely imagine Missouri without it. As one well-to-do settler from Vermont advised his brother, who was also considering a move to the far side of the Mississippi, "There is one thing you must reconcile your mind to when you get in this region, that is the owning of slaves."[3]

However, because so many of the first arrivals came from Kentucky (often originally from Virginia), where slaveholdings were relatively small, Missouri did not evolve into a plantation state.[4] Instead, properties of various sizes were cultivated. Not far from sprawling tobacco- and hemp-producing estates sprang up modest-sized farms, on which grew corn, wheat, and other crops, tilled by the owner and members of his family, with the help of a few slaves.[5] These small

---

1. Quoted in Roger G. Kennedy, "The Louisiana Purchase," www.common-place.org: 3:3 (April 2003).
2. The number of slaves in Missouri increased by nearly 240 percent between 1810 and 1820. See Trexler, "Slavery in Missouri, 1804-1865," in *Slavery in the States: Selected Essays* (New York: Negro Universities Press, 1969), 11.
3. Quoted in William E. Foley, *The Genesis of Missouri: From Wilderness Outpost to Statehood* (Columbia: University of Missouri Press, 1989), 239.
4. In 1860, the average slaveholding was smaller in Missouri than in Kentucky — namely, 4.72. See Ryle, "Randolph County," 226. By the end of the antebellum period, only four percent of white heads of household in Missouri's "Little Dixie" region could be considered "planters" by virtue of owning at least 20 slaves. In the Deep South, the proportion of planters was three times as great. Hurt, "Planters and Slavery," 408.
5. Cf. Trexler, *Slavery in Missouri*, 16-18. He notes, for example, that of the 636 slaveholders in Cooper County in 1850, 173 owned only one slave, and 102 owned two. Just prior to the Civil War, the average size of slaveholdings in Jackson County, in the western part of Missouri, was 4.5, and in Pike County, bordering the Mississippi, it was 3.14. Trexler, "Slavery in Missouri," 17. In 1830, half of all Missouri slaveholders owned only between one and four slaves. See "Manuscript Census Schedules, Slaves, 1830, 1840, 1850, 1860," in R. Douglas Hurt, *Agriculture and Slavery in Missouri's Little Dixie* (Columbia: University of Missouri Press, 1992), appendix, 307. For a more recent analysis of the uneven distribution of slaves in "Little Dixie," see Robert W. Frizzell, "Southern Identity in Nineteenth-Century Missouri: Little Dixie's Slave-Majority Areas and the Transition to Midwestern Farming," *Missouri Historical Quarterly* 96:3 (April 2005), 241-3.

farms became more numerous than large littoral tracts as Missouri emulated the diversified economic development of other border states like Kentucky. And, much as had taken place there, relations between masters and their black bondsmen were generally informal and reasonably humane. Slaves worked beside whites in the home as well as in the fields, and they were considered part of the household.[1] Slave gangs were rarely seen on this frontier,[2] although owners did treat their chattel brutally on occasion.[3] Blacks thus became part of the territory's population without causing whites to draw a clear line between the races: Missouri became another "society with slaves," rather than a "slave society," as existed in the Deep South.

While Missouri was clearly pro-slavery in philosophy, the great majority of early settlers did not own slaves. Many were rugged frontiersmen who preferred to hunt and trap in the wooded interior and eke out a living without relying upon anyone else's help. Among these independent types was Daniel Boone, who, having lost almost all his property in Kentucky as a result of unpaid taxes and land disputes, settled on 850 acres north of the Missouri River, which were granted him in 1799. Other non-slaveholding migrants were yeoman farmers. Even as the "peculiar institution" was taking hold on the territory's best farmland, whites in this group bought up cheaper acreage away from the riverbanks. As they had done previously in Kentucky and Virginia, these "plain folk" opted to coexist with slaveholders: they accommodated themselves to an economic and social system that not only did not well protect their own self-interest but also put their way of life at risk.

Why did they do this? Because many Upland Southerners made a *different* choice — namely, to cross over to "free" soil in the Old Northwest — one has to wonder what prompted several thousand small, independent farmers to relocate to a territory where slavery was becoming firmly entrenched. There are several

---

1. Such an observation was made by a native of New England who visited Missouri during the antebellum period. See John G. Haskell, "The Passing of Slavery in Western Missouri," *Transactions of the Kansas State Historical Society* 7 (1901-02), 31. Peter H. Burnett, who later became a leader in the settlement of Oregon and then the first governor of California, moved to Franklin, Missouri, as a young boy, shortly before it became a state. Many years later, he recalled spending his first winter in a "large camp with a dirt floor," with the members of his family living on one side, and their black slaves on the other. Peter H. Burnett, *Recollections and Opinions of an Old Pioneer* (New York: D. Appleton, 1880), 7.

2. Trexler, *Slavery*, 27.

3. A visitor from England in 1846 was dismayed by the violence he saw inflicted upon slaves in isolated parts of Missouri. At New Madrid, he noted that "the condition of the negroes is least enviable in such out-of-the-way and half civilized districts, where there are many adventurers, and uneducated settlers, who have little control over their passions, and who, when they oppress their slaves, are not checked by public opinion, as in more advanced communities." Charles Lyell, *A Second Visit to the United States of North America*, vol. 2, (New York: Harper & Brothers, 1849), 182.

explanations. One is strictly economic. Whites who could not afford slaves could also not afford expensive real estate, and Missouri appealed to independent farmers because land there was considerably cheaper than comparable acreage north of the Ohio. By moving west of the Mississippi River these farmers could gain the most for their dollar. On top of this, many farmers of modest means saw long-term economic advantages in homesteading where the slave system had taken hold. They felt that the existence of the "peculiar institution" would eventually create greater prosperity for all whites.[1] Higher returns on land investments and greater profits from farming would ensue from the existence of this cheap labor force. As was noted above, Missouri also attracted many "free spirits" eager to strike out for the next untouched wilderness as their forebears had trekked across the Appalachians. Restless souls like Boone who could not abide to live in the crowded, "civilized" world of the Ohio Valley hankered after the greater personal freedom and independence that could be found across the Mississippi.

A third, compelling argument in favor of Missouri was the fact it was located along roughly the same parallel of latitude as Kentucky and Virginia. During the era of frontier settlement, American farmers tended to move to locales where they could grow the crops they knew, using time-tested methods, and on soils and in a climate equally familiar to them. This inclination kept them from straying far from a due westerly line.[2] For this reason, Missouri was logically the next step for many farmers from the Upper South to take in the 1820s and 1830s. Group cohesion and custom reinforced the decisions made by the earliest frontier families: friends, neighbors, and loved ones would usually follow the routes taken by these trailblazers and settle near them.[3] Once established, such migratory paths were difficult to deviate from: few settlers possessed the courage or eccentricity to branch off in some new and uncharted direction by themselves. Rather, as one historian has put it, "like stuck with like": migrants from one part of the country streamed across the continent like water flowing through a well-defined riverbed, recreating their unique form of life wherever they stopped to establish farms along the way.[4] So cultural continuity also played a major role in the choices made by Southerners — slaveholders and non-

---

1. Cf. March, *History of Missouri*, 400.
2. Some historians have argued that farming conditions outweighed the existence or absence of slavery in determining migratory decisions. See, for example, Lynch, "Westward Flow," 327.
3. "Little Dixie" counties bordering the Missouri River had particularly large percentages of residents originally from the slave states of Kentucky, Virginia, and Tennessee. In 1850, this proportion varied from a high of 42 percent in Lafayette County to 31 percent in Cooper County. See Table III, "Place of Birth by State for Settlers in Little Dixie," Hurt, *Agriculture and Slavery*, 55.
4. Oberly, "Westward Who?" 435.

slaveholders alike — to head for Missouri. For them, the chattel system was an integral part of the world they knew and in which they felt at home.[1]

Another reason why independent farmers from the South may have decided to migrate across the Mississippi is that the slave system was not as pervasive or as threatening to them economically in Missouri as it was in much of the South. True, the proportion of slaves in Missouri's population was nearly as high as it was in long-existing slave states — over 15 percent by 1820[2] — but the distribution of blacks was more geographically confined. They lived mainly in enclaves along the Missouri and Mississippi rivers, where large plantations had arisen. In fact, just eight river-bordering counties — Cape Girardeau, Ste. Genevieve, St. Louis, St. Charles, Pike, Montgomery, Cooper, and Howard — accounted for 80 percent of the 10,222 slaves living in the Missouri Territory.[3] Since "plain folk" farmers from the Upland South gravitated toward less fertile parts of the territory, where land was cheaper, they did not have to worry about unwelcome contact with black chattel.[4] This was especially so in the northern plains and in the southwestern foothills of the Ozarks.[5] Furthermore, as large numbers of non-slaveholding whites entered Missouri in the decades leading up to the Civil War, the proportion of slaves in its population declined sharply: from 15.3 percent in 1820 down to 9.7 percent in 1860. On the eve of that conflict, only about one white family in eight owned any slaves.[6] Thus, over time, the Show Me State became "whiter" and hence more appealing to settlers uncomfortable living near blacks.

In addition, since most slaveholding Missourians kept only two or three slaves, the "peculiar institution" was less visible — and less worrisome. The division between planters with large holdings and yeoman farmers who employed only a few or no slaves was not at all as clear in Missouri as it was in the Deep South. In relocating to the other side of the Mississippi, settlers of limited means

---

1. Partially for this reason, over half — 52.9 percent — of migrating Virginians had opted to settle in slave states by 1850. See Table 2, "Free Virginia-born people living in states outside Virginia, 1850 and 1860," Schwarz, *Migrants Against Slavery*, 9.
2. In 1820, the slave proportions of the populations in Kentucky and Tennessee were 22.4 percent and 18.9 percent, respectively.
3. At that time, in 1820, two counties — Howard, on the north shore of the Missouri, in the middle of the territory, and the one encompassing the city of St. Louis — had a combined slave population of 3,899, or 38 percent of the state's total.
4. When Missouri became a state, more than a fifth of all whites lived in counties with fewer than 500 slaves.
5. Gerlach, *Settlement Patterns*, 28, and Wiley Britton, "Pioneer Life in Southwest Missouri," *Missouri Historical Review* 16:3 (April 1922), part three, 393. At the time of the Civil War, only 60,000 blacks lived in the Ozarks. Rafferty, *Ozarks*, 60, *passim*.
6. Howard W. Marshall, *Folk Architecture in Little Dixie: A Regional Culture in Missouri* (Columbia: University of Missouri Press, 1981), 12. In some counties, of course, this percentage was much higher. For example, in 1859, 33.8 percent of white households in Pike County kept slaves, and in 1860, the proportion of white slaveholding families in Boone, Jackson, and Cooper counties was 33.2, 20.5, and 6.1, respectively. For these figures, derived from county tax records, see Trexler, *Slavery in Missouri*, 17.

did not have to fear domination by a landed elite. Instead, there was a fluid socio-economic continuum in this territory. With land plentiful, families of different income levels could live close to one another, and, as a result, an egalitarian milieu developed. Whites who kept many slaves, those who owned one or two, and those who had none did not constitute mutually exclusive social classes. Small farmers could aspire to join the ranks of slaveholders, or move up within that class. If they could buy a few slaves, this would allow them to cultivate more land, produce more crops, increase their income, improve their standard of living, and then purchase more slaves. Thus, Missouri appealed to them as a place where the chattel system supported white social mobility.

At the same time, a slave workforce gave many disadvantaged Southern whites a degree of psychological security they would otherwise not have had. In free states, poor whites were consigned to the bottom rungs of society, scorned and ridiculed by their "betters." However, when slaves were present, "plain folk" farmers had an even lowlier group to look down upon, and, consequently, they gained stature and self-respect. If they could manage to procure just a few slaves, they would rise significantly in the estimation of other whites.[1] Such a benefit could offset the potential threat to their livelihood posed by slave labor.

Moving across the river also protected non-slaveholding whites against another racial nemesis — the Ohio Valley's growing population of free blacks. This group was practically non-existent in Missouri. Fewer than 350 former slaves resided in the territory just prior to its entering the Union, and this number was 250 less than it was a decade before.[2] Whites in Missouri wanted to maintain this status quo. They were as allergic to free blacks as were most whites in the Old Northwest.[3] Delegates revising Missouri's first constitution several years later would reveal this animosity by voting emphatically for a provision that would prevent free blacks and mulattoes from entering the state.

Just how many Southern migrants fell into the category of small slaveholder cannot be accurately determined, as there are no extant data on the property holdings of Missouri settlers during this period. However, it is possible to draw some inferences from the statistical information that is available. In particular, facts on migration from Kentucky — the leading "feeder" state for antebellum Missouri — reveal some telling trends.

---

1. In Missouri, a farmer who owned six or more slaves was called "Colonel," while one who kept only one or two slaves was referred to as "Mister." However, owning just one slave gave a farmer of modest land holdings a higher stature than a non-slave-holding neighbor with more land. See Britton, "Pioneer Life," 394.
2. Foley, *Genesis of Missouri*, 254.
3. Germans migrating to Missouri were dismayed to find that the free black was "looked upon as a pest." A.A. Dunson, "Notes on the Missouri Germans on Slavery," *Missouri Historical Review* 59:3 (April 1965), 361.

One genealogical survey of over 4,000 Missourians who arrived from Kentucky during the 19th century has found that roughly 30 percent of these migrants came from just seven counties.[1] All of them — Bourbon, Madison, Fayette, Clark, Shelby, Mason, and Scott — are located in the eastern half of the state, within or close to the fertile Bluegrass region. During the first decades of the century, each of these counties had several demographic factors in common with the others. For one thing, because of their suitability for hemp and tobacco production, they had attracted large slaveholders and become densely populated with slaves: the proportion ranged from 40.3 percent of Fayette residents to 24.6 percent in Shelby.[2] The number of slaves in these counties continued to increase up until 1830. Secondly, as was previously noted, the trend in these counties during the antebellum period was toward a greater consolidation of slaveholdings in the hands of fewer owners. As this elite grew more powerful, small slaveholders and farmers without slaves were marginalized, and many of them had to leave the Bluegrass. This displacement is evident in the sharp decline of the white population in this part of Kentucky. By 1840, six of the seven counties in question had lost between 42.5 percent (Bourbon) and 13.8 percent (Scott) of their white residents; only Mason, situated some distance from the Bluegrass along the Ohio River, experienced a net gain of whites.[3]

While many of these uprooted farmers established new homesteads in other parts of Kentucky, others joined the exodus out of state — to the Old Northwest or to Missouri. Among those seeking to better their fortunes in the newly opened trans-Mississippian West were many small slaveholders. Their economic aspirations and status can be partially inferred from their choices of destination within Missouri. For the several thousand migrants documented in *Kentuckians in Missouri*, the most popular locales were counties along the Missouri River in the central and western parts of the state — Howard, Boone, Saline, Clay, and Platte. Several of these counties also happened to be ones in which slavery quickly took hold and spread. In 1840, Howard had the highest proportion of slaves (28 percent) in the state and the second largest total number (3,683), behind only St. Louis County. Boone had Missouri's fourth highest concentration of slaves, and the fifth highest largest population. Nearly one of three residents of Saline County was a slave. Only far western Platte and Clay, on or near the Kansas border, contained relatively small numbers of bondsmen. (Statewide,

---

1. For these migration demographics, see Stuart S. Sprague, *Kentuckians in Missouri* (Baltimore: Genealogical Publishing Co., 1983).
2. The slave proportion of the populations in these counties exceeded the statewide average of 22.3 percent in 1820.
3. Between 1818 and 1840, two of these counties — Shelby and Scott — decreased in size, so that these statistics do not reflect the somewhat larger decline in white population in the areas that they originally encompassed.

slaves made up just over 15 percent of Missouri's population in 1840.) Tellingly, the largest contingents of Kentuckians migrating to the Show Me State settled in counties that not only had numerous slaves, but also black population densities approximating what could be found in the counties they had left. The data indicate that these migrating Southerners — whether slaveholders or not — were not uncomfortable living and working among slaves. Despite their negative experiences in the Bluegrass, they apparently did not feel that slavery in Missouri presented a serious danger to their future well being. If they did have any strong aversion to the "peculiar institution," this was apparently outweighed by the likelihood of prospering on rich farmland where blacks were also being introduced.

It should be emphasized that the majority of small slaveholders and non-slaveholding whites did *not* migrate out of Kentucky or, indeed, out of any other Southern slave state, during the antebellum period. One can find evidence of this fact by looking at migratory statistics collected for the federal census in 1850. At that time, 257,643 white and free colored persons who had been born in the Bluegrass State were living in other states or territories, compared to 601,764 who were then still residing in Kentucky. By 1820, the white population of Kentucky was already close to half a million, or nearly twice the number of all native-born residents who had left the state — and who were still alive — three decades later. Similarly, 241,606 natives of Tennessee were residing outside its borders in 1850, but 585,084 were not.[1] This out-migration amounts to roughly 30 percent of the natives of each state. (Earlier censuses did not elicit information on migration, so it is impossible to determine what percentages of persons born in these states moved elsewhere before 1850.) A population outflow on a much larger scale occurs very rarely in human history — usually as a result of some overwhelming natural catastrophe, war, or political upheaval. Farmers of modest means did not face such dire circumstances in the Upper South. Their decision to leave their lands and strike out to the north or west was based on a calculation of the relative benefits of staying where they were versus staking out homesteads on new land. (This having been said, it should also be noted that several Atlantic slave states did experience a net loss of their native white populations before the Civil War — that is, the number of natives who moved to another state exceeded the in-migration of out-of-staters. For example, 387,531 free persons born in Virginia were residing in other states in 1850, whereas only 53,717 persons from other states had moved to the Old Dominion.)

---

1. Table XX, "Place of Birth of the White and Colored Population of the United States, 1850," *Mortality Statistics of the Seventh Census*, 38-9.

The weighing of pros and cons resulted in different destination choices for migrating Kentucky families. But there were also regional agricultural proclivities, and these also figured prominently in the decisions about moving on. Perhaps the single most significant factor was the type of crops that could be grown in a particular area. Cotton and tobacco had specific soil, climate, and labor requirements, and they directly influenced how these cash crops would be produced. Tobacco was most profitably grown on large tracts, tended and harvested by cheap slave labor. The rich soils and the moist, warm climate in which the plant thrived were not widespread, particularly in the border states, and so a small planter class, with large slaveholdings, could buy up the most desirable lands and control the tobacco market. Invariably, many small growers were forced out of business. However, such a consequence was less common where cotton was king.

The explosion in cotton production following Eli Whitney's invention of the cotton gin in 1793 breathed new life into the South's economy. This development helped offset a decline in tobacco farming, as prices fell and soils were exhausted at about this time. At just the right moment, the region had a new source of wealth. The prospect of reaping huge profits by growing cotton spurred migration to virgin lands in the Old Southwest — in the states of Tennessee, Mississippi, Alabama, Arkansas, and Louisiana. It also provided badly needed employment for slaves who would otherwise have been dangerously idle and a drain on their owners' finances. With prices for cotton in Europe high, Southern cotton plantations flourished. In short order, cotton became the largest commercial crop in the United States, accounting for as much as 60 percent of the total value of its exports in the years preceding the Civil War. Like tobacco, cotton was grown most efficiently on large plantations, by slaves. But, unlike tobacco at that time, cotton could also be produced at a profit on smaller farms. This was largely due to market demand: much as had occurred during the early years of tobacco growing in Virginia, high prices enabled both large and small farmers to make a living off the crop. Although wealthy plantation owners did drive most of the yeomanry and small slaveholders out of the choice alluvial regions, this removal did not necessarily lead to their being driven out of business, or out of the state. Instead, these small farmers continued to grow cotton as well as other crops, largely without the aid of slaves. Census-derived statistics from later in the century support this contention.

By 1860, over half — 54 percent — of the farms in cotton-producing counties of the New South did not employ slaves.[1] Furthermore, over 70 percent of the region's rural white population lived on farms with seven or fewer slaves.[2] In other words, on the eve of the Civil War, this part of the South supported a large population of small slaveholders. In addition, more than 10 percent of the farms in the so-called New South were small, consisting of between 10 and 19 acres; by contrast, only 4.2 percent of farms in the Old South fell into this category.[1] In 1860, some 38 percent of New South farms contained 50 or fewer acres; only 19 percent of those in the Old South did.[2] These statistics indicate that farmers of modest means and holdings had managed to hold their ground against an expanding plantation system in the Cotton Belt. Many of them did so by growing their own food along with the cash crop, as small farmers in Virginia had done in the 18th century. This diversification helped them withstand the increasing concentration of cotton production on slave plantations. In 1860, 82.5 percent of New South cotton was produced on farms having at least 10 slaves. But one has to bear in mind that these figures pertain to a period some four decades after the first major influx of settlers from the Old South. The distribution of land and slave ownership may well have been different at this earlier point.

In coping with the consolidation of cotton production, the yeoman farmers of the Cotton South appear to have been more successful than their counterparts in the tobacco-growing Upper South. In the latter region, making a profit was so dependent upon slave ownership that small farmers without such workers frequently could not compete. To survive, many of them had to move on to neighboring territories or states. The fact that land planted with tobacco was rapidly depleted added to this pressure to relocate. Their periodic displacement produced a geographically narrow stream of western migration.[3] It flowed chiefly out of Virginia into Kentucky, and from there divided into two branches — one flowing north across the Ohio River, the other westward to Missouri.

In opting for Missouri, poor Southern whites clearly considered many factors. As in the past, the search for better opportunities weighed heavily in their decision-making process. Considerations of race could pull these "plain folk" in two different directions. From a strictly economic perspective, they were generally better off living solely among their fellow whites: both free blacks and slaves could cost them jobs. Blacks also "degraded" white labor and supposedly weakened the moral fiber of the "superior" race. Sexually unrestrained black males

---

1. Table 2, "Percentage of Slaveless Farms in Cotton Regions of Eleven Southern States, 1860," James D. Foust, *The Yeoman Farmer and Westward Expansion of U.S. Cotton Production* (New York: Arno Press, 1975), 20. These statistics are derived from a sampling of 5,229 farms covering 382 of the 409 "cotton counties" in the South.
2. *Ibid.*, 93.
1. Table 10, "Size Distribution of Farms by Region, 1860," *ibid.*, 64.
2. *Ibid.*, 104.
3. Farmers in the tobacco-growing counties of Tennessee were an exception to this migration pattern. An analysis of farms in those regions in 1850 and 1860 does not indicate that the yeomanry was being forced off the land by the planter elite. See Donald L. Winters, "'Plain Folk' of the Old South Reexamined: Economic Democracy in Tennessee," *Journal of Southern History* 53:4 (Nov. 1987), 565-86.

endangered white women and risked creating an "amalgamation" of the races. Enslaved blacks were a constant danger: violent retaliation against their masters could come at any time. For all these reasons, yeoman farmers and skilled workers wanted nothing to do with blacks. But, as was noted above, the existence of a black subclass benefited poor and landless whites. In class-conscious Southern society, slaves made these somewhat marginal whites feel more psychologically and socially secure. This advantage, together with strong attachment to the cultural traditions associated with the "peculiar institution," kept many Southerners from moving outside the slave states. This was particularly true in the Cotton South. But this dependence upon a system that worked counter to their own economic self interest would become more troubling as "plain folk" whites moved further west. Competition from the slave system would only intensify, and pressure to escape from its pernicious impact would only grow stronger.

When Missouri sought to join the Union, these complex feelings about blacks would be subsumed by a single burning question: should this new state tolerate slavery within its borders? Up until this point, newly arrived settlers had not spent much time debating the merits of the "peculiar institution." For the most part, they had been busy buying land, clearing fields, planting crops, and forging new homesteads to question this system. Since so many came from the South, slavery was a fact of life they tended to accept without question. Only a minority of whites objected to this practice as being morally repugnant. And they had made little effort to argue this case in public. During the 1817 campaign to choose the territory's congressional representative, the issue of slavery did not come up. None of the early statehood petitions sent to Washington made any mention of slavery, or expressed any desire to sanction or prohibit it. These documents only requested that the territory be admitted "on an equal footing with the original states."[1] Furthermore, no editorials or letters published in Missouri newspapers broached this subject. It was almost as if the chattel system's continuation was simply taken for granted. But all this would abruptly change when the passions of the entire nation became enflamed over the fate of the "peculiar institution" on Missouri soil.

The catalyst for this dramatic confrontation came in the form of an amendment that was tacked on to the congressional enabling bill dealing with Missouri's statehood on February 15, 1819. Proposed by an upstate New York Republican, James Tallmadge, Jr., this amendment imposed two conditions: first of all, the "further introduction" of slavery in Missouri was to be banned; secondly, the children of slaves already there were to be granted their freedom upon

---

1. See, for example, *Memorial and Resolutions of the Legislature of the Missouri Territory* (Washington: Gales & Seaton, 1819), 4.

reaching the age of 25. Tallmadge's proposal expressed an emerging consensus in the North that slavery was simply wrong, but it also clearly advanced a regional political agenda. At this point, a delicate balance of power existed between North and South. There were 11 free states and 11 slave states. Although this meant that each section had an equal number of votes in the Senate, Southerners tended to vote as a bloc and thus controlled that chamber. On the other hand, due to their greater population, Northerners made up a majority in the House of Representatives,[1] so the two legislative bodies held each other in check. By imposing a ban on slavery in Missouri, the free states would tip this balance in their favor by gaining two Senate seats. And, by opposing this extension of the slave system, congressmen from the Northeast hoped to find common cause with colleagues from the Old Northwest, thus creating a powerful coalition that would isolate and weaken the South politically.

Missouri also presented a test case for the future of slavery throughout the entire trans-Mississippian West. In states east of the Mississippi that had been admitted to the Union after 1787, geography and political history had often determined the legal status of the chattel system. For instance, Kentucky and Tennessee had originally been parts of Virginia and North Carolina, respectively, and had only been allowed to break away from those "parent" states under condition that slavery not be abolished within their borders. Conversely, in states north of the Ohio River, the Northwest Ordinance had established a legal basis for barring the "peculiar institution" there. Sharply contrasting climates, terrains, and agricultural systems had set the two regions apart and made slave labor indispensable in the South while rendering it redundant above the Mason Dixon Line. After passage of the Ordinance of 1787, Congress had taken no action whatsoever to interfere with slavery or its expansion. Following acquisition of the Louisiana Territory, federal lawmakers had considered a proposal to exclude the slave system west of the Mississippi, but the South-leaning Senate had ultimately rejected this, 17-11, fearing such a ban would upset the national political equilibrium.[2]

Geographically as well, the country was evenly divided into northern and southern halves. The free states filled the northeastern quadrant of the present-day continental United States, whereas the slave ones encompassed roughly the same size area to the south. Only Louisiana, which had entered the Union in

---

1. In 1820, the Northern states had 121 seats in the House of Representatives, and the Southern states 98 seats. On the basis of its white population alone, the South should have had fewer representatives, but the three-fifths clause of the Constitution enlarged the region's total.
2. Robinson, *Structure of American Politics*, 399. A split among northern Whigs and Federalists had led to the defeat of this measure. Fehrenbacher, "Missouri Controversy," 13.

1812, disturbed this territorial symmetry by extending to the other side of the Mississippi River. Because its alignment would alter this sectional status quo, Missouri — located squarely in the middle of the nation's Western frontier — took on tremendous importance. If Congress voted to prohibit slavery there, this might establish a precedent for other Western territories seeking to join the Union. Such action would prevent slave-based Southern agriculture from expanding, and expansion was essential for the system to survive. Denying the "peculiar institution" a political base west of the Mississippi would also weaken the power of the slave states at the federal level and possibly, some Southerners feared, lead to the triumph of abolitionism. Conversely, admitting Missouri as a slave state would be "tantamount to condoning the extension of black bondage beyond the limits of the traditional South, and such a decision would be a legal recognition of the slaveholders' right to emigrate westward."[1]

The ensuing congressional brouhaha over Tallmadge's amendment galvanized the country. The postwar "Era of Good Feelings" between North and South was suddenly over. Reacting to the news at his Monticello home, the 75-year-old Jefferson said the rapidly unfolding crisis resounded like "a fire bell in the night," filling him with "terror." He considered the Missouri controversy the "knell of the Union."[2] Not surprisingly, this proposal ignited a firestorm of protest among his fellow Southerners, in and outside the halls of Congress. Economically, they felt they were being throttled. They countered that slavery was the key to development of Western states like Missouri.[3] But many Southern politicians based their objections on legal grounds: they accused Northerners of violating the Constitution by making statehood contingent upon the prohibition of slavery, thereby interfering in matters that should properly be left to individual states to decide. There was angry talk of some slave states seceding from the Union, and even of civil war. In the North, antislavery groups quickly mobilized against any extension of the "peculiar institution." Fired-up speakers told mass gatherings in several cities that a fateful moment in the nation's history had

---

1. Ronald C. Woolsey, "The West Becomes a Problem: The Missouri Controversy and Slavery Expansion as the Southern Dilemma," *Missouri Historical Review* 77:4 (July 1983), 410.
2. Letter of Jefferson to John Holmes, 22 April 1820. Quoted in Fehrenbacher, "Missouri Controversy," 13. Jefferson went on to state: "The cession of that kind of property, for so it is misnamed, is a bagatelle which would not cost me a second thought, if, in that way, a general emancipation and *expatriation* could be effected; and gradually, and with due sacrifices, I think it might be. But as it is, we have the wolf by the ears, and we can neither hold him, nor safely let him go. Justice is in one scale, and self-preservation in the other." For the complete text, see http://odur.let.rug.nl/-usa/P/tj3/writings/brf/jefl260.htm.
3. So argued, for instance, an editorial in the Richmond *Enquirer*, reprinted in the *Missouri Gazette*, 31 Mar. 1819.

arrived. Warned an editorial in the antislavery New York *Advertiser*: "This question involves not only the future character of our nation, but the future weight and influence of the free states. If now lost — it is lost forever."[1]

After three days of stormy debate, and over the strenuous objections of Speaker Henry Clay, the House of Representatives voted — strictly along regional lines — to adopt Tallmadge's amendment. The ban on slavery in Missouri passed by 87-76, and the provision for the gradual emancipation of the territory's slaves by 82-78.[2] However, this measure was subsequently defeated by a considerable margin in the Senate, with several pro-slavery Northerners joining their Southern colleagues in voting "nay."[3] Thus, Congress was deadlocked. Neither chamber was willing to back down from its position, and so the fate of Missouri was left hanging as the legislative session came to a close. This impasse exposed the nation's sensitive fault line on the slavery question. For decades, this had remained quiescent: North and South had developed in their separate ways, without overt tension or animosity estranging them. The exclusion of slavery from the Old Northwest (endorsed by Southern members of Congress back in 1787) had not raised any hackles below the Mason Dixon Line. Even as recently as a few months before Tallmadge introduced his amendment, most Southern lawmakers had tacitly acknowledged the federal government's power to restrict or permit slavery in new states.[4] And Northerners had been generally content to have territories south of the Ohio River enter the Union as slave states. Now it was apparent that further growth of the United States would bring an end to this laissez-faire attitude and draw the two sections into direct conflict. The only question was whether or not this could be resolved peacefully.

When Congress reconvened, in December 1819, Missouri statehood stood at the top of its agenda. Once again, the debate was bitterly divisive — and inconclusive. To break this legislative logjam in the Senate, John Holmes, of Massachusetts, offered a compromise solution: Missouri could be admitted as a slave state as long as Maine was simultaneously allowed to join the Union as a free

---

1. Quoted in "The Missouri Crisis," http://www.digitalhistory.uh.edu/database/article_display.cfm?HHID=574.
2. Only one representative from a slave state (Delaware) voted for restricting slavery in Missouri, while 10 of the 96 Northern congressmen voted against this proposal. See Table 1, "Tallmadge Amendment, 1819, House" in Woolsey, "West Becomes a Problem," 416. The House then voted, 91-82, to adopt both parts of Tallmadge's amendment. See Calvin Colton, *The Life, Correspondence, and Speeches of Henry Clay*, vol. 1, *Life and Times* (New York: A.S. Barnes, 1857), 277.
3. The Senate rejected the proposal for gradual emancipation by a 37-11 margin, with many Northern members agreeing that Congress could not impose such a condition. The vote defeating a restriction on slavery in Missouri was closer — 22-16. David E. March, "The Admission of Missouri," *Missouri Historical Review* 65:4 (July 1971), 429.
4. This was in the context of Arkansas's petition to join the Union. See Fehrenbacher, "Missouri Controversy," 16-7.

state. But the Northern-controlled House refused to go along with this proposal, once again rebuffing Clay's impassioned plea for moderation.[1] Then, in joint conference, Northern representatives were offered another concession to gain their support: Sen. Jesse B. Thomas (of Illinois) proposed that slavery be excluded from any other part of the Louisiana Territory north of 36.30 latitude — a line marking Missouri's southern border and extending west below Kansas and Colorado. The Senate eagerly adopted this compromise, 34-10, with some Northerner "yes" votes influenced by a blunt Southern threat to leave the Union if it failed to pass.[2] Clay had to use all of his persuasive powers to convince the House to accept this solution,[3] overriding similar Northern objections to allowing slavery in Missouri.[4] Thanks to this impressive feat of legislative legerdemain, the national crisis over Missouri was temporarily defused.

In Missouri itself, news of this outcome in Washington triggered spontaneous celebrations: bells rang, cannons roared, and fireworks filled the skies.[5] After seemingly interminable wrangling, Congress had granted what the majority of residents wanted — the right to own slaves. Now they were free to do so. The battle over slavery in the nation's capital had both perplexed and annoyed them. White Missourians, overwhelmingly from the South, had few objections to the "peculiar institution" and could not imagine that the federal government had any business dictating what was permissible for them to do. This is not to say that all were delighted to have slaves living among them. In the Deep South and the border states, a considerable number of whites had become disenchanted with the "peculiar institution" and now considered it a "necessary evil." The slave system had not brought widespread prosperity. Many farmers realized that oppressed

---

1. During a speech that lasted close to four hours, Clay argued against restricting slavery. He appealed to Northerners by contending that the spread of the slave system would spell its downfall, as it would prove unable to compete with free labor. At the same time, "The Great Compromiser" cautioned against imposing any restrictions on Missouri's admission and thus making it a "vassal" state. See *The Papers of Henry Clay*, vol. 2, *The Rising Statesman, 1815-1820*, ed. James F. Hopkins (Lexington: University Press of Kentucky, 1961), 776-7.
2. The warning issued by Sen. Charles Pinckney of South Carolina was particularly ominous. See letter of William Plumer, Jr. to William Plumer, Sr., 20 Feb. 1820, in William Plumer, *The Missouri Compromises and Presidential Politics, 1820-1825, from the Letters of William Plumer, Jr.*, ed. Evert Somerville Brown (St. Louis: Missouri Historical Society, 1926), 11.
3. "It was with great reluctance that many of the Southern members voted for the resolution, — & nothing but the exertions of Clay brought them to it — No other man could have effected it." Letter of William Plumer, Jr. to William Plumer, Sr., 26 Feb. 1821. Plumer, *Missouri Compromises*, 43.
4. In the Senate, Southerners backed the compromise by 20-2, whereas Northerners opposed it, 18-4. In the House, Southerners voted 98-0 to remove the restriction on slavery in Missouri, joined by 19 Northerners. (102 of them were opposed.) On the proposal to accept the 36.30 line, Northerners in the House voted in favor, 115-7, while Southerners supported it by 53-45. Fehrenbacher, "Missouri Controversy," 17-8.
5. March, "Admission of Missouri," 439-40.

blacks did not make for highly productive workers. Generally speaking, reliance on chattel labor tended to slow a state's development. This was becoming increasingly apparent as manufacturing flourished in the North and that region's economy boomed, while the South's stagnated. As one opponent of slavery, the journalist Joseph Blunt, pointed out in an 1819 pamphlet, the worth of goods produced annually in Massachusetts alone outstripped the wealth generated by *all the slave states* south of Maryland.[1] How much these states lagged behind their Northern neighbors had already become apparent in their sharply contrasting land prices, levels of agricultural production, and farm income. Up and down the Atlantic seaboard, slaves had evolved from a cheap source of labor into a financial burden. As their numbers had increased due to a high birth rate, they had exceeded their usefulness. Owners ended up having to feed and house slaves they could not profitably put to work, and these expenses cut into their profits. Only the demand for more slaves in the Cotton South had helped to alleviate this problem. The only other recourse for slaveholders was to emancipate their unwanted chattel, thus adding to the population of undesired black freemen.

Both morally and socially, the presence of slaves had a corrosive influence on whites, some Southerners now concluded. They had come to appreciate the wisdom in Thomas Jefferson's admonition against allowing the two races to coexist over a long period of time. Instead of raising blacks up, such contact only dragged whites down. As a non-slaveholding Kentucky planter told a visitor from England, "Kentucky is morally and physically ruined. We have been brought up to live without labour; all are demoralized."[2] Blunt used the very same language to describe slavery's impact on whites: "So great a number of ignorant, degraded beings must necessarily affect the whole mass of society. When the lowest order of citizens is very ignorant and depraved, the corruption gradually seizes the adjoining members, until the nobler parts are invaded, and the disease pervades the whole social body."[3] In addition, fears of a slave uprising kept whites from feeling secure. Finally, the owning of slaves so blatantly contradicted the principles of freedom and justice embedded in the Declaration of Independence that many Americans — south as well as north of the Mason Dixon Line — now recognized how harmful continuing this practice would be to the nation's psyche. Even their representatives in Washington concurred. On the floor of the House, Georgia congressman Robert Reid confessed that he would "hail the day as the most glorious in our dawning" when slavery no longer existed.[4]

---

1. "Marcus" [Joseph Blunt], *An Examination of the Expediency and Constitutionality of Prohibiting Slavery in the State of Missouri* (New York: C. Wiley & Co., 1819), 8.
2. William Faux, *Early Western Travels*, vol. 12, *Memorable Days in America*, Part II, 13.
3. *Ibid.*, 9.
4. Quoted in Woolsey, "West Becomes a Problem," 418.

So, at the same time that the debate over Missouri's status was taking place, the value of the chattel system was being questioned. How widespread opposition to slavery may have been in the territory itself is impossible to say since public opinion was never sampled.[1] The Virginia native who represented Missouri in Congress, John Scott — a Republican from Ste. Genevieve — voiced his "regret" over the existence of slavery in the United States, and he probably would not have done so if a large percentage of his constituents had not shared this view.[2] Evidence of disapproval also surfaced in the pages of the *Missouri Gazette & Public Advertiser* (St. Louis) a year before the convening of a territorial constitutional convention in 1820. An anonymous reader who identified himself as a farmer in St. Charles County wrote several letters condemning the slave system as an "evil" and a "curse" in other states, and claiming that many of his neighbors shared his sentiments. For example, in one letter published on April 7, he opined:

> I have seen an attempt in several papers to induce abroad that the people of this territory are almost unanimously opposing to prohibiting the future introduction of slavery. What are the wishes of people in other counties, I will not pretend to say; but in my neighborhood and as far as my acquaintance extends, the people with scarce one exception declare that they wish to have no more slaves brought into this territory. There are, to be sure, a few slave holders; but even they do not wish to saddle their posterity with what both reason and experience have convinced them is a curse. I do not know but all the people of St. Louis are in favor of slavery; but I cannot see why they should be so, if it is true, as I have heard, that several attempts have been made there, by slaves, to burn the houses and poison the families of their masters. My neighbors unanimously declare, that even if they really believed that Congress had no right to prohibit the introduction of slavery, they would raise a clamor about it. They are well convinced that slavery is always accompanied by the most disgraceful and beastly vices — that those who have slaves to do all their work for them, are too apt to spend their time in gambling and drinking — in dirking and duelling. They are convinced that it is impossible to keep the slaves always in a state of ignorance, especially in a country like this — that, as slaves have few inducements to be virtuous, the people will frequently suffer from their depredations. They cannot see how it can be constitutional for Congress to prohibit slavery entirely in Ohio, Indiana, and Illinois — and unconstitutional to prohibit the intro-

---

1. At the time, some Missourians argued that "the people are divided on the slave question." See unsigned "Communication" to the Printer, *Missouri Gazette*, 23 June 1819. Two decades later, a visiting Englishman noted that a "respectable minority" of Missouri's residents had opposed slavery at the time of statehood. Lyell, *Second Visit*, 182.
2. Trexler, *Slavery in Missouri*, 105. But, in 1819, Scott attacked Congress's attempt to restrict slavery as "unwarrantable" and unconstitutional. See "Remarks of Mr. Scott, of Missouri," reprinted in the *Missouri Gazette*, 12 May 1819. The fact that his county, Ste. Genevieve, had the state's largest proportion of slaves in its population may have influenced Scott's position.

duction of slaves in Missouri. Slavery, they say, must be abolished sooner or later; and there can never be a better time to commence its abolition than the present period — for "an ounce of prevention is worth a pound of cure."[1]

The nameless but well-educated farmer's comments sparked a heated exchange in the editorial pages of the *Gazette*, with several correspondents defending the right to own slaves and others agreeing that the system had an "unhappy influence" on whites.[2] The fact that both points of view were aired suggests each had backing in the territory, but one cannot say how much. The anonymous St. Charles farmer contended that wealthy slaveholders were relying on newspapers like the *St. Louis Gazette* and a "lawyer junto" to hoodwink voters into defending slavery, at the expense of the economic interests of Missouri's mostly poor farmers.[3] No friend of the black man himself, he was concerned that slaves unwanted in Southern states would move to Missouri and turn it into another "Botany Bay."[4] But proponents of the slave system retorted that the territory's residents had no wish to see Congress "rob us of our lands and negroes."[5]

What is most revealing in this correspondence is the line of argument adopted by the supporters of slavery. Instead of refuting the St. Charles farmer's charge that slavery was "evil" and slaves "troublesome and dangerous to keep at home," pro-slavery writers dwelled at length upon Missourians' right to decide this matter for themselves. In a letter published on April 14, 1819, "Sydney" claimed that territorial residents were not prepared to yield such power to Congress. In two subsequent letters, a correspondent using the *nom de plume* of "Hampden" upheld the "sovereignty of the states" over and above any pronouncements from Washington.[6] While he was opposed to slavery as "monstrous in principle" and detrimental to Missouri's economic development, "Pacificus" declared that the federal government had no right to ban the institution in any state.[7] He preferred to accept the wishes of local voters even if these ran counter to what he felt was best for Missouri. With heavy irony, "Pacificus" pointed out that, in making up their minds, Missourians would have to consider not only the anticipated adverse effect of slavery on the new state's growth, but

1. Letter of "A Farmer" to the Printer, *Missouri Gazette*, 7 April 1819.
2. Letter of "An American" to the Printer, *Missouri Gazette*, 26 May 1819. For other comments on the slavery question, see letters published in the issues of 14 April, 21 April, 28 April, 5 May, 12 May, 2 June, 9 June, 16 June, 23 June, 30 June, and 4 Aug. 1819.
3. Letter of "A Farmer" to the Printer, *Missouri Gazette*, 4 Aug. 1819.
4. Letter of "A Farmer" to the Printer, *Missouri Gazette*, 21 April 1819. "Botany Bay" referred to Britain's exporting of convicts to this part of Australia.
5. Letter of "Sydney" to the Printer, *Missouri Gazette*, 14 April 1819.
6. Letters of "Hampden" to the Printer, *Missouri Gazette*, 28 April 1819 and 5 May 1819.
7. Some Missourians did not dare to oppose slavery for fear of discouraging well-to-do Southerners from migrating to the territory. See Trexler, "Slavery in Missouri Territory," 196.

also the "pride, personal gratification or ambition of a few moderately rich slave proprietors, and the safety and advantage of those States who keep slaves out of their dominions, but are charitably disposed to have us alleviate their apprehensions by taking a share of a burdensome black population upon our young and athletic shoulders."[1] Other white Missourians came out against the chattel system but also defended their right to resolve this matter without outside interference. At a public meeting held in mid-May in St. Louis, it was agreed that slavery was "contrary to the term freedom and . . . to the laws of nature," but also that Congress could not impose its will on the state.[2]

Because the focus shifted away from the merits of the slave system to the question of Congress's power to set conditions for admission to the Union, those opposed to the "peculiar institution" had little chance of convincing others to join their cause. Instead, they were overwhelmed by a groundswell of popular outrage at politicians in Washington meddling in this "local matter." Residents in several counties passed resolutions denouncing Congress, and grand jurors in St. Louis came out with a statement saying all the slave states were threatened by any attempt to keep slavery out of Missouri.[3] Editorials in all five territorial newspapers sounded the same theme. On May 15, the St. Louis lawyer Thomas Hart Benton, shortly to be elected Missouri's first senator, told an enthusiastic throng that federal lawmakers had no authority to exclude the slave system from any state or territory.[4]

Even those opposed to slavery, such as the territory's representative in Congress, were loath to go against the will of the people on this question.[5] When delegates were being selected at the county level to draft the new state's constitution, any candidate who spoke out against slavery was loudly denounced.[6] Northerners inspired the most severe condemnation.[7] As the Congregationalist minister Timothy Flint noted with some dismay, no aspirant stood the slightest

---

1. Letter of "Pacificus" to the Printer, *Missouri Gazette*, 2 June 1819.
2. *Missouri Gazette*, 23 June 1819. This article also reported that other counties were holding meetings to address "this growing evil and threatening curse of the further admittance of involuntary slavery" in Missouri.
3. Trexler, *Slavery in Missouri, 1804-1865*, 106-7. Cf. Trexler, "Slavery in Missouri Territory," 197.
4. March, *History of Missouri*, 389.
5. In 1819, Scott declared that even though he believed slavery to be wrong, he remained "an advocate of the people's rights to decide on this question . . . for themselves." Quoted in Trexler, *Slavery in Missouri*, 105.
6. "When a few citizens in the territory had the temerity to question if Missouri should consider limiting the further introduction of slavery, the proslavery majority raised a hue and cry against the menace of restrictionism." Foley, *Genesis of Missouri*, 295. For more details, see Arvarh Strickland, "Aspects of Slavery in Missouri, 1821," *Missouri Historical Review* 65:4 (July 1971), 517.
7. To discredit them, Benton attacked restrictionists as "preachers from the North." Quoted in March, "Admission," 441.

chance of getting votes unless "his sentiments [in favor of slavery] were unequiv-ocally expressed."[1] As a consequence, candidates favoring restrictions ran in only five of Missouri's 15 counties, and almost none of them were elected.[2] In a lead-mining district in Franklin County, one slavery opponent lost by a lopsided vote of 1,147 to 61, and another went down to defeat by a 3-to-1 margin in St. Louis.[3] In the salt-producing region known as "Boone's Lick Country," (where large num-bers of migrants from Kentucky and Virginia had settled, including many non-slaveholders), none of the 20 candidates came out for the exclusion of slavery.[4] Thus a minority of slaveholders gained political power in Missouri, neutralizing most opposition by diverting attention away from the issue of slavery to the issue of states' rights. This shift in tactics suggests that support for the chattel system itself was waning. Still, many non-slaveholders did join the pro-slavery camp out of perceived economic self-interest, having witnessed how the terri-tory had prospered under the chattel system.[5]

When the delegates gathered early in June 1820, several months after Con-gress had reached a compromise on Missouri statehood, the conservative, planter faction in the pro-slavery forces took control — just as it had previously in the territorial legislature.[6] (Among its members was Edward Bates, a St. Louis lawyer from a distinguished Virginia family, who would later serve as Abraham Lincoln's attorney general.[7]) This outcome assured that the new constitution would fully protect the institution of slavery.[8] Indeed, the document included provisions prohibiting emancipation without the consent of the slave owner and preventing the legislature from ever voting to restrict the future entry of slaves

---

1. Timothy Flint, *Recollections of the Last Ten Years* (New York: DeCapo Press, 1968), 214. Flint also observed that many proslavery candidates had never run for office before and displayed "unblushing effrontery" in attacking their opponents.
2. March, "Admission," 440. Trexler cites Benjamin Emmons, of St. Louis, as "rumored" to have been the sole opponent of slavery elected as a delegate. But Emmons' views on the subject are not well documented. See Trexler, *Slavery in Missouri*, 103, note 9.
3. Trexler, *Slavery in Missouri*, 103-4, 109-10. He quotes the pro-slavery positions of several candidates elected to the constitutional convention.
4. March, *History of Missouri*, 400.
5. Cf. Strickland, *Aspects of Slavery*, 516-7.
6. Because of their larger white populations, counties with high concentrations of slaves elected the bulk of representatives to the territorial assembly in 1818. Howard, St. Charles, and St. Louis counties accounted for 20 of the 35 legislators. See *Journal of the Territory of Missouri, 4th General Assembly*, 29 Oct. 1818. As one historian has summed up, conservatives played upon antislavery fears and "positioned themselves as champions of the antirestrictionist majority. For the moment, statehood and the future of slavery in Missouri were the paramount issues, and a majority of the voters played it safe by selecting well-known, proslavery property holders to represent them in the constitu-tional convention . . ." Foley, *Genesis of Missouri*, 296.
7. Marvin R. Cain, *Lincoln's Attorney General: Edward Bates of Missouri* (Columbia: University of Missouri Press, 1965), 9-10. Bates would also serve briefly as president of the Missouri Colonization Society.
8. Cf. March, *History of Missouri*, 193.

into the state.[1] But the delegates, still smarting from Congress's attempt to set conditions for Missouri's admission to the Union and determined to have their own say this time, also added a provocative clause to the constitution. Mirroring similar restrictions in slave states like Delaware, Article 3, Section 26 required the General Assembly to enact laws to "prevent free negroes and mulattoes from coming to and settling in this State, under any pretext whatsoever."[2]

On the surface, this provision appeared to be nothing more than a gratuitous retaliatory slap in the face of Congress.[3] Since there were fewer than 300 free blacks in all of Missouri in 1820, they did not pose any immediate concern to white residents. But it was also true that the delegates — and the voters they represented — were worried that more blacks *might* soon migrate westward. As an editorial in the *Missouri Gazette* had pointed out a few years before, there was pervasive unease about the "prospect . . . of the whole mass of white population in the country being gradually corrupted by the admixture of the blacks." White Missourians were particularly apprehensive that free blacks might lead a slave revolt. To reduce this danger, territorial lawmakers had previously attempted to discourage black freemen from residing in Missouri by limiting their rights — making it a crime for former slaves to travel freely or hold gatherings, even for educational purposes.[4] For the same reason, the *Gazette*, along with many white residents of Missouri, heartily endorsed the American Colonization Society's proposal to remove this "meaner race" to the coast of Africa, impracticable as that scheme might be.[5] Like their counterparts in the "butternut" states, white Missourians were bent upon doing everything possible to keep emancipated blacks from being "dumped" inside their borders.

This action taken by the elected delegates gathered in St. Louis showed how nearly universal antipathy toward black freemen was among whites in the United States. Regardless of whether they lived in the Northeast, the Southeast, the Old Northwest, the Old Southwest, or the Western frontier, most white Americans plainly despised this group. Wherever they could do so, whites set up barriers to keep free blacks from settling in their vicinity. Thus far, these legal impediments at the state level had gone unchallenged by the federal government.

---

1. Foley, *Genesis of Missouri*, 296.
2. Missouri Constitution of 1820, Article III, Section 26: http://www.doprocess.net/lees%20summit/missouri%a0%20constitution%20of%a0%201820.htm.
3. In adopting such an inflammatory provision, members of the convention were defying the advice of leaders such as acting governor Frederick Bates (brother of Edward). In a letter published in 1818, he had urged delegates to steer away from controversial issues until after Missouri became a state: "the less we do the better," Bates had recommended. See letter of Frederick Bates to the Printer, *Missouri Gazette*, 30 Oct. 1818.
4. Greene, et al., *Missouri's Black Heritage*, 63. This legislation was adopted in 1817.
5. See editorial, "Black Colony," *Missouri Gazette*, 22 Mar. 1817.

This was because of tacit approval of such discriminatory measures in Congress and indifference in the White House and Supreme Court toward the rights of freed slaves and their descendants. At best, free blacks were regarded as second-class citizens and, at worst, as not citizens at all. Exactly what protections were afforded them under the Constitution would remain unresolved for some time.[1] In the meanwhile, provisions requiring emancipated slaves to leave states like Virginia and blocking their entry into ones as diverse as Mississippi and Ohio remained in force.

But Missouri's explicit exclusion of free blacks and mulattoes went further than any previous measures. Coming on the heels of the defeat of the Tallmadge amendment and Congress's subsequent decision to accept Missouri as a new slave state, this amendment enraged antislavery Northerners. Vermont's General Assembly declared that Missouri's efforts to "prevent citizens of the United States, on account of their origin, color, or features" from entering its territory were "repugnant to a republican government and in direct violation of the constitution of the United States."[2] In Washington, Congress renewed its battle over Missouri, "bitter beyond precedent."[3] Northern foes of slavery — looking for an excuse to keep Missouri out of the Union — vowed not to accept such an "obnoxious" provision in a state's basic law.[4] But, weary from so much contentious arguing, their opposition to admitting Missouri as a slave state wavering, and alarmed by more Southern talk of secession, many of their colleagues wanted to put the matter behind them.[5] After more backroom maneuvering, failed resolutions, and renewed threats,[6] both houses of Congress finally agreed upon a second Missouri compromise in March. This called for the territory's legislature to revise the constitution so that it guaranteed that subsequent lawmakers would "never pass any law preventing any description of persons from going to, and settling in, the said state, who now are, or hereafter may become, citizens of any states in this Union."[7] Otherwise, Missouri would not become a state.

1. This issue was not legally settled until the Supreme Court ruled, in the 1857 Dred Scott case, that blacks were not citizens.
2. Resolution of the General Assembly, State of Vermont, 15 Nov. 1820, in the *Journal of the Senate of the United States*, 9 Dec. 1820, 52.
3. James G. Blaine, *Twenty Years of Congress: From Lincoln to Garfield* (Norwich, Ct.: Henry Bill, 1884), vol. 1, 17.
4. Rep. William Plumer of New Hampshire wrote to his father on Feb. 2, 1821, that a group of 20 Northern congressmen had met to plan their course of action: all remained steadfastly opposed to accepting this discriminatory clause in Missouri's constitution. Plumer, *Missouri Compromises*, 29.
5. See letter of William Plumer, Jr. to William Plumer, Sr., 14 Dec. 1820. Cf. letter of 2 Feb. 1821. *Ibid.*, 24, 29.
6. "Many of the southern people, & particularly the Virginians, talk coolly & deliberately of a separation of the States, or at least of an attempt to deprive the General Government of some portion of its powers." Letter of William Plumer, Jr. to William Plumer, Sr., 25 Feb. 1821. Plumer, *Missouri Compromises*, 41.

Faced with this ultimatum, the territory's legislators convened a special session in June 1821. Holding their noses, they backed off and partially agreed to abide by Congress's wishes. But they did so defiantly, camouflaging their contempt for Washington in convoluted legal language. The lawmakers acknowledged the Constitution as the "supreme law of the land," while reaffirming that the federal government had no right to "annex any condition to the admission of this state into the Federal Union." The delegates refused to alter the original version of the constitution and only consented not to pass any future laws limiting the rights of free blacks and mulattoes. Missouri's House of Representatives passed this resolution, 36-6 — with two dissenting members going on record as bitterly opposed to this forced compliance on states' rights grounds. How stubbornly opposed this body remained to Washington's intervention is evident in the report of the committee tasked with settling this matter. The report declared, in part:

> That the general government have [*sic*] no right, when a territory as Missouri was, shall have been authorized to form a constitution of state government for herself, to interfere in the free and unrestrained exercise of that right, by imposing any previous conditions or restrictions whatever . . . It is, therefore deeply regretted, that Congress should have changed this liberal, just and pacific course as heretofore pursued and extended towards the other new states, coming into the union, by adopting a very different one towards Missouri.

Reflecting the view of most Missouri whites, the committee also asserted that "by far the greatest part of the free negroes and mulattoes of the different states, have no pretention [*sic*] whatever to the claim of such privileges and immunities [that is, the right of citizenship] under the constitution or laws of the respective states where they inhabit, consequently cannot be considered as within the meaning of the aforesaid resolution of congress . . ."[1] (Thanks again to the efforts of Henry Clay, Congress accepted this compromise, but stipulated that no other prospective state could include any such anti-black provision in its constitution. However, some four years after the House and Senate voted to admit Missouri, on August 10, 1821, Missouri legislators in Jefferson City would score a final victory when, disregarding their earlier pledge, they went ahead and approved laws making it more difficult for free blacks to enter the state.[2]) The tenor of the committee's comments showed how explosive an issue Missouri's

---

7. Quoted in Clay, *Papers*, vol. 2, 18. Cf. "Resolution providing for the admission of the State of Missouri into the Union on a certain condition," reprinted in *Journal of the House of Representatives of the Extra-Session of the First General Assembly of the State of Missouri*, 4 June 1821, 13.
1. Report of the Committee on Constitutional Provisions, *Journal of the House of Representatives*, 23 June 1821, 104, 106.
2. This 1825 legislation required free blacks and mulattoes wishing to enter Missouri to produce a certificate attesting to their citizenship.

status had become —arraying not only free states against slave states, but also state against federal authority. Under these politically fractious circumstances, Southern slaveholders and non-slaveholders were inclined to band together despite any disagreements over the benefits derived from the slave system.[1] This conflation of states' rights and proslavery positions would later prove a powerful tool for mobilizing Southern backing for efforts to introduce the "peculiar institution" in other territories and states west of the Mississippi.

Historically, the famed Missouri Compromise is regarded as the first in a series of legislative bids to avert a breakup of the Union over slavery. During these rancorous congressional debates between 1819 and 1821, Northerners developed a dread of the chaos and violence that would engulf the nation if they could not somehow patch over their differences with their Southern counterparts. As pioneers pushed the frontier further and further west, these disputes would center on the disposition of newly settled territories — namely, would they be "slave" or "free"? In one confrontation after another, North and South would seek to gain a political advantage over the other, but fail to do so. Given the roughly equal distribution of power in Congress, neither side could impose its will, and thus another compromise would have to be struck — to satisfy both regions and keep the nation intact. But these increasingly intense battles would leave North and South more embittered, antagonistic, and polarized than ever before. As a consequence, the likelihood of secession and civil war would increase. The compromises struck in the halls of Congress would only stave off the inevitable.

But the Missouri Compromise had another seminal significance in shaping the sectional rivalries that led to the Civil War. For the agreements hammered out in Washington not only established that Congress had the authority to decide whether or not territories west of the Mississippi River could adopt the slave system (thereby ensuring that slavery's extension would remain a national bone of contention), they also brought to the fore another highly controversial and politically explosive issue — the legal status and future of free blacks in the United States. As has been noted earlier, this issue had been growing in importance, especially in the Deep South and Ohio Valley, as the number of slaves manumitted by their masters had risen sharply. While the nation's free black population remained numerically tiny, the perception that it

---

1. Of the six legislators who voted against complying with Congress's condition for statehood, five came from counties with large slave populations, but the sixth was one of two representatives from Franklin County, where few slaves lived — only 186 out of a population of 1,928. This suggests that opposition to allowing free blacks into Missouri extended to whites of all social classes. For details on the slave population in 1821, see the census figures reported in the *Journal of the House of Representatives*, 9 Nov. 1821, 61.

was inimical to whites was pervasive. Both economic anxiety and racial preju-dice intensified this feeling. The passage of black laws in several states was but one strategy for alleviating it. Formation of the American Colonization Society and the popularity of its objectives in those states with large slave or free black populations further attest to the depth of this anti-black fear. The likelihood that more slaves would be freed as they became too costly for their owners to keep only added to it.

Because the U.S. Constitution had not defined the rights of blacks, or explicitly granted them citizenship,[1] the individual states had exercised these powers — without having their decisions reviewed or challenged by federal courts. The result was a legal hodgepodge, with a few Northern states making blacks equals under the law, while most other states relegated them to second-class stature. This practice made "citizenship" a tentative and ambiguous con-cept for black freemen.[2] For example, a black citizen of Massachusetts could not move to Indiana with any confidence of retaining the rights he or she had previously enjoyed. Now, in the imbroglio over Missouri's entry into the Union, Congress had gone on record upholding the right of black and mulatto citizens to settle in that state. It was, therefore, more than possible that future legal efforts to keep blacks out of Western states would also fail. While a territory might be admitted as either a free or a slave state — depending on its location north or south of the 36.30 line — its white citizens would still be forced to accept the coming of former slaves in either eventuality. One could certainly interpret the Missouri Compromise as creating a legal framework for this mat-ter. Given the surprisingly broad, interregional support in Congress for this guarantee of free blacks' right of access, such a precedent was likely to be hon-ored.[3]

This new political consensus in favor of opening up new states to black set-tlement greatly perturbed white Americans who felt that the growing presence of this other race posed a grave danger to the nation's future. In their view, blacks not only endangered white morals, but also undermined the white work

---

1. This did not occur until ratification of the 14th and 15th amendments, in 1868 and 1870, respectively.
2. Southerners pointed out that no state legislature had designated free blacks citizens and almost all states denied them the right to vote. Northerners like Sen. James Burrill, Jr., of Rhode Island, retorted that many blacks had served in the military, owned land, and enjoyed other rights exercised by citizens.
3. Perhaps indicative of a desire to put this issue behind them, both houses of Congress had quickly passed the second Missouri Compromise in February 1821, with legisla-tors from Southern states crossing lines to cast affirmative votes, thus offsetting the opposition of some Northern colleagues. For example, in the Senate, the Missouri resolution was approved 28-14, with 11 Northern and 17 Southern senators voting "aye." Two senators from the South joined 12 from the North in voting against this measure. See *Senate Journal*, 28 Feb. 1821, 16th Congress, 2nd Session, 240.

ethic upon which the future development and growth of the United States depended. These whites believed it was not enslaved blacks but *free* blacks who constituted the most serious and intractable racial problem. The slave system had inherent economic shortcomings and geographical limitations that, many predicted, would ultimately lead to its decline and demise. But the residue of this system — millions of ex-slaves and their issue — would remain on American soil long afterward. To borrow an image from our own day, the enduring existence of so many emancipated blacks could be likened to the radioactivity of discarded nuclear fuel: long after its usefulness had been exhausted, this remnant would be a source of concern, anxiety, and potential harm to the rest of society. Hence, it was best to find a way to "drain them off."[1]

The political figure who used this phrase was none other than the Great Pacificator himself, Henry Clay. That is scarcely surprising. Long known as a moderate on slavery — philosophically opposed, convinced it was an "evil" and committed to its gradual elimination[2] — Clay had a negative opinion of blacks in general and thought the country would be better off without them.[3] Both to benefit blacks and to spare whites the negative consequences of interracial contact, Clay had helped to found the American Colonization Society and worked diligently to advance its cause.[4] Even if removing all of the country's free blacks would turn out to be an impossible task, the Kentucky lawmaker (and slaveholder) hoped that the country's expansion westward would ultimately resolve its racial conflict by separating whites from blacks. Clay foresaw that free white labor would demonstrate its economic superiority over slave labor in the West and thus bring about the downfall of the institution he abhorred.[5] This geographic segregation would also prevent the emergence of "one homogeneous

---

1. Henry Clay, paraphrase of remarks delivered at the organizing meeting of the American Colonization Society, 21 Dec. 1816, in Clay, *Papers*, vol. 2, 263.
2. In 1798, as a young lawyer in Lexington, Clay had written (under the pseudonym "Scaevola") a moving plea on behalf of the slaves: "Can any humane man be happy and contented when he sees near thirty thousand of his fellow beings around him, deprived of all the rights which make life desirable, transferred like cattle from the possession of one to another; when he sees the trembling slave, under the hammer, surrounded by a number of eager purchasers . . . when he beholds the anguish and hears the piercing cries of husbands separated from wives and children from parents . . ." Quoted in Robert V. Remini, *Henry Clay: Statesman for the Union* (New York: W.W. Norton, 1991), 27.
3. In a letter to James Madison, Clay, C. James Laurie and Jon Peter wrote: "The utility of a separation of the persons in question from the residue of the population of the U. States, as it respects the interest and the happiness of both parties, must be quite obvious." Letter of 22 Sept. 1817, quoted in Clay, *Papers*, vol. 2, 384.
4. Clay was elected president of the society in 1836 and held this post until his death in 1852.
5. Speech of Henry Clay, House of Representatives, 8 Feb. 1820, cited in Remini, *Henry Clay*, 182.

mass" out of two incompatible and unequal races. Such integration would likely ensue from emancipation: freed slaves would "mingle" socially and sexually with whites. Such an outcome Clay, a disciple of Madison and Jefferson, could not abide. Many years later, as he was preparing to run for President in 1844, he would ask rhetorically,, "Does any man recommend amalgamation — that revolting admixture, alike offensive to God and man . . .?"[1] Because he had the goal of racial separation in mind, Clay welcomed Senator Thomas's amendment excluding slavery from all of the Louisiana Purchase north of the 36.30 line.[2]

Clay's thinking about America's racial future placed him squarely in the midst of a newly emerging political camp. Geographically as well as philosophically, it was staking out a mollifying middle ground in an increasingly fractured and fragile nation. While North and South remained at loggerheads over the issue of slavery's extension — ever more suspicious of and hostile toward each other, and seemingly incapable of finding a way of settling their profound differences — this new political force was developing a new approach to the problem of race. Because it held the balance of power between these two intractably estranged sections of the country, it could exert a profound influence on government policies and the course of events at both the state and national levels. Like Clay, this movement was a product of the border states — a bridge between North and South by circumstance as well as by necessity. Like Clay, too, it upheld seemingly contradictory positions. While its roots were Southern — deeply embedded in the slave system and the way of life that this sustained — its outlook was unabashedly democratic, not aristocratic. This new political force — as yet not identified with any party and, indeed, nameless — took seriously the values of the American Revolution: freedom, independence, equality, and self-reliance. But it limited these, without any qualms, to those whose skin color happened to be white.

Whereas the politics of North and South were formed in states along the Atlantic coast, with strong ties to their European ancestry, this nascent movement was a product of Western settlement: it was strongest on the frontier, where its democratic values could flourish and give shape to the politics in emerging territories and states. It was a populist movement, attracting to its ranks not men of great means and lofty stature, but small farmers, aspiring businessmen, shrewd land speculators, hardheaded merchants, and other ambitious individuals who possessed the vision, the courage, the drive, and the perseverance to pursue successfully the continent's boundless opportunities for wealth and social advancement. It drew to it men looking to realize the American Dream

---

1. Speech of Henry Clay, 1 Oct. 1842 (Richmond, Ind.), quoted in Remini, *Henry Clay*, 618.
2. James D. Bilotta, *Race and the Rise of the Republican Party, 1848-1865* (New York: Peter Lang, 1992), 79.

through their own dogged efforts, much as the United States would seek to do in advancing relentlessly westward under the banner of Manifest Destiny. In undertaking their quest, these self-made men faced many obstacles — not the least of which was the presence on the frontier of other races, innately unlike European Americans, indifferent to their dream, and detrimental to its fulfillment. These were the Native American and Hispanic peoples who already inhabited these lands — and the black people who seemed on the verge of populating them as well. And, because of centuries of unwelcome and distasteful contact, it was this latter group that loomed as the greatest threat to the well being of whites.

The political philosophy embraced by Henry Clay (and likeminded Americans of his day) was particularly schizophrenic about slavery. On the one hand, their democratic orientation led them to consider the enslaving of human beings to be utterly reprehensible, and they did not hesitate to condemn the practice as "evil." But, on the other hand, they respected individual rights — including property rights — and could not countenance any interference with them. Thus, they did not advocate the radical step of abolition, only a gradual, voluntary manumission of slaves. Where there was consistency in their thinking it was on the subject of the black race itself. Blacks were inherently inferior to whites in all important respects, and bringing them together with whites only highlighted this inequality, worsened the situation for blacks, and imperiled white morality. Therefore, in the short term — until slavery was done away with, or blacks transported to some other corner of the world — both races would benefit greatly from being kept apart from one another. Spared white contempt and hostility, blacks could develop their own way of life; spared black "contamination," white farmers and workers could develop the West and prosper. In practical terms, such segregation could only be enforced by individual states, enacting laws to keep blacks at bay or pressure them to leave.

Accordingly, those Westerners who shared Henry Clay's outlook and hopes were both *antislavery* and *anti-black*. In their minds, there was no inconsistency in holding these two positions. Rather, they were conjoined by one overarching consideration: whether free or enslaved, the black race brought only "degradation" upon whites. From a political perspective, however, this was problematic. In the North, an antislavery stance was associated with being *pro-black*: New England abolitionists wanted to end slavery in order to stop the brutal treatment and dehumanization of blacks, out of a sense of common humanity. But Westerners had little compassion for this other race; it was the negative impact of slavery on *whites* that they wanted to curtail. Southerners also eyed blacks with contempt and derision, but, at the same time, they depended upon the slave system for their well being. They were prepared to do whatever was necessary to uphold the "peculiar institution" and establish it elsewhere in the country. This unshakable commitment to slavery, if only as a "necessary evil," made them hostile toward whites who opposed the extension of the chattel system to Western territories — namely, the vast majority of settlers there. Conversely, since the complex racial attitudes in the Northern and Southern states — and the policies that emanated from them — did not match the needs or wishes of these settlers, they were inclined to develop their own ways of dealing with the nation's blacks.

By the 1820s, this process had already begun. First, in Ohio, non-slaveholding migrants from the South had succeeded in fashioning that state's laws so that both slaves *and* free blacks were excluded. Now, in the congressional debate over Missouri's admission to the Union, strong support from border state legislators had helped to pass the amendment placing territory north of the 36.30 parallel off-limits to the "peculiar institution."[1] As the United States continued to expand into the West, and the political power of that region increased accordingly, this antislavery, anti-black outlook would gain strength and have a major national impact. In the decades leading up the Civil War, it would give rise to two major new national political entities — first, the Free Soil movement of the late 1840s, and then, as the inheritor of this movement's mantle, the Republican Party. How this new political force articulated and advanced the desire of frontier settlers to create a racially homogeneous region in the West will be discussed in the following chapter.

Paradoxically, Congress's acceptance of slavery in Missouri was followed not by the flowering of slavery there, but by a slowing of its growth. After an initial post-statehood in-migration of settlers bringing slaves with them, that state's white population grew much more rapidly than its slave population. From 50,753 in 1821, the former increased to 80,677 in 1824, and then rose to 92,801 four years later. But during the same seven-year period, the number of slaves jumped even more dramatically, from 9,808 to 19,124.[2] However, after 1830, the white population soared while the black one did not keep pace. By 1850, Missouri had more than five times as many white settlers as it had had in 1830, but only about three times as many slaves. This was mainly due to economic developments. For one thing, slavery did not prove to be suitable for most parts of the state. Hence, the concentration of slaves in just a few counties — chiefly those producing hemp, wheat, and tobacco along the banks of the Mis-

---

1. Representatives from Delaware, Kentucky, and Maryland had voted 16-2 in favor of this amendment. Congressmen from Virginia had strongly opposed the measure, 18-4, while representatives from the other slave states had been almost equally divided. Fehrenbacher, "Missouri Controversy," 19.
2. For these population statistics, see *Journal of the House of Representatives of the State of Missouri*, 5 Nov. 1821 and 20 Nov. 1824, and *An Abstract of the Census of the Several Counties of the State of Missouri for the Year 1828*.

souri — grew more pronounced.[1] (Unlike states in the Cotton South, the Show Me State did not depend on slave labor to harvest cotton.[2]) On the eve of the War Between the States, the proportion of slaves in these seven counties ranged from 25 to 37 percent, whereas no other county in the state had more than a 20 percent black population. Within this bottomland region, Missouri followed the pattern established in Kentucky's Bluegrass: farms with large slaveholdings displaced those with fewer slaves.[3] In 1860, this region — which, after the Civil War came to be known as "Little Dixie" — accounted for 27.7 percent of all the slaves in Missouri; in 1830, the percentage had been just over 21. Statewide in 1860, slaves made up only 9.76 percent of Missouri's population, down sharply from 17.4 percent in 1810. As a result, the Show Me State never evolved into a slave state on the order of Virginia, Maryland, or South Carolina.

Secondly, a change in federal land policy made Missouri more inviting to small farmers who could not afford slaves. After having initially set the minimum purchase at a quarter section (160 acres), Congress reduced this by half in July 1820 and also lowered the base price to $1.25 per acre. These steps were designed to aid would-be settlers who had suffered financially in the Panic of 1819. Left in force for the next four decades, this policy did much to encourage yeoman farmers, largely from neighboring Southern states, to migrate to Missouri and thus altered the socioeconomic composition of the state's white population.[4] Many poor farmers from Tennessee and Kentucky, who could not pay even these lower prices for good farming tracts, bought property in the Ozark Mountains and the southwestern part of the state.[5] Like the Cumberland Mountains in Kentucky,

---

1. Between 1830 and 1860, the number of whites living in Boone County increased by 52 percent, while the slave population increased 56 percent. In Cooper County during the same period, whites *decreased* by 10 percent as slaves increased by 60 percent. In Howard, the increases for whites and slaves were 21 and 98 percent, respectively. This shift toward a proportionately more black population in "Little Dixie" continued in the 1840s: during that decade, Clay saw a 226 percent rise in the number of slaves, but only a 53 percent increase in the white population. Similar demographic disparities occurred in five of the seven river counties. Hurt, *Agriculture and Slavery*, Table IV, "Population Growth in Little Dixie, 1820-1860," 218.
2. The six counties that produced the most cotton had very small slave populations, ranging from 7.38 percent of the total (Dallas Co.) to 73 percent (Shannon). See James Fernando Ellis, *The Influence of Environment on the Settlement of Missouri* (St. Louis: Webster, 1929), 109.
3. Whereas, in 1830, only 32 percent of slaveholders owned five or more slaves, this percentage had grown to 42.5 by 1850. Furthermore, the percentage owning 15 or more slaves doubled over these 20 years, going from 3.5 to 6.2. Hurt, *Agriculture and Slavery*, appendix, "Number of Slaves Per Holder, 1830, 1850," 307, 309. For evidence of this trend in one river county, see Fig. 5, "A Comparison of Slave Ownership Patterns in Callaway County," Scarpino, "Slavery in Callaway County," 33.
4. March, *History of Missouri*, 250. These Scotch-Irish migrants from Kentucky and Tennessee settled mainly in the Ozark Mountains, in southwestern Missouri. Gerlach, *Settlement Patterns*, 23.

this region could not support slave-based agriculture, and only a handful of the predominantly Scotch-Irish families there owned slaves.[1] In general, the successive waves of new settlers following statehood were composed of non-slaveholders. This trend further increased their statewide majority. As was noted above, only about 12 percent of white families owned slaves by 1860, making Missouri statistically less of a slave state than even Kentucky. Expectations that the legalizing of slavery would lead to a massive in-migration of wealthy Southern slaveholders proved to be illusory, as growth of the white population in the river counties fell behind the rate elsewhere in the state.[2]

Not only small Southern farmers without slaves were drawn to Missouri despite the existence of slavery there: European immigrants also found the new state's agricultural resources enticing. Ironically, many of them — chiefly from Germany and Ireland — had been victims of tyranny and oppression in their home countries. Given this personal history, moving to a place in faraway America where nearly one in five persons was enslaved seems wildly implausible. The fact that they did overcome any reservations about living in a slave system speaks to the powerful pull of greater economic opportunity in Missouri. Particularly persuasive for would-be German immigrants was Gottfried Duden's glowing account of life west of the Mississippi, which appeared in his native country in 1829. To reassure politically liberal émigrés, Duden conceded that slavery was an evil, but then went on to argue that Missouri tolerated only a "milder form" of this institution. It did not pose a real problem for his fellow Germans since the number of slaves was relatively small. Taking a more pragmatic tack for the sake of his more affluent readers, Duden pointed out that a shortage of white workers made slaves a *sine qua non* for a settler "who either cannot or does not wish to" work himself.[3] Largely because of Duden's book and others published after it,[4] thousands of Germans (many of them members of a "mottled aristocracy"[5]) flocked to eastern Missouri in the 1830s and 1840s. By 1850, more than 45,000

---

5. By 1858, 1.89 million acres in the Ozarks had been sold, with most land going for 12.5 cents per acre. Milton D. Rafferty, *The Ozarks: Land and Life* (Fayetteville: University of Arkansas Press, 2001), 51. The white population in counties in southwestern Missouri grew by 418 percent between 1840 and 1860, compared to a 258 percent increase statewide.

1. According to one estimate, most mountain counties had only a dozen or so slave owners. Britton, "Pioneer Life," 393.

2. The "Little Dixie" counties experienced a 146.8 percent increase in their white populations between 1830 and 1860, but Missouri's overall white population grew by 929 percent.

3. Gottfried Duden, *Report on a Journey to the Western States of North America and a Stay of Several Years Along the Missouri*, trans. George H. Kellner, Elsa Nagel, Adolf E. Schroeder, and W.M. Senner (Columbia: University of Missouri Press, 1980), 115.

were living in the Show Me State. They were joined there by a contingent of Irish immigrants numbering 14,734.[1]

As Missouri developed — along the lines of Kentucky and Virginia — into a frontier state in which the best land, the most slaves, and the greatest wealth were possessed by a small minority of whites, the economic and social conflicts between this elite and the small landholding majority would intensify.[2] Contrary to the theories Frederick Jackson Turner expressed in his influential writings on the West, the peopling of these states did not so much promote the flowering of democracy as expose that system's limitations: original hopes entertained by small farmers for more personal freedom and economic prosperity would run afoul of harsh realities. As was true back east, greater wealth, status, and political power tended to accrue to those who already had these attributes. With the passage of time, the imbalance between the haves and have-nots only widened. This growing disparity, in turn, made existing conditions less tolerable — and the grass on distant pastures appear greener. Within a quarter century of Missouri's entering the Union, a large proportion of its white residents would decide to move on once again — to seek another land of milk and honey further west, far beyond the reach of the slaveholders and their slaves.

---

4. More than a dozen German-language travel accounts published in the 1830s and 1840s encouraged migration to Missouri. Gerlach, "Population Origins," 12. Novels by Charles Sealsfield, Friedrich Armond Stubberg, Friedrich Gerstäcker, and Balduin Möllhausen also helped to create a romanticized view of the West. See George R. Brooks, "The American Frontier in German Fiction," in *The Frontier Re-Examined*, 155-62.
5. Quoted in Milton D. Rafferty, *Historical Atlas of Missouri* (Norman: University of Oklahoma Press, 1981), 33. Following in the wake of working-class Germans, many "counts, barons, scholars, preachers, gentlemen farmers, officers, merchants, and students" migrated to Missouri. Gerlach, *Settlement Patterns*, 24.
1. Table XX, "Place of Birth," *Seventh Census*, 39.
2. According to the 1850 federal census, only about one in seven Missouri farms employed slave labor. See Nevins, *Fruits of Manifest Destiny*, 502.

VII. The Politics of Exclusion

The bitter battle over Missouri augured badly for the nation's future. This protracted crisis had revealed how tenuous the bonds holding North and South together were and how easily they could be rent asunder. Further westward expansion promised more trying tests of national unity to come. For each new outpost on the frontier — each new territory clamoring for statehood, each new uproar over slavery — inexorably pitted section against section, imperiling the political power, economy, values, way of life, and even survival of each one. But, while the steady advance toward the Pacific increased the tensions over race and other divisive issues, it also offered an escape from them. Indeed, much of the frontier's appeal lay in being ostensibly removed from the conflicts that afflicted much of American life. In large part, the frontier drew settlers because of what it appeared to lack, of what had not yet arrived there — restrictive laws, "civilized" customs, constraining walls, intruding neighbors, and unwelcome races. This absence — this sheer emptiness — imbued the West with much of its mystique. When the frontier faded away under the onslaught of large-scale and permanent settlement, much of this allure disappeared.

Throughout its history, the West has served as a place of refuge as well as opportunity. In its early days, this vast wilderness attracted many individuals who did not fit easily into their staid New England communities — "shiftless" and "discontented people" who, as Timothy Dwight, the Calvinist president of Yale feared, might have soured and turned into revolutionaries if they had stayed at home.[1] Later on, the West was seen as a land of second chances for those who could not find work or support their families further east. Still others ventured there to avoid run-ins with the law, an irate tax collector, or an intemperate

---

1. Quoted in Stewart Holbrook, *The Yankee Exodus: An Account of Migration from New England,* (New York: Macmillan, 1950), 108.

spouse. By absorbing all these restless and impetuous types, the frontier served as a "safety valve" for the young nation, allowing social pressures to be harmlessly released while affording new arrivals a heavy dose of freedom and independence. It also offered them sanctuary.

Among those pressures and conflicts chronically welling up in American society were ones born of racial animosity. Many whites who were socially uncomfortable or economic insecure living among blacks, who were unable to keep members of this race "in their place" or drive them away, resorted to fleeing themselves. The phenomenon of "white flight" that has been associated with post-World War II suburban sprawl actually has a much longer history, dating back to colonial days. It characterized much of the nation's westward expansion during the 19^(th) century. Because half the country was committed to enslaving blacks — and to extending this system of involuntary servitude over ever-larger stretches of terrain — escaping from what was regarded as a pernicious black "taint" became more and more difficult. Efforts to establish whites-only havens on farmland in the continent's interior invariably failed, as slave owners assiduously pursued the same paths west, seeking the same economic opportunities, and settling in the same places. Even moving on to sparsely inhabited "free" territories and states did not afford racially threatened whites any lasting refuge, for liberated slaves, seeking the freedom these lands professed to offer all Americans, came there as well.

If, in the years preceding the Civil War, there was one a place left on the North American continent where migrating whites might build homesteads with little worry that slaves — or emancipated blacks — would ever follow in their footsteps and "degrade" the surrounding environment, it was the trans-Mississippian West. This sprawling domain, immense beyond comprehension and believed to be largely uninhabited, thus beckoned racially intolerant white pioneers irresistibly. Those who did not own chattel, and who considered slavery a "curse" upon the white race, could hope to escape the system's corrupting influence by penetrating deep into this latter-day Garden of Eden and staking out claims where only supposedly superiorly endowed Anglo Saxons could ever be expected to survive and prevail. These whites reasoned that, by virtue of its remoteness and inhospitality to the black man, the Far West would prove to be an insurmountable racial barrier — far more effective than discriminatory laws and outright hostility in dissuading former slaves from flowing out of the Deep South into the free states. Sheer geographic space — the New World's greatest asset — would save the white race by swallowing it up.

After practically coming to a halt following Missouri's admission to the Union, the pushing back of the frontier resumed with great fervor in the 1840s. This time the usual reasons for moving west — an abundance of cheap land, a love of adventure, the perennial quest for a better life — were bolstered by the lure of fabulous wealth: the discovery of gold nuggets in a California streambed provoked a frenzied rush across the continent. But, to a large extent, this rekin-dled desire of white settlers to light out for the country was also racially moti-vated: they wanted to flee from an increasingly volatile national dilemma over slavery and the unwelcome arrival of black freemen in their midst.

During a hiatus lasting roughly a quarter century, when the United States did not grow any larger (except for the acquisition of Florida, in 1821), the ten-sions created by the presence of blacks intensified. The underlying cause was the steady rise in the number of blacks living in the United States — an increase of over one million, from 1,772,000 to 2,874,000, in just two decades (between 1820 and 1840). Although the proportion of blacks in the overall U.S. population actu-ally *fell* by 1.6 percent during these 20 years and, in fact, had been declining since the colonial era (as it would continue to do up until World War II), blacks had spread to many parts of the country by 1840. The "peculiar institution" was no longer confined to the Old South, but had become deeply entrenched in Ken-tucky, Tennessee, Mississippi, Alabama, Arkansas, and Louisiana, as well as Missouri.[1] And numerous free blacks now lived not only in southern New England and the mid-Atlantic states, but also throughout the country's midsec-tion — from northern Ohio to central Tennessee.[2] Most troubling to racially biased whites, slave owners were manumitting their superannuated and surplus bondsmen at an alarming pace. While many of these slaveholders hoped that gradual emancipation would be linked to African repatriation, this exodus was not taking place at a rate that could reduce — let alone stabilize — the free black population. Instead, the number of former slaves in the United States grew by over 64 percent between 1820 and 1840, surpassing one third of a million.[3]

As the next generation of pioneers started to head westward in the 1840s, many non-slaveholding Southerners in their ranks worried that blacks would be joining this migration as well. The establishing of slavery in Missouri (and Arkansas) had shown that slavery *could* thrive on the other side of the Missis-

---

1. By 1840, virtually the same numbers of slaves were living in the Old South (1,110,031) as in the New South states of Georgia, Florida, Alabama, Mississippi, Tennessee, Arkansas, and Louisiana (1,126,850). Between 1820 and 1840, the proportion of the slave population in the latter region rose from 25 to 44 percent of the national total. See McClelland and Zeckhauser, *Demographic Dimensions of the New Republic*, Table B-3, "United States Slave Population by Regions, 1800-60," 118.

2. See Zelinsky, *Population Geography of the Free Negro*, Fig. 2, "Free Negro Population, 1810 and 1830," 390. The dispersion of former slaves within Western states is evident in Kentucky. There, in 1820, 20 or more black freemen lived in 29 of 58 counties. Ten years later, 52 of Kentucky's 83 counties had this many free black residents. By 1840, 20 or more resided in 59 of 90 counties. Statewide, the number of free blacks increased by 165.2 percent between 1820 and 1840, while Kentucky's white popula-tion grew by only 35.8 percent.

3. In the ensuing decades, the free black population grew much more slowly, as Southern fears of rebellion discouraged manumissions. Between 1840 and 1860, the nation's free black population increased by only 26 percent, from 377,757 to 476,748.

sippi, and it was certainly possible that it might spring up in other parts of the West as well. (As it would turn out, slavery would spread only to Texas in the two decades before the Civil War.) Furthermore, since some black freemen had already relocated to the southern-tier states of the Old Northwest — Illinois, Indiana, and Ohio — to escape the slave system, they might soon move further northward and westward within that region, into the white bastions of Michigan, Wisconsin, and eastern Minnesota.[1] If lands beyond the Mississippi were more welcoming, free blacks might move there as well.

Non-slaveholding whites could do little to stop the expansion of slavery: more than a century of unsuccessfully competing against the planter elite had taught Southern yeoman farmers that much. Even though they were a small minority, large slaveholders invariably came to control the political and economic systems wherever they settled and thereby ensured that their interests were well served. Indeed, *no state* in which slavery could profitably exist had ever kept the chattel system out. But non-slaveholders could band together to craft laws aimed at impeding the flow of former slaves into free territories and states. This was the lesson they had learned in the Old Northwest. As long as their next frontier destinations did not support slave-based agriculture, pioneers of modest means stood a good chance of replicating the legal barriers already raised against blacks in the "butternut" states. And, all across the West, this is precisely what they would proceed to do.

The hostility of non-slaveholding frontier settlers toward black people dates back to pre-Revolutionary Virginia. There and in other slave states, abhorrence of this race stemmed largely from economic competition and from a profound antipathy toward human beings who would submit to enslavement. Independent-minded "plain folk" farmers prized their stature as free men above else and regarded slaves as a grave affront to their values. Ironically, they blamed the slaves, not the slave owners, for their own dismal fate. But, as individual blacks were set free and entered a different racial category, Northern as well as Southern whites found other reasons for their intractable animus. In a "free" society, the prospect of blacks and whites commingling now emerged as their deepest dread, and the concerted actions of settlers all across the trans-Mississippian West displayed an almost pathological wish to prevent this from happening. The strength and depth of this racial hostility can be measured by the attitudes that persisted on this new frontier during the antebellum period, as well as by the positions taken by many territories and states on matters relating to blacks.

1. In 1830, Michigan had only 261 free black residents (compared to 31,346 whites), the second smallest number (after Arkansas) in the Union. This amounted to 0.8 percent of the territory's population, the lowest such density outside northern New England. Comparable census figures for Minnesota and Wisconsin prior to 1850 are not available.

This chapter will examine how anti-black bias influenced the West's outlook on three key issues — the in-migration and legal rights of non-whites, the Wilmot Proviso, and the Free Soil movement of the late 1840s.

In order to assess the importance of racial motives in the settling of the trans-Mississippian West, it is important first of all to establish who moved there. The most reliable statistics on the origins of Western settlers were compiled as part of the federal census, from 1850 on.[1] From these, one can discern a decided regional difference: the exodus toward the frontier prior to mid-century consisted largely of Southern whites. At the outset, considerably more persons born in slave states crossed the Mississippi than natives of free states.[2] For instance, as of 1850, a total of 418,973 Southerners (overwhelmingly *non-slave-holders*) had moved west of this river, compared with only 226,060 Northerners.[3] This disparity looms larger if considered in relation to the total population of the two regions: by mid-century, seven percent of free persons born in the southeastern quadrant of the nation had relocated to the West, versus only two percent of those born in the Northeast. However, if one excludes from these migratory data the four slave states located in the western half of the United States — Arkansas, Louisiana, Missouri, and Texas — this imbalance is reversed. In the six Western free territories and states that existed in 1850 (not counting Wisconsin), settlers born east of the Mississippi and north of the Mason Dixon Line outnumbered natives of the South by nearly three to one — 139,172 to only 47,282. In the four Western slave states, this regional concentration was even more pronounced, with 81 percent of their white residents hailing from the South. So, in fact, this western migration was made up of two separate and distinct streams — one out of the North, the other from the South.

By 1860, this sectional disparity in the origins of settlers moving across the Mississippi had all but disappeared. At that point, nearly 400,000 additional natives of Northeastern states were living west of the Mississippi, while fewer than 200,000 new migrants from the Deep South had settled in this region. As a result, the population of the West was almost evenly split — 865,802 Southern natives, versus 800,307 from the North — along sectional lines. This demographic shift is partially the result of slavery's proving unsuitable in most of the nation's western half. In fact, large-scale plantation agriculture established only

---

1. For the demographic figures cited here and elsewhere in the text, see Table XX, "Place of Birth of the White and Free Colored Population," *Mortality Statistics of the Seventh Census*, 38-9.
2. In terms of overall population, a higher percentage of persons born in Southern states east of the Mississippi moved west than did Northern natives. In 1850, 7.3 percent of Southerners, versus only 3.3 percent of Northerners, were living west of the Mississippi.
3. This number includes whites and free blacks. In this compilation, Louisiana is considered a state west of the Mississippi, although part of it is situated east of the river.

one base beyond the Mississippi Valley — in Texas. The failure of the slave system to take hold made the West less inviting to subsequent Southern migrants
— slaveholders and independent farmers alike. Between 1846 and 1861, six new
states in that part of the country entered the Union, and all but Texas joined as
free states.[1] Not surprisingly, this trend encouraged more migration from the
North than from the South. Western free states attracted non-slaveholders and
pioneer families who preferred to live where slavery was not present. Large in-
migration from states like Ohio, New York, and Illinois gave several of these new
states a decidedly Northern character and thus made them seem unwelcoming
to Southerners. For example, by 1860, nearly as many natives of New York were
living in Iowa as persons born in all of the slave states east of the Mississippi
combined.[2]

For all the influence exerted on it by neighboring Missouri, Kansas actually
had slightly fewer residents from the Show Me State than from Ohio.[3] Just
before the outbreak of the War Between the States, 104,006 free-state natives
were living in California, compared to only 26,111 from the slave states; for Iowa,
the comparable figures were 320,368 and 48,310, and for Kansas they were 50,918
and 15,342. In analyzing these data, one has to bear in mind that many white
natives of southern Ohio, Illinois, and Indiana were the children of Southerners
and therefore should more properly be considered as coming from the South.
Their migration further west, chiefly to Missouri, Iowa, Nebraska, and Oregon,
played a major role in transmitting anti-black and anti-slavery views to those
territories and states. Nonetheless, it still remains true that, aside from an anomalous relocation of non-slaveholding white Southerners north to the Old Northwest, settlers headed west during the antebellum decades along two parallel
routes: Southern-born settlers (and their descendants) gravitated toward areas
that tolerated slavery, while Northern ones went where it was either prohibited
or unlikely to take root.[4]

Because they were familiar with the slave system, natives of the South
showed little inhibition about moving into areas where it already existed or
might be introduced. Of course, some of them were directly responsible for
bringing slaves west of the Mississippi. But that does not mean that all, or even
most, of these Southerners were slaveholders. Quite the opposite was true.
According to the 1860 federal census, 21,878 persons owned slaves in Texas, out

---

1. The five free states admitted were Iowa (1846), California (1850), Minnesota (1858),
   Oregon (1859), and Kansas (1861).
2. Census figures show that 46,053 New Yorkers were residing in Iowa at that time,
   compared to 48,310 persons from the Deep South.
3. In 1860, 11,356 Missouri natives were living in Kansas, as well as 11,617 natives of Ohio.
4. This having been said, it should be pointed out that, by 1850, nearly as many of the
   Southern natives not moving to Missouri had settled in free states and territories
   (65,728) as had in Texas (77,879).

of an adult white male population of 100,790.[1] In other words, only about one in five white men were slaveholders. This ratio approximates that found, at least initially, in border states such as Kentucky and Missouri. Any economic disadvantage stemming from the presence of slaves did not stop these non-slaveholding whites from heading to another slave state. Rather, they moved to Texas for many of the same reasons that their fathers and grandfathers had previously migrated to those states. They were familiar and comfortable with the Southern way of life, including its subjugation of blacks. These pioneers of little means concluded that the economic (and social) benefits of living within a slave society outweighed the drawbacks.

Settlement of the trans-Mississippian West along regional and cultural lines was more pronounced than it was in the Ohio Valley, where many Southerners living in Kentucky and Tennessee had crossed over to free states. In the West, greater distances and disparities in climate and terrain kept Northern and Southern migrants apart: for example, only a handful of slave-state natives ventured as far north as Michigan, while a similarly small number of Yankees ended up in Texas.[2] But slavery was also a major sorting out factor. If one puts aside Arkansas, Louisiana, and Missouri (states settled decades earlier than others in the West), this becomes starkly apparent. The Lone Star State had attracted nearly ten times as many Southerners as Northerners by 1860, and they were almost exclusively natives of the Deep South — strong proponents of the plantation system, eager to transplant their way of life further west. According to the 1850 census, fully 84.3 percent of Southern-born migrants to Texas came originally from the South, compared to 54.8 percent in Louisiana, 46.9 percent in Arkansas, and only 36.1 percent in Missouri.[3]

The fact that Texas became the main Western outpost for slavery made it a magnet for whites whose livelihood and lifestyle depended upon the "peculiar institution." At the same time, Texas was *terra non grata* for white settlers opposed to either the slave system or the large-scale presence of blacks. On the eve of the Civil War, 1,573,751 Americans then alive had migrated to the western side of the Mississippi, but only 189,567 of them — or 12 percent — were residing in the sprawling and agriculturally rich Lone Star State. By putting down roots elsewhere, these newcomers were, in effect, voting with their feet against

---

1. This applies to men between the ages of 20 and 59. In earlier decades, this percentage was somewhat higher. More than 30 percent of white families owned slaves in 1850, for example. Randolph B. Campbell, *An Empire for Slavery: The Peculiar Institution in Texas, 1821-1865* (Baton Rouge: Louisiana State University Press, 1989), 68.
2. In 1860, only 5,768 of Michigan's 303,500 non-native residents came from slave states. In Texas, 2,254 — out of a non-native, free white and black population of 223,923— were originally from New England states.
3. In these statistics, the Deep South includes Virginia and North Carolina, as well as Arkansas, but not the border states of Tennessee, Kentucky, Maryland, Delaware, and Missouri.

slavery. Their actions, coupled with the West's general unsuitability for cotton or tobacco growing, exposed the inherent limitations in this system of labor and foreshadowed its eventual demise. The forthcoming national conflict over the extension of slavery into newly acquired territories was actually resolved before it even began. Not politics or economic clout, but climate and soil were the key factors determining where the slave system would take hold and grow. Almost the entire West was geographically pre-destined to be "free."[1]

As a consequence, the more pressing racial question of the day was this: *would the rest of the West be reserved exclusively for whites?* Once it became clear that the chattel system was unlikely to spread beyond the Mississippi Valley and the Gulf coast, pioneers and prospective migrants began to worry more about the coming of an even more unwanted racial minority — free blacks. Unwanted and distrusted in the South, despised and ostracized in the North, former slaves had to find some part of the country where they could live and earn a living in relative peace. For them, too, the West represented a new, and perhaps final, frontier. But they had to overcome tremendous hurdles to move there. Determined to preserve their racial homogeneity, white settlers who had begun to build new lives beyond the Mississippi were now prepared to take all steps necessary to keep this black population out.

One way of excluding non-whites was to pass laws making their entry and residence difficult, if not impossible. Although "blacks laws" adopted in Ohio, Illinois, and Indiana had not completely stopped the northward stream of ex-slaves, they had reduced it. These discriminatory measures thus provided a model for legally thwarting black migration to the West. However, as anti-black Missouri whites had discovered in 1820, Congress was not going to admit territories to the Union if their constitutions contained an explicit ban on black migration. An alternative strategy pursued by territorial legislatures was to adopt a provision denying or severely restricting black rights, chiefly the franchise. (States were still free to define "citizenship" as they saw fit.) Doing so telegraphed white hostility and — lawmakers believed — thus dissuaded black freemen from coming in large numbers. Racial "purity" could thus be maintained. This strategy appeared to work. In 1840, free blacks were virtually non-existent in the trans-Mississippian West. Fewer than 30,000 of them could be found, scattered over an area stretching from the shores of Lake Superior to the Gulf of Mexico and as far west as the banks of the Missouri River. Of these blacks, almost all (over 25,000) were located in Louisiana, principally in New Orleans, as a result of a policy adopted by Spanish authorities in the late 18th century that

---

1. In 1860, there were 740,338 slaves west of the Mississippi. Of these, 331,726 were in Louisiana, 182,566 in Texas, 114,931 in Missouri, and 111,115 in Arkansas. Census figures for that year show slaves living in only two other Western states — Nebraska (15) and Kansas (2).

had enabled slaves to purchase their own freedom.[1] Territorial and state legislatures (outside the Northern Plains) wanted to keep these numbers from rising. When they sat down to draft or revise their states' constitutions, this became a top priority.

In his landmark, if deceptively titled, book, *The Frontier Against Slavery*, Eugene Berwanger has described in considerable detail the effort made by Western lawmakers to prevent blacks from settling in their vicinity. (Berwanger's title is misleading because these measures dealt primarily with excluding free blacks, not slaves.) He contends that migrants from the Old Northwest were largely responsible for exporting anti-black prejudice to the West. These frontier settlers, mostly the offspring of Southern yeoman farmers who had headed north a generation before in search of more opportunities and less black competition, now hoped to create on the far side of the Mississippi the kind of racially homogeneous society their parents had previously attempted to establish in Ohio, Indiana, and Illinois. Egged on by lawmakers, newspaper editors, and other agitators, "these pioneers," Berwanger writes, "pushed westward with an increased determination to keep the Negro, free or slave, out of the new lands" they were populating.[2]

But a firm resolve to keep free blacks out of the West was not limited to these "plain folk" farmers originally from the South. Slaveholders concentrated along the Mississippi River and the Gulf Coast were just as eager to bar the door to former slaves, if for other reasons. The security of these whites depended upon their maintaining control over the large numbers of enslaved blacks they owned, and the coming of often better educated, more outspoken, and independent-minded free blacks potentially jeopardized the slaveholders' dominance. The fact that it was an ex-slave (and leader of the African Methodist Church), Denmark Vesey, who had plotted a slave revolt in Charleston, South Carolina, in the late spring of 1822 only heightened white misgiving about these blacks.[3] Consequently, various steps were taken to expel black freemen from the Western slave states or discourage them from migrating there. Such efforts intensified as the free black population increased. For example, during the 1840s Louisiana authorities grew alarmed at this growing minority and began enforcing a law that required all black freemen who had entered the state after 1825 to leave.

1. The free black population of New Orleans peaked at 19,226 in 1840. See Laura Schafer, *Becoming Free, Remaining Free* (Baton Rouge: Louisiana State University Press, 2003), 9. By 1860, only 7 percent of the city's population consisted of free blacks.
2. Berwanger, *Frontier Against Slavery*, 59. As an historian of blacks in the American West has succinctly put it: "The black laws moved westward with the pioneer's wagon." William L. Katz, *The Black West*, rev. ed. (Garden City: Anchor Press, 1987), 54.
3. See Harold Schoen, "The Free Negro in the Republic of Texas," *Southwestern Historical Quarterly* 40:3 (Jan. 1937), 185. Vesey had purchased his freedom after winning $1,500 in a lottery. He had been inspired to challenge white authority by the slave revolt in Haiti.

This crackdown led to a precipitous decline in the state's free black population by 1850.[1] Similarly, under the terms of Arkansas's 1836 constitution, black freemen were prohibited from settling within the state unless they first produced a certificate of freedom and a $500 bond. A few years later, because of fears of another slave revolt, the state imposed a total ban on their entry.[2] And, in Texas, once slavery was introduced by American settlers in the 1820s, free blacks were no longer welcome. Under first Spanish and then Mexican rule, Texas had previously been a haven for emancipated slaves, and there had even been talk of creating a colony for them there, but a series of draconian laws deterred subsequent in-migration and drastically reduced their numbers.[3] In 1850, only 397 free blacks were still living in the Lone Star State, out of a total population of 212,592.

On the "free" frontier, however, more tolerance could still be found. Whether this was due to a genuinely more liberal attitude toward blacks, or to scant exposure to them, residents of the Old Northwest territories of Wisconsin, Michigan, and Minnesota were more divided on the subject of racial coexistence. Indeed, some whites there favored granting blacks additional rights, in particular the franchise. In Wisconsin, a territorial lawmaker first proposed extending this right in 1844, although his motion was defeated, 21-5.[4] Two years later, a similar proposal was tabled in the territorial Council by a single vote, 7-6, and then defeated in the House by a margin of 16-10.[5] And when delegates to the territory's constitution convention convened in Madison a few months later, they received a number of petitions asking that the existing prohibition on black suffrage be lifted. Opposition to slavery was also growing inside Wisconsin at that time, thanks to local Protestant churches. (However, many whites simply wanted to keep the chattel system out in order to protect their own self-interest. For example, the avowedly antislavery Liberty party argued that slavery tended to "erode the liberties of white men."[6]) The fact that, as of 1850, more than half of

---

1. Another reason is that slaves who had been freed under Spanish rule — that is, prior to 1807 — had largely died by 1850. Once Spain had ceded control over Louisiana, it became far more difficult for a slave to gain his or her liberty.
2. Florence R. Beatty-Brown, "Legal Status of Arkansas Negroes Before Emancipation," *Arkansas Historical Quarterly* 28:1 (Spring 1969), 8, 11.
3. Texas's 1836 constitution required any free black wishing to reside in the Republic to petition its legislature for permission. In 1840, that body voted that *all* free blacks had to leave, but this law was not enforced. However, after Texas joined the Union, even more punitive measures were enacted. For instance, any black who insulted, abused, or verbally threatened a white person was subject to between 25 and 100 lashes. Alwyn Barr, *Black Texans: A History of Black Americans in Texas, 1528-1995* (Norman: University of Oklahoma Press, 1996), 5, 9. During their war for independence, Anglo Texans had worried about free blacks joining the Mexican side. See Schoen, "Free Negro in Texas," 171.
4. Michael J. McManus, *Political Abolitionism in Wisconsin, 1840-1861* (Kent, Ohio: Kent State University Press, 1998), 20.
5. Moses M. Strong, *Annual Address Before the State Historical Society of Wisconsin, Feb. 4, 1870* (Madison: Atwood & Culver, 1870), 35.
6. McManus, *Political Abolitionism*, 1, 8.

this state's non-native, American-born residents came from the New England and mid-Atlantic states largely explains this pro-black sentiment.[1]

However, this was still a minority viewpoint. At the Democrat-dominated convention of 1846, delegates soundly defeated (91-12) an amendment to the state constitution that would have given blacks the vote.[2] Some did so in order to ensure that the constitution would be approved.[3] (A proposal to put the question of non-white suffrage before Wisconsin's voters was also rejected, 51-47.) Opposition was particularly strong in the southwestern part of the territory, which had been largely settled by persons from Kentucky, Tennessee, and other Southern states, attracted by the presence of lead mines there.[4] But some European immigrants in eastern Wisconsin, as well as delegates who came from the Northeast, also wanted to keep blacks out. Racial animosity extended over a broad geographical range. A representative from Racine County who had been born in Ireland, Edward Ryan, told his fellow delegates he did not want to see his adopted home "overrun with runaway slaves from the South."[5] Neither did he wish to see the two races "mingle," counter to God's plan. And Moses Strong, a lawyer from Rutland, Vermont, delivered a "violent speech" against black suffrage.[6] As one recent historian has noted, "the debates revealed that racist attitudes prevailed even among supporters of black enfranchisement."[7] When asked to decide this controversial issue in an April 1847 referendum, voters all across Wisconsin, overwhelmingly from the free states, rejected broadening the right to vote by a 2-1 margin — 15,959 to 7,704.[8] By doing so, they sent a clear signal that free blacks would not be welcomed.[9]

Similarly, in 1835, Michigan lawmakers debated ending the territory's whites-only restriction on voting but ultimately decided against doing so,

---

1. Ibid., 3.
2. See *Publications of the State Historical Society of Wisconsin*, vol. 27, *The Convention of 1846*, ed Milo M. Quaife (Madison: Wisconsin State Historical Society, 1919), 268. Of the 12 delegates who supported black suffrage, six came from New York, three from Massachusetts, two from Connecticut, and one from New Hampshire. Several were members of the Whig Party. But leading opponents of this proposal, including Moses Strong (Vermont), W.H. Clark (New York), and D.A.J. Upham (Mass.,) also came from the New England and mid-Atlantic states.
3. McManus, *Political Abolitionism*, 28.
4. Delegates pointed out that an amendment to grant blacks the right to vote would be overwhelmingly rejected by voters in western Wisconsin. See, for example, remarks of Moses S. Gibson, 21 Oct. 1846, *Convention of 1846*, 217.
5. Remarks of Edward G. Ryan, 21 Oct. 1846, 214.
6. Remarks of Moses S. Strong, 21 Oct. 1846, 215.
7. McManus, *Political Abolitionism*, 31.
8. The counties that opposed this amendment by a margin of 3-to-1 or more included several in western Wisconsin (Grant, Lafayette, Green, Crawford, Richland, and St. Croix), but also Portage and Columbia, in the central part of the state, and Brown, Manitowoc, and Milwaukee, in the east. See *Publications of the State Historical Society of Wisconsin* vol. 28, *The Struggle Over Ratification, 1846-1847*, ed. Milo M. Quaife (Madison: Wisconsin State Historical Society, 1920), 698. In 1850, over 95 percent of American-born, out-of-state natives came from free states, with more than half of this group (68,595) being from New York

largely out of concern about a resulting black influx. (Previously, the territorial legislature had also passed laws requiring would-be black residents to produce certificates of freedom and post bonds of $500; another measure banned interracial marriage.) Representative of the opposition to such a constitutional change are the comments of Isaac Crary, a lawyer from Connecticut, who cautioned his fellow delegates that former slaves were looking for an "asylum" in the free states and might head straight for Michigan if they were given the vote. "Erase the word white from this part of our constitution," Crary declared, "and the unsettled portions of this territory may very soon be filled up with a race that can you can never remove without doing violence to their right."[1] Echoing this view was Kentucky native John Norvell, who wondered why the convention would want to "hold out inducements" to the black race.[2] The 1835 convention ended up reserving the franchise for whites only, with just 17 of the 80 delegates voting to grant it to black freemen.[3] This result came out of a legislative body made up predominantly of men from the Northeast.[4]

When Michigan voters had a chance to express their own opinions on black suffrage, they turned it down just as emphatically. Upholding the state's restriction on voting rights indicates how determined residents were to keep blacks from entering and "commingling" with whites in their new home.[5] That such laws were adopted in a state in which *over 98 percent* of the non-native, American-born population came from free states attests to how pervasive anti-black prejudice was in the northern half of the United States.[6] Likewise, during Minnesota's 1857 constitutional convention, Democrats defeated a proposal to award the suf-

---

9. In 1849, another state referendum was held on black suffrage, and this measure was approved. However, since a majority of voters did not participate, the results were discounted. McManus, *Political Abolitionism*, 65. For blacks to have the right to vote was rare in the free states. As of 1840, 93 percent of Northern free blacks lived in states that denied them the franchise. Litwack, *North of Slavery*, 75. The five New England states — Maine, New Hampshire, Vermont, Massachusetts, and Rhode Island — that extended equal rights to free blacks accounted for only 3.6 percent of this population group in 1850.

1. Remarks of Isaac E. Crary, 22 May 1835, *The Michigan Constitutional Conventions of 1835-1836*, ed. Harold M. Dorr (Ann Arbor: University of Michigan Press, 1940), 162.

2. Remarks of John Norvell, 22 May 1835, *Conventions*, 157.

3. See Appendix A, roll call vote #17, *Conventions*.

4. At the convention, 56 delegates were natives of New England or mid-Atlantic states, with 27 from New York alone.

5. When Michigan lawmakers met to revise the state's constitution in 1850, they received a petition asking that blacks be given the vote. The chief argument against taking this step was that it would lead to a rise in the state's non-white population. One delegate asserted that an overwhelming majority of white voters was opposed to extending the franchise. And, in fact, when the issue was put to the voters in November, they turned it down by a margin of nearly three to one (32,000 to 12,800). The convention also voted against so changing the constitution by 59-21. Of those opposed, all but one came from a Northeastern free state or a foreign country. See *Report of the Proceedings and Debates in the Convention to Revise the Constitution of the State of Michigan, 1850* (Lansing: R.W. Ingals, 1850), vi, vi, 288, 289, 482, 483.

frage to blacks, by appealing to belief in white supremacy. They argued that the coming of an "enervated and ignorant race" would bring "in our system an element of dissatisfaction, danger and corruption."[1] Even after the Civil War, voters in Minnesota twice rejected a constitutional amendment that would have extended the franchise to non-whites. Only on the third try, in 1868, did this bill finally pass, with 56 percent of voters in favor.

Whites in this part of the United States were already "protected" against extensive interracial contact by the Ordinance of 1787. By outlawing the "peculiar institution" in the Old Northwest, this act had sought to guarantee that black bondsmen would never come to these territories and that, therefore, down the road, white residents would never have to deal with a population of emancipated slaves. Other territories and states created further west could depend upon a similar barrier — namely, the Missouri Compromise — to keep slaves out. Extension of the 36.30 parallel had placed most of these lands, except for present-day Oklahoma, Texas, New Mexico, and southern California, off limits to the chattel system. This demarcation line remained in effect until Congress enacted the Kansas-Nebraska Act in 1854.[2] Antipathy toward blacks also prompted lawmakers in the free territories of Iowa, Kansas, Nebraska, Utah, Colorado, and Oregon to consider racially exclusive laws similar to those already adopted in the Old Northwest.[3] In 1858, Nebraska came close to prohibiting the in-migration of black freemen. After narrowly passing a bill to abolish slavery, the lower chamber of its territorial legislature went on to adopt an amendment stating that "all free blacks shall be prohibited from settling in this Territory."[4] (Ultimately, this measure was tabled in the Council.) In Kansas, delegates to the "Free State" Topeka constitutional convention in 1855 banned slavery, but also denied free blacks the vote and excluded them from the territory.[5]

---

6. In 1850, 197,273 of Michigan's 200,907 native American residents born outside the state came from free states. Of these, 133,756 were born in just one state, New York. At the constitutional convention held that year, only two of the 100 elected delegates had been born in a slave state.

1. Quoted in Beverly Smith, "Black Suffrage," *Session Weekly* (St. Paul: Minnesota House Public Information Office, 1991), 1; www.house.leg.state.us/hinfo/swkly/1995-9/select/black.txt.

2. The Supreme Court's ruling in the Dred Scott case (1857) that the federal government lacked the power to ban slavery in the territories legally invalidated the Missouri Compromise.

3. According to Eugene Berwanger's calculations, 79.5 percent of voters in Indiana, Illinois, Kansas, and Oregon wanted free blacks excluded. Berwanger, *Frontier Against Slavery*, 140.

4. Quoted in William G. Cutler, *The Andreas' History of the State of Nebraska* (Chicago: Andreas' Western Historical Publishing Co., 1882), 182. www.kancoll.org/books/andreas-ne/state/state-pl.html#state.

5. Three-quarters of the delegates originally from the Midwest supported the exclusion of blacks. Berwanger, *Frontier Against Slavery*, 112.

Only New Englanders at this gathering argued that blacks should be treated as equals under the law. Other elected representatives cared little about slavery, only about land.[1] They adopted a nominally "antislavery" posture in order to keep *all* blacks out of Kansas.[2] Asked to ratify this racial ban, voters in December did so overwhelmingly. At a subsequent convention, held in Wyandotte in 1859, a delegate from Ohio proposed that Kansas become not just a free state but a "free white state" so that it would not become a "receptacle of free negroes and runaway slaves" from neighboring slave states.[3] After much discussion, capped off by an impassioned speech by Solon O. Thacher, a 28-year-old lawyer from New York, this proposal was defeated by a vote of 26-21.[4] Nonetheless, the convention did retain the "whites-only" restrictions on rights written into previous Kansan constitutions, and this action had the desired effect of discouraging black migration. By 1860, only 0.6 percent of Kansas' population was black.[5]

As the national debate over slavery and black freemen heated up in the years prior to the Civil War, some of these race-based laws were tightened. Whites in states ranging from Ohio to Oregon feared that the slightest improvement in the official status of blacks would cause members of this race to head in their direction. Hence, white hostility in Ohio toward such in-migration was even stronger at the 1850 constitutional convention than it had been nearly half a century before. The same tendency was evident in Iowa. In drafting its territorial laws in 1839, and writing two state constitutions in the 1840s, the Southern-dominated legislature had passed measures (modeled on ones previously approved in Virginia, Kentucky, and Louisiana) to reduce the likelihood of black migration, even though only about 200 blacks were then living there.[6] These included a ban on

---

1. Cf., for example, David M. Potter, *The Impending Crisis, 1848-186* (New York: Harper & Row, 1976), 202.
2. Cf. Katz, *Black West*, 54.
3. Remarks of William C. McDowell, 14 July 1859, *A Reprint of the Proceedings and Debates of the Convention Which Framed the Constitution of Kansas at Wyandotte in July 1859* (Topeka: Kansas State Printing Plant, 1920), 178. Cf. Berwanger, *Frontier Against Slavery*, 106.
4. Benjamin F. Simpson, "The Wyandotte Constitutional Convention," Appendix C, *Proceedings and Debates of the Convention*, 660. Thacher spoke eloquently for preserving Kansas as "the inheritance of free men and free institutions" and denied that his willingness to allow blacks in was based on belief in "Negro equality." Thacher felt that white animosity would suffice to keep free blacks from migrating to Kansas. See remarks of Solon O. Thacher, 14 July 1859, *ibid.*, 179-81. At the time, some argued that anti-black feeling in Kansas was so strong that voters would not approve a constitution unless it included an exclusionary provision. This turned out not to be the case, however. See Appendix D-2, "Sources of the Constitution," *ibid.*, 697.
5. In his book on "Bleeding Kansas," James Rawley argues that pervasive anti-black prejudice "justified excluding blacks from the territories." James A. Rawley, *Race and Politics: "Bleeding Kansas" and the Coming of the Civil War* (Philadelphia/New York: J.B. Lippincott, 1969), vii. The statistic on Kansas' black population is cited in Quintard Taylor, *In Search of the Racial Frontier: African Americans in the American West, 1528-1990* (New York: W.W. Norton, 1994), 76.

interracial marriage and the denial of educational rights to blacks. Although this "black code" was rarely enforced (and was denounced by abolitionists in the territory), it did clearly convey Iowa's inhospitality to non-whites.[1] Efforts to relax these restrictions were met with counterproposals to strengthen them. In 1844, delegates even approved an amendment making black migration into the territory illegal, but this was eventually overruled as federally unconstitutional.[2] When a petition was introduced to treat blacks as equals under Iowa law, a Democratic representative, Jonathan C. Hall, responded by saying white Iowans could "never consent to open the doors of our beautiful State and invite him [the black freeman] to settle our Lands."[3] In January 1851, both houses of Iowa's legislature approved a measure that would have prevented non-whites from coming to the territory, with Democrats voting heavily in favor.[4]

At a third convention, in 1857, delegates again took up the matter of black migration. In the interim, opposition to blacks had intensified, even though the state's non-white population had scarcely increased.[5] This more intransigent position was fortified by legislative steps taken elsewhere in the country — in particular, Florida's joining the Union in 1845 with a clause in its constitution giving lawmakers the power to pass laws to prevent free blacks and mulattoes from entering the state and congressional debating of the Wilmot Proviso, which sought to exclude slavery from Southwestern territories acquired from Mexico.[6] Some delegates argued strenuously that, if Iowa did not take steps to bar blacks, they would soon inundate the state. This would "degrade" its white population. One member of the convention protested loudly against Iowa's becoming "an asylum for the superannuated, the worn and broken down [slaves] of other states."[7] Others contended that the presence of blacks would deter whites from migrating to Iowa and slow its economic development. At the same time, lawmakers more favorably disposed toward blacks proposed that they should be given the same citizenship rights as whites.[8] A few of these delegates

---

6. In 1840, there were 188 blacks in Iowa. Robert R. Dykstra, *Bright Radical Star: Black Freedom and White Supremacy on the Hawkeye Frontier* (Cambridge: Harvard University Press, 1993), viii. Dykstra notes that the major concern was an influx of manumitted slaves from Missouri's "black belt." More than half of the representatives at the 1838 session of Iowa's legislature came from slave states.

1. *Ibid.*, 44.

2. *Ibid.*, 60.

3. *Ibid.*, 53.

4. Democrats voted 29-13 for this amendment, but all nine Whigs opposed it. *Ibid.*, 112.

5. During the proceedings, delegates stated that a state census showed that 272 blacks were residing in Iowa in 1857. However, the federal census for 1850 lists 333 free blacks, and the 1860 one has 1,069 living in Iowa.

6. Dykstra, *Bright Radical Star*, 108.

7. Remarks of Amos Harris, 31 Jan. 1857, *The Debates of the Constitutional Convention of the State of Iowa* (Davenport: Luse, Laue & Co., 1857), vol. 1, 134.

felt that Iowa ought to extend a welcoming hand to both races, while others questioned the constitutionality of banning their entry.[1]

A third faction at this 1857 convention wanted to see slavery come to Iowa (now that this was legally permissible, in light of the recent Supreme Court ruling, in the Dred Scott case, that Congress could not prohibit slavery in the territories), but vehemently opposed letting in free blacks. These representatives regarded a proposed constitutional amendment to give free blacks the vote as designed to entice members of this group to come to Iowa.[2] Criticizing it, one delegate pointed out that he and a number of his fellow Kentuckians had been driven out of their native state because of slavery, which they considered "a curse upon the poor, free, laboring white man."[3] In the end, the proposal to enfranchise blacks was rejected by a two-to-one margin.[4] This outcome reflected a broad consensus among white Iowans — encompassing Republicans and Democrats alike — that blacks were unwanted. (This hostility was further expressed when the state's voters gave a thumbs-down to non-white voting in a referendum held later in 1857.) When the convention then took up the question of whether or not blacks should be allowed to testify in court, one speaker noted with regret that prejudice against this race was actually stronger in Iowa than in the Deep South, where an "amalgamating and unmistakable bleaching process is going on."[5] He thus held out little hope for passing an amendment bestowing this right on blacks, and, indeed, it was quickly tabled.

In the ensuing debate over black suffrage, only a few took the position that the convention should support it. Two delegates issued an minority committee report that described a dire future for Iowa if blacks were to settle there in large numbers:

> However your committee may commiserate with the degraded condition of the negroes, and feel for his [sic] fate, yet they can never consent to open the doors of our beautiful State, and invite him to settle our lands. The policy of other States would drive the whole black population of the Union upon us. The ballot-box would fall into their hands, and a train of evils would follow, that, in the opinion of your committee, would be incalculable. The rights of persons would be less secure, and private property materially impaired. The injustice to the white population would be beyond computation . . . No one can doubt that a degraded prostitution of

8. The proponent of this amendment was Rufus L.B. Clarke, a 37-year-old attorney from Connecticut.
1. One opponent of giving blacks more rights argued that white voters would reject the new constitution if such provisions were added. Remarks of George Gillaspy, 3 Feb. 1857, *Debates*, vol. 1, 189.
2. Remarks of George Gillaspy, 21 Jan. 1857, *Debates*, vol. 1, 130.
3. Remarks of John Edwards, 23 Feb. 1857, *Debates*, vol. 2, 682.
4. Supporting this proposal were 10 delegates, whose roots lay in Maine, Massachusetts, Connecticut (2), New York (3), Pennsylvania, Indiana, and Ohio. *Debates*, vol. 1, 180.
5. Remarks of John T. Clark, 3 Feb. 1857, *Debates*, 192.

moral feeling would ensue; a tendency to amalgamate the two races would be superinduced; a degraded and reckless population would follow; idleness, crime and misery would come in their train, and government itself fall into anarchy or despotism.[1]

Ultimately, the legislature sidestepped the issue of black suffrage, allowing Iowa's voters to decide. They flatly rejected any extension of the right to vote. The state's whites-only restriction remained in effect until three years after the Civil War ended.[2]

It is instructive to correlate the various positions on race taken by delegates with where they — and their constituents — came from. The two most outspoken opponents of black settlement and legal rights in Iowa were George Gillaspy, a 42-year-old farmer born in Kentucky, and the above-mentioned Jonathan Hall, a lawyer from upstate New York. Gillaspy represented the 8th District, which encompassed Wapello County. Hall was elected by voters in Des Moines County. Both of these counties are located in the southeastern corner of Iowa — near slave enclaves along the Mississippi River in neighboring Missouri. It was to this part of the state that runaways were apt to flee, making their presence a particularly inflammatory issue. (Most delegates who wanted to deny blacks rights in Iowa came from its southern counties.) Two counties represented by leading proponents of black rights were Henry, also in the southeast part of the state, and Alamakee, in the extreme northeast, bordering Wisconsin. Their spokesmen at the constitutional convention were Rufus L. B. Clarke, a lawyer born in Connecticut, and John T. Clark, another attorney, who had migrated to Iowa from New York. Despite their differing positions on bills dealing with free blacks, these four delegates represented remarkably similar constituencies. All four had overwhelming majorities of out-of-state, Northern natives (between 73.5 and 92.3 percent). In all four districts, the single largest regional bloc consisted of persons born in the "butternut" states of Illinois, Indiana, and Ohio. This proportion ranged from a low of 32.9 percent in Alamakee County to a high of 64.1 percent in Wapello.[3] Geographical proximity likely accounts for this variation, as Alamakee was more distant from Illinois than the other three counties.

---

1. J.C. Hall and D.W. Price, minority report, Special Committee on Suffrage, *Debates*, vol. 2, 651.
2. As late as 1860, Sen. James Harlan of Iowa delivered a speech denouncing Democratic policies that would "fill the virgin Territories [of the Southwest] with negroes, wherever negro labor can be made profitable." James C. Harlan, "Shall the Territories Be Africanized?" Speech delivered in the U.S. Senate, 4 Jan. 1860. www.hti.umich.edu/cgi/t/text/pageviewer-idx?c=moa;cc=moa;sid=d7495dbd56b672debfb3e48f77283522;q1=Iowa;rgn=title;view=image;seq=0001;idno=ABJ4929.0001.001

Given the predominance of Northern natives in these four counties — and, in fact, throughout Iowa prior to the Civil War[1] — there are two possible explanations for their generally anti-black posture. Either migrants from the North were as prejudiced against blacks as Southerners, or else a large percentage of "butternut" state natives who moved to Iowa had family roots below the Mason Dixon Line and thus held the racially intolerant views common to that region. Existing information about migratory patterns in the Old Northwest strongly suggests that the latter is more likely. It is well known that many settlers left Ohio, Illinois, and Indiana in the three decades prior to the Civil War. This trend continued after the war as well. By 1900, for example, 178,000 natives of the Buckeye State had moved to other states. By far the greatest number of them went to neighboring Indiana, but Kansas, Michigan, and Iowa also had large numbers of Ohio natives. In 1860, persons born in the "butternut" states accounted for 53 percent of Kansas's American-born, non-native residents, 42.5 percent of this contingent in Iowa, and 13.4 percent in Michigan.

While these residents were officially "Northerners," they were actually the descendants of transplanted Southerners. For the exodus from the "butternut" states was primarily out of the lower tier counties that had been initially been settled by migrants from the South. One can see this pattern clearly in Ohio. Between 1810 and 1850, the population in 18 southern counties grew by over 400,000, but the number of people living in 18 northern counties increased by 1.7 million. A decade before the Civil War, there were nearly four times as many people living in northern Ohio as in the southern part. But the same outflow occurred in Indiana and Illinois as well. Why did so many Southern natives and their offspring leave these states? A primary reason was the coming of settlers from the Northeast. The opening of the Erie Canal in 1825 and the advent of steamships on the Great Lakes a few years later spurred their journey west. As a result, by 1850, New Yorkers constituted the largest single bloc of migrants living in Illinois, and six of the top ten "donor" states were situated north of the Ohio River.[2] New arrivals from free states thickly populated the northern counties of all three "butternut" states and thus changed these states' predominantly Southern character. This increase in the number of Northern natives residing in Ohio helps to explain its somewhat more receptive attitude toward blacks by

---

3. These statistics are derived from *The Census Returns of the Different Counties of the State of Iowa for 1856* (Iowa City: Crum & Boye, 1857): http://www.hti.umich.edu/cgi/t/text/pageviewer-idx?c=moa;cc=moa;sid=cd48a1b4c303bc020aa8ab6aabed8cad;q1=Iowa;rgn=title;view=image;seq=00000001;idno=AFP3813.0001.001

1. According to the 1850 federal census, persons born in free states constituted 74.5 percent of the non-native residents of Iowa born in the United States.

2. Davis, *Frontier Illinois*, 306.

mid-century. Because of this greater Northern presence, families with roots in the South no longer felt as at home in the Old Northwest as they once had. But the growth of the free black population also contributed to their wanderlust. Such an assertion is difficult to corroborate, but the animosity toward blacks later expressed by some migrants from Ohio do lend it credence. During the debates at the 1857 Iowa constitutional convention, for instance, Amos Harris, an native of the Buckeye State, pointed out that many other whites in Ohio would gladly migrate to Iowa if the latter adopted anti-black laws.[1] At the 1859 Republican-dominated Wyandotte convention in Kansas, natives of the "butter-nut" states accounted for 21 of the 52 attending delegates and therefore bore much responsibility for upholding constitutional restrictions on the rights of black residents.[2]

Discriminatory laws did discourage free blacks from moving to the territories and states that had enacted such measures, but these barriers did not assure that blacks would not find a home in some other, more hospitable part of the West. Denying them access to the entire region called for more sweeping measures, such as the Missouri Compromise's ban on slavery north of the 36.30 parallel. But this long-standing dividing line had left a large swath of territory to its south open to slavery and, as the urge to expand the nation's domain gained momentum in the 1840s and the United States government cast its eye covetously toward lands belonging to Mexico, there was mounting concern in the North that any such territorial acquisition would facilitate the spread of the "peculiar institution." And, wherever slaves went, manumitted blacks were bound to appear as well. The successful revolution of American settlers in Texas (1835-1836), the establishment of an independent republic there, and its incorporation into the United States as a slave state in December of 1845 had presaged such a biracial outcome. The ensuing Mexican War of 1846-48 was seen as an excuse for a naked land grab on the part of an aggressively expansionist Polk administration, and antislavery groups worried this conflict was being fought to enlarge the slave system further.

But a pent-up lust for new territorial and a desire to demonstrate Anglo-Saxon superiority over a racially "backward" and "powerless" Mexican people swept aside these reservations. The resolution to declare war passed in the Senate by an overwhelming vote of 41-2, and an equally jingoistic House voiced its approval, 174-14.[3] Even though support for this conflict quickly cooled in those

1. Remarks of Amos Harris, 31 Jan. 1857, *Debates*, vol. 1, 133.
2. All told, 41 delegates to the Wyandotte convention came from free states, seven from slave states, and four from abroad. However, a coalition of delegates from the Old Northwest and the slave states made up a majority of those attending.
3. Ray Allen Billington, *The Far Western Frontier, 1830-1860* (New York: Harper & Row, 1956), 191, 174.

parts of the country that had little to gain from it (chiefly the Northeast), the U.S. army's successes on the battlefield assured that an immense land mass would soon fall into the victor's lap. (And, indeed, when the Treaty of Guadalupe Hidalgo was signed, in February 1848, the United States gained, at one fell swoop, an area of some 500,000 square miles, increasing the size of the nation by two thirds.) The fate of these lands — that is, their position vis-à-vis slavery — was difficult to predict. What was clear was that they were not off-limits to chattel labor under federal law. Each annexed territory would have the right to decide for itself whether it wanted to be "slave" or "free."

It was in this atmosphere of uncertainty and congressional impotence over the possible extension of slavery that a 32-year-old freshman lawmaker from Pennsylvania named David Wilmot and several of his Democratic colleagues in the House went out for dinner in Washington one warm August night in 1846.[1] Out of their discussions that evening emerged a novel proposal — one that was destined to become one of the most controversial and divisive pieces of 19th-century legislation.[2] This proviso was drafted by Jacob Brinkerhoff, a representative from northern Ohio. However, Wilmot, being a new face in Congress and a loyal backer of the Polk administration, was thought to be a more politically palatable spokesman, and so he took the lead in introducing it.[3] Rising to speak on the House floor on August 8, the portly Pennsylvanian first duly offered his support for the "necessary and proper" war being fought against Mexico, as well as for any future acquisition of Mexican land — as long as this occurred as the result of negotiations or outright purchase, not of "conquest." But Wilmot's support for any such territorial expansion came with another major condition — that any land so annexed remain forever off limits to slavery.[4] His amendment to a $2 mil-

---

1. Those present included Martin Grover of New York, Brinkerhoff of Ohio and Hannibal Hamlin of Maine — Abraham Lincoln's first vice president. See Oliver C. Gardiner, *The Great Issue or The Three Presidential Candidates, Being a Brief Historical Sketch of the Free Soil Question in the United States* (Westport: Negro Universities Press, 1970), 60.
2. Charles Buxton Going, *David Wilmot Free Soiler: A Biography of the Great Advocate of the Wilmot Proviso* (New York: D. Appleton, 1924), 128.
3. George Pierce Garrison, *The American Nation: A History*, vol. 17, *Westward Extension, 1841-1850*, ed. Albert B. Hart (New York: Harper & Row, 1906), 256. Brinkerhoff, a native New Yorker, switched to the Republican Party in 1856. Eric Foner has taken the position that Preston King was more likely the author of the Proviso. See Foner, "The Wilmot Proviso Revisited," *Journal of American History* 56:2 (Sept. 1969), 265. In this article he points out that Van Buren Democrats from New York figured prominently in crafting this amendment and suggests that members of this branch of the party felt that identification with "Southern principles" was undermining Democrats' popularity in the state. He writes: "For western Democrats, and for many easterners as well, the Proviso represented a revolt against Southern control of the administration and the political power of the South." *Ibid.*, 274.
4. Remarks of David Wilmot, 8 Aug. 1846, 29th Congress, 1st Session, *Congressional Globe*, House of Representatives, 1214-5.

lion appropriations bill for working out a settlement with Mexico, thereafter known as the "Wilmot Proviso," stated that, "as an express and fundamental condition to the acquisition of any territory from the Republic of Mexico by the United States, by virtue of any treaty which may be negotiated between them, and to the use by the Executive of the moneys herein appropriated, neither slavery nor involuntary servitude shall ever exist in any part of said territory, except for crime, whereof the party shall first be duly convicted."

David Wilmot was, indeed, an unlikely rebel within the Democratic Party. While he had declined to back Polk during the 1844 election, Wilmot had shown himself to be a strong congressional proponent of the President's expansionist agenda. Twice he had voted to annex Texas, and in his maiden House address Wilmot had pledged his support for a war against Great Britain if that country refused to recognize legitimate American rights to the Oregon Territory.[1] The Pennsylvania Congressman's previous voting record on slavery gave little hint of a burning desire to exclude the "peculiar institution" from new territory. On the contrary, he had helped to defeat an amendment that would have kept slavery out of Texas, voted for its admission to the Union as a slave state, and, in December 1845, voted to restore the "gag rule" that for nearly a decade had kept anti-slavery petitions from being brought before Congress.[2]

In fact, Wilmot was not an opponent of slavery at all. Nor did his famed proviso indicate a change of heart on his part. Like many of his Northern colleagues, Wilmot remained wedded to a laissez-faire position on the slave system. As he would tell the House when it took up his proviso during its next session, in February 1847, "I make no war upon the South nor upon the slaves in the South. I have no squeamish sensitiveness upon the subject of slavery, nor morbid sympathy for the slave."[3] What prompted the Northern Congressman to introduce this amendment was his antipathy toward any further *extension* of slavery in the West. And, while his proviso could thus be seen as an antislavery measure, this was not why Wilmot wanted it to become law. An unabashed foe of abolitionists, he opposed the spreading of slavery not because this harmed and denigrated blacks, but because it harmed and denigrated *whites*. To Wilmot and many nominally "antislavery" politicians, it was only the welfare of the white race that mat-

---

1. Going, *David Wilmot*, 51. Remarks of David Wilmot, 7 Feb. 1946, 29th Congress, 1st Session, *Appendix to the Congressional Globe*, House of Representatives, 184-5. While uncertain that the United States' claim to all of Oregon was "clear and unquestionable," Wilmot said Americans should not "submit to be plundered of our rights" in order to avoid war.
2. Going, *David Wilmot*, 51, 49. Wilmot contended that since slavery already existed in Texas, he was simply respecting the right of its residents to decide this matter.
3. Remarks of David Wilmot, 8 Feb. 1847, 29th Congress, 2nd Session, *Appendix to the Congressional Globe*, House of Representatives, 354.

tered. In the West, white settlers were hoping to establish new homesteads and realize the American dream of freedom, independence, and material prosperity. If slavery came to these Western territories it would imperil this dream, for free white labor and enslaved black labor could not coexist. Unwilling to move where slaves lived, white workers would remain in the East, growing so numerous in the eastern half of the country that their wages and standard of living would fall sharply. Ultimately, white labor itself would become "enslaved" by these adverse economic developments.[1] Wilmot well understood fears that this might happen — and he hoped to rally opponents of slavery by evoking them.[2] This is why he was wont to refer to his amendment as the "White Man's Proviso."

When Wilmot presented his proviso, at the very end of Congress's session in August 1846, he did not spell out his reasons for wanting to keep any land wrested away from Mexico free of the "peculiar institution." The amendment passed the House along sectional lines, 77-58, but the Senate failed to act on it, and thus a final decision on the proviso was carried over to the next gathering of the 29th Congress, the following winter. When it came up for debate this time, Wilmot expanded the scope of his proposal so that it would pertain to *all* future territory absorbed by the United States.[3] During a speech on February 8, 1847, he also explained the reasons for his opposition to any continental extension of slavery:

> I plead the cause and the rights of white freemen. I would preserve to free white laborers a fair country, a rich inheritance, where the sons of toil, of my own race and own color, can live without the disgrace which association with negro slavery brings upon free labor. I stand for the inviolability of free territory. It shall remain free, so far as my voice or vote can aid in the preservation of its character . . . The white laborer of the North claims your service; he demands that you stand firm to his interests and his rights; that you preserve the future homes of his children, on the distant shores of the Pacific, from the degradation and dishonor of negro servitude. Where the negro slave labors, the free white man cannot labor by his side without sharing in his degradation and disgrace.[4]

---

1. Bernard Mandel, *Labor: Free and Slave, Workingmen and the Anti-Slavery Movement in the United States* (New York: Associated Authors, 1955), 117. White workers in both the North and South felt the Wilmot Proviso would free them from unfair competition with slaves. An article that appeared in the 24 July 1851 issue of the antislavery *National Era* noted that white mechanics meeting in Virginia and Georgia endorsed the proviso as "redemption and deliverance to them, until the final struggle comes." Quoted in *Contributions in American History*, vol. 157, *Northern Labor and Antislavery: A Documentary History*, ed. Philip S. Foner and Herbert Shapiro (Westport: Greenwood Press, 1994), 85. See also White, "*It's Your Misfortune, and None of My Own,*" 159.
2. Civil War historian Bruce Levine has argued that Wilmot felt adopting this position was the best way to reverse the popular decline of the Democratic Party. See Levine, *Half Slave and Half Free: The Roots of Civil War* (New York: Hill and Wang, 1992), 180.
3. When he introduced his proviso during this session of Congress, Wilmot was prepared to accept a congressional declaration of support for this anti-extension measure, in lieu of having it added to the Mexican appropriations bill. He revealed his position in a conversation with President Polk in late December. See, James K. Polk, *The Diary of James Polk During his Presidency, 1845-1849* (New York: Kraus Reprint Co., 1970), vol. 2, diary entry for 23 Dec. 1846, 288-90.

As far as Wilmot was concerned, whether or not a black was enslaved did not alter his negative impact on whites. He did not believe that a bondsman could improve either his character or his work ethic through emancipation. In his mind, the terms "slave labor" and "Negro" were virtually synonymous. Because the black race was innately inferior, its presence was necessarily detrimental to whites. On occasion, Wilmot likened blacks to a disease.[1] He could see evidence of the harm they wrought in the contrasting economic conditions that existed in free and slave states. In the latter, "there is always a lack of . . . energy and enterprise," whereas the "enterprise, the diligence, and the economy of free labor . . . has built up new Empires in the West."[2]

In arguing this case, Wilmot was making common cause with anti-black lawmakers and settlers, while distancing himself from Northerners who found slavery morally repugnant, inhumane, and contrary to the nation's basic principles.[3] This longstanding opposition to the chattel system, based in abolitionist societies and some churches, was largely, but not exclusively, confined to New England and the mid-Atlantic states. Its political appeal was therefore limited. By themselves, the abolitionists and others sympathetic to the plight of slaves could not hope to win many victories for their cause. The indifference, if not outright hostility, of the majority of whites stymied such aspirations. However, forging an alliance with *anti-black* voters on the basis of their shared dislike of the slave system offered a more promising political strategy. As was previously noted, such collusion between anti-slavery and anti-black groups in several western territories and states had led to the excluding of slavery as well as the forestalling of free black migration. (A number of congressmen backed Wilmot's proviso for other reasons, including disaffection with their Southern colleagues for not having fought to extend Oregon's northern boundary, political opposition to the "Slave Power," and unhappiness with President Polk's policies.[4] Furthermore, many Northern Democrats sided with Wilmot to display their displeasure over the South's control of their party.) Now this same approach was

---

4. Remarks of David Wilmot, 8 Feb. 1847, 29th Congress, 2nd Session, *Appendix*, 354-5.

1. Bilotta, *Race and the Rise of the Republican Party*, 83.

2. Remarks of David Wilmot, 8 Feb. 1847, *Appendix*, 355.

3. For example, during a speech in the House on Jan. 5, 1847, Rep. Preston King (New York) argued "The labor of the free white men and women, and of their children, cannot and will not eat and drink, and lie down, and rise up with the black labor of slavery; free white labor will not be degraded by such association. If slavery is not excluded by law, the presence of the slave will exclude the laboring white man." Remarks of Preston King, 5 Jan. 1847, 29th Congress, 2nd Session, *Congressional Globe*, House of Representatives, 114. Cf. "The Position of the Democratic Party," *National Era* 1:1 (7 Jan.1847), 3.

4. See Chaplain W. Morrison, *Democratic Politics and Sectionalism: The Wilmot Proviso Controversy* (Chapel Hill: University of North Carolina Press, 1967), 13, 15.

to be tested in the halls of Congress. When looked at in this light, it becomes evident that Jacob Brinkerhoff's yielding to David Wilmot as the point man for this proviso was an astute political calculation. For an appeal for votes was not to be made on the basis of principle, but rather of white self-interest. In so couching his case, Wilmot was reaching out particularly to many Western legislators, who were especially concerned about blacks settling on their side of the Mississippi.[1]

How views on slavery differed within this nascent alliance can be gleaned from comparing Wilmot's and Brinkerhoff's speeches on the proviso. Whereas Wilmot (and others) dwelt upon the concerns of white settlers contemplating a move west, Brinkerhoff invoked higher authorities — Thomas Jefferson, George Washington, the Declaration of Independence — in laying out his argument that slavery was an evil wholly incompatible with American values. In his House speech of February 10, Brinkerhoff declared that slavery was wrong, and that "there are some wrongs so great I cannot consent to commit them; some rights so sacred, that I cannot consent to be instrumental in their violation." He called upon his fellow Democrats to stand up for "the preservation of the great principles of liberty and of right" on which the nation was founded. Otherwise, by tolerating slavery, they would continue to make common cause with tyranny.[2]

While the differences between Wilmot and Brinkerhoff were philosophical, they also had a regional basis. A lawyer of Dutch extraction from upstate New York, Brinkerhoff expressed the moral objections to slavery raised more often in the Northeast than any other part of the country. By contrast, Wilmot came from rural northern Pennsylvania, where few whites opposed slavery on these grounds.[3] As he freely attested, his constituents had not the least affection for abolitionists.[4] Like him, many elected officials in the free states identified

---

1. It should be pointed out that some Western lawmakers, such as Ohio's George Fries, a Democrat, opposed the extension of slavery on moral and religious grounds. See remarks of Fries, 9 Feb. 1847, 29th Congress, 2nd Session, *Congressional Globe*, House of Representatives, 444. Historian Eric Foner has rejected the theory that the authors of the Wilmot Proviso hoped to create an "antiexpansionist arrangement between North and South." He concludes they were motivated mainly by concern that the growing popularity of antislavery groups would undermine their own electability. See Foner, "Wilmot Proviso," 278.
2. Remarks of Jacob Brinkerhoff, 10 Feb. 1847, 29th Congress, 2nd Session, *Appendix to the Congressional Globe*, House of Representatives, 378, 379.
3. Eric Foner points out that many New England natives settled in Wilmot's district, giving it an antislavery outlook, but this did not mean that their opposition had a religious or moral basis. Eric Foner, *Free Soil, Free Labor, Free Men: The Ideology of the Republican Party before the Civil War* (New York: Oxford University Press, 1970), 107.
4. See Wilmot's remarks, 8 Feb. 1847, *Appendix*, 355.

more with Western values — namely, a wish to keep blacks at bay.[1] They regarded the proviso as a means of securing a new American frontier for their own race.[2] One such politician was Abraham Lincoln. As a newly elected Whig congressman from Illinois, Lincoln did not arrive in Washington until several months after this debate took place, but he hinted at his own reasons for supporting Wilmot's proviso in an 1848 speech in the House. In these remarks, Lincoln represented himself not as a Northerner but as a "Western free state man, with a constituency I believe to be, and personal feelings I know to be, against the extension of slavery."[3]

Thanks to this proviso, the lines were more clearly and firmly drawn between North and South.[4] Congressmen from the slave states attacked Wilmot as an "abolitionist" whose proposal would tear the Union apart. Exclaimed one prominent Southern senator: "If by your legislation you seek to drive us from the territories of California and New Mexico . . . thereby attempting to fix a national degradation upon half the States of this Confederacy, I am for *disunion*."[5] Northerners vowed to make no more compromises with the detested slave system: not one more inch of territory would fall into its grasp. Both North and South balked at giving the other a decisive political advantage in these new territories.[6] After a

---

1. This wish was not limited to Western legislators, however. During the House debate on the Wilmot Proviso, Democratic congressman George O. Rathbun (New York) declared there was "no place" for freed slaves in the North. "As far as New York is concerned," he said, "should the refuse part of the population of Virginia reach our territory, we shall carry them back to Virginia." Remarks of George Rathbun, 9 Feb. 1847, 29th Congress, 2nd Session, *Congressional Globe*, House of Representatives, 365.
2. Ronald Takaki has made this point: "This northern concern for white racial purity was a basis for the opposition to the expansion of slavery into the western territories." Ronald Takaki, "The Black Child-Savage in Ante-Bellum America," in *The Great Fear: Race in the Mind of America*, ed. Gary B. Nash and Richard Weiss (New York: Holt, Rinehart & Winston, 1970), 35.
3. Remarks of Abraham Lincoln, 27 July 1848, "Speech on Taylor and the Veto," *The Abraham Lincoln Papers at the Library of Congress*, Gen. Correspondence, 1833-1916, *American Memory*: http://memory.loc.gov/cgi-bin/query/P?mal:7:./temp/~ammem_VxjW: Subsequently, Lincoln would vote for the proviso when it was again brought before the House.
4. Some Northern legislators did oppose the proviso because they reasoned that legalizing the "peculiar institution" in the Southwest would absorb excess slaves who otherwise might head north after being given their freedom. So argued, for example, Democratic congressman William Sawyer, from northwestern Ohio's 5th District. Sawyer vowed that he would "join his constituents in forming armed columns a mile deep to repel any black invasion of Ohio." Thomas R. Hietala, *Manifest Destiny: Anxious Aggrandizement in Late Jacksonian America* (Ithaca: Cornell University Press, 1985), 169. Nonetheless, pro-proviso sentiment unified lawmakers from the North more than the effort to prohibit slavery in Missouri more than a quarter century earlier, when one of every 10 free-state congressmen had sided with the slave states.
5. Remarks of Sen. Robert Toombs (Ga.), delivered in the House, 13 Dec. 1849. Quoted in Fehrenbacher, "The Wilmot Proviso and the Mid-Century Crisis," *Three Sectional Conflicts*, 20.
6. Morrison, *Democratic Politics*, 59-60.

series of incendiary speeches, the House again passed Wilmot's proviso, 115-106. Significantly, congressmen from states in the Old Northwest voted overwhelming for it, across party lines — 28 to 6.[1] Indeed, without their support, the measure would not have passed. This outcome marked the forging of a new political bond between Northerners and Westerners based on their shared opposition to the extension of slavery.[2] With tensions riding high all over the nation, South Carolina's John C. Calhoun then orchestrated adoption of the appropriation bill — minus Wilmot's proviso — in the Southern-dominated Senate. On the evening of February 26, with the gallery packed and gas lights illuminating the chamber with a dazzling, surreal glow, four free-state senators, most notably Lewis Cass of Michigan, joined forces with their slave-state colleagues to make this possible.[3] Subsequently, backers of the proviso in the House attempted to tack it on to the bill approved by the Senate, but failed to do so when several Northern legislators switched sides.[4] Thus, the Wilmot Proviso was defeated.[5]

For Northern opponents of the "peculiar institution," the lesson of this controversy was clear. Since their region of the country was less solidly unified *against* slavery than the South was *for* it, a more encompassing political strategy was needed to advance the antislavery cause. The enlisting of legislators desirous of preserving the West for the white race was a shrewd maneuver toward attaining that goal. As one historian has pointed out, the proviso (and, later, the Free Soil movement) "offered whites a way to oppose slavery without necessarily embracing blacks . . . the future of the nation, or certainly of the North, lay in the West. If whites were to enjoy that future as free men, they would have to keep

---

1. Of the representatives from Ohio, Indiana, Illinois, and Michigan who supported the proviso, 11 were Whigs and 17 Democrats. The six Old Northwest opponents of this amendment, however, were all Democrats. For this breakdown of the congressional vote, see "The Wilmot Proviso," *National Era* 1:8 (2 Feb. 1847), 2.
2. Of the 106 representatives who opposed the proviso, 18 came from the free states. Southern congressmen, by contrast, were almost unanimous in rejecting this amendment: only a lone Whig congressman from Delaware voted "yes."
3. "The Closing Debate in the Senate on the Three Million Bill," *National Era* 1:10 (10 Mar. 1847), 2. Cass, who would become the Democratic candidate for President in 1848, angered many of his Northern colleagues by not supporting the proviso. On the Senate floor, he contended that passage of this amendment would undermine the nation's war effort against Mexico. "The choice before us is the proviso or the war," he said. "One or the other must be given up." Remarks of Lewis Cass, 1 Mar. 1847, 29th Congress, 2nd Session, *Congressional Globe*, Senate, 550.
4. There was speculation that President Polk had persuaded these representatives to change their votes by awarding them favors such as diplomatic assignments and military postings for their sons. See "Freedom Betrayed," *National Era* 1:9 (4 Mar. 1847), 3. Cf. "How It Was Done," *National Era* 1:12 (25 Mar. 1847), 4.
5. President Polk had indicated that he would veto the proviso if it had passed both houses of Congress. He felt that slavery was a "domestic question," best left to individual states to decide. See, *Diary of James Polk*, vol. 4, diary entry for 9 March 1849, 364-5.

the region free of slaves. From that simple assumption grew an overarching anti-slavery argument that linked unlikely allies all across the continent."[1]

***

The North-South split over the Wilmot Proviso had exposed a political fault line deeper and more significant than party affiliation. Whigs and Democrats north of the Mason Dixon Line had banded together against their counterparts to the south. In the final House vote to reinstate the proviso as part of the Senate bill, all 36 Northern Whigs had sided with Wilmot, while all Southern ones had joined with the pro-slavery bloc. (Free-state Democrats were divided 41 to 22.) As long as these two national parties were so divided, the forces opposed to slavery could not muster a reliable majority in Congress (certainly not in the Senate) and, therefore, could not hope to shape national policy on this highly explosive issue. Frustrated by this stalemated state of affairs, Northern lawmakers at both the state and national levels began to ponder the creation of a new political movement that could give a decisive edge to the antislavery campaign.

As the presidential election of 1848 neared, unhappiness within the Whig and Democratic parties over their accommodating positions on slavery turned into open revolt. In New York State, radical Democrats allied with former President Martin Van Buren broke away from the party establishment when it was taken over by a conservative group known as the "Hunkers" in 1847.[2] These upstart "Barnburners" — so named because they wanted to "burn down" the state's Democratic Party in order to get rid of its corruption[3] — held their own convention in the fall of that year, endorsing free trade as well as the Wilmot Proviso. (Wilmot addressed this gathering, as did Van Buren's son, John, who embraced this anti-extension position on behalf of "the free white laborers of the North and South . . ."[4]) Committed to establishing libertarian, republican values

---

1. Gregory H. Nobles, *American Frontiers: Cultural Encounters and Continental Conquest* (New York: Hill and Wang, 1997), 164. Thomas R. Hietala makes a similar argument. He sees white vulnerability vis-à-vis other races driving western settlement: " . . . the country's black population provided a powerful impetus behind territorial expansion in the 1840s." Hietala, *Manifest Destiny*, 10. Reginald Horsman concurs: "Debates on slave expansion in the 1850s revolved as much around the issue of preventing blacks from degrading new white areas as they did around the issue of the evils of slavery." Horsman, *Race and Manifest Destiny: The Origins of American Racial Anglo-Saxonism* (Cambridge: Harvard University Press, 1981), 275.
2. This faction gained its name from its members' reputed "hunger" for power and political office. See Gardiner, *Great Issue*, 46.
3. This was how a Dutch farmer reputedly got rid of rats. See John Mayfield, *Rehearsal for Republicanism: Free Soil and the Politics of Antislavery* (Port Washington, N.Y.: Kennikat Press, 1980), 9. Cf. Gardiner, *Great Issue*, 46.
4. Quoted in Joseph G. Rayback, *Free Soil: The Election of 1848* (Lexington: University Press of Kentucky, 1970), 77.

in the West, the Barnburners firmly opposed any introduction of slaves there.[1] They stood for "Free Soil, Free Labor, Free Trade, and Free Speech."[2] When these radical Democrats gathered again, in Utica the following February, they reaffirmed their steadfast support for the rights of white labor. Keynote speaker Martin Grover, a congressman from the western part of the state, proclaimed: "The question is not whether black men are to be made free, but whether we white men are to remain free."[3] After they were refused recognition at the 1848 Democratic national convention in Baltimore, the Barnburners watched in dismay as the delegates nominated Cass — an expansionist in favor of letting Westerners decide the slavery question for themselves.[4] To carry on the fight to keep this region of the country "free," in light of waning party support for the Wilmot Proviso, these radical Democrats would have to mount their own separate campaign.

Meanwhile, in Massachusetts, Whigs unhappy with their party's support for Texas annexation and the war against Mexico had staged an uprising of their own. Fearful that a more powerful "slavocracy" would endanger Northern free labor, these so-called "Conscience Whigs" also rejected the slave system as immoral.[5] Turning their backs on the "Cotton Whigs" who held sway at both the state and national levels,[6] they reached out increasingly to popular abolitionist elements in Massachusetts and sought to build ties with them to halt slavery's expansion.[7] The fractious congressional vote on the Wilmot Proviso

---

1. In emphasizing republican values, the Barnburners "implicitly contrasted a system that was essentially black to one that was white." Mayfield, *Rehearsal for Republicanism*, 84.
2. This was the headline for a report on the Herkimer convention published in the *New York Post. Ibid.*, 100. "Free Trade, Free Labor, Free Soil, Free Speech, and Free Men" was the title of John Van Buren's speech before the Barnburner convention at Utica in February 1848. Gardiner, *Great Issue*, 92.
3. Quoted in Morrison, *Democratic Politics*, 61. The argument that blacks would "ruin" Western lands was popularized by James Russell Lowell in his widely read, allegorical *Bigelow Papers*.
4. Cass had recently adopted this new doctrine of "popular sovereignty." In a 30 Dec. 1847 letter to A.O.P. Nicholson, Cass stated that he supported "leaving to the people of any territory, which may be hereafter acquired, the right to regulate it for themselves, under the general principles of the Constitution." Quoted in Gardiner, *Great Issue*, 43.
5. The most notable Whig opponents of slavery were John Quincy Adams, his son Charles Francis Adams, Charles Sumner, Richard H. Dana, Samuel Gridley Howe, and J.G. Palfrey. See Kinley J. Brauer, *Cotton versus Conscience: Massachusetts Whig Politics and Southwestern Expansion, 1843-1848* (Lexington: University Press of Kentucky, 1967), 24, and Rayback, *Free Soil*, 82.
6. The Cotton Whigs, representing cotton manufacturers in the state, had dominated the Massachusetts party since its inception. Brauer, *Cotton versus Conscience*, 1.
7. During the election of 1844, the abolitionist Liberty party had attracted larger numbers of voters in all but two of Massachusetts' counties. Two years later, this abolitionist movement gained more strength, and "Conscience Whigs" feared that their party would be swept aside unless it took a more unequivocal stance against the "peculiar institution." *Ibid.*, 97, 149.

convinced the Conscience Whigs that the existing national party could not survive intact for much longer.[1] They, too, needed to find a new political platform on which to promulgate their antislavery agenda.

Thus, the year 1848 was ripe for the emergence of a new political party. To bring this into being, leaders of the Barnburner Democrats, the Conscience Whigs, and the abolitionist Liberty Party agreed to hold a mass meeting in Buffalo, New York, that August. Literally as well as philosophically, this turned out to be a "big tent" affair, attracting a veritable army of over 20,000 opponents of slavery to a huge open-air forum in the city's courthouse square.[2] It was a motley assemblage, with delegates hailing from all of the free states and further south — from Maine, New Hampshire, Vermont, Massachusetts, Rhode Island, Connecticut, New York, New Jersey, Pennsylvania, Ohio, Michigan, Wisconsin, Illinois, Indiana, Iowa, Delaware, Maryland, Virginia, and the District of Columbia.[3] If politics now and then makes for strange bedfellows, this was certainly one of those occasions. From Boston came the Conscience Whig leader Charles Francis Adams, scholarly and "prepossessing,"[4] resolved to carry on the antislavery work of his late father, John Quincy, whom he so strikingly resembled. From Brooklyn came Walt Whitman, footloose, recently unemployed as an editor — his head full of dreams of a continental Anglo-American destiny, his heart with the free (white) workingmen who would forge this grand empire with their own hands, without any interference from blacks.[5] From nearby Rochester came the black abolitionist, Frederick Douglass, fresh from attending the first national conven-

---

1. In the March 1847 House vote to reinstate the Wilmot Proviso, the Whigs had split — 48 in favor, 21 opposed.
2. Overnight, the gathering thus increased Buffalo's population by at least 50 percent.
3. Before the convention commenced, one local Democratic newspaper predicted it would be a "fairly funny affair," with "politicians of every kind" in attendance, including "the disaffected of all parties" and "advocates of the most reckless ultraisms." "The Buffalo Convention," *Daily Courier* (Buffalo), 2 Aug. 1848. Afterwards, another Buffalo newspaper described the convention's organization as "the most peculiar that has probably ever been known in the political history of parties. It was constituted of material that heretofore has stood at opposite points of the political compass." "The Free Soil Convention," *Morning Express* (Buffalo), 12 Aug. 1848.
4. "The Buffalo Convention," *Daily Courier*, 10 Aug. 1848.
5. In the *Brooklyn Daily Eagle* of 7 July 1846, Whitman had written: "We love to indulge in thoughts of the future extent and power of this Republic — because with its increase is the increase of human happiness and liberty . . . . What has miserable, inefficient Mexico — with her superstition, her burlesque upon freedom, her actual tyranny by the few over the many — what has she to do with the great mission of peopling the New World with a noble race? Be it ours, to achieve that mission! Be it ours to roll down all of the upstart leaven of old despotism, that comes our way!" Over a decade later he would warn about a "black tide" threatening to engulf white workingmen and reiterate his opposition to letting free blacks settle in the Western territories. But, at the same time, Whitman considered black workers the equals of whites and advocated that all immigration barriers against other races be removed. See, for example, his unpublished 1856 manuscript entitled "The Eighteenth Presidency!"

tion for women's rights, at Seneca Falls, eager to advance the cause of black rights, too. From Ohio, bringing his wife, children, and nurse maid in tow, came a 40-year-old lawyer, Salmon Portland Chase, a zealous convert to the antislavery cause, fortified by "a great deal of faith" that its time had finally arrived.[1]

Starting on the morning of August 9, a "vast moving multitude, whose tumult was like the roaring of the sea," packed the Buffalo park in the mid-summer heat to hear ardent abolitionists, including a former slave, rail against slavery.[2] The crowd responded to their fiery words with shouts of "Amen!" and "So be it!" And when one Democratic speaker from Michigan dared to refer to Lewis Cass as "our candidate," silence from the assembled throng conveyed its stern disapproval. Ohio's Jacob Brinkerhoff mockingly proposed that his party's presidential nominee should drop the first letter from his last name. Zachary Taylor was denounced as a "Benedict Arnold" for spurning Whig principles. Joshua Giddings claimed it was Martin Van Buren who had remained true to these: he — Giddings — was now prepared to take the ex-president "to his bosom." There were repeated calls for Frederick Douglass to come forward to the podium. (He declined, pleading a sore throat.) Roused by the soaring rhetoric, the gathering evinced all the excitement and unanimity of a college pep rally.[3]

Meanwhile, sequestered in a nearby church, the pragmatic-minded, racially biased Barnburners quietly took charge of the proceedings.[4] While the speeches droned on under a sweltering sun, Chase — a future Chief Justice of the Supreme Court, already famed for his defense of fugitive slaves and their white protectors — worked with several others to hammer out a platform for the new party.[5] Reflecting Chase's paramount desire to build a united front against the extension of slavery,[6] this document was largely devoted to defending "free democracy" against the "slave power."[7] At the insistence of Barnburner represen-

---

1. Letter of Salmon P. Chase to Charles Sumner, 2 Dec. 1847, *The Samuel P. Chase Papers*, vol. 2, *Correspondence, 1823-1857*, ed. John Niven (Kent State: Kent State University Press, 1995), 161.
2. "Buffalo Free Soil Convention," *Morning Express* (Buffalo), 10 Aug. 1848.
3. "The Free Soil Convention," *Morning Express*, 11 Aug. 1848.
4. Untitled editorial, *Daily Courier*, 10 Aug. 1848. The Barnburners' opposition to slavery's expansion was based solely on its negative impact on free white workers. See Eric Foner, "Politics and Prejudice: The Free Soil Party and the Negro, 1849-1852," *Journal of Negro History* 50:4 (Oct. 1965), 239.
5. Chase had formerly belonged to the Liberty Party, but had quickly come to the realization that he had to find another forum to popularize the antislavery message among Northerner voters. See Foner, *Free Soil*, 79.
6. See letter of Chase to John P. Hale, 20 June 1848, Box 8, File 2, John P. Hale Papers, Special Collections, New Hampshire Historical Society, Concord, N.H.
7. In a letter written shortly after the convention, Chase stated: "The contest is between the Democracy disenthralled from subjection to the Slave Power & Hunkerism submitting to slaveholding dictation for the spoils of office." Letter of Chase to Benjamin F. Butler, 2 Aug. 1848, *Correspondence*, 182.

tatives, it said nothing about emancipating the slaves or giving blacks equal rights.[1] In order to reach consensus behind this new party's goals, Chase had to be circumspect about its underlying rationale.[2] In fact, the slogan that was inscribed on the party's banner — *Free Soil, Free Speech, Free Labor, and Free Men* — was almost diabolically ambiguous. These ringing phrases left much room for interpretation. "Free soil" evoked the populist goal of giving public lands in the West to poor settlers under the Homestead Laws, but also implied that these territories should be made available only to "free" (that is, white) men. This was not a new proposal. Previous free soil organizations such as the Workingmen's Party had fought since the late 1820s to preserve these lands for white yeoman farmers.[3] A group of Land Reformers had recently picked up support for this policy among industrial unions in New York and Ohio.[4]

But there was a subtle anti-black message here, too. This racial aspect would become more transparent a few years later.[5] In 1852, for example, Free Soil supporters in Congress would explicitly seek to limit land ownership to

---

1. Foner, "Politics and Prejudice," 239. Because he understood that only support for the Wilmot Proviso could unify the Free Soil movement, Chase agreed to say "nothing about abolitionism" in the party's platform. Frederick J. Blue, *Salmon P. Chase: A Life in Politics* (Kent State: Kent State University Press, 1987), 59. According to a Chase biographer, a small group of delegates "scuttled the Liberty party and the Hale candidacy." John Niven, *Salmon Portland Chase: A Biography* (New York: Oxford University Press, 1995), 109. Chase felt that freeing the slaves would harm the South's economy as well as blacks themselves. See Stephen Middleton, *Ohio and the Antislavery Activities of Attorney Samuel Portland Chase, 1830-1849* (New York: Garland Press, 1990), 88. At one point, Chase had expressed a desire to keep the population of his own state of Ohio "homogenous." Quoted in Rawley, *Race and Politics*, 30.

2. Chase tended to conceal his underlying beliefs and motives in order to build political alliances. For example, in letters seeking to convince John Hale to run on a "Free Territory platform," Chase expressed his regret that the Utica convention had nominated Martin Van Buren. Chase felt Hale would make a more "popular candidate." However, in writing to Martin Van Buren's son, John, just a few days later, Chase saluted the convention for making "the best possible nomination for the Presidency." See letters of Chase to Hale, 2[5] June 1848 and 15 June 1848, and letter of Chase to John Van Buren, 19 June 1848, Chase, *Correspondence*, 172, 175, 176.

3. George Henry Evans, the editor of an early Free-Soil newspaper, the *Working Man's Advocate*, felt strongly that blacks should be kept out of the West. In an 1844 exchange with the abolitionist Gerrit Smith, Evans made his position clear: "I was formerly, like yourself, sir, a very warm advocate of the abolition of slavery. This was before I saw that there was white slavery. Since I saw this, I have materially changed my views as to the manner of abolishing negro slavery. I see now clearly, I think, that to give the landless black the privilege of changing masters now possessed by the landless white would hardly be a benefit to him in exchange for his surety of support in sickness and old age, although he is in a favorable climate. If the southern form of slavery existed at the north, I should say the black would be a great loser in such a change." Quoted in Wendy McElroy, "The Free Soil Movement, Part I," *Freedom Daily*, May 2001: http://www.fff.org/freedom/0501e.asp

4. Rayback, *Free Soil*, 221.

whites.[1] Three years later, the House approved just such an amendment to the Homestead Laws. During subsequent debate over this bill, Sen. James Doolittle, a Democrat from Wisconsin, called for opening up public lands "for the free white men of this country."[2] Under the measure eventually passed by Congress in May 1862, racial discrimination was less overt. Access to these lands was to be reserved for American citizens and immigrants intending to become citizens. In effect, this provision restricted the public tracts almost entirely to whites, since blacks held this status in only a handful of states.

Similarly, the phrases "free men" and "free labor" resonated with anti-slavery sentiment, but whites hostile to blacks could read into them an aversion to this race: in the minds of many Americans, blacks lacked the capacity to be truly "free" even if the chains of the chattel system were eventually lifted from their shoulders.[3] A parsing of the fine print in the Free Soil platform reveals this underlying anti-black bias. The party was resolved to "secure free soil to a free people" — not to *all* peoples; it was only concerned with preventing the *extension* of slavery, not its elimination; it offered no condemnation of the slave system; it affirmed solidarity with "our brethren in Oregon" who wished to establish a "free government" there, but who were equally bent upon keeping free blacks out.[4] Similarly, the term "free labor" spoke not only to white farmers but also to workers in Northern cities who feared competition from emancipated slaves arriving from the South, and who wished to secure the urban labor market exclusively for themselves. These workers had mixed feelings about non-whites. To some extent, they sympathized with the slaves' plight as debased laborers, but they also considered blacks to be their inferiors and wanted little to do with them.[5] Many of these Northerners looked to the frontier as a "safety valve" that would protect them against blacks and also promote white social

---

5. As early as 1841, and on several subsequent occasions, "exclusionist sentiment" had led Congress to bar blacks from purchasing public lands. Litwack, *North of Slavery*, 48-9. In Kansas, Free Soil supporters were largely responsible for promptly enacting legislation to keep that state "free" of both slaves and free blacks. See White, *"It's Your Misfortune*," 158.

1. See "Latest Intelligence," *New York Daily Times*, 8 Mar. 1852. This article reports that this effort has just been abandoned, but may be resumed in a "new quarter."

2. Quoted in George M. Stephenson, *The Political History of the Public Lands, from 1840 to 1862* (New York: Russell & Russell, 1917), 194. See remarks of James R. Doolittle, 25 Feb. 1859, 35th Congress, 2nd Session, *Congressional Globe*, Senate, 1351-63.

3. Wilmot, for example, was wont to contrasting "free labor" with "black labor."

4. "Freedom of opportunity for the free man was the common desire of the elements gathered at Buffalo." Rayback, *Free Soil*, 224

5. While the free labor movement was philosophically opposed to slavery, it also appealed to Democratic voters in both the North and the South who "did not regard the enslavement of blacks as significantly compounding the degradation of a race they deemed inferior to their own." Jonathan A. Glickstein, *Concepts of Free Labor in Antebellum America* (New Haven: Yale University Press, 1991), 13.

mobility.[1] In fact, by the late 1840s, urban workers were becoming a significant component of the westward exodus, accounting for roughly one fourth of all white migrants.[2] Their desire to keep blacks from following them thus had to be implicitly articulated in the Free Soil platform. (Abolitionists had already sought to appeal to white laborers and craftsmen by pointing out that "free labor and slave labor were fundamentally antagonistic." Antislavery leaders had stirred fears of competition among white workers by pointing to Southern plans to build factories that would employ slave labor.[3]) Despite these racial undertones to the new party's rhetoric, the resolutions were met with great enthusiasm when they were presented before the Buffalo gathering — a sign, no doubt, that antislavery unity mattered far more than agreement on the party's specific positions regarding blacks.

All in all, the Free Soil platform mirrored the racist attitudes of most white Americans of the day: Northerners indifferent to the well being of blacks, free or slave, could find little to object to in the Free Soil philosophy.[4] At the same time, abolitionists could take some comfort from the party's vow to "limit, localize, and discourage slavery" and to ban it from the District of Columbia.[5] Across the country, many Americans did flock to the Free Soil movement out of a genuine wish to abolish the chattel system. In Iowa, for example, supporters of the new party took up the cause of racial equality.[6] While skeptical of its being "a party for keeping Free Soil and not for setting men free," William Lloyd Garrison reluctantly gave his blessing to the new movement, as did his abolitionist comrade-in-arms, Frederick Douglass.[7]

---

1. Lacy K. Ford, Jr., "Frontier Democracy: The Turner Thesis Revisited," *Journal of the Early Republic* 13:2 (Summer 1993), 153.
2. One study of westward migration between 1850 and 1870, involving a sample of 4,938 adult males taken from census manuscript schedules, determined that 24 percent had been living in urban areas prior to moving west in the 1850s. Joseph P. Ferrie, "Migration to the Frontier in Mid-Nineteenth Century America: A Re-Examination of Turner's 'Safety Valve,'" 8. www.faculty.econ.northwestern.edu/ferrie/papers/munich.pdf.
3. Williston H. Lofton, "Abolition and Labor," *Journal of Negro History* 33:3 (July 1948), 252, 258.
4. The new party's leaders realized that a platform endorsing equal rights for blacks would be extremely unpopular in the North. See Foner, "Politics and Prejudice," 239.
5. This latter plank had been proposed by Preston King.
6. Dykstra, *Bright Radical Star*, 86-7.
7. In a 10 Aug. 1848 letter to the antislavery writer Edmund Quincy, Garrison conceded that the recently adopted Free Soil platform included "all that the Liberty party dare claim Congress is constitutionally empowered to do," but said he was not satisfied with the document because it did not go beyond endorsing the Wilmot Proviso. *The Letters of William Lloyd Garrison* vol. 3, *No Union with Slaveholders, 1841-1849*, ed. Walter M. Merrill (Cambridge: Belknap Press, 1973), 581. Douglass was dismayed to find racially prejudiced politicians like Wilmot at the Buffalo convention and had mixed feelings about this new movement. See See James Brewer Stewart, *Holy Warriors: The Abolitionists and American Slavery* (New York: Hill and Wang, 1976), 145. However, his newspaper, *The North Star*, endorsed the Free Soil ticket in its issue of 10 Sept. 1848. Douglass believed the new party could create a powerful antislavery force all across the country.

John Hale, a senator from New Hampshire and influential figure in the Liberty party, also decided it was better to work within the new antislavery alliance "than to stand aloof and oppose."[1] In return for accepting the controversial (but popular) Martin Van Buren as the party's nominee for president,[2] Liberty members were given a chance to help shape the platform; this was the most they — being a small minority in Buffalo — could expect to accomplish.[3] By merging into this Free Soil coalition, the Liberty party hoped its cause would thrive as it, as a political organization, had not.[4]

During the presidential campaign that fall, the Free Soil party played a historically pivotal role, even though it failed to carry a single state. Van Buren made a particularly strong showing in New England, capturing close to a fifth of all votes cast there.[5]

Throughout the North, Free Soil ideology attracted primarily rural voters — that is, farmers for whom land ownership was a central concern, especially those who might be thinking of migrating to the West. Van Buren's ticket achieved its best result in Vermont — 29.6 percent — but fared poorly in cities like Boston and New York.[6] This discrepancy suggests that urban workers saw less relevance to their own needs in Free Soil's emphasis on making Western public lands freely available to all white settlers. While the party had virtually no sup-

---

1. Letter of John P. Hale to Lewis Tappan, 6 July 1848, Box 8, File 4, Hale Papers. Salmon Chase had dissuaded Hale from running for President on the Liberty ticket in 1848. Blue, *Salmon Chase*, 61.
2. In balloting for the party's nomination, Van Buren defeated Hale, 244-181. See "The Buffalo Convention," *Daily Courier*, 12 Aug. 1848. Charles Francis Adams was chosen as Van Buren's running mate. Many Liberty men considered the latter's nomination a "slap in the face," and Free Soil Whigs "hated" Van Buren. Theodore Clarke Smith, *The Liberty and Free Soil Parties in the Northwest* (New York: Longmans, Green & Co., 1897), 145, 151. Many opponents of slavery had doubts about the New Yorker's "conversion" to their cause. A hostile editorial in the local *Daily Courier* (9 Aug. 1848) castigated the former president for his "utter selfishness" and "absolute hypocrisy" for accepting the Free Soil presidential nomination. As president, Van Buren had felt decisions about slavery should be left up to the states, and he had pledged to veto any attempt to abolish slavery in the District of Columbia. See Joel H. Silbey, *Martin Van Buren and the Emergence of American Popular Politics* (Lanham: Rowman & Littlefield, 2002), 171. By declaring, in 1848, that Congress could exclude slavery in Western territories, he made himself acceptable to many antislavery Northern Democrats. However, many of the Free Soil delegates at the Buffalo convention (and voters elsewhere) remained skeptical of Van Buren's commitment to the antislavery cause.
3. Letter of Henry B. Stanton to John P. Hale, 20 Aug. 1848, Box 8, File 10, Hale Papers.
4. Addressing the Buffalo convention, the New York abolitionist leader Joshua Leavitt reassured his fellow Liberty members that the party was "not dead, but translated" into the Free Soil party. Quoted in Vernon L. Volpe, *Forlorn Hope of Freedom: The Liberty Party in the Old Northwest, 1838-1848* (Kent State: Kent State University Press, 1990), 134.
5. In the mid-Atlantic states of New Jersey and Pennsylvania, the Free Soil party gained only 1 and 3.1 percent, respectively. Rayback, *Free Soil*, 287.
6. While the Free Soil ticket captured 28.3 percent of the votes in Massachusetts, it picked up only 15 percent in Boston. In Philadelphia, Van Buren received only 877 votes, out of over 53,000 cast. *Ibid.*, 283, 287.

port in the South, a dozen of its candidates — including two in Ohio's Western Reserve — did win election to Congress, and votes for this third party had a decisive impact on the outcomes in New York and several other states.[1] Paying heed to the popularity of the new party's platform, both the Whig candidate for president, Gen. Zachary Taylor, and his Democratic opponent, Cass, espoused Free Soil positions in appealing for Northern votes, while declaring themselves opposed to the Wilmot Proviso in front of Southern audiences.[2] This tactic undermined support for Van Buren, and, nationally, the Free Soil party ended up with only 291,616 votes out of 2,882,120 cast. (And nearly half of these, 120,514, came from Van Buren's home state of New York.) But this upstart organization — the first mass, grass roots movement in American history — reshaped the national political landscape. By unequivocally opposing any extension of the "peculiar institution," the Free Soil movement acted as a wedge, driving the two wings of the established parties apart, gravely weakening both, and widening the inter-sectional chasm over slavery.[3] On top of this, it paved the way for the rise of the Republican Party in the coming decade.

What does support for the Free Soil cause reveal about Northern attitudes towards blacks and slavery? Clearly, it did not indicate any growing desire to do away with the slave system. For one thing, the Free Soil platform did not advocate emancipation, except within the District of Columbia, and neither did very many antebellum voters. At its height, during the 1846 congressional elections, the abolitionist Liberty Party had drawn only 75,000 votes in the entire nation,[4] and its support had then waned due to its opposition to annexing Texas. Only in New England and areas settled primarily by migrants from this part of the country was there a groundswell of sentiment in favor of freeing all the slaves. Such views were highly unpopular in the Old Northwest.[5] When James G. Birney ran

---

1. Van Buren actually outpolled Cass by over 6,000 votes in New York State. In Maine, Massachusetts, Vermont, and Connecticut, turnouts for the Free Soil ticket exceeded the margin of victory for Taylor. In the Old Northwest states of Ohio, Illinois, Indiana, Michigan, and Wisconsin (as well as Iowa), Free Soil support helped Cass come out on top. Support for the Free Soil party was mainly concentrated in the eastern parts of those states.
2. For a harsh critique of the two candidates' "duplicity," see "The Movement," *National Era* 2:80 (14 Sept. 1848), 146. Cf. Rayback, *Free Soil*, 238. Abraham Lincoln, William Seward, Horace Greeley, and other prominent Whigs persuaded many voters that Taylor, if elected, would not veto the Wilmot Proviso. William O. Lynch, "Anti-Slavery Tendencies of the Democratic Party in the Northwest, 1848-50," *Mississippi Valley Historical Review* 11:3 (Dec. 1924), 319. The appeal of the Free Soil platform in the Old Northwest also induced many Democrats in that region to endorse the proviso.
3. Van Buren's candidacy drew more votes from the Democrats than from the Whigs. For a detailed analysis of how the Free Soil party weakened its Democratic and Whig rivals, see Mayfield, *Rehearsal for Republicanism*, 192-202.
4. The party's presidential candidate in 1844, James G. Birney, garnered only some 62,000 votes.

as the Liberty candidate for president in 1840, he picked up a grand total of 903 votes in Ohio, out of over a quarter million cast.[1]

Yet, eight years later, the Free Soil party attracted *more than 30 times* as many votes in the Buckeye State. The fact that a former president, Van Buren, was the party's nominee partially accounts for this impressive showing — garnering some 10 percent of all votes cast nationally after having been in existence only three months. (When Van Buren returned to the fold of the Democratic Party, and John Hale ran on the Free Soil ticket four years later, support for the latter party fell sharply in most states.[2]) Unhappiness with the two established parties also contributed to this defection from their ranks. But a desire on the part of many Northern voters to take a firm stand against any further expansion of the chattel system figured most prominently in the Free Soil party's success.

Free Soil fared well in parts of the country where opposition to the extension of slavery was most pronounced. These happened to coincide with areas of abolitionist strength — namely, western New York, and northern sections of Ohio, Illinois, and Indiana[3] — but there does not appear to have been a great deal of Liberty crossover voting for Free Soil in 1848.[4] The two parties diverged too sharply on the question of race relations.

By and large, abolitionists wanted to treat blacks as equals and assimilate them on these terms into American society, whereas the Free Soil party generally made no bones about its desire to "contain" this "inferior" race within the

---

5. The proselytizing activities of evangelical abolitionists in the 1830s were met with strong hostility throughout Ohio, even in the Western Reserve. A Cleveland gathering condemned these agitators as "unwise, dangerous, and deserving the emphatic reprehension and zealous opposition of every friend of peace and of the country." Several towns in the state barred abolitionists from holding public meetings, and Ohio Methodists joined in condemning abolitionists at the church's General Conference of 1835. For more details of anti-abolitionist attitudes in Ohio, see Buley, *The Old Northwest*, vol. 2, 620-1.

1. Volpe, *Forlorn Hope*, xi. The "resistance and apathy of the overwhelming majority of Northern voters" prevented the Liberty party for spreading its abolitionist message. Birney's appeal was limited almost exclusively to the Western Reserve. In Illinois he picked up only 160 votes and in Indiana just 30.

2. Nationally, the Free Soil party netted only 156,297 votes — down 46 percent — in the 1852 presidential election.

3. Levine, *Half Slave and Half Free*, 156. The single largest concentration of Liberty voters was to be found in the 20th Congressional District of Ohio (south of Cleveland), represented by an unabashed abolitionist, Joshua Giddings. See Stewart, *Holy Warriors*, 100. A native of Pennsylvania, Giddings had served in the House as a Whig up until 1842, when he resigned after being censured for making remarks in defense of slaves who had mutinied on a ship bringing them over from Africa. The Western Reserve was a Whig bastion, and unhappiness with that party's nomination of a slaveholder (Taylor) for president, in addition to Giddings' influence on Whigs, accounts for much of the Free Soil vote in that region. See Niven, *Salmon Chase*, 114. Democratic anti-slavery sentiment was widespread in northeastern Illinois (including Chicago) and parts of southern Wisconsin. Smith, *Liberty and Free Soil Parties*, 122.

South.[1] (This was not the case in all states, however. For example, in Ohio, Free Soilers pushed hard for repeal of that state's infamous black laws and for legal parity between whites and blacks.[2]) Nominally, the party was *antislavery*, but, in fact, it was *anti-black*.[3]

Its presidential candidate, Van Buren, had made clear his opposition to blacks entering the West, "In [sic] behalf of the free white laborers of the North and South, in behalf of the Emigrants from abroad, in behalf of posterity, and in the name of freedom."[4]

Its opportunistic strategist, Salmon Chase, eager to build a broad political base for the Free Soil movement, made black exclusion a dominant campaign

---

4. So contends Frederick J. Blue, *The Free Soilers: Third Party Politics, 1848-54* (Urbana: University of Illinois Press, 1973), 2. But Theodore C. Smith takes the opposite view, contending that most Liberty backers did vote for the Free Soil ticket. Smith, *Liberty and Free Soil Parties*, 151. It is not possible to determine with any certainty how many Liberty members did, in fact, switch to Free Soil in 1848, however. It is true that several prominent abolitionists did join the Free Soil cause, such as western New York congressman Seth M. Gates, a Whig who ran unsuccessfully for lieutenant governor on the Free Soil line in 1848. A Liberty party faction opposed to the merger with the new party — led by James Birney, William Goodell, and Gerrit Smith — ran its own ticket that year, with Smith as the presidential candidate, but picked up only 2,733 votes.

1. One historian has noted that abolitionists regarded the Free Soil emphasis on keeping blacks out of the West as a "distasteful expression of prejudice." See Ronald G. Walters, *The Antislavery Appeal: American Abolitionism After 1830* (Baltimore: Johns Hopkins University Press, 1976), xiii. But at least some white political leaders who favored freeing the slaves held this view only out of self-interest: they felt that emancipation would keep slaves from streaming north. One such figure was Sen. Benjamin F. Wade, a Free Soil advocate from Ohio. See Louis Filler, *The Crusade Against Slavery, 1830-1860* (New York, Evanston: Harper & Row, 1960), 224. In the 1850s, Wade and a congressman from Ohio, L.D. Campbell, opposed a scheme to relocate freed slaves to the West. Nevins, *Fruits of Manifest Destiny*, 521. During a 18 Jan. 1860 speech on the Senate floor, Wade declared: "There is in these United States a race of men who are poor, weak, uninfluential, incapable of taking care of themselves. I mean the free negroes, who are despised by all, repudiated by all; outcasts upon the face of the earth, without any fault of theirs that I know of; but they are the victims of a deep-rooted prejudice ... It is perfectly impossible that these two races can inhabit the same place, and be prosperous and happy. I see that this species of population are just as abhorrent to the southern states, and perhaps more so, than to the north. Many of those states are now, as I think, passing unjust laws to drive these men off or subject them to slavery; they are flocking into the free states, and we have objections to them. Now, the proposition is, that this great government owes it to justice, owes it to those individuals, owes it to itself and to the free white population of the nation, to provide a means whereby this class of unfortunate men may emigrate to some congenial clime, where they may be maintained to the mutual benefit of all, both white and black. This will insure a separation of the races." Quoted in A.G. Riddle, *The Life of Benjamin F. Wade* (Cleveland: William W. Williams, 1886), 231-2.

2. Foner, "Politics and Prejudice," 240. Leaders of the Free Soil party in Massachusetts, including Charles Sumner, also endorsed equal rights for blacks.

3. Free Soil advocates "saw no contradiction between racial prejudice and anti-slavery feeling." Foner, "Politics and Prejudice," 248-9.

4. Quoted in Gardiner, *Great Issue*, 52.

theme.[1] And the party's organ, *The National Era*, called for blacks to migrate to Africa cr some other remote region since white Americans considered their presence an "inconvenience."[2]

Thus, it seems plausible to conclude that most of those who voted for the Free Soil ticket regarded this emerging party as the most reliable champion of "free labor" and racial exclusion in the Western territories. As one historian has summed up, the "unspoken objective of white people searching for 'free soil' was a combination of 'free soil, free labor, free men, and no free blacks.' Land without slavery made this objective look attainable."[3] Other scholars have reached the same conclusion: one has written that the Free Soil movement attained popularity due to a "a deep-seated and long-existing desire on the party of many white Americans for a racially homogeneous society."[4]

There is further evidence to support this interpretation of Free Soil's appeal. During the late 1830s and early 1840s, former President John Quincy Adams, elected to the House by loyal Plymouth voters, fought a stubborn and often lonely battle against slaveholding interests. A *bête noire* of his was the "gag rule" passed by Congress in 1836, which prevented antislavery petitions from being received. Adams got around this by accepting such memorials himself. While a number of groups sent him petitions asking that slavery be abolished because it was "unjust," "a heinous sin," and a "violation of the laws of nature and of God," the majority of these documents objected only to the extension of slavery, the admission of additional slave states such as Texas, the slave trade, the existence of the "peculiar institution" in the nation's capital, and the Fugitive Slave Act.[5]

---

1. Foner, *Free Soil*, 95. One historian has found Chase marked by a "willingness to advance his own interests without concerning himself too much about his political friends." Theodore Clarke Smith, *Parties and Slavery, 1850-1859* (New York: Haskell House, 1968), 48-9. Early in his career, Chase adhered to the prevalent view that God intended the races to remain separate. Later, while endorsing their right to the vote, he expressed the hope that blacks would move to warmer climates and stay away from his state of Ohio. See Foner, "Politics and Prejudice," 240. Chase was not concerned by the "wrongs of the slave but by the dangers to free white men." See Albert B. Hart, *Salmon Portland Chase* (Boston: Houghton Mifflin, 1899), 48. But his exposure to mob attacks on blacks and white abolitionists such as Birney helped to moderate his racial outlook. As a member of the U.S. Senate, Chase worked with other Free Soil leaders in Ohio to repeal the state's infamous black laws. For details on his antislavery involvement in Ohio, see Middleton, *Antislavery Activities*.
2. *National Era*, 19 April 1849, quoted in Foner, "Politics and Prejudice," 249. This publication also criticized blacks for showing reluctance to leave the United States.
3. Schwarz, *Migrants Against Slavery*, 14.
4. Frederickson, *Black Image in the White Mind*, 131. Another historian has observed: "The Free Soil leaders, in fact, came to put so much emphasis on the racial reasons for keeping slavery out of the West that they seemed at times to be arguing that the struggle for supremacy in the territories was not so much a struggle between the North and the South, or even between slavery and freedom, as one between the black race and the white race." Bilotta, *Rise of the Republican Party*, 74.

After the gag rule was repealed, in 1844, the steady stream of memorials (now directed to the House judiciary committee) focused on the extension issue and on the harm that slavery's growth would do to the nation. (Many of these appeals to Congress warned that the chattel system would bring about the Union's demise.) Typical of them was a flyer originally addressed to the citizens of Philadelphia, conceding that most of them might not side with abolitionists but pointing out that they did agree that slavery's "tendency is to deteriorate the condition of free laborers in the regions where it exists."[1]

While these antislavery petitions are by no means an objective barometers of public opinion, they do tend to confirm that Northern opposition to the slave system was based mainly on the system's ill effects on whites. Since the "peculiar institution" was so well entrenched in the South, hopes for weakening or under-mining it could only blossom in the West. At the same time, this was where the white race's destiny would now unfold. For Anglo-Saxon Americans to bring the rest of the continent under their control, develop it economically, infuse it with the bounties of civilization, and thus fulfill their special historical mission, blacks would have to be kept out. Free blacks presented an additional concern because they could compete for land and jobs with in-migrating whites. Hence, efforts were made to impede their settlement west of the Mississippi. The dis-criminatory legal barriers raised by new territories and states largely succeeded. Just before the start of the Civil War, only 10,283 black freemen were living in states located in the western half of the country[2] — fewer than the number then residing in New York City. This number amounted to 0.2 percent of the total population in those states. (Tellingly, the West's racial homogeneity has not changed appreciably over the last 150 years. According to the 2000 federal cen-sus, blacks then made up only 2.9 percent of the population in Western states that had never legalized slavery.)

Erecting these impediments was a core objective for the Free Soil movement as well as for the organization that would inherit most of its supporters — the Republican Party. In future elections, the latter would reach out to whites opposed to black Americans settling on the frontier. Masquerading as opposi-tion to slavery, this exclusionary credo would also help motivate the next wave

---

5. For the text of these petitions, see HR 26A-H1.4: "Admission of Slave States to the Union"; HR 26A -H1.5: "Annexation of Texas"; HR 27A -G10.7: "Committee on the Judiciary — Slavery"; and HR 27A -H1.7: "Slavery," Chap.13: Committee on Territo-ries (1825-1946), Record Group 233, "Records of the U.S. House of Representatives," National Archives, Washington, D.C.

1. Attachment to petition to the Committee on the Judiciary from citizens of Sandwich, N.H., 7 April 1846, HR 29 A- G8.9: "Committee on the Judiciary — Petitions — Slavery and Slave Trade," RG 233, National Archives.

2. This population statistic does not include Louisiana, which was settled considerably earlier. In 1850, the comparable figure was only 5,208.

of pioneers as they pushed across the arid, inhospitable prairies and soaring, snowcapped Rockies to reach the unsullied shores of the Pacific. There, the dream of creating a white Garden of Eden on the North American continent would have one last chance to become a reality.

VIII. Manifest Necessity

Less than two months before tens of thousands of enthusiastic Free Soilers descended upon the city of Buffalo, Sen. John Adams Dix of New York rose on the Senate floor in Washington to deliver a speech on a question of pressing concern to him and his colleagues. The subject was Oregon — specifically, whether or not this remote, sparsely settled territory, located some three thousand miles from the spot where he was standing, was to be "free" or "slave."[1] Erect in bearing, with piercing black eyes, Dix, a patriot and former soldier who had pulled strings to enlist as a 14-year-old stripling in the War of 1812 and who, half a century later, would be commissioned a major general in the Union Army by President Abraham Lincoln, spoke eloquently that June day against the extension of slavery to the faraway Pacific. It was not so much the inherent evil of enslaving human beings that perturbed this officer-turned-politician[2] — Dix professed no wish to interfere with the system wherever it now existed— but slavery's incompatibility with his messianic vision of the nation's future.[3] Describing Oregon and environs as a land akin to Italy in climate and agricultural riches, he saw this territory as the crowning jewel in a sprawling American empire, reaching from coast to coast across forests, prairies, deserts, and mountain ranges, on a scale exceeding even what the Romans had accomplished some 2,000 years before.

---

1. The Buffalo convention endorsed a resolution supporting a "free" Oregon.
2. Dix did consider slavery to be an "evil," which did "violence to all the dictates of nature." See his remarks delivered in the Senate, 26 July 1848, 30th Congress, 1st session, *Appendix to the Congressional Globe*, Senate, 1182. He .was a protégé of Sen. Thomas Benton Hart. See Elbert B. Smith, *Magnificent Missourian: The Life of Thomas Hart Benton* (Philadelphia: J.B. Lippincott, 1958), 209.

But unlike the polyglot imperium the legions of Rome had cobbled together with "brute force," this New World colossus would offer a lasting testimonial to peace-loving Anglo-Saxon civilization, marked by superior "industry," ambition, prowess, superiority, and self-reliance. "I believe it is the order of Providence," the Democratic senator from upstate Cooperstown intoned, "that the continent of North America, with the exception, perhaps, of some inconsiderable districts, is ultimately to be peopled by the same race which has overspread Europe, and made it what it is in science, in art, in civilization, and in morals . . . It is in the vast and fertile spaces of the West that our own descendants, as well as the oppressed and needy multitudes of the old world must find the food they require, and the rewards for labor, which are necessary to give them the spirit and the independence of freemen. I hold it to be our sacred duty to consecrate these spaces to the multiplication of the white race." For this reason, and this reason alone, the virgin lands of Oregon had to be kept clear not only of slaves, but also of free blacks — an "inferior caste" — "a burden and encumbrance to the white race, and an impediment to its moral and physical development." If not checked, these most "undesirable" of blacks would point their own footsteps westward in a futile search for the American dream of freedom.[1]

Dix did not use the phrase "Manifest Destiny" in his Senate remarks, but he did succinctly capture the racial rationale for territorial conquest that initially underlay American expansionist ideology in the 1840s.[2] It was the editor John O'Sullivan who had coined this jingoistic slogan a few years before the Free Soil gathering in Buffalo, in a piece that appeared in the July 1845 issue of *The United States Democratic Review.* Reacting to a population surge registered by the latest federal census, O'Sullivan hailed the nation's "manifest destiny to overspread the continent allotted by Providence for the free development of our yearly multiplying millions." He saw the acquisition of Western lands as the solution to an oth-

---

3. Dix felt that containing slavery in the South would lead to the slow decline of the nation's black population. In his July speech before the Senate, he further contended that the degrading of free blacks in free states like New York will have the beneficial consequence of causing their numbers to decline. See remarks of Dix, 26 July 1848, *Appendix to the Congressional Globe*, 866. As one historian has put it: "By promising that the [Wilmot] Proviso would mean the elimination of the Negro everywhere in the republic except in the South, where it would be localized, Dix was able to appeal directly to the hostility which the white man of the North felt for the colored race." Morrison, *Democratic Politics and Sectionalism*, 72-3.

1. Remarks of Dix, 26 June 1848, *Appendix to the Congressional Globe*, Senate, 865-66.

2. A highly critical article that appeared in 1847 attacked the proponents of Manifest Destiny for urging that "the Spanish race on this continent, and all others, must fade away before the face of the Anglo-Saxons, or rather of the Yankees, as shadows fly before the coming light. The Indians have receded and wasted at our approach, and so must all the rest of the dwellers on this side of the globe, except, perhaps, so far as we may see fit to embrace them and inoculate them with our blood." See "The Whigs and the War," *American Whig Review* 6:4 (Oct. 1847) 338.

erwise unavoidable commingling of white and black peoples. O'Sullivan was strongly influenced by the position advanced — somewhat disingenuously[1] — by Mississippi's Pennsylvania-born Senator, Robert J. Walker, who argued that the territories of Texas, New Mexico, and California were worth acquiring because they would "drain off" slaves, leading ultimately to their removal to Mexico and South America. Shorn of this unwanted racial element, Anglo-Saxon America would be able to attain the greatness that constituted its historical uniqueness — "to establish on earth the noblest temple ever dedicated to the worship of the Most High — the Sacred and the True . . . its congregation a Union of many Republics, comprising hundreds of happy millions, calling no man master, but governed by God's natural and moral law of equality, the law of brotherhood — of 'peace and good will amongst men.'"[2] Whereas he and other Northern advocates of Manifest Destiny described the Far West as a pristine wilderness in which Americans could live more freely than anywhere else,[3] what they really wanted was a sanctuary for whites. In their minds, "white exclusivity" and "freedom" were practically synonymous. In *Leaves of Grass*, Walt Whitman expressed this linkage in poetic phrases what many of his fellow countrymen felt but could not articulate:

> COME, I will make the continent indissoluble;
> I will make the most splendid race the sun ever yet shone upon;
> I will make divine magnetic lands,
> With the love of comrades,
> With the life-long love of comrades.

An anonymous essayist in *The American Literary Magazine* made the same points in equally evocative prose calling for the settlement of California. "It becomes us to see the finger of Providence in all these gigantic [westward] moves, and to believe that Providence is confiding such great power and resources to the Anglo-Saxon race with some vast ulterior views . . . An intelligent, moral, cultivated, industrious and Christian race is permitted to fill every corner of the earth with its influence . . . above the din of hurrying masses, the boasts of human pride, and the applause of admiring nations, may be heard . . .

---

1. Walker was strongly in favor of expansion, particularly in Texas, and used this argument to win over Northerners to his position. He contended that slaves would be relocated to newly gained lands in the Southwest, thus reducing their presence in the eastern half of the country. See Frederick Merk, "A Safety Valve Thesis and Texas Annexation," *Mississippi Valley Historical Review* 49:3 (Dec. 1962), 414-18. Cf. White, "It's Your Misfortune," 75.
2. John O'Sullivan, "The Great Nation of Futurity," *United States Democratic Review* 6:23 (Nov. 1839), 429.
3. Cf. Albert K. Weinberg, *Manifest Destiny: A Study of Nationalist Expansionism in American History* (Chicago: Quadrangle Books, 1935), 100-2.

the echoes of Omniscient Energy, as it drives on the machinery of human progress, and works by invisible but unappreciated means, the destiny of the world."[1]

But much of this talk about "Manifest Destiny" merely applied a camouflaging, self-serving gloss to what can best be described as naked land greed: one unsympathetic scholar has bluntly labeled the doctrine "white savagery in the garb of civilization."[2] Although such a lofty, God-given historical purpose was cited by politicians, poets, and presidents alike to justify the nation's expansion, it is doubtful that many ordinary settlers murmured John O'Sullivan's fabled phrase as they trudged across the Great Plains. They, too, may have wanted to live in a West "free" of undesirable, darker-skinned races, but, for the most part, their aspirations were far more pragmatic and concrete. Like generations of pioneers before them, they mainly wanted to build new lives under more propitious circumstances, fulfilling not so much the nation's grandiose dream of an empire stretching from sea to shining sea but their own, more modest hopes of buying more land, lifting themselves out of poverty through hard work, and achieving a modicum of material well being on the uncharted frontier. The exclusion of blacks from Western territory mattered to them as a way of achieving these goals.

In fact, the slogan "Manifest Destiny" did not enter the American vernacular until the mid-1840s, and by then several thousand families had already completed the Great Migration westward from the Mississippi River to the Pacific coast.[3] Moreover, this phrase was mostly invoked in the decades before the Civil War not to inspire pioneers to migrate across the continent, but rather to justify American economic expansion *beyond* the nation's natural boundaries. While still couched in hyperbolic language, this urge to plant the flag on foreign shores actually bespoke the commercial ambitions of the well to do, including many slaveholders, to reach new sources of wealth. For them, engagement with other races was economically imperative: blacks, Mexicans, Asians, and other non-whites in distant places would supply the cheap, inexhaustible labor and readily accessible raw materials upon which the continuing prosperity of their own enterprises depended. Rather than shrink from contact with such "inferiors," these captains of trade, agriculture, and industry desperately needed to bring these other races under their control. Thus, they came to envision the nation's future on a global scale. They developed their own interpretation of "Manifest Destiny" — one that was sharply at odds with the exclusionary (and, indeed,

---

1. Anon., "California," *American Literary Magazine* 3:6 (Dec. 1848), 337.
2. Clarence Merton Babcock, *American Frontier: A Social and Literary Record* (New York: Holt, Rinehart and Winston, 1964), 7.
3. By 1850, some 5,000 Americans were living in the Willamette Valley. White, *"It's Your Misfortune,"* 72.

isolationist) doctrine O'Sullivan had first proposed. For the sake of its burgeoning capitalist system, America needed to become a multinational and multiracial empire, not a sheltered, lily-white oasis securely bounded by the lapping waves of the Pacific.

In 1851, for example, an editorial in the *New York Daily Times* suggested that the nation's historical mission compelled it to reach far beyond its continental boundaries and annex the Sandwich Islands (now the Hawaiian Islands), even though they were peopled by another race. "Manifest Destiny and the horizon move together," the newspaper affirmed. "The individual who thirsts for freedom in the far west ends of the earth finds it here without money or price."[1] Another opinion piece in the same publication asked Americans to overcome their racial bias so that they could begin to trade with Japan.[2] The term "Manifest Destiny" was also frequently used by those favoring the annexation of Cuba.[3] Just as American designs on Mexican territory had necessarily brought whites into contact with another race, so would any further acquisitions overseas. What had been originally conceived as a way for the Anglo-Saxon race to fulfill its unique potential apart from other peoples was transformed by the realization that the quest for greater economic prosperity would inevitably bring Americans to lands inhabited by non-whites. "Manifest Destiny" had to be modified to meet this need: its ideological rationale would now become an obligation to shoulder the "white man's burden" and bring a higher level of civilization to those remote and backward shores.

However, for wagon trains of pioneers negotiating the narrow ruts of the Oregon Trail in the 1840s and 1850s, preserving racial "purity," attaining freedom, and achieving material prosperity were still inextricably linked. This generation of restless farmers, traders, shopkeepers, skilled laborers, and small businessmen had not the slightest desire to live or work among persons unlike themselves. On the contrary, just like "plain folk" from the Upper South who had been forced to move west because of economic competition from slaves and fears of social "contamination" by their emancipated offspring, the pioneers bound for Oregon wanted to put as much distance as possible between them and blacks — both free and slave. Indeed, a major attractiveness of the Far West was its geographical removal from this other race. That they had this aspiration turns out to perfectly logical, since a large proportion of these "Oregon or Bust" settlers were the children and grandchildren of the same Southern yeoman farmers who had previously moved west in part to escape such unwanted contact. They were seeking what their forebears had over and over again failed to find — their own version of "racial freedom." The journey of these settlers to the Pacific would

---

1. "Annexation in the Pacific," editorial, *New York Daily Times*, 11 Nov. 1851.
2. "Desultory Notes about Japan," editorial, *New York Daily Times*, 7 Feb. 1852.
3. See, for example, untitled article, *National Era* 1:32 (12 Aug. 1847), 2.

write the final chapter not only of American continental settlement, but also of the effort of poor whites to escape the presence of other races that frustrated this desire.

Race, of course, was not the sole reason for this next wave of migration. Movement to new areas, both domestically and across national boundaries, is almost always the outgrowth of complex "push" and "pull" factors, and the Great Migration to Oregon was no exception to this rule. But, to a surprising degree, animosity toward other races did figure in the decision of early pioneer families to undertake this arduous, historic trek. To assess its importance, one has to examine the origins and particular circumstances of these settlers, the factors that may have induced them to head further west, and the steps they took once they reached their new homes in Oregon. The most striking demographic fact about this stream of migrants in the 1840s is the disproportionate number of Missouri natives within it.[1] According to the federal census of 1850, more than 18 percent of Oregon residents from elsewhere in the United States — or nearly one in five — had been born in the Show Me State.[2] Furthermore, there were more than twice as many Missourians living in the territory at that time as natives of any other state in the Union. The Midwestern states contributed the next-largest contingent of new arrivals. Illinois, the second biggest "donor" state, had contributed 1,023 settlers, less than half the number hailing from Missouri.[3]

But to state that a large percentage of Oregon settlers had roots in Missouri (or the Midwest, for that matter) is somewhat misleading. In fact, many of these newcomers were descendants of transplanted Southerners.[4] This is indicated by what is known of the settlement patterns in the Show Me State. For one thing,

---

1. The major group promoting emigration, the Oregon Pioneer Association, had branches in a number of states in 1843, but by far the greatest number of members lived in Missouri. M.L. Wardell, "Oregon Immigration Prior to 1846," *Oregon Historical Quarterly* 76:1 (March 1926), 59.
2. This percentage remained the same 10 years later. A study of land claim recipients prior to Dec. 1855 has shown that, nationally, the greatest concentration of these families came from central and western Missouri. See Map 13, "Counties of Birth and Marriage of Oregon Donation Land Claim Recipients," William A. Bowen, *The Willamette Valley: Migration and Settlement on the Oregon Frontier* (Seattle: University of Washington Press, 1987), 41. In 1870, natives of Missouri still constituted the largest contingent of residents born out of state: according to the census taken that year, 7,000 Oregonians had been born in Missouri, compared with 4,700 in Illinois, 4,000 in Ohio, 3,700 in Iowa, and 3,400 in Indiana.
3. "Place of Birth of the White and Free Colored Population," *Seventh Census*, 38-9. Some 39 percent of these early pioneers came from seven Midwestern states — Missouri, Kentucky, Tennessee, Illinois, Indiana, Iowa, and Ohio. See Robert W. Johannsen, *Frontier Politics and the Sectional Conflict: The Pacific Northwest on the Eve of the Civil War* (Seattle: University of Washington Press, 1955), 6. Furthermore, 86.9 percent of Oregon residents in 1850 had been born in just ten states — Iowa, Missouri, Illinois, Indiana, Tennessee, Kentucky, Ohio, New York, Pennsylvania., and Virginia. Jesse S. Douglas, "Origins of the Population of Oregon in 1850," *Pacific Northwest Quarterly* 41:2 (April 1906), 105.

persons originally from out of state made up 42 percent of Missouri's white population in 1850;[1] of these in-migrants, nearly three fourths had been born in other slave states.[2] In other words, roughly a third of the state's population came from the South. Secondly, a survey of census data has shown that many Missouri natives living in Oregon were not adults but the children of settlers who had grown up in the Upper South.[3] For many of these families, Missouri — and other states in the Mississippi Valley or Old Northwest — were merely stepping-stones on their odysseys from Virginia or Kentucky to the Pacific Northwest.[4] In looking at the backgrounds of delegates to Oregon's constitutional convention in 1857, one finds that 27 of the 61 members listed slave states as their place of birth. Of the 16 who had resided in Missouri most recently, 11 had been born either there or in another slave state. Significantly, a fourth of these delegates had left their places of birth in the South to live in a free state such as Illinois, Indiana, or Iowa before migrating to Oregon.[5] While the large size of this group could be explained by Missouri's being a jumping off point for wagon trains heading across the Great Plains, this proximity alone does not appear to be a sufficient reason for migration. If it were, what would account for more natives of a distant state like New York moving to Oregon than from Indiana, Tennessee, or Kentucky?[6]

Not only were so many Oregon-bound pioneers from Missouri, but also they belonged largely to a particular socioeconomic stratum — they were "plain folk" farmers, small merchants, and skilled workers with little education and equally small incomes, who did not own slaves. Furthermore, nearly half of these

---

4. An historian analyzing the background of Oregon migrants in the 1840s concluded that the bulk of them were Scotch-Irish yeoman farmers, with roots in Virginia, Maryland, and the Carolinas; they had previously migrated from those Southern states to Missouri, Kentucky, and Tennessee. John Minto, "Antecedents of the Oregon Pioneers and the Light These Throw on Their Motives," *Quarterly of the Oregon Historical Society* 5:1 (Mar. 1904) 53.

1. Table XIV and XV, "Nativities of White and Free Colored Population," *Mortality Statistics*, 36. It should be noted that the figure given here for Missouri's overall free population in 1850 — 592,004 — is the same as that for its white population only, according to data compiled by the University of Virginia for its Historical Census Browser.

2. This statistic is derived from place-of-birth data provided in the Seventh Census.

3. One scholar has calculated that three-quarters of Missouri natives in Oregon were children, compared to 41 percent of the territory's total population in 1850. See Douglas, "Origins of the Population," 106.

4. Migratory information available at an Internet site that registers the movements of individuals based on family genealogical research shows that a large number of migrants to Oregon came originally from the Upper South and lived briefly in the Old Northwest states of Illinois, Ohio, Indiana, and Iowa, or in the border states Kentucky, Tennessee, and Missouri, before heading further west. For more details, see www.migration.org.

5. "List of Delegates to the Constitutional Convention," *The Constitution of Oregon, Framed by the Constitutional Convention* (Portland: S.J. McCormick 1857), 3-4.

6. By 1870, more than a third of Oregon's total population of 90,923 were natives of New York.

migrants — 4,284 out of 8,810 Oregon residents in 1850 — were natives of slave states.[1] This was a unique and telling statistical anomaly, as all other territories in the northwestern corner of the present-day United States initially attracted settlers mostly from free states.[2] That so many pioneers reached Oregon by pursuing a migratory route at variance with the normal east-west path followed by frontier families suggests that an aversion to slavery played a role in their decision.[3]

In their predominantly non-slaveholding status and antislavery attitude, migrants from Missouri were typical of the larger settler cohort. Almost none of these early pioneers brought black bondsmen with them to Oregon,[4] and strong opposition to legalizing the "peculiar institution" in the territory was expressed by residents as early as 1841.[5] (A few emigrants did argue that cheap slave labor was needed to spur agricultural growth on the Pacific frontier, but their reasoning did not persuade many skeptical farmers.[6]) This hostility is evident in the migratory path of delegates to Oregon's 1857 constitutional convention — that is, their movement out of slave states to free ones. If one adds these "refugees" from slavery to the number of delegates (26) who had never resided in a Southern state, this amounts to a large majority of elected representatives — 67 percent — who were presumably opposed or unsympathetic to the slave system. But emigrants from Missouri were also representative of the great majority of those who settled in Oregon in the 1840s in other ways — namely, in their background and their motives for undertaking this journey. Because this is so, and because Missourians figured so prominently in the economic development and political organization of this Western settlement, understanding why they decided to relocate to the Pacific Northwest takes on a broader historical importance.

---

1. Emigrants from the Upper South and Midwest settled in rural, agricultural areas of Oregon, whereas new arrivals from the Northeastern states and Europe tended to congregate in towns and cities. See Bowen, *Willamette Valley*, 95.
2. The only other Far Western free territory that had a sizeable proportion (38 per cent) of slave-state natives in 1850 was California.
3. One historian has calculated that, in 1850, 83.4 per cent of Americans living outside the states of their birth could be found along the same parallel of latitude. White, *"It's Your Misfortune,"* 184-5.
4. There are records of some slaves being kept in Oregon during the 1850s. For details, see Fred Lockley, "Some Documentary Records of Slavery in Oregon," *Quarterly of the Oregon Historical Society* 17:1 (Mar. 1916), 107-15. Census data from 1850 and 1860 show a number of blacks identified as "servants" in white households. One historian has concluded that at least 14 of the 135 blacks living in Oregon during this period were "clearly" slaves. Quintard Taylor, "Slaves and Free Men: Blacks in the Oregon Country, 1840-1860," *Oregon Historical Quarterly* 83:2 (Summer 1982), 166-7.
5. Meeting at French Prairie early in 1841, Oregon settlers had drawn up a set of "Organic Laws" which included a ban on slavery. See Dale L. Walker, *Pacific Destiny: The Three-Century Journey to the Oregon Country* (New York: Tom Doherty Associates, 2000), 294-5.
6. Robert W. Johannsen, *The Frontier, the Union, and Stephen A. Douglas* (Urbana: University of Illinois Press, 1989), 62.

As in earlier migrations, farmers predominated on the Oregon Trail. The agricultural bent of these early colonists can be deduced from contemporary census data as well as from the land policies devised to encourage their moving to Oregon.[1] These policies appealed particularly to Missourians. A prime force in promoting settlement of the Pacific Northwest was one of their U.S. senators, Lewis Linn, who was anxious to establish an American outpost there as a bulwark against feared British encroachment.[2] In 1843, Linn proposed that the federal government grant each white male settler 640 acres (plus another 160 acres for his wife and each child) as long as this land was occupied for five years. Even though it was tabled in the House, this piece of legislation, together with the assiduous efforts of Linn and his fellow Missourian in the U.S. Senate, Thomas Hart Benton, convinced a large number of land-hungry farmers to leave for Oregon, including many living in the Show Me State.[3] Congress finally adopted a similar measure in 1850, known as the Oregon Donation Land Act. It, too, restricted land ownership to whites — and "half-breed Indians."

Economic conditions lent a sense of urgency to this outbreak of "Oregon Fever." By the early 1840s, Missouri was feeling the ill effects of the Panic of 1837:[4] agricultural prices were falling, banks were withholding credit, and many small farmers were losing their land due to foreclosure.[5] Those who managed to hold onto their property during these difficult years saw more and more of the state's agricultural resources consolidated in the hands of well-to-do slaveholders. For instance, in central Callaway County, which contained the third largest number of slaves in the state, the wealth of slave owners and small farmers contrasted starkly. A survey of 179 slaveholders and 120 non-slaveholders in the county showed that the former owned farms worth five times more than the latter group. Farmers with slaves also held an average of 97.7 acres, versus only 33.5

---

1. For instance, the 1850 federal census for one part of Clackamas County, (where a large number of Missouri migrants resided), lists 36 farmers, 18 merchants, and 17 carpenters. A number of heads of households were also classified as millers, teamsters, and sawyers. For more complete demographic data for this county, see http://ftp.rootsweb.com/pub/usgenweb/or/clackamas/census/1850/pg00023.txt
2. See Elizabeth A. Linn, *The Life and Public Services of Dr. Lewis F. Linn* (New York: D. Appleton, 1857), 195, 412.
3. For the impact of these grants on the decision to migrate, see Henry Nash Smith, *Virgin Land: The American West as Symbol and Myth* (Cambridge: Harvard University Press, 1950), 26. See also March, *History of Missouri*, 764. Benton had argued for developing Oregon as early as 1823. His vision of agricultural and commercial opportunities there had resonated well with his farming constituents. In May 1846, Benton delivered a Senate speech that stretched over three days in support of Oregon settlement. William Nisbet Chambers, *Old Bullion Benton- Senator from the New West: Thomas Hart Benton, 1782-1858* (Boston: Little, Brown, 1956), 84-5, 299.
4. Ray Billington, among others, cites the Panic of 1837 as a major "push" factor causing settlers to head for Oregon. See Billington, *Far Western Frontier*, 69.
5. Perry McCandless, *A History of Missouri*, vol. 2, *1820 to 1860* (Columbia: Univ. of Missouri Press, 1972), 121. Cf. Bowen, *Willamette Valley*, 18.

for those without slaves.[1] Other sectors of the state's economy were faring relatively well — manufacturing in St. Louis was booming, as were lead mining in the southwestern corner of the state, freight traffic along the Mississippi, and trade with the Western frontier. But the profits from these enterprises did not improve the lot of small farmers in the interior counties.[2] On the contrary, they saw their fortunes further decline as, starting in the late 1830s, German immigrants bought up much of the choice farmland still available along the Missouri.[3] Although these European newcomers kept mostly to themselves, their prosperity stirred up envy and dislike on the part of some American-born residents. For instance, the prominence of Germans in St. Louis led to rioting there in 1836, and more anti-immigrant violence during the 1852 mayoral election.[4]

While these incidents per se were not of major significance, they indicated that hostility toward foreigners — nativist or Know-Nothing sentiment — clearly existed in Missouri prior to the Great Migration. The fact that many German immigrants — like the recently arrived Irish — were Catholics added fuel to this local prejudice. However, such feelings contributed only marginally, if at all, to the decision of American-born Missourians to leave the state for the Pacific Northwest. Far more important was a series of calamitous natural disasters from the mid-1830s on, including several major floods and the attendant spread of diseases such as typhoid, malaria, and cholera. Some historians have estimated that unhealthy conditions in Missouri were as responsible for migration west as the lure of better economic opportunities.[5] One of the well-publicized advantages of life in Oregon was its mild and healthy climate.[6] Another, related "pull" factor was the territory's reputed agricultural resources — the

---

1. Scarpino, "Slavery in Callaway County," Fig. 1, "A Random Sample Comparing 179 Slaveholders and 120 Nonslaveholders for the Year 1850," 27.

2. While factory workers in St. Louis at this time could expect to earn between $2 and $2.50 an hour, workers elsewhere had average wages of only about $12 a week. McCandless, *History of Missouri*, 160.

3. A large percentage of these German immigrants bought land: this was what had enticed them to the New World. Walter D. Kampfhoefner, *The Westfalians: From Germany to Missouri* (Princeton: Princeton University Press, 1987), 167. Many Germans settled in central Osage County, and "Little Germany" was established at Hermann, just to the east on the southern banks of the Missouri. Robyn Burnett and Ken Luebbering, *German Settlement in Missouri: New Land, Old Ways* (Columbia: University of Missouri Press, 1996), 35, 44.

4. Burnett and Lueberring, *German Settlement*, 63. By 1850, a third of St. Louis's population was German.

5. Malaria caused more settlers to move to Oregon than any other disease. Bowen, *Willamette Valley*, 19.

6. The superiority of Oregon's climate was cited by several early settlers. See, for example, Overton Johnson and William H. Winter, *Route Across the Rocky Mountains* (Princeton: Princeton University Press, 1932), 66. See also letter of Alvin T. Smith to C.T. and S.F. Smith, 24 June 1845, Sm515, Western Americana Collection, Beinecke Library, Yale University. Smith writes: "the climate it is healthy mild and delightful in the latter part of the fall winter . . ."

"abundance of grass and most excellent timber" to be found in the western Blue mountains, and the "high hills, rich, fertile valleys, and beautiful plains" south of the Columbia River, as one early guidebook put it.[1] (A church newspaper rhapsodized about Oregon as a "great empire — yet to be," featuring fertile soil, a benign climate, good harbors, and "a back country teeming with all the gifts of nature . . ."[2]) On top of this was the mystique of the Far Western wilderness, as described in the journal of Meriwether Lewis and Washington Irving's widely read *Astoria* — an 1836 account of John Jacob Astor's building of a frontier outpost in Oregon.[3]

All of these elements may have made Oregon attractive to would-be migrants from the Mississippi Valley, but one has to wonder — as Horace Greeley did in the pages of the *New York Weekly Tribune* — if it was really these factors that convinced thousands of families to pull up stakes and "brave the desert, the wilderness, the savage, the snow precipes of the Rocky Mountains, the wary summer march, the storm-drenched bivouac, and the gnawings of famine."[4] Traversing some two thousand miles over the Oregon Trail extracted a heavy toll, and many pioneers never reached their destination.[5] What made them take on such hardships? Certainly, Missourians could have found suitable places to settle closer to home — in neighboring Iowa, for instance. It appears that they were drawn westward by more than the promise of material reward. Some less tangible but more compelling reason figured in their decision.

To a large extent, this was a hunger for "freedom" — a desire similar to that which had brought yeoman farmers to the hills of backcountry Virginia and Kentucky nearly 100 years before. In a petition to Congress, a leading Oregon politician would later write, "We believed that in settling in this far off region we were extending and enlarging the 'area of freedom,' and by planting civilization, liberty, and Christianity upon the shores of the great Pacific, we should render a lasting benefit to mankind."[6] On the way to Oregon, this romantic frontier spirit could assert itself once again.[7] As one of the early wagon train leaders noted in an account of his journey, "we had proceeded only a few days travel, from our native land of order and security, when the 'American character' was fully exhibited. All

1. Lansford W. Hastings, *The Emigrants' Guide to Oregon and California* (Cincinnati: George Conclin, 1857), 25, 32.
2. Zion's Herald, 31 Oct. 1838, quoted in A. Atwood, *The Conquerors: Historical Sketches of the American Settlement of the Oregon Country* (Tacoma: Jennings & Graham, 1907), 77.
3. Minto, "Antecedents of the Oregon Pioneers," 42.
4. Article dated 19 July 1843, quoted in Michael Golay, *The Tide of Empire: America's March to the Pacific* (New York: John Wiley & Sons, 2003), 265.
5. Of the 875 pioneers who set off in the Great Migration of 1843, 16 died en route. See Walker, *Pacific Destiny*, 370.
6. Quoted in Johannsen, *Frontier Politics*, 10. These were the words of George L. Curry, who served in Oregon's territorial legislature and later as a U.S. senator from the state just prior to the Civil War.
7. Cf. Bernard DeVoto, *The Year of Decision: 1846* (Boston: Little, Brown, 1943), 49.

appeared to be determined to govern, but not to be governed. Here we were, without law, without order, and without restraint; in a state of nature, amid the confused, revolving fragments of elementary society!"[1] But to be "free" on the frontier connoted more than the absence of civilization's cloying bonds. It was tinged with a disdain for slavery — and for those who would allow themselves to be enslaved. Being inherently "unfree" and, indeed, antithetical to the very notion of freedom, slaves were considered anathema by these pioneers — an economic as well as social impediment to the latter's wish to live without constraining law or power, only as they saw fit.

The platform of the Free Soil movement had obliquely linked racial exclusion and "freedom" in the West: it had demanded "freedom and established institutions for our brethren in Oregon now exposed to hardships, peril, and massacre, by the reckless hostility of the slave power to the establishment of free government for free territories." But such a denunciation of the slaveholders only masked a masked a deeper, but politically more controversial, disdain for blacks, regardless of whether they were free or slave. Generally speaking, the role of such racial animosity is difficult to gauge in analyzing what prompted settlers to head further west. But in the case of the Oregon pioneers, especially those from Missouri, there is considerable historical evidence that such prejudice did, indeed, play a major role.

White Missourians had already expressed their inhospitality toward free blacks by defying the will of Congress and passing a law in 1825 that severely restricted the freedom of non-whites to enter that state. This measure stemmed from anger toward the federal government for attempting to dictate conditions in Missouri, as well as white unhappiness with having blacks as neighbors and co-workers. The state's economic hardships following the Panic of 1837, along with a shrinking of its slave population relative to its white population, made black bondsmen less important or desirable for economic reasons and made black freemen even less popular.[2] Additional laws were enacted in 1847 to prevent free blacks and mulattoes from settling in the Show Me State.[3] (Because of the growing concentration of slaves in riverside counties with large plantations and in cities like St. Louis, most Missouri whites had little or no contact with blacks and wanted to maintain this racial separation.) Hostility toward blacks was frequently expressed by leading state politicians. Frank Blair, an attorney and former slaveholder from Kentucky, who first served as a state representative and then as a Republican congressman in the 1850s, stated in a January 1858 House speech — supporting the federal purchase of land in South America for

---

1. Hastings, *Emigrants' Guide*, 6.
2. Whereas Missouri's white population increased more than fivefold between 1830 and 1850, the number of slaves grew by only 248 percent.
3. March, *History of Missouri*, vol. 1, 820.

former slaves — that the "strong repugnance of the free white laborer to be yoked with the negro refugee, breeds an enmity between races, which must end in the expulsion of the latter."[1] Edward Bates, a Missouri congressman briefly during the 1820s, also supported the forced removal of all blacks once a "tide" of white settlers swept westward across the country.[2]

The state's most eminent statesman, Thomas Hart Benton, was desirous of seeing Oregon developed economically and, largely for this reason, wanted to keep blacks from settling there, as well as throughout the West.[3] "Old Bullion" Benton thought all of this territory should be "clean of negroes."[4] Although he had fought against congressional restrictions on Missourians' right to own slaves at the time of statehood, the senator had later come around to favoring the Wilmot Proviso's ban on slavery in Western territories. A strong believer in Manifest Destiny, Benton believed that the superiority of the white race would ultimately result in its conquering the West for its own exclusive benefit.[5] He also spoke out against the annexation of all of Texas as a slave state,[6] even though this position was not very popular among his constituents.[7] In Missouri, Benton secretly became involved in a scheme to emancipate its slaves, because their presence would retard development of the prairies.[8]

But, if any one person played a critical part in persuading his fellow Missourians to head two thousand miles across the Great Plains to escape the deleterious influence of blacks, it was a self-taught attorney of humble origins by the name of Peter Hardeman Burnett. In the annals of the West, Burnett stands out as a larger-than-life figure. A natural leader of considerable intelligence, courage, and fortitude, he not only helped to guide settlers west during the Great Migration, but also went on to dominate the politics of two states, Oregon and California (where he was elected as the first governor in 1849). While his accomplishments were extraordinary by any measure, Burnett was also representative of thousands of Western pioneers in terms of his background, family circumstances, aspirations for a better life, and motives for undertaking the

---

1. Quoted in William E. Parrish, *Frank Blair: Lincoln's Conservative* (Columbia: University of Missouri Press, 1998), 71.
2. Cain, *Edward Bates*, 99.
3. Richard White has written that Benton relied upon "racial mysticism" to advance his cause of Western economic development. White, "*It's Your Misfortune*," 57.
4. Quoted in Gardiner, *Great Issue*, 134.
5. Hietala, *Manifest Destiny*, 152.
6. Benton proposed a compromise, under which slavery would be barred from the northern and northwestern parts of Texas. See Frederick Merk, *Slavery and the Annexation of Texas* (New York: Knopf, 1972), 155.
7. Most white Missourians, slaveholders and non-slaveholders alike, continued to regard any congressional ban on slavery as unwarranted federal interference in a local matter. See Paul C. Nagel, *Missouri: A Bicentennial History* (New York: W.W. Norton, 1977), 115-6.
8. Trexler, *Slavery in Missouri*, 112. This scheme was hatched in 1828.

Pacific trek, as well as in his jaundiced approach to blacks and race relations in the United States. For this reason, too, Burnett's life is worth close examination. While migration is a complex phenomenon, best understood in the statistical aggregates of population shifts, political trends, social interactions, and economic developments, there is also much to be learned from analyzing the thoughts and actions of individual settlers. These add an illuminating personal dimension to the larger sweep of humanity across the North American continent and help to bring this process into sharp relief and clarify its driving forces.

Burnett was born on November 15, 1807, in Nashville, Tennessee — an appropriate birthplace for a man destined to become one of the West's most prominent pioneers and political leaders. For, at that time, Nashville was the northern terminus of the Natchez Trace — the starting point for pioneer families eager to plant cotton and other cash crops on the black alluvial soils of the Lower Mississippi Valley. Burnett's family had lived in that port town since the turn of the century. His grandfather on his mother's side had been a friend and neighbor of Andrew Jackson's. (The Hardemans, Burnett would explain in his memoirs, were more sophisticated, better educated and more successful than his father's people, who "cared little for riches, being content with a fair living."[1]) His father was a dirt-poor carpenter and occasional farmer who had spent only three months of his life inside a schoolhouse. The family struggled to make ends meet, and "when Peter was still a boy," his grandfather Hardeman joined a host of fellow Tennesseans hoping for better opportunities by migrating northwest to the newly opened Missouri Territory. Burnett's family followed shortly thereafter, living for a while in a "large camp with a dirt floor," divided into racially segregated halves — the whites on one side, the black help (presumably his grandfather's slaves) on the other.

By 1822, his father had saved enough money from his carpentering to purchase 160 acres of bottomland (at $1.25 per acre) in far western Clay County, on the north side of the Missouri River. There he grew wheat and other crops. While this part of the state was not a true frontier, living conditions were primitive, and survival was not easy, with settlers dependent on expensive goods brought up the river from St. Louis. The family lived off local game — quail, raccoons, deer, wild turkeys and bear — as well as nuts and fruits, and what little they could earn from selling grain. After having attended school briefly, the 19-year-old Burnett returned to Nashville in the fall of 1826, moving in with his "rich kin" in that city. For a while, he took on some odd jobs, including waiting tables for one of his uncles in western Tennessee. There, he met his future wife, Harriet Rogers. After they married, Burnett made up his mind to better his lot by teaching himself the law. After studying nights for only half a year, he returned to

---

1. Burnett, *Recollections and Opinions of an Old Pioneer*, 2,4.

western Missouri — his new wife and infant son in tow, 62 and a half cents in his pocket, $700 in debt, and desperate for work — in 1832. Not yet prepared to hang out his shingle, Burnett eventually found a job as a clerk in a store owned by a friend of his father. In a small town outside Kansas City, fittingly named Liberty, he rented a log cabin for his growing family: the couple soon produced six children.[1]

After holding down this position for several years, Burnett returned to his self-guided law studies in 1838 and shortly thereafter opened a practice, working at first on cases related to the expulsion of Mormons from Missouri. (He also served as one of the defense counsels for Joseph Smith and some of the latter's associates who had been indicted for murder and other crimes. Burnett apparently helped these prisoners to escape in February 1839.) His keen intelligence, persuasive speaking ability, and grasp of the nuances of the law soon earned him a reputation, and in 1838, Burnett was named district attorney for the recently acquired Platte country. But this job did not pay particularly well,[2] and in order to support his growing family, Burnett had to go deeply into debt. His precarious financial situation was compounded by Harriet's poor health: like many settlers in that part of the state, she had contracted some of the various infectious diseases common there.[3] Burnett now vowed to break out of his impoverished circumstances once and for all and "make a fortune." In the early 1840s, "Oregon Fever" struck western Missouri, with reports from missionaries and early explorers stirring up tremendous excitement about this tantalizing Garden of Eden. Burnett proposed a novel scheme to his creditors: he would pay off what he owed them by organizing a party to make the trek with him overland to Oregon and then turn a quick profit by selling land and goods needed by other arriving pioneers.[4] The chance to obtain nearly 2,000 acres through grants to his family members made the Western territory particularly attractive to him, as did it salubrious climate, for his wife's sake.

Starting in the fall of 1842, Burnett traveled around several neighboring Missouri counties and gave a series of rousing talks to crowds eager to hear about this new Western paradise.[5] It is not clear how Burnett picked up his knowl-

---

1. For more details of Burnett's life, see his *Recollections*.
2. Burnett was earning $1,000 a year as a circuit court attorney. See *The American Almanac and Repository of Useful Information for the Year 1845* (Boston: Gray and Bowen, 1830-61), 287.
3. For example, Asa L. Lovejoy, Burnett's future law partner in Oregon and later governor of that state, moved from Sparta, Missouri, in the southwestern part of the state, to the Far West in 1842 because of his poor health. See A.L.Lovejoy, "Lovejoy's Pioneer Narrative," ed. Henry E. Reed, *Oregon Historical Quarterly* 31:3 (Sept. 1930), 240. Burnett himself was also prone to illness; in 1838 he was laid up for several months due to an unspecified condition.
4. Minto, "Antecedents," 43. Minto implies that Burnett exaggerated the positive aspects of Oregon in order to increase the number of migrating families and thus more easily pay off his debts.

edge of Oregon (having not yet visited there himself), but his lectures were apparently persuasive.[1] An article published in the *Platte Eagle* reported that his remarks contained a great deal of information "calculated to impress those who had the pleasure of hearing him with the advantages attendant on an early settlement of our western demesne." The paper described Burnett as "one of our most estimable citizens," in the forefront of "exciting a laudable spirit" for the Oregon adventure.[2] This opinion was seconded by an impressionable immigrant from England named John Minto, who heard Burnett speak on at least one occasion and later praised him as "the most influential leader of the immigration from Missouri" during the early wagon train years.[3] The ambitious 35-year-old Missourian would continue to promote Oregon by writing numerous articles about his own trek west for local papers and the *New York Herald.*[4] These glowing accounts of Oregon (" . . . the grass is now as luxuriant as a wheat field . . . The country exceeds my expectations, and certainly, if a man cannot supply all his wants here, he cannot any where. . . .[5] the climate is the finest you ever saw"[6]) later got Burnett into hot water as emigrants lured west the following year discovered that life in this "paradise" actually entailed a relentless struggle for survival.[7]

5. According to one historian of Oregon, Burnett spent a year "lecturing in western Missouri, calling for the other fever-stricken comrades to join him in Independence to start the journey. He had patched together the funds to buy two wagons and the oxen to pull them and by the time he arrived in Independence he had many followers and seemed a natural leader." Walker, *Pacific Destiny,* 364.

1. When John Minto reached Oregon in 1844, he asked a number of new arrivals what had prompted them to travel to Oregon. Many, particularly those from the South, cited Burnett's talks. Minto, "Antecedents," 39.

2. The *Ohio Statesman,* 14 Mar. 1843, reprinted from the *Platte Eagle,* "Documents Relating to the Oregon Emigration Movement, 1842-1843," *Oregon Historical Quarterly* 4:2 (June 1903), 174-5.

3. John Minto, *Reminiscences of Experiences on the Oregon Trail in 1844-* II, *Oregon Historical Quarterly* 2:3 (Sept. 1901), 232. Elsewhere, Minto opined that Burnett "succeeded beyond his own expectations" in promoting migration to Oregon. Minto, "Antecedents," 43.

4. Within Missouri, Burnett's letters appeared in the *Jefferson Inquirer,* the *St. Louis Republican,* the *Platte Argus,* the *Missouri Reporter,* the *Independence Journal,* and the *Platte Eagle.*

5. Letter of Peter H. Burnett to "Friend Penn," *Jefferson Inquirer* (Mo.), 29 Aug. 1844. Cf. letter of Burnett to James G. Bennett, *New York Herald,* [?] Feb. 1844, reprinted in "Crossing the Plains: Letters from a Tualatin Pioneer," *Talking on Paper: An Anthology of Oregon Letters and Diaries,* ed. Shannon Applegate and Terence O'Donnell (Corvallis: Oregon State Univ. Press, 1994), 19: "Our country is most beautiful, fertile, and well-watered, with the most equable [sic] and pleasant climate."

6. Burnett, "Letter from Oregon," *St. Louis Republican,* reprinted in *Niles' National Register,* 2 Nov. 1844.

7. When he wrote his memoirs, Burnett was more candid, conceding that the journey to Oregon was "slow" and "wearisome," game was scarce, and supplies were nearly exhausted en route. When the next band of pioneers reached Oregon, in 1844, they complained loudly about poor conditions, which they had been led not to expect. Burnett came in for his "full share of censure" for this unpleasant surprise, but protested that he had told the truth about Oregon. He pointed out to the new arrivals that in this territory one had to "work or starve." See Burnett, *Recollections,* 181.

Aside from settling his debts and improving his wife's health, Burnett had more complex personal reasons to cast his eye longingly on Oregon. For one thing, he relished the chance to live in virtually unconstrained freedom, in a community of equals far beyond the reach of established law and order.[1] Here was the perfect arena for a man like himself — a man with abundant drive, talent, and brains — to thrive and live out the American dream. But Burnett, product of the poverty that so often befell non-slaveholding whites in the South, was equally desirous of starting a new life in a place where blacks did not live — and where they were not likely to come. Without question, one of the chief appeals of the Far West, in his mind, was the absence of both slaves and a free black population there. Understandably, Burnett did not dwell upon this reason in the accounts he later published about the early days in Oregon, but contemporary records do indicate that he sought to persuade many of his fellow Southerners to migrate to this remote land because it offered a refuge from racial tensions and conflict.[2] The Oregon territory was the last best hope for poor whites like him to build prosperous lives free from competition from and "degradation" by blacks. Burnett emphasized this point during his lectures, which attracted local farmers who already had a well-developed bias against both slaves and the system that enslaved them. Most were little-educated yeoman farmers who had moved to Missouri from the Upper South. They were true Jeffersonian democrats, who chafed under any kind of yoke and who considered slavery philosophically as well as materially intolerable. One of the leaders of the 1843 migration, Jesse Applegate, would write to a fellow Oregonian some years afterward: "You and I made our livings by honest labor. We both expect to leave our children in Oregon. One of the worst features of slavery is to degrade labor. If slavery is introduced into Oregon our children must blush for themselves or their fathers; if forced to labor they will be degraded from social equality, and blush for themselves; if rich and slave owners, they will blush to confess that their father toiled by the 'sweat of his face.'"[3]

---

1. Burnett later wrote that he wanted to participate in building up a new colony in the Far West. *Ibid.*, 192.
2. Burnett's racist thinking emerged in comments he made about the people living in Oregon when he arrived there. He was surprised and disappointed to discover that as many as a third of the residents were Canadians, French, or persons of mixed blood. Burnett expressed his distaste for intermarriage between white trappers and native American "squaws," which was fairly common. Still, he felt these were bonds of necessity on the frontier. See letter of Peter H. Burnett to David R. Atchinson, 8 Dec. 1844, *Platte Argus*, reprinted in *Jefferson Inquirer*, 26 Nov. 1845. For further evidence of the diversity in frontier Oregon, see undated 1845 letter of Claiborne C. and Wellington B. Walker to members of the Walker family, Purvine family records. They note that the Willamette Valley community at that time consisted of "people from all parts of the world, English, Americans, French, half-breeds, Quartroons, and Sandwich Islanders."

These Missouri "plain folk" were equally disdainful toward the well-to-do slaveholding whites who now controlled the state's economy and made their own existence precarious. They were resolved to escape this economically injurious situation, to end their subjugation by escaping the influence of the slave system once and forever. In the words of one historian, "Slaveowning neighbors had moved in beside their small farms in the hills of Kentucky or southern Missouri and had scorned them for working their ground with their own hands . . . No niggers whatsoever (the word is theirs) — whether free or slave — would be allowed inside the new territory [Oregon] if the more rabid of the migrants had their way, as for a short time they would."[1] They looked at the Far West as the independent white working man's last bastion — the final chance for Jacksonian democracy on the North American continent.[2] Similarly, when a group of missionaries had journeyed to Oregon during the 1830s, they had declared their goals to be civilizing the Indians and establishing a "white Christian society" in this wilderness.[3] Many families who decided to participate in the Great Migration "had the getting away from the institution of slavery very generally as a motive," sums up a contemporary observer.[4] A prominent Oregon migrant from the South, R.W. Morrison, subsequently acknowledged that he had responded so positively to Peter Burnett's portrayal of the territory for this reason. Morrison was tired of competing with slave-produced goods and declared he had come to Oregon "where there would be no slaves, and all would start in life even."[5] Specifically, he wanted to calm his wife's fears about the territory's being inundated by runaway slaves.[6]

Further evidence that this "plain folk" distaste for the slave system was a major factor in migration can be found in letters written by Oregon missionaries. Ezra Fisher, a Baptist minister living in Washington Butte in the 1850s, wrote to a colleague back east that a "large portion of our members are from slave-holding states, and a larger portion are professedly opposed to slavery, 'but all their sympathies are with the South.' What a paradox!"[7] (Later in the year this letter was written —1857 — white residents would register their feelings toward the "peculiar institution" and black freemen by voting overwhelmingly to keep both

3. Letter of Jesse Applegate to Medorem Crawford, 4 Feb. 1855, Medorem Crawford Papers, University of Ore. Library, quoted in Johannsen, *Frontier Politics*, 28.
1. David Lavender, *Land of Giants: The Drive to the Pacific Northwest, 1750-1950* (Garden City: Doubleday, 1956), 225.
2. Jeff LaLande, "'Dixie' of the Pacific Northwest: Southern Oregon's Civil War," *Oregon Historical Quarterly* 100:1 (Spring 1999), 37.
3. Lavender, *Land of Giants*, 197.
4. Minto, "Antecedents," 54.
5. *Ibid.*, 40.
6. *Ibid.*, 45. According to Minto, anti-black legislation adopted in 1857 "represented the just fears of girlhood and womanhood of slaves fleeing for life and liberty."
7. Letter of Rev. Ezra Fisher to Rev. Benjamin M. Hill, 31 March 1857, "Correspondence of Reverend Ezra Fisher," *Oregon Historical Quarterly* 20:1 (March 1919), 135.

out of Oregon.) There was a whiff of utopian escapism about this impulse to flee westward, away from the intractable complexities of black-white relations, back to a simpler, more harmonious time in the distant past when race largely defined community and secured one's place in it. For many Oregon-bound settlers, heading west meant moving back to that fabled age.[1]

Like many 19th century white Americans, Peter Burnett firmly believed that any close contact between the two races brought harm to both, but he was most worried about how it affected his own kind.[2] In his view, Oregon — and the Far West in general — afforded whites the last chance to establish a bastion based on racial exclusivity. Shortly after he arrived in Oregon, Burnett made his intentions perfectly clear. He desired to "keep clear of the most troublesome class of population" — that is, blacks.[3] As he gained political clout within the new territory, Burnett would be largely responsible for taking some of the most hostile, discriminatory, and barbaric legal measures ever enacted on the continent to discourage black migration. By raising such barriers in Oregon, and attempting to do so later in California, he would seek to perpetuate racial prejudice in this part of the country and ensure that white dominance would never be seriously contested.

By the spring of 1843, Burnett had managed to scrape together enough cash to purchase two wagons and some oxen to transport him and his family to Oregon.[4] He resigned his position as district attorney and, in May, led his small party to Independence, where a sizeable group of emigrants had already assembled. Later that month, Burnett's family joined one of the first groups heading west as part of the Great Migration. Crossing the Kansas River on a pontoon bridge, they organized into a company of 111 wagons, and, in quintessentially democratic fashion, sat down on the far bank to choose their leaders, with each male over 16 having an equal say in this decision. Burnett was elected captain, and 22-year-old James W. Nesmith — a Maine native, later to serve as one of Oregon's first senators — chosen orderly sergeant.[5] However, poor health forced Burnett to resign his post a week later.[6] Probably as a result of personal disagreements, the party then split into two companies, crossing the arid, alien prairies that spread all the way to the Rocky Mountains separately.

---

1. For a discussion of this theme, see Malcolm Clark, Jr., *Eden Seekers: The Settlement of Oregon, 1818-1862* (Boston: Houghton Mifflin, 1981), 261. He notes that, by keeping blacks out, white Oregons sought to "set themselves permanently apart from the increasingly passionate controversy over slavery they left behind them in the States."
2. So argues, for example, Lockley, "Documentary Records of Slavery," 109.
3. Letter of Peter Burnett to the Editor, 25 Dec. 1844, *Jefferson Inquirer*, 23 Oct. 1845.
4. Walker, *Pacific Destiny*, 364.
5. James W. Nesmith, "Diary of the Emigration of 1843," *Oregon Historical Quarterly* 7:4 (Dec. 1906), 331.
6. Letter of Burnett to James G. Bennett, *New York Herald*, [?] Feb. 1844.

Each group made its way through Indian territory without encountering any hostility on the part of local tribes. Despite problems finding food and firewood en route, Burnett's party reached the pass through the Rockies in relatively good time — by early August — after having only lost one of its members.[1] Apparently, their chief problems were boredom and the (doubtless related) chronic "grumbling and quarreling" among the pioneers themselves.[2] Downplaying these, the unfailingly upbeat Burnett wrote back to Missouri that "We have come so far with great ease and safety, the difficulties of the way not coming up to our anticipations."[3] Lt. John Charles Fremont, the "romantic cavalier" then in the midst of surveying the Oregon Trail,[4] joined the party for a short spell, as did the legendary Kit Carson.[5] Reaching the first missionary outpost in Oregon in early October, the wagon train of hopeful emigrants continued on to the Willamette Valley. In November, Burnett left his family temporarily to accompany Fremont on an exploration of the upper Willamette River by canoe. Burnett was delighted by the economic conditions he found near Fort Vancouver: "Business is very brisk, and labor finds ready employment and prompt payment, at high prices."[6] With a keen eye for making a fast dollar, the self-made Tennessean quickly staked out a claim on one of the best parcels in Oregon — ten miles from Vancouver on the banks of the Willamette — and began selling off lots for a tidy profit.[7] A piece of land bought for $50 sold a few weeks later for $200.[8] Burnett and an emigrant from Iowa named McLaughlin founded on this site one of the earliest towns in Oregon, naming it Linnton in honor of the Missouri senator who had done so much to foster settlement of the Pacific Northwest. The two pioneers were now reaping the economic rewards of that policy. As Burnett wrote in one letter to the New York *Herald*, "There is no country in the world where the wants of man can be so easily supplied, upon such easy terms as this; and none where the beauties of nature are displayed upon a grander scale."[9]

---

1. Buffalo (bison) turned out to be much more scarce than the pioneers had expected.
2. "The tedium of so long a journey is considerable," Burnett conceded. Letter of Burnett to "Friend Penn," 25 Oct. 1843, *Missouri Reporter*, reprinted in *Jefferson Inquirer*, 15 Aug. 1844.
3. Letter of Burnett to the Editor, *Platte Eagle*, 5 Aug. 1843, reprinted in *Jefferson Inquirer*, 25 Jan. 1844.
4. This pithy description of Fremont comes from William H. Goetzmann, *Exploration and Empire: The Explorer and the Scientist in the Winning of the American West* (New York: Knopf, 1966), 244. Goetzmann argues that the real agenda of Fremont's expeditions was to "dramatize the West as the American destiny" and to gather economic and scientific information about the region.
5. Nesmith, "Diary of the Emigration," 349.
6. Letter of Burnett to "Friend Penn," Nov. 1843, *Jefferson Inquirer*, 29 Aug. 1844.
7. Letter of Burnett to the Editor, 25 July 1844, *Jefferson Inquirer*, 19 Sept. 1844
8. Burnett, "Letter from Oregon," *St. Louis Republican*, reprinted in *Niles' National Register*, 2 Nov. 1844.
9. Letter of Burnett to the Editor, New York *Herald*, 6 Jan. 1845.

By the fall of 1844 this latest wave of Oregon pioneers reluctantly came to the conclusion that some rules and laws had to be established in order to regu-late their affairs. Doing so clashed with their fervent individualism, but conten-tious disputes over land ownership had made such a course of action inevitable: Burnett wrote with resignation that "stern invincible necessity" gave the settlers no choice.[1] (Dislike of government interference was unmistakable on this new frontier: the 1843 migrants went so far as to make the paying of taxes voluntary, although those who opted not to contribute lost the right to pursue their land claims in court. As a consequence, nearly all the settlers agreed to pay their taxes.) The colony's legal status was then very much in limbo, as neither the United States nor Great Britain had extended its dominion to this wilderness. But settlers in the Willamette Valley were not deterred by this unresolved state of affairs and vowed to go ahead and set up their own independent, provisional government, if need be.[2] In June of 1844, they elected representatives to craft a set of laws, with Peter Burnett being one of the nine chosen for this task.[3] Con-sidered the best legal mind in Oregon, he easily dominated the group and ended up writing most of the first legislation adopted by Americans living there.

Along with drafting measures prohibiting alcohol and protecting the rights of indigenous tribes, Burnett focused his attention on preserving the colony's racial homogeneity. He was anxious to make Oregon as inhospitable to blacks as possible. As he put it, "We are in a new world, under most favorable circum-stances, and we wish to avoid most of those great evils that have so much afflicted the United States and other countries."[4] He first drew up a law that prohibited slavery and required slaveholders to remove any slaves they had brought to Oregon within two years or else free them. But Burnett was even more determined to exclude free blacks. For, given Oregon's location, climate, and type of agriculture, these blacks were more likely to arrive than ones bound in shackles. Their coming posed a threat to the livelihood of white settlers.[5] To prevent this from happening, Burnett proposed a law that, in its final version, included an extremely harsh penalty (although Burnett apparently did not actu-

1. Letter of Burnett to James Bennett, 4 Nov. 1844, reprinted in *Talking on Paper*, 19.
2. Most Oregonians were openly disdainful of the federal government and its attempts to regulate their affairs through officials sent out from Washington.
3. Taylor, "Slaves and Free Men," 154-5.
4. Letter of Burnett to unknown correspondent, 25 Dec. 1844, published in *Jefferson Inquirer*, 23 Oct. 1845.
5. Concern about free blacks in Oregon increased greatly after one of them provoked a violent confrontation in Oregon City in March 1844 that left two white men and a Native American dead. See William E. Franklin, "The Political Career of Peter H. Burnett," (Ph.D. diss., Stanford Univ., 1954), 65. Franklin also notes that "many of the men of 1843 were ex-Southerners who had suffered poverty under the plantation regime and who wanted to escape association with Negroes — free or slave — in Oregon."

ally favor this[1]): any free black who refused to leave Oregon within two years was to be arrested and then "receive upon his or her bare back not less than twenty nor more than thirty-nine stripes, to be inflicted by the constable of the proper county."[2] This so-called "lash law" was adopted by the territory's Legislative Committee in June 1844, although the whipping provision was never enforced and was, in fact, nullified a few months later.[3] Meeting in September 1849, lawmakers would reaffirm their wish to thwart black migration.[4] At that time, Burnett once again sought to close Oregon's borders to free blacks by proposing that those who continued to live there would be forced into slavery.[5] These draconian measures had the desired effect: by 1870, only 318 blacks and mulattoes were living in the state of Oregon.[6]

While the introduction of slavery into Oregon was, at best, only a remote possibility, the firm position against it taken by the territorial legislature riled some Southerners in the U.S. Senate.[7] They did not want to give the Northern states a voting edge[8] — or create a dangerous precedent — by allowing an anti-slavery Oregon into the Union. Consequently, they twice blocked House-adopted bills to create a free territory in the Pacific Northwest. Pro-expansion

1. In his memoirs, Burnett claimed that he had been opposed to whipping as a way of discouraging black migration and that he had been unhappy with this provision of the bill and had worked to nullify it. See his *Recollections*, 218-9. Cf. Franklin, "Political Career," 66.
2. Quoted from "Laws against Slaves, Negroes and Mulattoes," 25 June, 1844, in Taylor, "Slaves and Free Men," 155.
3. Instead of being whipped, any free blacks who chose to stay in Oregon would be subject to involuntary servitude. (However, there is only one known case of a person of color being forced to leave the territory under such a threat.) In his memoirs, Burnett sought to deflect criticism over this cruel and inhuman form of punishment. He claimed that it was best to exclude blacks from Oregon because of the strong white prejudice against them. Burnett went on to explain his own reasons: "To have such a class of men in their midst is injurious to the dominant class itself, as such a degraded and practically defenseless condition offers so many temptations to tyrannical abuse. One of the great objections to the institution of slavery was its bad influence upon the governing race." He claimed he wanted to establish a state where "the evils of intoxication and of mixed races, one of which was disfranchised," would not take hold. Burnett, *Recollections*, 220-1.
4. The House approved the measure, 12-4, on 19 June 1849, and the Council voted in favor, by a margin of 5-4, on 21 Sept. 1849. See *Journal of the House of Representatives of the Territory of Oregon*, (Oregon: Asahel Bush, 1854), 56, and *Journal of the Council of the Territory of Oregon*, (Oregon: Asahel Bush, 1854), 94.
5. This proposal was adopted in Dec. 1844. For a brief description of Burnett's role, see Lockley, "Documentary Records of Slavery," 110.
6. Of those, 78 had been born in the state. From 1840 to 1875, Oregon's black population never exceeded 0.3 percent of the total. K. Keith Richard, "Unwelcome Settlers: Black and Mulatto Oregon Pioneers, Part II," *Oregon Historical Quarterly* 84:2 (Summer 1983), 190-1.
7. For the tenor of the Senate debate, see "Speeches in the Senate on the Bill to Establish the Territorial Government of Oregon," 23 June 1848, 860ff. 30th Congress, 1st Session, *Appendix to the Congressional Globe*, Senate.
8. At that time the Union consisted of 15 slave and 15 free states.

Northern Democrats were incensed by this Southern opposition because they thought they had forged a *quid-pro-quo* agreement with their slave-state colleagues to back the acquisition of Texas in exchange for designating Oregon a federal territory.[1] In addition to Senator Dix of New York, several free-state lawmakers were openly sympathetic with the desire of whites living on this isolated frontier to maintain its racial exclusivity.

As a result of this impasse, as well as protracted congressional debate over its northern boundary,[2] Oregon was not organized as a free territory until August 1848.[3] The following year, its legislature passed restrictions on non-white migration (having removed the provision for physical punishment) out of fear that new black arrivals would join forces with local Native Americans in fomenting a revolt against white settlers.[4] But Oregonians were also worried that the coming of even a small number of free blacks would destroy the racially "pure" enclave they had created in the Pacific Northwest and thus make it less likely that other white pioneers would undertake the trek west.[5] During the territorial period, most Oregonians remained steadfastly opposed to allowing blacks of any sort to settle among them (although racial attitudes did soften somewhat with the arrival of emigrants from Northern states and Europe).[6] In the words of one territorial representative, "niggers . . . should never be allowed to mingle with the whites. They would amalgamate and raise a most miserable race of human beings . . . If niggers are allowed to come among us and mingle with the whites, it will cause a perfect state of pollution. Niggers always retrograde, until they get back to the state of barbarity from whence they originated . . . I don't see that we should equalize ourselves with them by letting them come among us."[7]

---

1. See, for example, Goodwin, *Trans-Mississippi West*, 377. Bills to acquire Texas and organize Oregon into a territory were introduced in 1844 and passed that same year by both houses of Congress. But Northern Whigs remained opposed to expansion into either of these regions.
2. President Polk angered many in his party by backing away from his inaugural pledge in agreeing to make Oregon's northern boundary the 49th parallel, rather than insist on the 54.40 line sought by arch-expansionists.
3. This occurred under the relevant provision of the Northwest Ordinance.
4. White Oregonians were particularly fearful of Indian uprisings as a result of a massacre that occurred in 1847. Thinking that the missionary Marcus Whitman had deliberately spread measles among them, members of the local Cayuse tribe slaughtered him, his wife, and 12 other whites. Free blacks had already sought to incite Native Americans against whites in Oregon. See Johannsen, *Frontier Politics*, 20-1.
5. In the words of one historian, white Oregonians "simply believed that the fewer blacks and mulattoes around the better the quality of the society." They did not want to compete for jobs against either slaves or free black workers. Richard, "Unwelcome Settlers," 191. Cf. LaLande, "'Dixie' of the Pacific Northwest," 37.
6. Minto, "Antecedents," 45.
7. Portland *Weekly Oregonian*, 16 Jan. 1855. Quoted in Johannsen, *Frontier Politics*, 23.

It came, therefore, as no surprise that a central question facing delegates to Oregon's first constitutional convention was black migration.[1] This issue had re-emerged in the wake of congressional passage of the Kansas-Nebraska Act of 1854, which supplanted the Missouri Compromise and gave territories the right to decide the slavery question for themselves, under Stephen Douglas's doctrine of "popular sovereignty." This meant that Oregon was no longer off limits to the "peculiar institution" solely because of its geographical location. As a result, the "sense of security against the black evil was succeeded by uncertainty, if not positive alarm."[2] Oregonians opposed to slavery held their first convention in June 1855 and denounced the expanding Slave Power. In February 1857, members of the recently constituted Oregon Republican Party affirmed their unshakable opposition to any extension of slavery into free territories, while two months later the territory's Democrats declared that this matter was properly left up to each individual territory to resolve. So the stage was set for a major political confrontation.

Convening in Salem's county courthouse on August 18, 1857, 60 representatives from all over the territory took up the question of how the prospective state would deal with this explosive issue.[3] As had been the case in Missouri some 35 years before, Oregon politicians were mindful of the national repercussions of their decisions — adopting too extreme a stance ran the risk of Congress's rejecting the state's constitution and bid for statehood. But, like their counterparts in Missouri, these delegates were independent-minded Westerners, constitutionally predisposed to thumb their noses at federal authority.[4] Slightly more than half were farmers. Almost all were Democrats.[5] A quarter of them were native Southerners who had previously moved north of the Ohio River before making the long and arduous journey across the Great Plains.[6] Most, but

---

1. Slavery was the "only real issue before the people" at the 1857 convention. Walter C. Woodward, *The Rise and Early History of Political Parties in Oregon, 1843-1868* (Portland: J.K. Gill, 1913),107.
2. *Ibid.*, 89.
3. When it was proposed to refer the slavery question to a standing committee for resolution, several members objected, but unsuccessfully so. One characterized slavery as "the most important of subjects for consideration" before the convention. Quoted in Charles H. Carey, "The Creation of Oregon as a State," *Oregon Historical Quarterly* 27:1 (March 1926), 4. A similar motion to bar floor debate on the "peculiar institution" was defeated.
4. At a state Democratic convention held in April, delegates from both wings of the party had agreed that "all negroes should be excluded" from Oregon. Charles H. Carey, *The Oregon Constitution and Proceedings and Debates of the Constitutional Convention of 1857* (Salem: State Printing Office, 1926), 24.
5. Only one delegate, J.R. McBride from Yamhill County, listed his affiliation as Republican.
6. Nearly as many — 14 delegates — had spent all of their lives in slave states. All told, of the 60 elected representatives, 28 were free-state natives, and 26 slave-state natives.

not all, were opposed to legalizing the "peculiar institution" in Oregon, largely for economic reasons: they worried about competition from slave labor.[1]

Moral considerations did not affect their positions in the slightest. These were tough frontier pragmatists, concerned only about their own self-interest.[2] As one Democratic delegate put it, "I shall vote against slavery, but if it carries I shall get me a nigger."[3] But some well-to-do migrants from the Upper South wanted to allow slaves to be brought into the territory — both to cultivate their own large landholdings and to tilt the national political balance in favor of the slave states.[4] Pro-slavery forces were also keen to employ this form of labor in the search for gold, which had recently been discovered in the southern part of the territory.[5] They further contended that making the slave system unlawful would only encourage free blacks to come to Oregon.[6] The men favoring slavery had powerful local allies. At the time of the convention, five of the territory's eight newspapers had come out in favor of tolerating slavery in Oregon, and several leading politicians had also endorsed this policy. But the vast majority of delegates gathered in the Salem courthouse were Jeffersonian democrats, philosophically averse to any form of human bondage. While somewhat reluctant to go on record against slavery for fear of being labeled "abolitionists" or "black Republicans," these Democrats held the fate of the proceedings in their hands. Even though the "hard," or party-line, Democrats elected the convention's president — 33-year-old Matthew P. Deady, a Maryland native of Irish ancestry who was then serving as a territorial judge[7] — as well as the chairs of its various committees, they had no chance of carrying the day on the slavery issue. A proposal to protect the property rights of slaveholders in Oregon was soundly rejected.

---

1. A 31 March 1857 editorial in the Oregon *Statesman* had advised voters to approach the question of slavery solely from this point of view, and this piece had considerable influence on the positions taken at the convention. Carey, "Creation of Oregon," 7, note 6. Another territorial judge, George H. Williams, wrote in July that free labor was economically superior to slave labor. He argued that "one free white man is worth more than two negro slaves in the cultivation of the soil, or any other business that can be influenced by zeal or the exercise of discretion." See *Statesman*, 28 July 1857, quoted in Charles H. Carey, *A General History of Oregon Prior to 1861*, vol. 1, *To the Great Civil War* (Portland: Metropolitan, Press, 1936), 509.
2. The slavery issue boiled down to an economic question: "Will it pay?" Quoted in Woodward, *Political Parties in Oregon*, 115.
3. Quoted in Carey, *A General History*, 507.
4. For more on the political aspects of becoming a slave state see remarks of J. Kelsey, 25 Aug. 1857, *Proceedings and* Debates, 174. The Supreme Court's ruling in the Dred Scott case a few months before had nullified the Missouri Compromise and seemingly made it possible for Oregonians to decide that they wanted to establish a slave state.
5. For a while, settlers eager to pursue gold mining proposed that southern Oregon join with northern California to form a new territory that would allow slavery. But Californians did not want to cede any land for this purpose.
6. Carey, "Creation of Oregon," 12.
7. Paradoxically, Deasy was the only delegate to the 1857 convention who had publicly declared himself in favor of slavery.

Although this issue had generated a great deal of discussion in the Oregon press prior to the convention, delegates were disinclined to have the final say on legalizing slavery — one way or the other — preferring to let the territory's voters decide in a referendum. This strategy would let the politicians off the hook. Still, many of those attending the Salem convention were not shy about speaking their minds on the subject of race. In the course of expounding on the need for "free and equal" elections, a representative from New York explained to the presiding officer that in using this term he certainly did not mean to include "Chinese or niggers." [1] Another native of the Empire State, territorial judge George H. Williams — a Democrat who later switched to the Republican Party — vowed that he would "consecrate Oregon to the use of the white man, and exclude the negro, Chinaman, and every race of that character. He believed the interests of Oregon would be promoted by such course." [2] Even a delegate (still another New Yorker) who felt that the rights of blacks already residing in the territory should be respected was opposed to opening Oregon to any more of their race: he did not "wish to see Oregon filled with so undesirable a population as either negroes or Chinamen. I have an instinctive dislike of all mongrel races, be they red or black, and I am certain that nothing could more impede the progress and prosperity of this country, morally, politically and financially, than to have it filled with hungry hordes of docile men, born to servility; and I would do nothing to encourage their migration hither." [3] While agreeing to put this matter into the hands of voters, the representatives in Salem backed a provision excluding from Oregon all persons who were not U.S. citizens and approved sections of the state's Bill of Rights that prohibited slavery as well as the entry of free blacks and mulattoes. [4] So written, the constitution was adopted by a vote of 34-11.

The remarks made at the 1857 convention and the strong backing for the constitution's discriminatory clauses make two points evident. First of all, the delegates did not want other peoples to come to Oregon. The new state was to be founded on a doctrine of racial exclusivity, to protect the well being of white settlers. Secondly, this animosity toward non-whites was by no means limited to Oregonians who had come from the South. Natives of the Northeast were just as adamant about keeping blacks out. That this was so confirms the pattern of nearly universal prejudice found in other Western states and tends to invalidate the conclusion of some historians that only Southern migrants were responsible for spreading racial intolerance and hatred throughout this region of the United States.

---

1. Remarks of Delazon Smith, 10 Sept. 1857, *Proceedings*, 318.
2. Remarks of George H. Williams, 15 Sept. 1857, *Proceedings*, 362.
3. Remarks of William H. Watkins, 15 Sept. 1857, *Proceedings*, 385.
4. It has been argued that the ban on free-black migration was designed to appease proslavery Oregonians, or, in the more colorful language of the times, "a tub thrown to the whale." Quoted in Carey, *Proceedings*, 34.

Throughout the fall, the slavery question dominated public debate in Oregon, but when voters finally went to the polls in November 1857 to approve the new constitution and register their views on admitting slaves or free blacks, the outcome left no doubt about their sentiments. While strongly endorsing the constitution, by a better than two-to-one (7,195 to 3,195) ratio, residents even more resoundingly rejected the legalization of slavery in Oregon, with 7,727 against versus only 2,645 in favor. But the most one-sided result was on the question of allowing free blacks and mulattoes into the state. Eight Oregonians opposed this proposal for every one who marked his ballot with a "Yes." The final tally was 8,640 against, and 1,081 in favor. As had been true in the territorial legislature, settlers from different parts of the country showed aversion to free blacks. For example, far northern Clatsop County had more New York natives than persons from any other state (17.9 percent of the total population), but nearly three quarters of its voters rejected black migration. However, counties with the highest proportion of Missouri natives were even more decidedly opposed: 91.6 percent of voters in Polk County, in which over a third of residents had been born in the Show Me State; 85.9 percent in Yamhill (with 29.4 percent from Missouri); and 93.6 percent in Marion (where 28.4 percent were Missouri-born).[1] In the succinct view of one scholar, "The anti-Negro sentiment in Oregon was emphatic."[2] Another historian of Oregon's constitutional convention has sought to explain this popular result as motivated by a desire to gain congressional approval for entering the Union as a free state, but this interpretation overlooks the territory's racist climate.[3] While some Oregonians supported the coming of slavery for economic reasons, the arrival of free blacks would bring no benefits to any whites. On the contrary, this racial group was considered undesirable on all counts — economically, socially, morally, and politically. Black freemen would cost white workers jobs and dissuade other whites from trekking to Oregon. Free blacks would weaken white morality and work ethic; they also might intermarry with whites and thus blur the important dividing line between the races. Finally, emancipated slaves would set a "bad example" for other oppressed people, such as Native Americans, and might inspire them to revolt. For all of these reasons, early pioneers in the Pacific Northwest wanted to keep these blacks out. The lopsided vote on November 9, 1857, sent an unmistakable signal across the nation that only whites would be welcomed in this new "paradise."

---

1. These data are derived from Jesse S. Douglas, "Origins of the Population of Oregon in 1850," *Pacific Northwest Quarterly* 41:2 (April 1950), Table III, "Places of Birth of Native-born White Population, Oregon Territory, 1850,"170, and Woodward, *Political Parties*, Appendix I, "The Vote on the Adoption of the Oregon Constitution, Nov. 9, 1857," 341.
2. Woodward, *Political Parties*, 89.
3. Carey, *General History*, vol. 2, 511.

The Supreme Court's recent ruling in the Dred Scott case — that free blacks did not enjoy the rights of citizenship — gave Oregon's lawmakers confidence that the racially discriminatory provisions of the state's constitution would not face legal or political challenge in Washington. And, indeed, Northerners in Congress did not raise the same objections as they had nearly 40 years before, when Missouri had sought to join the Union. Both the Senate and the House accepted Oregon's petition for statehood without prolonged discussion,[1] and, on February 14, 1859, this white bastion on the Pacific became the 33rd state — and the second west of the Rockies — to join the Union.[2]

Oddly enough, as Oregon's "free state" status was being officially endorsed in the nation's capital, the state's voters seemingly reversed themselves in June by spurning Republican candidates who had condemned the slave trade at their 1858 state convention and electing a slate of officials who held *pro*-slavery views. Democratic candidates won all contested statewide offices and captured most of the seats in the state legislature. "Honest John" Whiteaker, a Democrat who hailed from northeastern Indiana, was chosen to be Oregon's first governor, in part because he reasoned that introducing slavery was the best way to maintain white superiority. Similarly, in 1859, voters picked two pro-slavery Democrats — Joseph Lane (who had previously been appointed territorial governor by President Polk) and Delazon Smith, an Oberlin-educated New Yorker — to represent them in the U.S. Senate. And Lafayette Grover, a Democratic lawyer from Maine with sympathy for slaveholders, was elected as Oregon's first congressman. Why would Oregonians, who had so decisively rejected the "peculiar institution" just a few months before, now vote into office so many "violent advocates of slavery"?[3]

The explanation for this apparently paradoxical behavior lies with a central concern of Westerners — namely, states' rights. Having voiced their own strongly anti-slavery feelings through the state constitution, white Oregonians were now free to express their equally intense dislike of outside interference in their internal affairs. This time, residents looked at the differences between Democrats and Republicans not in terms of their positions on slavery (as this was now a moot issue), but rather their degree of support for local autonomy, or "popular sovereignty." At their March 1858 convention, Oregon Democrats had

---

1. Ironically, it was antislavery Republicans who now opposed Oregon's admission. Some took umbrage at the constitutional ban on free-black migration, while others were simply worried about adding another Democrat-dominated state to the Union. Despite this opposition, the Oregon statehood bill passed the House, 114-108 on Feb. 12, 1859, after having been approved by the Senate the previous year. See Woodward, *Political Parties*, 147-8.
2. After losing his Senatorial race to Stephen Douglas in 1858, Abraham Lincoln had been offered the post of territorial governor in Oregon, but had turned this down, in part due to his wife's reluctance to move so far away from friends and family.
3. Carey, *General History*, 519.

clearly sided with those who believed the federal government had no business telling states whether they could be "free" or "slave." By contrast, the state's Republicans, adopting a Free Soil platform the following year, went on record firmly against allowing any new states to legalize slavery. Oregonians had already been concerned that President James Buchanan, a proponent of popular sovereignty, might try to impose slavery upon them, and their voting for state Democratic candidates was intended to help forestall any such attempt by Washington to regulate their affairs. In short, Western abhorrence of outside control determined the outcome at the polls. The complexities of Oregon's politics on the eve of the Civil War show that the nation was now divided as much over the question of ultimate legal power in the land as it was over the fate of the "peculiar institution."

Oregon's hostility toward non-white migrants would continue for a considerable period of time. During the Civil War, its legislature passed a law forcing black freemen and mulattoes, as well as Chinese and Hawaiians, to pay an annual tax of $5, or else perform manual labor for ten days to earn that amount. After the war, Oregon citizens failed to approve the 14th Amendment (making blacks citizens) when it first came up for a vote, and it was not until 1868 that they finally did so. Likewise, Oregonians voted against the 15th Amendment (granting blacks the vote) in 1870. The state's legal exclusion on black in-migration was not repealed until 1926. Repeated efforts to change Oregon's constitution so as to grant black residents the suffrage did not succeed until 1927. And it was not until 1959 — nearly a century after it became part of the U.S. Constitution — that Oregon's voters endorsed the 15th Amendment. Given this history, it is hardly surprising that, in 2000, only about 1.6 percent of the state's population of 3.5 million persons was black.

***

During all of these contentious deliberations concerning Oregon's statehood, the name of Peter H. Burnett was wholly absent. This is because the peripatetic frontiersman was no longer living in the Emerald State. After he had served two terms in the territorial legislature (where he had introduced a bill to ban slavery, in June 1844,[1] and, four years later, drafted a petition asking Congress to incorporate Oregon as a federal territory[2]) and secured a lucrative appointment as associate justice in Oregon's judiciary,[3] wanderlust and his perennial need for more cash got the better of Burnett. In July of 1848, word reached the Pacific Northwest of the discovery of gold at Sutter's saw mill, in

---

1. "Journal of the Legislative Committee, June 18, 1844," *The Oregon Archives, Including the Journals, Governors' Messages, and Public Papers of Oregon* (Salem: Asahel Bush, 1853), 47. Burnett also proposed a ban on alcoholic beverages in Oregon.
2. "Petition of Citizens of Oregon," 30th Congress, 1st Session, Misc. No. 136, 8 May 1848. This document is signed by Burnett, George L. Curry, and L.A. Rice, but was written by Burnett.

Coloma, California, six months earlier. "Gold fever" struck with a vengeance: along with an estimated two-thirds of the able-bodied men then living in Oregon, Burnett impulsively headed south to become rich.[1] In September, he organized a wagon train in Oregon City and was named its captain. The party reached the Sacramento Valley about a month later and traveled on to the gold mines.

There, Burnett found a number of old friends and acquaintances from Oregon already hard at work, toiling in the stream beds and extracting gold worth about $20 a day — the equivalent of over $400 today. ("Men are here nearly crazy with the riches forced suddenly into their pockets," Burnett wrote. "The gold is positively inexhaustible.")[2] At Long Bar, on the Yuba River, Burnett purchased a claim for $300, and after a month he had earned enough to pay off all his debts back in Oregon, with a comfortable cushion of cash left over.[3] Drawing upon his prior political experience and ties, he then became involved in efforts to preserve California's new wealth from "undesirables." He and other Oregonians lobbied successfully to keep blacks — slaves and freemen alike — out of the burgeoning mining camps.[4] The number of blacks had grown rapidly after the discovery of gold. Some came as slaves, accompanying owners from states such as Texas.[5] But others arrived as free individuals — the first blacks to come this far west of their own volition. Black freemen were, in fact, among the first Americans to be drawn west by the promise of instant riches, as well as by somewhat misleading reports of "social fluidity" on this frontier.[6] Consequently, the black population in California doubled in the three years after gold was discovered there, and in the gold-mining counties alone between 600 and 700 blacks had taken up residence. Half of them were freemen.[7] By the beginning of the Civil

---

3. Burnett was paid $2,000 a year, only $1,000 less than the territorial governor. See "Oregon Territory," *The American Almanac and Repository of Useful Information for the Year 1849*, (Boston: Gray and Bowen, 1850), 311. He was appointed to this post by President Polk on 14 Aug. 1848.

1. Exact figures on migration from Oregon to California are not available. The 1850 federal census shows there were 5,890 Missouri natives then living in California — the second-largest out-of-state contingent after New York (10,160). Most of these Missourians likely came to California via Oregon. At that time, Oregon's American-born population totaled 11,992.

2. Letter of Burnett to Col. Alexander Doniphon, reprinted in the *Saturday Evening Post* 28:1453 (2 June 1849), 3.

3. For details on Burnett's prospecting days, see *Recollections*, 273-5, 283-6, and Donald Dale Jackson, *Gold Dust* (New York: Knopf, 1980), 56-7.

4. F. G. Yang, "The Lewis and Clark Centennial," *Oregon Historical Quarterly* 4:1 (March 1903), 11.

5. California officials allowed this to happen, in defiance of the state's ban on slavery, in order to avoid confrontation with these Southern slave owners. Lawrence B. de Graaf and Quintard Taylor, "Introduction," *Seeking El Dorado: African Americans in California*, ed. Lawrence B. de Graaf and Quintard Taylor (Seattle, London: University of Washington Press, 2001), 9.

War, this number had risen to over 4,000, making California home to 75 percent of all free blacks in the West.[1]

For a while, Burnett dabbled in real estate, acting as agent for "General" John Sutter — helping the German immigrant to settle debts of his own and manage his estate, New Helvetia. Burnett profited handsomely from selling Sutter's lots in newly established Sacramento and soon found himself again caught up in local politics.[2] Early in 1849, he was instrumental in organizing a citizens' group to lobby for California's setting up a provisional government, without waiting for Washington's approval. On June 12, Burnett gave a speech at the first political gathering ever held in the territory, railing against Congress's oppressive and unjust treatment of California as well as its purported efforts to impose slavery. He advised members of the audience to resist paying taxes to the federal government, just as American colonists had refused British demands a century before. There was some apprehension at that time that prominent national politicians might force the territory into the ranks of the slave states — fears fueled by Pres. Zachary Taylor's appointment of a Georgia slaveholder, Thomas Butler King, as his special representative in California. Some Californians felt that only a prohibitory clause in its constitution could stop Southerners from bringing more slaves into their midst.[3] Burnett was a leader in this antislavery camp.[4] Known as "Locofocos," radical Democrats opposed to the banks and wealthy businessmen ran a slate of candidates for state office, with Burnett taking on his former employer, Sutter, in the contest for governor. Thanks to the large number of former Oregonians then living in California, Burnett won the election handily, defeating both Sutter and William Sherwood in November of 1849.[5]

Burnett delivered his inaugural address on December 20, lauding the new constitution for having outlawed the "great social and political evil" of slavery,

---

6. Defeat of a proposal to restrict black in-migration had given them hope. So did the existence of an all-black mining company in California and the migration of some New England abolitionists to the territory. Because of the informal living arrangements in the camps, and the need for them as cooks, blacks gained some acceptance, and "a fragile and spotty democracy . . . prevailed between free black men and white men in the mines." Rudolph M. Lapp, *Blacks in Gold Rush California* (New Haven: Yale University Press, 1977), 15-17, 77.

7. *Ibid.*, 49.

1. De Graaf and Taylor, "Introduction," 8.

2. According to one historian, Burnett had acquired assets worth nearly $400,000 by 1851. William E. Franklin, "A Forgotten Chapter in California History: Peter H. Burnett and John Sutter's Fortune," *California Historical Quarterly* 41:4 (Dec. 1962), 323.

3. "Late — Important from California," *National Era* 3:31 (2 Aug. 1849), 123. White miners worried about blacks gaining any share of the wealth being extracted from the California beds. Berwanger, *Frontier Against Slavery*, 62.

4. However, the antislavery publication *National Era* named Burnett as one of the "proslavery men" seeking to make California a state. See "Danger Ahead — Freemen Faltering," *National Era* 3:38 (20 Sept. 1849), 151.

5. For Burnett, the governorship was financially lucrative, giving him an annual salary of $10,000.

but then asking the assembled legislators to go farther than this document had gone (in denying free blacks the vote) and make it illegal for "free people of color" to live in California. He made his case thusly:

> If we permit them to settle in our State, under existing circumstances, we consign them, by our own institutions, and the usages of our own society, to a subordinate and degraded position, which is in itself a species of slavery. They would be placed in a situation where they would have no efficient motives for moral or intellectual improvement, but must remain in our midst, sensible of their degradation, unhappy themselves, enemies to the institutions and the society whose usages have placed them there, and for ever fit teachers in all the schools of ignorance, vice, and idleness.

While conceding his proposal to exclude manumitted slaves was "harsh," Burnett tried to convince the lawmakers that adopting it was best for both blacks and whites, who would otherwise suffer "a most serious injury."[1] Some wholeheartedly agreed with Burnett about the desirability of preserving California — particularly its gold mines — for the white race.[2] But others greeted his speech with considerable hostility.[3] The assembly did approve the exclusion of free blacks, but Burnett's measure was killed in the senate. Sensing he would not be able to accomplish in his new state what he hoped to do in this post, Burnett resigned the governorship a little over a year later.[4] In his final message to the legislature, in January 1851, he once again urged lawmakers to take steps to stop free blacks from settling in the state, predicting that "When those who come after us shall witness a war in California between the two races . . . they will have as much cause to reproach us for not taking timely steps . . . to prevent this state of things, as we now have for reproaching our ancestors for the evils entailed upon us by the original introduction of slavery into the Colonies."[5] But the legislators did not go along with him. (However, they did deny black freemen the rights to testify in court, marry whites, serve on juries, and own homesteads.)

Although the desire among many white settlers to bar black freemen from California increased during the next decade as more of them arrived in the state,[6]

---

1. Peter H. Burnett, Inaugural Address, 20 Dec. 1849, http://www.governor.ca.gov/govsite/govsgallery/h/documents/inaugural_1.html. He feared that, in the coming years, slaves in the eastern half of the country would be freed once they were no longer profitable for their owners, and that this would result in a large number of blacks coming to California to work in its mines. See Franklin, "Political Career," 143.
2. Lapp, *Blacks in Gold Rush California*, 127.
3. At least some of Burnett's critics feared that his attempt to exclude blacks would stir up an unwelcome controversy in California, which already had an ethnically and racially diverse population. See Franklin, "Political Career," 145.
4. In his last message to the California legislature, in January 1851, Burnett worried about the threat posed by local Indians to the gold mines, urged that a "war of extermination" be waged "until the Indian race should become extinct." Quoted in Annie R. Mitchell, "Major James D. Savage and the Tularenos," *California Historical Quarterly* 28:4 (Dec. 1949), 329.
5. Quoted in Franklin, "Political Career," 170.

mostly to work in the mines, a more hospitable racial climate slowly developed. Blacks themselves organized to fight for their rights: the first convention of "colored citizens" of California took place in 1855.[1] This and subsequent gatherings kept up the pressure to liberalize the state's policies regarding blacks. But whites also took up their cause, signing petitions to permit blacks to testify in court. In January 1858, the governor, J. Neely Johnson, spoke out for this change in California law.[2] Even though a bill bestowing this right was rejected, racial attitudes were clearly beginning to change. The election of Leland Stanford as governor in 1862, for example, led to repeal of the state's prohibition on black testimony in court. And, in this gradual evolution, California was not alone. As more immigrants from Europe and Asia reached the nation's shores, both in the East and in the West, and as more white Americans adjusted their preconceptions about other peoples as a result of greater contact with them, the current of history started to flow in another direction — away from an Anglo-Saxon hegemony toward a more complex, multiracial future.

***

In his later years, Burnett returned to the practice of law, served briefly on California's supreme court, and presided for 17 years over a corporation that became the Pacific Bank.[3] He also wrote several books, including a spiritual autobiography entitled *The Path Which Led a Protestant Lawyer to the Catholic Church* and a treatise on American government.[4] Burnett died in San Francisco at the ripe old age of 87, on May 17, 1895 — some five years after the superintendent of the census concluded that the Western frontier no longer existed, and that the pioneering era in American history had come to an end.

Up until then, and even afterwards, open spaces in the Far West continued to attract restless, adventurous, fiercely independent, self-reliant men and women, much as generations of like-minded individuals before them had pursued their individual destinies on the fringes of American civilization — in places as disparate but equally enticing as the backwoods of Maine, the red-clay hills of Virginia, the Cumberland Mountains of Kentucky, the banks of the Ohio River, the rich bottomland of Missouri, the cornfields of Iowa, the streambeds of

---

6. The black population rose from 672 in 1850 to 2,206 in 1852. Berwanger, *Frontier Against Slavery*, 73. In 1858, California's legislature again debated a proposal to restrict black in-migration, although this was not adopted.
1. See *Proceedings of the First State Convention of the Colored Citizens of the State of California* (Sacramento: Democratic State Journal Printer, 1855).
2. Lapp, *Blacks in Gold Rush California*, 203-4.
3. While on the court, Burnett wrote the majority opinion in a highly controversial case that resembled the one involving Dred Scott. Under this decision, a slave who had been brought to California and then escaped was ordered returned to his owner.
4. In the latter, *The American Theory of Government, Considered in Reference to the Present Crisis* (New York: D. Appleton, 1861), Burnett argued that division of the Union would lead to constant war between North and South, the rise of despotism, and the failure of republican government.

California, and the billowing meadows of Oregon. They would continue to seek greater opportunity, solitude, liberty, and independence where law and civilized ways interfered only minimally with the exercise of their own will. Still deeply embedded in this impulse to seek freedom was a wish — now largely unutterable socially, as well as legally impermissible — to live, if not alone, then near only those of their own kind. The Civil War, the abolition of slavery, the granting of equal rights to blacks, and the subsequent migration to the United States of people from all corners of the world – persons of many different races and colors, forever changed the character of American society, making the pioneers' atavistic wish to reverse time by establishing a white redoubt on the Western frontier an ever more elusive fantasy. But, despite the inexorable flow of history, this desire would stubbornly persist. The frontier era may have ended, but the frontier spirit lingered on. Despite, or perhaps because of, America's great diversity in the second half of the 19th century and into the 20th, the impulse to withdraw — to retreat into a more comforting, homogeneous enclave — would not wholly die. All across the land, in places large and small, the quest after a white sanctuary would continue.

EPILOGUE

The decades-long struggle to shape the nation's racial landscape culminated in the most traumatic conflict in U.S. history. The Civil War proved "irrepressible"[1] because the opposing values, aspirations, economic systems, political objectives, and cultures in two sections of the country could not be indefinitely accommodated within the framework of a single Union. It would require four years of slaughter, taking over 600,000 lives and leaving permanent scars on the American psyche, to decide whether one region — the North — would be able to impose its will and preserve the bonds that held the nation together, or whether the other, the South, would go its separate way and become an independent country. The fate of the United States hung in the balance.

The various causes of the Civil War are intimately intertwined, and race is the thread that binds them all together. The nation was polarized — not over slavery itself, but over the *extension* of slavery. This was a far more volatile matter because it was heavily laden with national, rather than only regional, consequences. The West was still up for grabs, and whether it would be the North or the South that would ultimately bring this vast domain under its sway would determine the racial composition, ideology, and identity not only of these new lands, but also of the United States as a whole. The political compromises struck since the writing of the Constitution in 1787 to avoid confronting this fundamental question would no longer suffice. There was no middle ground left on to which to retreat.

---

1. The memorable phrase "irrepressible conflict" was first used by William Seward in a campaign speech in Rochester, delivered on 25 Oct. 1858.

The irreconcilable needs and agendas of the two regions now clashed head on. The South felt its very survival was at stake. Politically (that is, geographically) as well as economically, it believed the North was gaining an unmistakable advantage that could only lead to the destruction of its way of life. Any further restrictions on the spread of slavery would cripple Southern agriculture, but also create racial upheaval. If they were unable to sell or move their excess slaves westward, planters all over the South would have no choice but to let them go free, and the presence of so many emancipated blacks in Dixie and elsewhere in the country would create an intolerably perilous situation for whites. As one Southern lawmaker gloomily foresaw, "Either the black race must be sent out free, as emigrants, at the cost of the structure and habits of our society, or the white must . . . emigrate, leaving in the end the graves of their sires to be trodden under the heel of the African."[1]

From the North's point of view, the issues at stake were more complex, even contradictory. Certainly this was true of the racial aspect. While the South's need to defend and expand the "peculiar institution" was unequivocal and straightforward, one could not say the same about the North's hostility toward slavery. After all, the free states had long ago adopted a live-and-let-live attitude toward their Southern brethren on this issue, disavowing over and over again any ulterior motive of wishing to crush the slave system under foot. Nor was the possible extension of slavery into the territories and future states of the Far West objectively a concern for the North, as these lands, by and large, had not shown themselves to be adaptable to slave-based agriculture. Even if local residents were granted the right — under the doctrine of popular sovereignty — to decide if they wanted to be "free" or "slave," it was unlikely that they would opt for the latter status. The North could, therefore, feel reasonably confident that time and the course of Western settlement were on their side. Already, in 1860, its representatives held a numerical advantage in the chambers of Congress, with 18 free states arrayed against only 15 slave states. But, if this was the case, what, then, led the free states to gird their loins for battle, protesting as they did so that *their* very existence was now in mortal peril?

Officially, the North went to war not because of slavery but to undo the South's dissolution of the Union: the secession of South Carolina on December 17, 1860, followed by that of 10 other Southern states, placed the nation's fate in jeopardy and forced the North to respond. The House of Representatives made this abundantly clear in the resolution it adopted on July 22, 1861, stating that "this war is not waged upon our part in any spirit of oppression, nor for any pur-

---

1. Remarks of Sen. David Yulee, quoted in Michael A. Morrison, *Slavery and the American West: The Eclipse of Manifest Destiny and the Coming of the Civil War*, (Chapel Hill: University of North Carolina Press, 1997), 114.

pose of conquest or subjugation, nor purpose of overthrowing or *interfering with the rights or established institutions of those States* [italics added], but to defend and maintain the supremacy of the Constitution and to preserve the Union with all the dignity, equality and rights of the several States unimpaired . . ."[1] President Lincoln reaffirmed this rationale with rhetorical flourish just over a year later, in a letter to Horace Mann: "My paramount object in this struggle is to save the Union, and is not either to save or to destroy slavery. If I could save the Union without freeing any slave I would do it, and if I could save it by freeing all the slaves I would do it; and if I could save it by freeing some and leaving others alone I would also do that."[2] A desire to defend the Constitution, national honor, and the rule of law, coupled with outrage over the South's shelling of Fort Sumter, similarly aroused an almost universal "patriotic furor" among ordinary Northern citizens at the war's outset.[3] Few young men from Massachusetts or New York marched off to battle in order to free the slaves or to secure equal rights for black Americans.[4] This was a war fought by, for, and about the white race.

But, in fact, motives on the Northern side were more complicated, and they did encompass the slave system, although not for the reasons that one might suppose. Indeed, the region's attitude toward the "peculiar institution" was highly ambivalent. On the one hand, the North *was* adamantly opposed to any enlargement of the slave system. As long as slavery was contained within the states where it already existed, the odious system would gradually disappear, because — like a malignant cancer — its survival depended on constant growth. On this point, North and South were in full agreement. Thus, many Northerners had been dismayed by the 1857 Dred Scott decision, which determined that Congress had no power to regulate slavery in the territories. This ruling took away the North's *quasi* veto power in Congress over the admission of any additional slave states and raised the prospect, albeit remote, that the institution might take root somewhere in the West.

---

1. *House Journal*, 37th Cong., lst sess., 22 July 1861, 123.
2. Letter of Abraham Lincoln to Horace Greeley, 22 August 1862. *Primary Sources: Workshops in American History*, http://www.learner.org/channel/workshops/primarysources/emancipation/docs/lin_greeley.html.
3. James M. McPherson, *For Cause & Comrades: Why Men Fought in the Civil War* (New York: Oxford University Press, 1997), 16. McPherson quotes from letters written by Union soldiers explaining their motives for enlisting. But he concedes that the abstract concepts of "honor," "duty," and "country" so often cited by these recruits may not fully explain why they rushed to enlist.
4. According to one study, only about one in ten Union soldiers fought to abolish slavery. Randall C. Jimerson, *The Private Civil War: Popular Thought During the Sectional Conflict* (Baton Rouge: Louisiana State University Press, 1988), 41. However, roughly a third of the people in the North believed that the demise of the slave system was essential to restoring national unity. McPherson, *For Cause & Comrades*, 118.

On the other hand, few persons living above the Mason Dixon Line wished to see slavery abolished.[1] Residing in a region with an overwhelmingly white population — and strong anti-black prejudice — Northerners were eager to maintain this homogeneity. By and large, they did not want to live near blacks or work alongside them. From their perspective, slavery was an instrument of social control that kept thousands, if not millions, of unwanted blacks from moving northward, into their cities, towns, and villages. So, like their Southern counterparts, they worried about the impact of this system collapsing and, out of concern for their own well being, hoped this would not happen. Even staunch abolitionists had no desire to see liberated slaves come stampeding north.[2]

Mixed feelings about the likely end of slavery reflected the North's equally conflicted views about black people. These were well served by the emerging Republican Party. For it encompassed virtually all points of views on race relations — from unabashed abolitionism to equally unabashed contempt for blacks as "degrading" and "inferior." The party's seemingly contradictory positions had attracted voters of various persuasions, helped it rise to national prominence in just a few years, and enable it to capture the presidency in 1860. But this political strength was also a major liability: it prevented the Republicans from developing a coherent and consistent approach to dealing with the race question. Instead, it "contained multitudes." Without question, the party espoused moral, philosophical, and religious antipathy towards the chattel system, because this was seen as antithetical to American ideals. Slavery was a blot on the nation's soul. Slavery also violated the sacred principles of freedom and equality enshrined in the Declaration of Independence. In this sense, the Republican Party could present itself as the standard bearer of Jeffersonian principles.

The Republican embrace of freedom was particularly popular in the West, for there the right to live and prosper as "free" men and women took on a special meaning. In the West, the word "free" often meant the opposite of "slave," and what it implied was the absence not only of slaves, but of *all* blacks, since they were considered innately incapable of attaining true freedom. Slavery and "free labor" could not exist side by side. Neither could blacks and whites. This was the coded message conveyed through the word "freedom" in parts of the country where blacks had not yet settled: *we support your desire to stay clear of this undesirable race.* Republican candidates had borrowed this connotation from the political organization whose mantle they had seized — the Free Soil party of the late 1840s.

---

1. One historian has concluded that a majority of Northerners "probably" opposed emancipation until the end of 1864. Jimerson, *Private Civil War*, 48.
2. See, for example, Nevins, *Fruits of Manifest Destiny*, 533.

Having witnessed how well this now-defunct party's stand on behalf of "freedom" had resonated with the Northern public in 1848 — being adopted by the two major parties running presidential campaigns that year — the Republicans had shrewdly echoed Free Soil themes during the election of 1856. Choosing a famed Western explorer, John Charles Fremont, as their standard bearer, the new party adopted the apt, alliterative slogan "Free soil, free labor, and Fremont." While their platform condemned slavery as a "relic of barbarism" and invoked the words of the Founding Fathers to vouch for its un-American nature, the Republicans shied away from calling for an end to the "peculiar institution." To do so would have risked provoking the South and precipitating the breakup of the Union. Taking such a position would also have alienated Northerner voters who had no desire to see emancipated slaves heading their way en masse. The party only declared itself to be against any *extension* of the slave system into "Free Territory."

At the same time, the party came out in favor of granting basic rights to blacks. Many Republican candidates and officeholders took up this cause. For example, some of them assailed exclusionary black laws in the states of Ohio, Indiana, and Illinois.[1] However, the Republicans were careful to tailor their remarks on race in ways that would resonate well with audiences in different parts of the country. Realizing that any hint of pro-black sentiment would cost the party votes in the West, Republican candidates there instead lambasted the Democrats as the "black" or "nigger" party for wanting to introduce slavery in the region.[2] Abraham Lincoln, defeated in his bid to become Fremont's running mate, stumped for the Republican ticket during the fall campaign, telling crowds in Illinois and Michigan that any additional territories acquired by the United States should be reserved solely for "free white people."[3] Like most in his party and throughout the North, he abhorred the thought of "race mixing."

Perhaps no single national figure better represented the conflicting needs and feelings of Northerners on the questions of race and slavery than Lincoln — the product of generations of poor white dislocation by an ever-expanding plantation system. Raised to consider the enslaving of other human beings morally repugnant, Lincoln had strong sympathy for the blacks' plight.[4] During the early

---

1. Foner, *Free Soil, Free Labor, Free Men*, 286. Many Republicans saw the granting of more rights to former slaves as consistent with the party's "free labor" ideology.
2. Bilotta, Race and Rise of the Republican Party, 271, 395.
3. Quoted in Rawley, *Race and Politics*, 151. During his Peoria speech on 16 Oct. 1854, Lincoln had said: "The whole nation is interested that the best use shall be made of these territories. We want them for the homes of free white people."
4. In 1858, Lincoln stated that he had "always hated" slavery. Quoted in Robert W. Johannsen, *Lincoln, the South, and Slavery: The Political Dimension* (Baton Rouge: Louisiana State University Press, 1991), 13.

years of his career, however, he said little publicly about the "peculiar institution" and its dire human consequences. In many ways, Lincoln was conventional in his prejudiced thinking about race and had no desire to stir up controversy about it.[1] There was no advantage for him to gain by doing so. By the 1850s, the future president came to view the slave system in the larger context of national politics. After Congress voted for the Kansas-Nebraska Act in 1854, nullifying the demarcating line between free and slave states drawn under the Missouri Compromise, Lincoln seized upon opposition to western extension of slavery as his politically defining issue.

But Lincoln was astute enough not to call for abolition. Slavery might be an evil, but it was also a social and political fact of life, and any Northern politician who attacked this system did so at his own peril. Nor was Lincoln personally inclined to champion black freedom.[2] He accepted as a given that blacks were inferior, conceding in his first debate with Stephen Douglas, in 1858, that "there is a physical difference between the two [races] which, in my judgment, will probably forever forbid the two races living together upon the footing of perfect equality." He mockingly dismissed any arguments to the contrary as "but a specious and fantastic arrangement of words, by which a man can prove a horse-chestnut to be a chestnut horse." Lincoln told the attentive crowd in Ottawa, Illinois, that he had "no purpose, directly or indirectly, to interfere with the institution of slavery in the States where it exists." He added: "I believe I have no lawful right to do so, and I have no inclination to do so." However, Lincoln made it equally clear that he believed a black man was entitled to basic rights granted all Americans under the Declaration of Independence. "I hold that he is as much entitled to these as the white man. I agree with Judge Douglas he is not my equal in many respects — certainly not in color, perhaps not in moral or intellectual endowment. But in the right to eat the bread, without the leave of anybody else, which his own hand earns, *he is my equal and the equal of Judge Douglas, and the equal of every living man.*"[3] For this reason alone, Lincoln condemned slavery as inimical to the American way of life.

For other reasons — chiefly, the well being of white settlers — Lincoln opposed any extension of slavery onto Western territory. When he was running for president in March 1860, the Republican candidate fired up white workers on strike in New Haven by telling them they had "a chance to strike and go

---

1. Lincoln realized that "The colored man throughout this country was a despised man, a hated man." Quoted in *Recollected Words of Abraham Lincoln*, ed. Donald and Virginia Fehrenbacher (Stanford: Stanford University Press, 1996), 144.
2. Lincoln once dismissed the term "abolitionist" as an "odious epithet." Quoted in Johannsen, *Lincoln*, 66.
3. Remarks of Lincoln, debate with Stephen Douglas, 21 Aug. 1858, Ottawa, Ill. http://www.nps.gov/liho/debate1.htm.

somewhere else, where you may not be degraded, nor have your family corrupted by forced rivalry with negro slaves."[1] New territories, he noted on another occasion, should be preserved so "that white men may find [a] home . . . where they can settle upon some new soil and better their condition in life." Lincoln also felt that restricting slavery geographically was the only way to bring about the demise of the system without bloodshed. He once said: "There is no way of putting an end to the slavery agitation amongst us but to put it back upon the basis where our fathers put it . . . Restrict it forever to the old States where it now exists."[2]

By emphasizing their resolve to draw a racial line in the West, Republicans like Lincoln were seeking to assuage fears that blacks — either as slaves or as freemen — would pour into the territories and states beyond the Mississippi and take away jobs from white workers by accepting lower wages.[3] Such black in-migration would also retard economic development in that region, as had already occurred in the South. The party also appealed to Western voters by supporting a provision in the Homestead Act that would, in effect, restrict land ownership almost entirely to whites. Publicly it argued that the populating of Western lands by "free" farmers would prevent the spread of slavery there, while remaining silent about this law's deterrent effect on black freemen.[4]

Likewise, during the 1860 presidential campaign, the Republican Party denounced the Kansas-Nebraska Act (for overturning the Missouri Compromise and opening up additional areas in the West to slavery) and popular sovereignty — a policy which ceded the final say on slavery to individual states. The party's platform demanded that Kansas be admitted to the Union as a free state. It further called for an exclusion of the chattel system from all territories on Constitutional grounds, but, once again, did not condemn the "peculiar institution" outright.[5] In the course of the fall campaign, an uncompromising foe of slavery, Sen. William H. Seward of New York (who would serve as Lincoln's Secretary of State), admitted that the Republicans' underlying motive for opposing the system's extension had "always really been concern for the welfare of the white

---

1. Quoted in Levine, *Half Slave and Half Free*, 222.
2. *Ibid.*, 209-10.
3. In his book *American Exceptionalism, American Anxiety: Wages, Competition, and Degraded Labor in the Antebellum United States* (Charlottesville: University of Virginia Press, 2002), 227, Jonathan A. Glickstein describes how labor reformers and some Republican leaders persuaded workers that slaves would "undersell, exclude, pollute, and demoralize" free white labor.
4. Cf. Foner, *Free Soil*, 28.
5. The platform stated that "the normal condition of all the territory of the United States is that of freedom." But, unlike its statement of principles four years before, this document avoided any castigation of slavery and only reaffirmed the party's backing for the Constitutional right of all persons not to be deprived of "life, liberty, or property" without due process of law.

man."[1] Indeed, solidarity with the aspirations of "free labor" lay at the heart of Republican ideology. For it was these workers who would develop the nation and make it economically robust. Disparaging the Democrats for their willingness to leave the matter of legalizing slavery up to local residents, the party professed no unhappiness about being labeled the "only white man's party in the country."[2] To defend the rights of this race, the party was prepared to take a firm, unshakable stand — even if this meant going to war.

The election of 1860 thus presented the American electorate with literally a black-or-white choice. The central debate was not about slavery versus abolition. It was about race — or, more specifically, the nation's racial future. The contest was not just between two parties, but also between two ways of life. The real dividing line was not political but regional. The southern half of the nation was irrevocably committed to forging a biracial nation, while the northern half refused to accept any such outcome. In the words of one historian, "By 1860, the North had clearly defined its position on race relations: white supremacy and social peace required a vigorous separation of blacks and whites and the concentration of political and judicial power in the hands of the superior race — the Caucasian."[3]

In advocating such an avowedly anti-black policy, the Republican Party had to remain mindful of its radical wing, which condemned slavery as an intolerable moral evil, demanded that all slaves be set free, and wanted to offer blacks equal rights. This was clearly a minority position in the North, but the Republicans could not afford to alienate any who supported it if they hoped to win the White House and gain seats in Congress. Thus, the party paid lip service to concepts like "inalienable rights," while going out of its way to reassure voters it did not intend to be a friend to the black man. Its racially exclusionary orientation is evident not only in the statements of Abraham Lincoln, dating back to his support for the Wilmot Proviso when he was an Illinois congressman,[4] but also in the positions taken by the men he chose to serve in his cabinet. To consolidate his leadership, Lincoln reached out to several of his rivals for the presidential nomination to join his administration. As fellow Republicans, they held Free-Soil views on Western settlement — namely, determination to keep it "free" for

---

1. Quoted in James M. McPherson, *The Struggle for Equality: Abolitionists and the Negro in the Civil War and Reconstruction* (Princeton: Princeton University Press, 1964), 24.
2. Quoted in Foner, *Free Soil*, 265.
3. Litwack, *North of Slavery*, 112. Cf. Rawley, *Race and Politics*, 268: "Northerners who joined the Republican Party intended to keep America a white man's country, with no black slaves and few free Negroes in the western territories, and with the national government in hands friendly to white northern interests. They did not intend to emancipate the South's Negroes or promote racial equality."
4. Lincoln voted for the proviso on five separate occasions. Johannsen, *Lincoln*, 17.

whites. Ohio governor Salmon P. Chase, who had crafted the Free Soil platform in 1848 and unified the movement around the rights of "free labor," was named Secretary of the Treasury. Seward, Lincoln's closest political ally, became Secretary of State. For the post of Attorney General, the president selected Edward Bates, the Missouri attorney who had played an important role in his state's adopting a ban on free black migration in 1820. And Caleb B. Smith, the conservative Indiana Whig turned Republican who served briefly as Secretary of the Interior, was so adamantly opposed to Lincoln's freeing the slaves that he declared he would resign and work to defeat the administration if the president ever dared to sign an emancipation proclamation.

Ironically, by working to limit slavery's scope, the Republicans and like-minded Northerners were hastening the day when the system would end and the slaves would be freed. For, if the North succeeded in bottling up the "peculiar institution" in order to preserve the West for the white man, racial "amalgamating" would likely occur in the eastern half of the country. How could the "free" states possibly absorb some four million former slaves (who would presumably "vote with their feet" and flee north following emancipation)? How could "white society" survive this influx? Most Northerners could only grimace at these questions. They continued to regard the presence of blacks as corrupting and detrimental to white labor.[1] Influenced by prevailing "scientific" notions of race, they accepted the inferiority of blacks as a given. This prejudice was reinforced during the Civil War, when the Sanitation Commission measured the physical dimensions of whites and blacks and discovered that those of the latter were generally smaller. Autopsies conducted on white Union soldiers ascertained that their brains weighed some five ounces more than those of blacks. This finding suggested that blacks were more closely akin to apes than to whites. Because of these putative anatomical (as well as mental) deficiencies, the black race was seen as evolutionarily disadvantaged. In 1862, the Superintendent of the Census predicted that its eventual eradication was an "unerring certainty," only to be accelerated by emancipation.[2]

Accordingly, most Northern whites regarded any further mixing of the races — let alone social or political equality — as contrary to natural law and inimical to their own welfare. Most of all, they dreaded the ultimate consequence of close contact between the races — miscegenation. Hence, they viewed with alarm developments that might induce more blacks to move above the Mason Dixon

---

1. Senator Dix, a Democrat, had argued that the roughly 50,000 free blacks then residing in New York tended to "exclude" white workers from the labor marker. See remarks of Dix, 26 June 1848, *Appendix to the Congressional Globe*, 866.
2. John S. Haller, *Outcasts from Evolution: Scientific Attitudes of Racial Inferiority, 1859-1900*, (Urbana: University of Illinois Press, 1971), 30-1, 40.

Line. Legal steps already taken by states such as Arkansas, Kentucky, North Carolina, and Tennessee to expel free blacks increased worry about such a northern exodus: even the slightest upswing in black migration seemed a harbinger of what would transpire after all the slaves were emancipated. Vote-seeking Democratic politicians in the "butternut" states and as far north as Michigan painted a dire picture of what would ensue. During the war, these fears intensified as escaping slaves reached the northern side of the Ohio River. Many came as freemen — as a result of an 1862 administration offer to give money to Southern states that liberated their black bondsmen.[1] Their arrival on "free" soil led to the worst race riot of the war years, at New Albany, Indiana, a way station on the Underground Railroad: during 30 hours of violence and looting, two blacks were shot, one of them fatally.[2]

For many Northerners who saw the end of slavery coming, visions of racial "amalgamation" seemed more nightmarish than the present situation of a nation divided against itself. For all its gross and regrettable inhumanity, the "peculiar institution" had managed to stratify the races, for the benefit of whites, and it was not at all clear how their superior status would be protected once slaves were given their freedom. At worst, blacks would reproduce more rapidly than whites and "Africanize" American society. The white race would slowly disappear. Such a bleak post-emancipation prognosis had convinced many Free Soil supporters that the proposed "cure" for slavery would be worse than the "disease" itself.[3] Lincoln himself had come to that conclusion early in the 1850s. In delivering a eulogy for Henry Clay in 1852, he had cited with approval the Great Compromiser's prognostication that slavery could not be "at once eradicated, without producing a greater evil, even to the cause of human liberty itself."[4]

In holding the line against slavery's extension, Lincoln and other leaders of the Republican Party faced criticism that the "containment" policy they were pursuing would make this "greater evil" inevitable. They tried to pooh-pooh such concerns, saying that blacks — then only about 14 percent of the American population — would be evenly distributed around the country following emancipation, and this dispersion would cause no great problem for any particular region. Others fell back on racial stereotypes to defend this position, claiming that blacks preferred to live in warm climates and therefore would not move north once the "peculiar institution" was abolished. On the contrary, Northern blacks would head south.[5] Lincoln prophesied as much during his second annual

---

1. Voegeli, "Northwest and the Race Issue," 237.
2. Thornbrough, *Negro in Indiana*, 185-6.
3. Bilotta, *Rise of the Republican Party*, 165.
4. Quoted in Johannsen, *The Frontier*, 259.
5. So argued, for example, Salmon P. Chase. Voegeli, "Northwest and the Race Issue," 242.

address to Congress, on December 1, 1862: "But why," he asked rhetorically, "should emancipation south, send the free people north? . . . Heretofore colored people, to some extent, have fled north from bondage; and now, perhaps, from both bondage and destitution. But if gradual emancipation and deportation be adopted, they will have neither to flee from..."[1]

"Deportation" was Lincoln's blunt term for "colonization." Despite the fact that, over the preceding four decades, only about 11,000 former slaves had crossed the Atlantic to Africa, many Republicans held out hopes that this plan could solve the country's post-emancipation race problems. In his remarks after Clay's death, Lincoln had also recalled the Kentuckian's observation back in 1827 that "there is a moral fitness in the idea of returning to Africa her children," adding that, in his own opinion, "every succeeding year has added strength to the hope of its realization. May it indeed be realized!" On October 16, 1854, during a Peoria speech in which he assailed the "monstrous injustice" of slavery, Lincoln gave his blessing to the colonization effort. In 1856, other Republicans proposed Central America as a destination. Four years afterward, party leaders thought about adding a plank to their platform supporting the removal of blacks but, in the end, decided against this.[2] However, Lincoln continued to promote schemes to remove blacks from the United States while he was serving as president, mentioning them during two of his annual addresses to Congress and in several meetings of his cabinet. The most notable discussion he ever held on this subject took place in the White House, on August 14, 1862, when Lincoln met with Frederick Douglass and other prominent black leaders. The president hailed the "success story" of the American colony on the coast of Liberia, while pointing out to his skeptical and somewhat bemused audience that many of the black settlers brought there had died from disease and other causes. He said that whites in the United States would never accept blacks as their equals and urged that they seek a better future elsewhere, far from the nation's borders.[3] The delegation listened respectfully but displayed no enthusiasm for the president's plan.[4] Nothing ever came out of this meeting. After considering plans to send freed blacks to Panama and Haiti, Lincoln grew discouraged. In 1864, the Republican Party quietly stopped talking about colonization.

---

1. Quoted in Voegeli, "Northwest and the Race Issue," 251.
2. Foner, *Free Soil*, 278.
3. In his hour-long remarks, Lincoln went so far as to blame blacks for the Civil War: "But for your race among us there could not be war, although many men engaged on either side do not care for you one way or the other." Quoted in William K. Klingaman, *Abraham Lincoln and the Road to Emancipation, 1861-1865* (New York: Viking, 2001), 168.
4. Frederick Douglass denounced Lincoln "as an itinerant Colonization lecturer, showing all his inconsistencies, his pride of race and blood, his contempt for Negroes and his canting hypocrisy." *Ibid.*, 169.

One has to wonder why Lincoln's party clung to this scheme for solving the nation's looming racial quandary. The removal of over four million African Americans to some faraway corner of the world — largely against their will — presented enormous financial, logistical, and social challenges. Furthermore, while Lincoln was advocating this plan, the United States was being torn in half by a war of incalculable cost, duration, and outcome. One plausible explanation is that many Northerners realized that the Civil War would spell the end of slavery and thus lead to a racially integrated society. Colonization was the best — and perhaps only — way of averting this unwelcome consequence. It was also the only way to make the freeing of the slaves palatable to many on the Union side, including the president himself.[1] The other, more cynical way of interpreting the Republicans' support for black repatriation is that it was essentially a political ploy: knowing full well that colonization was not a realistic option, the party's leaders embraced it simply to demonstrate that they were not going to give former slaves equal rights after the war ended. They were sending another disguised message to white voters worried about "black Republicans" running the country: *You can trust us.*[2]

Lincoln's decision to issue a proclamation in January 1863 declaring slaves living in states that had taken up arms for the Confederacy "thenceforward, and forever" free, made advocacy of colonization even more politically necessary. Indeed, affirmation of the administration's desire to remove blacks from the United States *preceded* Lincoln's statement granting them freedom in the Emancipation Proclamation. The president fully understood that abolition was widely unpopular in the North, and, in fact, his historic statement unleashed a "furious outcry" throughout the free states.[3] Outside of New England, it cost the Republican Party dearly at the polls during the 1864 election. Within the Union ranks, a number of soldiers attested that they never would have signed up in the first place if they had known the war would lead to the freeing of blacks. Some officers even resigned their commissions in protest.[4] Lincoln himself had not fundamentally changed his mind about the wisdom of freeing the slaves. He clearly foresaw the pitfalls that lay ahead. He had only come around to taking this controversial step for practical, military reasons: as the war threatened to drag on, with the outcome still unclear, he had become convinced by the summer of 1862

---

1. Both Lincoln and his attorney general, Edwards Bates, felt that the abolition of slavery had to go hand in hand with the removal of former slaves from the United States. See, for example, Klingaman, *Abraham Lincoln*, 156-7.
2. So argues, for example, Larry Kincaid, "Two Steps Forward, One Step Back: Racial Attitudes during the Civil War and Reconstruction," in *The Great Fear: Race in the Mind of America*, 50.
3. Jimerson, *Private Civil War*, 41.
4. Klingaman, *Abraham Lincoln*, 237-8.

that the recruiting of runaway slaves into the Union Army might make a crucial difference. Emancipation was the means to that end. Of course, regardless of his intentions, Lincoln's proclamation ultimately had a far greater impact on race relations in the United States than on the course of the Civil War.

The Emancipation Proclamation, the subsequent service of some 180,000 black troops in the Union army, the defeat of the South, the collapse of the slave system, and the passage of the 13th, 14th, and 15th amendments radically changed the status of black Americans and rendered talk of their "repatriation" obsolete. The Civil War ended one long, sordid chapter in American race relations, by — legally, at least — lifting from blacks the stigma of being subhuman creatures" or "second class" citizens in a nation founded on the assertion that all persons are created equal. In this sense, the conflict was a major triumph for blacks. But it would turn out to be a hollow triumph in many ways, as the increased status, rights, and opportunities that black slaves had hoped to attain once they were liberated were denied them. Still, the end of slavery and the constitutional affir-mation of their equal legal stature represented enormous progress for black peo-ple in the United States.

If one looks at the racial impact of the Civil War from the perspective of white Americans, the picture is equally complex. In terms of lives lost, property destroyed, and regional pride deflated, the South suffered a crushing defeat. Along with a humiliating Yankee invasion and the indignities of surrender at Appomattox Court House came economic collapse: two thirds of the South's wealth disappeared as a result of the War Between the States.[1] Moreover, the ending of slavery deprived the South of the labor force it needed to rebuild. An entire way of life based upon the subjugation, ownership, and degradation of blacks abruptly came to an end. Henceforth, there would be no more masters or slaves in the land. Under the newly amended Constitution, a black man or woman stood on a par with his or her white counterpart. The racially stratified "southern vision" of America no longer existed.[2] Yet, despite this demise of their way of life, white Southerners recovered much of their former economic, politi-cal, and social status in the decades after the war. Naïve abolitionist hopes that cotton and tobacco plantations would be broken up into small farms for black freemen to own came to naught.[3] So did visions of black farmers laying claim to public lands in former slave states under the Southern Homestead Act of 1866. Instead, aided by Northern indifference, discrimination, intimidation, and acts of violence, whites reestablished their power over Southern blacks. Rather than

---

1. James M. McPherson, *Battle Cry of Freedom: The Civil War Era* (New York: Ballantine, 1988), 818.
2. *Ibid,*, 861.
3. McPherson, *Struggle for Equality*, 247.

become independent farmers, most of them remained sharecroppers. Freed of their chains, these blacks could not cast off the other barriers that held them back, and they languished in poverty, ostracized and scorned, on the margins of society, until the civil rights movement of the 1960s finally transformed the South into a semblance of an integrated society. Up until that point, one could have argued that the South may have lost the war, but had still managed to preserve the white ascendancy that lay at the core of its culture and identity.

For the North, the situation was reversed. Its soldiers laid waste to cities like Richmond and Atlanta and then marched back home with their heads held high for having bested "Johnny Reb" and preserved the Union. The North prospered from its victory and attained even greater power vis-à-vis the states south of the Mason Dixon Line. But this glorious triumph over the "Slave Power" was alloyed by misgivings about its racial implications. The North may have won the war, but how it would maintain the peace between blacks and whites remained an open question. Many Northerners had rejoiced that the dark stain of slavery had been removed from the nation's conscience, but they were also worried about what this change would mean for them. Thus, out of sheer habit, fear, or intransigence, lawmakers in many free states failed to repeal laws that kept blacks out or kept them in a secondary position. If anything, hostility toward blacks only intensified, especially in those parts of the North where geographical and economic circumstances tempted former slaves to take up residence.

Largely as a consequence, but also due to long-standing family ties in the South and protective Reconstruction policies, the feared mass exodus of blacks to Northern cities and towns did not take place. Between 1860 and 1880, the free black population in 15 states located in the northeastern and north central sections of the United States rose only by about 200,000.[1] (During the 1870s alone, fewer than 29,000 blacks born in the South moved into these Northern states.[2]) As a percentage, this represented a major increase — nearly a doubling of the number of blacks. But in relation to the overall population of these states, the proportion of blacks remained virtually unchanged: over this 20-year period it only rose from 1.2 percent of the total to 1.5 percent. And, not all of this growth was due to in-migration; natural increase also contributed to the higher total. More significantly, this increase was merely a tiny fraction of the potential black migratory increase. Of the roughly four million slaves living in the South just prior to the Civil War, no more than *two percent* relocated north of the Mason

---

1. These included the New England and mid-Atlantic states, as well as Illinois, Indiana, Ohio, Iowa, Michigan, and Wisconsin.
2. Table 1832, "Migration of Blacks Out of and Into the South by States, 1870-1910," *Historical Statistics of Black America*, ed. Jessie Carney Smith and Carrell Peterson Horton (New York: Gale Research, 1995), vol. 2, 1632.

Dixon Line. Furthermore, the migration was highly concentrated in just a handful of states: Illinois, Ohio, and Indiana accounted for more than half of the postbellum growth in the Northern black population.

But even such a relatively small rise in the number of blacks distressed
racially intolerant whites. In their view, the only remaining "free" land lay in the
West, and so they turned their aspirations in that direction. Under the protection of U.S. army troops commanded by the unreconstructed white supremacist
Gen. William Tecumseh Sherman,[1] and tasked with creating a *cordon sanitaire*
through hostile Indian territory, thousands of white settlers — including many
Civil War veterans — streamed westward over the next several decades. Wherever they built their homes, they made it clear that black Americans were not
wanted.

Kansas was a case in point. Nowhere else in the West did Southern blacks
make a greater effort to plant new roots. More than 6,000 impoverished former
slaves, known as "Exodusters," traversed the nation's midsection fleeing
renewed acts of white terrorism in the Deep South, searching for Canaan in Kansas's wheat fields. But neither local whites nor the land itself proved as hospitable as they had been led to believe. Instead, they encountered latent white
hostility as well as poor farming conditions, and this tentative foothold on the
Great Plains never evolved into a thriving black community.[2] Elsewhere on the
far side of the Mississippi, blacks spread even more slowly and sparsely. By the
turn of the century, only about 1.25 million African Americans were living in the
western half of the United States, and 92 percent of them were to be found in the
former slave states of Texas, Missouri, and Arkansas. Most were descendants of
blacks brought there long before the Civil War.[3]

So, as blacks were effectively discouraged from migrating westward — by
racial animus as well as an agriculturally inhospitable environment — whites
populated the flat expanses of the Great Plains and pushed further west, to the
stream-fed foothills of the Rocky Mountains, and down on the other side into
the lush valleys of California, Oregon, and Washington. What were the salient
characteristics of this new wave of settlers? For one thing, it contained more and
more Northerners. In every decade following the Civil War, the numerical pre-

---

1. Robert G. Athearn, *William Tecumseh Sherman and the Settlement of the West* (Norman: Oklahoma University Press, 1956), 14. Sherman wanted whites, particularly veterans, to
populate the West, thus "substituting for the useless Indians the intelligent owners of
productive farms and cattle-ranches." William T. Sherman, *The Memoirs of Gen. William
T. Sherman*, 2nd ed., rev. (New York: Appleton, 1913), 414.
2. Although Kansas's black population had surpassed 43,000 by 1880, it only increased to
52,000 over the next 20 years. For more details on black settlement of Kansas, see
Robert G. Athearn, *In Search of Canaan: Black Migration to Kansas* (Lawrence: Regents
Press of Kansas, 1978).
3. Half of all blacks west of the Mississippi were living in Texas alone.

dominance of westward-bound settlers from the North increased — from 57.4 percent of all persons living in the trans-Mississippian West in 1860, to 67.7 percent in 1870, to 71.9 percent in 1880. Despite the devastation, economic hardship, and racial upheaval brought about by this conflict, Southerners were less inclined to pull up stakes and head for the frontier. In addition, this postwar exodus was largely made up of settlers from relatively few Northern states: Illinois (224,984), Ohio (106,195), New York (99,270), Pennsylvania (93,844), and Indiana (84,722) had by far the most native sons and daughters living west of the Mississippi in 1880. This is not particularly surprising, since, in terms of overall population, these states ranked ahead of all the others, with the sole exception of Missouri.[1]

Because these were also the Northern states with both the largest numbers of black residents and the greatest post-Civil War increase in this portion of the population, it is tempting to conjecture that there was a direct, causal relationship between the white *out*-migration and the black *in*-migration these states experienced. Demonstrating such a link would provide further evidence of 19th-century "white flight." However, such a connection is not so easily made. If, for example, one examines population trends in the "butternut" states of Ohio, Illinois, and Indiana, the data suggesting that whites left because many blacks moved into the same parts of those states are inconclusive. As one might expect, most black in-migration occurred in southern counties, adjacent to the former slave state of Kentucky. (Exceptions to this general rule were major metropolitan areas, such as those centered on Chicago, Cleveland, and Indianapolis.) For instance, 13 counties located in the southwestern corner of Ohio accounted for 43 percent of the additional 43,227 blacks living in the Buckeye State two decades after 1860. But, while Ohio lost roughly 200,000 white residents to Western states during that period, it is not possible to ascertain how many of them came from these lower tier counties. In fact, many of these counties *increased* their white populations substantially during the postbellum era. However, if Hamilton County — which contains the manufacturing and commercial magnet of Cincinnati — is left out of this group, the remaining southern Ohio counties boosted their white populations by only 23.6 percent between 1860 and 1880 — considerably less than the statewide growth of 35.3 percent. This discrepancy can also be found in Illinois: its eight southwestern counties with the greatest black influx recorded a smaller increase in their white populations than the rest of the state did.[2] (In Indiana, the growth in the number of white resi-

---

1. In 1880, Missouri had a population of 2.1 million, slightly ahead of Indiana's 1.9 million. The rank order of the other states with the largest populations in 1880 was New York (5.0 million), Pennsylvania (4.2 million), Ohio (3.1 million), and Illinois (3.0 million).

dents in counties with substantial upswings in their black populations matched the average increase statewide.)

White out-migration might explain these demographic anomalies, and it is also possible that whites may have left the "butternut" states because of an aversion to blacks — a continuation of the decades-long flight of transplanted Southerners from the Old Northwest. But other reasons are also plausible, namely, that superior economic opportunities drew more out-of-state whites to northern counties in these states than to ones further south. And, even if out-migration was a major factor, it is not the case that most departing white residents were bound for destinations on the far side of the Mississippi. Persons leaving Ohio, for example, were more apt to move to nearby Indiana or Illinois than to relocate further west.[1] What census data do reveal is a distinct predilection among persons leaving the "butternut" states for specific Western states. In 1880, of the 397,180 Ohio natives then living in the western half of the nation, nearly three fourths were residents of just three states — Iowa, Kansas, and Missouri. Moreover, these states were the top three choices for Ohioans throughout the 1860-1880 period, with Iowa consistently coming out on top. Illinoisans were also inclined to move to these states, settling in each in roughly equal numbers.[2] Migrants from Indiana were somewhat more likely to establish homesteads in Kansas than in either Iowa or Missouri, but the same overall concentration in these three states is evident. One could argue that the preference these Midwesterners showed for two Western states with few black residents (Kansas and Iowa) over a former slave state, Missouri, indicates a desire to evade contact with non-whites, but this cannot be conclusively proven, based upon available demographic evidence.

What is clear is that the settling of the Far West was undertaken almost entirely by white Americans who came primarily from heavily populated Northern states that also happened to have large numbers of black residents, including many who had moved to these states after the Civil War. Because of the makeup of this migration, if not by conscious design, the western United States thus

---

2. Alexander, Jackson, Madison, Massac, Perry, Pulaski, Randolph, and St. Clair counties in southwestern Illinois accounted for over a third of Illinois' black population in 1880. Only Cook County, with Chicago as its hub, had more black residents than any of these counties. From 1860 to 1880, these seven counties saw their white populations grow by 62.6 percent, compared to a statewide increase of 77.8 percent.

1. The 1880 federal census shows that 185,300 natives of Ohio were then residing in Indiana, and 136,208 in Illinois. Iowa had the largest contingent of Buckeye State natives — 120,329 — among states west of the Mississippi. See Table XI, "Native White Population of the United States, Distributed According to State or Territory of Birth: 1880," *Statistics of the Population of the United States at the Tenth Census* (Washington: Government. Printing Office, 1883), 486.

2. By 1880 there were 106,670 Illinois natives living in Kansas, 102,515 in Iowa, and 102,522 in Missouri.

remained largely a white preserve — or, more accurately, a region devoid of blacks (since Hispanics and Native Americans already lived there in large numbers, and Asian immigrants would later come there as well). This regional racial exclusivity would persist — aside from Texas and urban areas in California after the 1920s — up to the present day. One can regard this long-lasting segregation of whites from blacks in fully half of the United States as the inadvertent consequence of a pioneering spirit — a quest for freedom, independence, and self-reliance — in which blacks, because of the crippling effects of both slavery and poverty, could not fully participate. But, looked at through the lens of over 300 years of prejudice, subjugation, hatred, and violence directed at blacks, and an equally long history of anxiety among whites about preserving their dominance and identity on a continent peopled by other races, this geographical separation — evident not only in the West but in most rural areas of the country — seems to address a deeper need. The consistent pattern of white dispersal across the United States reveals an effort to achieve what oppression, ostracism, legal constraint, and outright hostility toward black people could not — that is, a cohesive, homogeneous, and exclusive society. From colonial days onward, this impulse to flee from a far more complicated and confounding racial reality has been an integral, if largely unacknowledged, aspect of the American Dream. And so it still is.

SELECTED BIBLIOGRAPHY

Aaron, Daniel. *Cincinnati: Queen City of the West, 1819-1838.* Columbus: Ohio State University Press, 1992.

Abernethy, Thomas P. *Three Virginia Frontiers.* Baton Rouge: Louisiana State University Press, 1940.

Allen, Theodore M. *The Invention of the White Race.* Vol. 2. New York: Verso, 1994.

Anbinder, Tyler. *Nativism and Slavery: The Northern Know Nothings and the Politics of the 1850s.* New York: Oxford University Press, 1992.

Anderson, Hattie M. *A Study in Frontier Democracy: The Social and Economic Bases of the Rise of the Jackson Group in Missouri, 1815-1828.* Columbia: Missouri Historical Review, 1940.

_____. "Missouri, 1804-1828: Peopling a Frontier State," *Missouri Historical Review* 31 (January 1937): 150-80.

Anderson, Richard Clough, Jr. *Diary Journal of Richard Clough Anderson, Jr., 1814-1826.* Edited by Alfred E. Tischendorf and E. Taylor Parks. Durham: Duke University Press, 1964.

Andrews, Charles M., ed. *Narratives of the Insurrections, 1675-1690.* New York: Charles Scribner's Sons, 1915.

Applegate, Jesse A. *Recollections of My Boyhood.* Roseburg, Ore.: Press of Review, 1914.

Aptheker, Herbert. "The Quakers and Negro Slavery," *Journal of Negro History* 25 (July 1940): 331-62.

"Archives of Oregon," *Oregon Historical Quarterly* 3 (December 1902): 338-426.

Arfwedson, Carl D. *The United States and Canada in 1832, 1833, and 1834.* Vol. 1. London: Richard Bentley, 1834.

Aron, Stephen. *How the West Was Lost: The Transformation of Kentucky from Daniel Boone to Henry Clay.* Baltimore: Johns Hopkins University Press, 1996.

_____. "Pigs and Hunters: 'Rights in the Woods' on the Trans-Appalachian Frontier." In *Contact Points: American Frontiers from the Mohawk Valley to the Mississippi, 1750-1850,* edited by Andrew R.L. Cayton and Fredrika J. Teute, 175-204. Chapel Hill: University of North Carolina Press, 1998.

_____. "Pioneers and Profiteers: Land Speculation and the Homestead Ethic in Frontier Kentucky," *Western Historical Review* 23 (May 1992): 179-98.

Arrington, Leonard J. and Davis Bitton. *The Mormon Experience: A History of the Latter-Day Saints.* New York: Knopf, 1979.

Ashton, John and Tom Whyte. *The Quest for Paradise: Visions of Heaven and Eternity in the World's Myths and Religions.* San Francisco: HarperCollins, 2001.

Athearn, Robert G. *In Search of Canaan: Black Migration to Kansas, 1879-80.* Lawrence: Regents Press of Kansas, 1978.

_____. *William Tecumseh Sherman and the Settlement of the West.* Norman: University of Oklahoma Press, 1956.

Atwood, A. *The Conquerors: Historical Sketches of the American Settlement of the Oregon Country.* Tacoma: Jennings and Graham, 1907.

Axton, W.F. *Tobacco and Kentucky.* Lexington: University Press of Kentucky, 1975.

Babcock, Clarence M. *The American Frontier: A Social and Literary Record.* New York: Holt, Rinehart & Winston, 1965.

Bacon, Nathaniel. "Bacon's Declaration in the Name of the People (30 July 1676)." Project Gutenberg (Champaign, Ill.). http://emedia.netlibrary.com/reader.asp?product_id=1028100.

Ball, Charles. *Slavery in the United States: A Narrative of the Life and Adventures of Charles Ball, A Black Man.* New York: Negro Universities Press, 1969.

Ballagh, James C. *A History of Slavery in Virginia.* Baltimore: Johns Hopkins University Press, 1968.

_____. *White Servitude in the Colony of Virginia: A Study of the System of Indentured Labor in the American Colonies.* New York: Burt Franklin, 1969.

Barnhart, John D. "The Southern Influence in the Formation of Ohio," *Journal of Southern History* 3 (February 1937): 28-42.

_____. *Valley of Democracy: The Frontier versus the Plantation in the Ohio Valley, 1775-1818.* Bloomington: Indiana University Press, 1953.

_____. "The Southern Influence in the Formation of Indiana," *Indiana Magazine of History* 33 (September 1937): 261-76.

Barnhart, John D. and Dorothy L. Riker. *Indiana to 1816: The Colonial Period.* Indianapolis: Indiana Historical Society, 1994.

Barry, Louise. "The Emigrant Aid Company Parties of 1854," *Kansas Historical Quarterly* 12 (May 1943): 115-55.

_____. "The Emigrant Aid Company Parties of 1855," *Kansas Historical Quarterly* 12 (August 1943): 227-68.

Bartram, William. *The Travels of William Bartram.* Edited by Mark Van Doren. New York: Macy-Masius, 1928.

Bean, William G. "An Aspect of Know Nothingism," *South Atlantic Quarterly* 23 (October 1924): 319-34.

Beatty-Brown, Florence R. "Legal Status of Arkansas Negroes Before Emancipation," *Arkansas Historical Quarterly* 28 (Spring 1969): 6-13.

Beeman, Richard R. *The Evolution of the Southern Backcountry: A Case Study of Lunenburg County, Virginia, 1746-1832.* Philadelphia: University of Pennsylvania Press, 1984.

_____. *The Old Dominion and the New Nation, 1788-1801.* Lexington: University Press of Kentucky, 1972.

Bellamy, Donnie D. "The Persistence of Colonization in Missouri," *Missouri Historical Review* 72 (October 1977): 1-24.

Belshaw, George. "Journey from Indiana to Oregon: Journal of George Belshaw, March 23 to September 27, 1853." WA MSS 31, Collection of Western Americana, Beinecke Library, Yale University.

Bergstrom, Peter V. *Markets and Merchants: Economic Diversification in Colonial Virginia, 1700-1775.* New York: Garland, 1985.

Berkhofer, Robert F., Jr. *The White Man's Indian: Images of the American Indian from Columbus to the Present.* New York: Knopf, 1978.

Berlin, Ira. *Generations of Captivity: A History of African-American Slaves.* Cambridge: Harvard University Press, 2003.

Berry, Thomas S. *Western Prices Before 1861: A Study of the Cincinnati Market.* Cambridge: Harvard University Press, 1943.

Berwanger, Eugene H. *The Frontier Against Slavery: Western Anti-Negro Prejudice and the Slavery Extension Controversy.* Urbana: University of Illinois Press, 1967.

Betts, Robert F. *In Search of York: The Slave Who Went to the Pacific with Lewis and Clark.* rev. ed. Boulder: Colorado Associated University Press, 2000.

Bigham, Darrel E. *Towns and Villages of the Lower Ohio.* Lexington: University Press of Kentucky, 1998.

Billington, Ray A. *America's Frontier Heritage.* New York: Holt, Rinehart & Winston, 1966.

_____. *The Far Western Frontier, 1830-1860.* New York: Harper & Row, 1956.

_____. *Westward Expansion: A History of the American Frontier.* 3rd ed. New York: Macmillan, 1967.

Bilotta, James D. *Race and the Rise of the Republican Party, 1848-1865.* New York: Peter Lang, 1992.

Birkbeck, Morris. *An Appeal to the People of Illinois on the Question of a Convention.* Shawneetown, Ill.: C. Jones, 1823.

_____. "The Illinois Prairies and Settlers." In *Prairie State: Impressions of Illinois, 1673-1967, by Travelers and Other Observers*, edited by Paul M. Angle, 62-7. Chicago: University of Chicago Press, 1968.

Birney, James G. and F.H. Elmore. *The Anti-Slavery Examiner No. 8: Correspondence Between the Hon. F.H. Elmore and James G. Birney.* New York: American Anti-Slavery Society, 1838.

Black, Lloyd D. "Middle Willamette Valley Population Growth," *Oregon Historical Quarterly* 43 (March 1942): 40-55.

Blane, William N. *An Excursion Through the United States and Canada during the Years 1822-23 by an English Gentleman.* New York: Negro Universities Press, 1969.

Blue, Frederick J. *The Free Soilers: Third Party Politics, 1848-54.* Urbana: University of Illinois Press, 1973.

_____. *Salmon P. Chase: A Life in Politics.* Kent State: Kent State University Press, 1987.

Blunt, Joseph. *An Examination of the Expediency and Constitutionality of Prohibiting Slavery in the State of Missouri.* New York: C. Wiley, 1819.

Bogue, Allan G. *Frederick Jackson Turner: Strange Roads Going Down.* Norman: University of Oklahoma Press, 1998.

_____. *From Prairie to Corn Belt: Farming on the Illinois and Iowa Prairies in the Nineteenth Century.* Chicago: Quadrangle Books, 1963.

Bogue, Donald J. *Principles of Demography.* New York: John Wiley & Sons, 1969.

Bolton, Charles K. *Scotch Irish Pioneers in Ulster and America.* Baltimore: Genealogical Publishing Co., 1967.

Bond, Beverley W., Jr. *The Civilization of the Old Northwest: A Study of Political, Social, and Economic Development, 1788-1812.* New York: Macmillan, 1934.

Bowen, William A. *The Willamette Valley: Migration and Settlement on the Oregon Frontier.* Seattle: University of Washington Press, 1978.

Brackenridge, H.M. *Journal of A Voyage up the River Missouri, Performed in Eighteen Hundred and Eleven.* Baltimore: Coale and Maxwell, 1815.

Branch, E. Douglas. *Westward: The Romance of the American Frontier.* New York: D. Appleton, 1930.

Brauer, Kinley J. *Cotton versus Conscience: Massachusetts Whig Politics and Southwestern Expansion, 1843-1848.* Lexington: University Press of Kentucky, 1967.

Breen, T.H. *Tobacco Culture: The Mentality of the Great Tidewater Planters on the Eve of the Revolution.* Princeton: Princeton University Press, 1985.

Bruce, Philip A. *Economic History of Virginia in the Seventeenth Century: An Inquiry into the Material Condition of the People, Based on Original and Contemporaneous Records.* New York: Macmillan, 1896.

_____. Social Life of Virginia in the Seventeenth Century. Lynchburg: J.P. Bell, 1927.

Bryan, William S. *A History of the Pioneer Families of Missouri.* St. Louis: Bryan, Brand, 1876.

Buchanan, John. *Jackson's Way: Andrew Jackson and the People of the Western Waters.* New York: John Wiley & Sons, 2001.

Buck, Solon J. *Illinois in 1818.* rev. ed. Urbana: University of Illinois Press, 1967.

Buley, R. Carlyle. *The Old Northwest: Pioneer Period, 1815-1840.* Vol. 2. Indianapolis: Indiana Historical Society, 1950.

Burnet, Jacob. *Notes on the Early Settlement of the North-West Territory.* New York: D. Appleton, 1847.

Burnett, Edmund C., ed. *The Continental Congress.* New York: Macmillan, 1941.

Burnett, Peter H. *Recollections and Opinions of an Old Pioneer.* New York: D. Appleton, 1880.

_____. "Crossing the Plains: Letters from a Tualatin Pioneer." In *Talking on Paper: An Anthology of Oregon Letters and Diaries*, edited by Shannon Applegate and Terence O'Donnell, 13-20. Corvallis: Oregon State University Press, 1994.

Burnett, Robyn and Ken Luebbering. *German Settlement in Missouri: New Land, Old Ways.* Columbia: University of Missouri Press, 1996.

Butler, James D. "British Convicts Shipped to American Colonies," *American Historical Review* 2 (October 1896): 12-33.

Byrd, William. *The Commonplace Book of William Byrd II of Westover.* Edited by Kevin Berland, Jan Kirsten Gilliam, and Kenneth A. Lockridge. Chapel Hill: University of North Carolina Press, 2001.

Cain, Marvin R. *Lincoln's Attorney General: Edward Bates of Missouri.* Columbia: University of Missouri Press, 1965.

Campbell, Randolph B. *An Empire for Slavery: The Peculiar Institution in Texas, 1821-1865.* Baton Rouge: Louisiana State University Press, 1989.

Captive Passage: The Transatlantic Slave Trade and the Making of America. Washington, D.C.: Smithsonian Institution Press, 2002.

Carey, Charles H. *A General History of Oregon - Prior to 1861.* Vol. 1, *To the Territorial Government.* Portland: Metropolitan Press, 1935.

_____. *A General History of Oregon - Prior to 1861.* Vol. 2, *To the Great Civil War.* Portland: Metropolitan Press, 1936.

_____. "The Creation of Oregon as a State," *Oregon Historical Quarterly* 27 (March 1926): 1-40.

Carmony, Donald F. and Howard H. Peckham. *A Brief History of Indiana.* Indianapolis: Indiana Historical Bureau, 1946.

Carter, Col. Landon. *The Diary of Colonel Landon Carter of Sabine Hall, 1752-1778.* Edited by Jack P. Greene. Richmond: Virginia Historical Society, 1987.

Cartwright, Peter. *Autobiography of Peter Cartwright, the Backwoods Preacher.* New York: Carlton & Porter, 1857.

Cayton, Andrew R. L. *Frontier Indiana.* Bloomington: Indiana University Press, 1996.

Cayton, Andrew R.L. and Peter S. Onuf. *The Midwest and the Nation: Rethinking the History of an American Region*. Bloomington: Indiana University Press, 1990.

Chaddock, Robert E. *Ohio Before 1850: A Study of the Early Influence of Pennsylvania and Southern Populations in Ohio*. New York: Columbia University Press, 1908.

Chambers, William N. *Old Bullion Benton: Senator from the New West: Thomas Hart Benton, 1782-1858*. Boston: Little, Brown, 1956.

Chase, Salmon P. and Charles Dexter Cleveland. *Anti-Slavery Addresses of 1844 and 1845 by Salmon Portland Chase and Charles Dexter Cleveland*. repr. ed. New York: Negro Universities Press, 1969.

Christian, Charles M. *Black Saga: The African American Experience*. Boston: Houghton, Mifflin, 1995.

Clark, Malcolm, Jr. *Eden Seekers: The Settlement of Oregon, 1818-1862*. Boston: Houghton, Mifflin, 1981.

Clark, Thomas D. *Agrarian Kentucky*. Lexington: University Press of Kentucky, 1977.

_____. *A History of Kentucky*. New York: Prentice-Hall, 1937.

Clay, Henry. *The Papers of Henry Clay*. Edited by James F. Hopkins. Lexington: University Press of Kentucky, 1961.

Clevinger, Woodrow R. "Southern Appalachian Highlanders in Western Washington," *Pacific Northwest Quarterly* 33 (1942): 3-25.

Coffin, Levi. *The Reminiscences of Levi Coffin*. New York: Arno Press, the New York Times, 1968.

Cole, Arthur C. *The Irrepressible Conflict, 1850-1865*. New York: Macmillan, 1934.

Coleman, J. Winston, Jr. *Slavery Times in Kentucky*. Chapel Hill: University of North Carolina Press, 1940.

Collier, Christopher and James L. Collier. *Decision in Philadelphia: The Constitutional Convention of 1787*. New York: Random House, 1986.

Collins, Lewis. *Collins' Historical Sketches of Kentucky: History of Kentucky*. Vol. 1. Covington, Ky.: Collins, 1878.

Colton, Calvin. *The Life, Correspondence, and Speeches of Henry Clay*. Vol. 1, *Life and Times*. New York: A.S. Barnes, 1857.

Conrad, Alfred H and John R. Meyer. *The Economics of Slavery and Other Studies in Econometric History*. Chicago: Aldine, 1964.

"Constitution of the State of Ohio — 1802," *Ohio Archaeological and Historical Quarterly* 5 (1897): 132-53.

Cowie, Leonard W. *Plague and Fire: London 1665-66*. New York: G.P. Putnam's Sons, 1970.

Cramer, Clayton E. *Black Demographic Data, 1790-1860: A Sourcebook*. Westport: Greenwood, 1997.

Craven, Frank W. *White, Red, and Black: The 17th-Century Virginian*. Charlottesville: University of Virginia Press, 1971.

Curti, Merle. *The Making of an American Community: A Case Study of Democracy in a Frontier County.* Palo Alto: Stanford University Press, 1959.

Curtis. Philip D. *The Atlantic Slave Trade: A Census.* Madison: University of Wisconsin Press, 1969.

Cutler, Julia P. *Life and Times of Ephraim Cutler.* New York: Arno Press, the New York Times, 1971.

Dabney, Virginius. *Virginia: The New Dominion.* Garden City: Doubleday, 1971.

Davenport, F. Garvin. *Ante-Bellum Kentucky: A Social History, 1800-1860.* Oxford, Ohio: Mississippi Valley Press, 1943.

Davis, David Brion. *The Problem of Slavery in Western Culture.* Ithaca: Cornell University Press, 1966.

Davis, James E. *Frontier America, 1800-1840: A Comparative Demographic Analysis of the Settlement Process.* Glendale: A. H. Clark, 1977.

_____. *Frontier Illinois.* Bloomington: Indiana University Press, 1998.

De Graaf, Lawrence B., Kevin Mulroy, and Quintard Taylor, eds. *Seeking El Dorado: African Americans in California.* Seattle and London: University of Washington Press, 2001.

Deal, J. Douglas. *Race and Class in Colonial Virginia: Indians, Englishmen, and Africans on the Eastern Shore During the Seventeenth Century.* New York: Garland, 1993.

The Debates of the Constitutional Convention of the State of Iowa. Davenport: Luse, Laue & Co., 1857.

Degler, Carl N. "Slavery and the Genesis of American Race Prejudice." In *Colonial Southern Slavery,* edited by Paul Finkelman, 39-56. New York: Garland, 1989.

DeJong, Gordon F. and Robert W. Gardner, eds. *Migration Decision Making: Multidisciplinary Approaches to Micro-Level Studies in Developed and Developing Countries.* New York: Pergamon, 1981.

DeVoto, Bernard. *The Course of Empire.* Cambridge: Riverside Press, 1952.

_____. *The Year of Decision, 1846.* Boston: Little, Brown, 1943.

Dick, Everett. *The Dixie Frontier: A Social History of the Southern Frontier from the First Transmontane Beginnings to the Civil War.* New York: Knopf, 1948.

Dicken Garcia, Hazel. *To Western Woods: The Breckenridge Family Moves to Kentucky in 1793.* Rutherford, N.J.: Fairleigh Dickinson University Press, 1991.

"Documents," *Oregon Historical Quarterly* 4 (June 1903): 168-84.

"Documents," *Oregon Historical Quarterly* 4 (September 1903): 270-86.

Doddridge, Joseph. *Notes on the Settlement and Indian Wars of the Western Parts of Virginia and Pennsylvania.* Pittsburgh: John S. Ritenour & William T. Lindsey, 1912.

Donald, David D. *Lincoln.* New York: Touchstone, 1996.

Dorr, Harold M., ed. *The Michigan Constitutional Conventions of 1835-36; Debates and Proceedings.* Ann Arbor: University of Michigan Press, 1940.

Douglas, Jesse S. "Origins of the Population of Oregon in 1850," *Pacific Northwest Quarterly* 41 (April 1950): 95-108.

Drinnon, Richard. *Facing West: The Metaphysics of Indian Hating and Empire Building.* New York: Schocken, 1980.

Duberman, Martin, ed. *The Antislavery Vanguard: New Essays on the Abolitionists.* Princeton: Princeton University Press, 1965.

Duden, Gottfried. *Report on a Journey to the Western States of North America and a Stay of Several Years Along the Missouri.* Translated by George H. Kellner, Elsa Nagel, Adolf E. Schroeder, and W.M. Senner. Columbia: University of Missouri Press, 1980.

Dumond, Dwight L. *Antislavery: The Crusade for Freedom in America.* New York: Norton, 1961.

_____. *A Bibliography of Antislavery in America.* Ann Arbor: University of Michigan Press, 1961.

Dunbar, Seymour. *A History of Travel in America.* Vol. 2. New York: Greenwood, 1968.

Dunn, Richard S. "Black Society in the Chesapeake, 1776-1810." In *Slavery and Freedom in the Age of the American Revolution,* edited by Ira Berlin and Ronald Hoffman, 49-82. Urbana: University of Illinois Press, 1986.

Dunson, A.A. "Notes on the Missouri Germans on Slavery," *Missouri Historical Review* 59 (April 1965): 355-66.

Egerton, Douglas R. "'Its Origin Is Not a Little Curious': A New Look at the American Colonization Society," *Journal of the Early Republic* 5 (Winter 1985): 463-80.

Ellis, David M., ed. *The Frontier in American Development: Essays in Honor of Paul Wallace Gates.* Ithaca: Cornell University Press, 1969.

Ellis, James F. *The Influence of Environment on the Settlement of Missouri.* St. Louis: Webster Publishing, 1929.

Emerson, Ralph Waldo. *Selections from Ralph Waldo Emerson: An Organic Anthology.* Edited by Stephen E. Whicher. Boston: Houghton, Mifflin, 1957.

Esarey, Logan. *A History of Indiana From its Exploration to 1850.* Indianapolis: W.K. Stuart, 1915.

Etcheson, Nicole. *The Emerging Midwest: Upland Southerners and the Political Culture of the Old Northwest, 1787-1861.* Bloomington: Indiana University Press, 1996.

Evans, S. Estyn. "The Scotch-Irish: Their Cultural Adaptation and Heritage in the American Old West." In *Essays in Scotch-Irish History,* edited by E.R.R. Green, 69-86. London: Routledge & Kegan Paul, 1969.

Evans, Nelson W. and Emmons B. Stivers. *A History of Adams County, Ohio, From its Earliest Settlement to the Present Time.* West Union, Ohio: E.B. Stivers, 1900.

Faragher, John M. *Women and Men on the Overland Trail.* New Haven: Yale University Press, 1979.

Faux, William. *Early Western Travels, 1748-1846.* Vol. 12, *Memorable Days in America, Part II,* 1-138. Edited by Reuben Gold Thwaites. Cleveland: Arthur H. Clark, 1905.

Fearon, Henry B. *Sketches of America: A Narrative of a Journey of Five Thousand Miles through the Eastern and Western States.* London: Benjamin Blom, 1969.

Featherstonhaugh, G.W. *Excursion through the Slave States.* New York: Harper & Brothers, 1844.

Fehrbacher, Don E. *The South and Three Sectional Crises.* Baton Rouge: Louisiana State University Press, 1980.

Ferrall, Simon E. *A Ramble of Six Thousand Miles Through the United States of America.* London: Effingham Wilson, 1832.

Ferrie, Joseph P. 2002. "Historical Statistics of the U.S., Millennial Edition: Internal Migration." www.faculty.econ.northwestern.edu/faculty/ferrie/papers/essay.pdf.

Filler, Louis. *The Crusade Against Slavery, 1830-1860.* New York, Evanston, and London: Harper & Row, 1960.

Finkelman, Paul. 1987. "The Northwest Ordinance: A Constitution for an Empire of Liberty." Paper presented at symposium, Pathways to the Old Northwest: An Observance of the Northwest Ordinance, 10-11 July, at Franklin College of Indiana, Franklin, Indiana.

Finley, James B. *Autobiography of Rev. James B. Finley.* Edited by W.P. Strickland. New York: Hunt & Eaton, 1853.

"First Constitutional Convention, Convened November 1, 1802," *Ohio Archaeological and Historical Quarterly* 5 (1897): 80-131.

Fischer, David H. *Albion's Seed: Four British Folkways in America.* New York: Oxford University Press, 1989.

Fischer, David Hackett and James C. Kelly. *Bound Away: Virginia and the Westward Movement.* Charlottesville: University Press of Virginia, 2000.

Fisher, Ezra. "Correspondence of Reverend Ezra Fisher," *Oregon Historical Quarterly* 20 (March 1919): 95-137.

Flanders, Stephen A. *Atlas of American Migration.* New York: Facts on File, 1998.

Flint, James. *Early Western Travels, 1748-1846.* Vol. 9, "Flint's Letters from America, 1818-1820." Edited by Reuben Gold Thwaites. Cleveland: Arthur H. Clark, 1904.

Fogel, Robert W. and Stanley L. Engerman. *Time on the Cross: The Economics of American Negro Slavery.* Boston: Little, Brown, 1974.

Foley, William E. *The Genesis of Missouri: From Wilderness Outpost to Statehood.* Columbia: University of Missouri Press, 1989.

Foner, Eric. *Free Soil, Free Labor, Free Men: The Ideology of the Republican Party before the Civil War.* New York: Oxford University Press, 1970.

_____. *Politics and Ideology in the Age of the Civil War.* New York: Oxford University Press, 1980.

_____. "Politics and Prejudice: The Free Soil Party and the Negro, 1849-1852," *Journal of Negro History* 50 (October 1965): 239-56.

_____. "Racial Attitudes of the New York Free Soilers," *New York History* 46 (October 1965): 311-29.

_____. "The Wilmot Proviso Revisited," *Journal of American History* 56 (September 1969): 262-79.

Ford, Lacy K., Jr. "Frontier Democracy: The Turner Thesis Revisited," *Journal of the Early Republic* 13 (Summer 1993): 144-63.

Ford, Thomas. A History *of Illinois From its Commencement as a State in 1818 to 1847.* Chicago: S.C. Griggs & Co., 1854.

Foust, James D. *The Yeoman Farmer and Westward Expansion of U.S. Cotton Production.* New York: Arno Press, 1975.

Fox, Dixon R., ed. *Sources of Culture in the Middle West: Backgrounds versus Frontier.* New York: Russell & Russell, 1964.

Fox, Early L. *The American Colonization Society, 1817-1840.* Baltimore: Johns Hopkins University Press, 1919.

Franklin, William E. "The Political Career of Peter Hardeman Burnett." Ph.D. diss. Stanford University, 1954.

Frederickson, George M. *The Black Image in the White Mind: The Debate on Afro-American Character and Destiny, 1817-1914.* New York: Harper & Row, 1971.

Freehling, William W. *The Reintegration of American History: Slavery and the Civil War.* New York: Oxford University Press, 1994.

Fremont, John Charles. *The Expeditions of John Charles Fremont.* Vol. 2, *The Bear Flag Revolt and the Court Martial.* Edited by Mary Lee Spence and Donald Jackson. Urbana: University of Illinois Press, 1973.

Galenson, David W. *White Servitude in Colonial America: An Economic Analysis.* Cambridge: Cambridge University Press, 1981.

Gardiner, O.C. *The Great Issue or The Three Presidential Candidates, Being a Brief Historical Sketch of the Free Soil Question in the United States.* Westport: Negro Universities Press, 1970.

Garkovich, Lorraine. *Population and Community in Rural America.* New York: Greenwood, 1989.

Garrison, George Pierce. *The American Nation: A History.* Vol. 17, *Westward Extension, 1841-1850.* Edited by Albert B. Hart. New York: Harper & Brothers, 1906.

Gay, Theressa. *Life and Letters of Mrs. Jason Lee, First Wife of Rev. Jason Lee of the Oregon Mission.* Portland: Metropolitan Press, 1936.

Genovese, Eugene D. *The Political Economy of the Slavery: Studies in the Economy: Society of the Slave South.* 2nd ed. Middletown: Wesleyan University Press, 1989.

Gerlach, Russel L. *Settlement Patterns in Missouri: A Study of Population Origins With a Wall Map.* Columbia: University of Missouri Press, 1986.

_____. "Population Origins in Rural Missouri," *Missouri Historical Review* 71 (October 1976): 1-21.

_____. "The Ozark Scotch-Irish: The Subconscious Persistence of an Ethnic Culture," *Pioneer America Society Transactions* 7 (1984): 47-58.

Gilmore, William E. *Life of Edward Tiffin.* Chillicothe, Ohio: Horney & Son, 1897.

Glickstein, Jonathan A. *American Exceptionalism, American Anxiety: Wages, Competition, and Degraded Labor in the Antebellum United States.* Charlottesville: University of Virginia Press, 2002.

_____. *Concepts of Free Labor in Antebellum America.* New Haven: Yale University Press, 1991.

Goetzmann, William H. *Exploration and Empire: The Explorer and the Scientist in the Winning of the American West.* New York: Knopf, 1966.

_____. *New Lands, New Men: America and the Second Great Age of Discovery.* New York: Viking, 1986.

Going, Charles B. *David Wilmot, Free Soiler: A Biography of the Great Advocate of the Wilmot Proviso.* New York: D. Appleton, 1924.

Golay, Michael. *The Tide of Empire: America's March to the Pacific.* New York: John Wiley & Sons, 2003.

Goodwin, Cardinal. *The Trans-Mississippi West, 1803-1853: A History of Its Acquisition and Settlement.* New York: Russell & Russell, 1922.

Gordon, John Steele. *An Empire of Wealth: The Epic History of American Economic Power.* New York: HarperCollins, 2004.

Graebner, Norman A. *Empire on the Pacific: A Study in American Continental Expansion.* New York: Ronald Press, 1955.

_____., ed. *Manifest Destiny.* Indianapolis: Bobbs-Merrill, 1968.

Gragg, Larry D. *Migration in Early America: The Virginia Quaker Experience.* Ann Arbor: UMI Research Press, 1978.

Greene, Lorenzo J. *The Negro in Colonial New England, 1620-1776.* New York: Atheneum, 1969.

Greene, Lorenzo J., Gary R. Kremer and Antonio F. Holland. *Missouri's Black Heritage.* rev. ed. Columbia: University of Missouri Press, 1993.

Gruenwald, Kim M. *River of Enterprise: The Commercial Origins of Regional Identity in the Ohio Valley, 1790-1850.* Bloomington: Indiana University Press, 2002.

Gwathmey, John H. *Twelve Virginia Counties: Where the Western Migration Began.* Richmond: Dietz, 1937.

Hale, John P. *Papers of John P. Hale.* New Hampshire Historical Society, Concord, N.H.

Hall, Basil. *Travels in North America in the Years 1827 and 1828.* Vol. 3. Edinburgh: Robert Cadell, 1830.

Haller, John S., Jr. *Outcasts from Evolution: Scientific Attitudes of Racial Inferiority, 1859-1900.* Carbondale: Southern Illinois University Press, 1971.

Hammon, Neal O. *Early Kentucky Land Records, 1773-1780.* Louisville: Filson Club, 1992.

Hancock, Samuel. 1860. "The Narrative of Samuel Hancock." WA MS 240, Collection of Western Americana, Beinecke Library, Yale University.

Hannah, Matthew G. *Cambridge Studies in Historical Geography*. Vol. 32, *Governmentality and the Mastery of Territory in Nineteenth-Century America*. New York: Cambridge University Press, 2000.

Hansen, Marcus. *The Atlantic Migration, 1607-1860: A History of the Continuing Settlement of the United States*. Cambridge: Harvard University Press, 1940.

Harrison, Lowell H. *Kentucky's Road to Statehood*. Lexington: University Press of Kentucky, 1992.

Harrold, Stanley. *The Abolitionists and the South, 1831-1861*. Lexington: University Press of Kentucky, 1995.

Hart, Albert B. *Salmon Portland Chase*. Boston: Houghton, Mifflin, 1899.

_____. *The American Nation: A History*. Vol. 16, *Slavery and Abolition, 1831-1841*. Edited by Albert B. Hart. New York, London: Harper & Brothers, 1906.

Hastings, Lansford W. *The Emigrants' Guide to Oregon and California*. Cincinnati: George Conclin, 1845.

Helper, Hinton R. *The Impending Crisis of the South: How to Meet It*. New York: Burdick Bros., 1857.

Hibbard, Benjamin H. *A History of the Public Land Policies*. Madison: University of Wisconsin Press, 1965.

Hickok, Charles T. *The Negro in Early Ohio, 1802-1870*. Cleveland: Press of the Williams Publishing & Electric Co., 1896.

Hietala, Thomas R. *Manifest Destiny: Anxious Aggrandizement in Late Jacksonian America*. Ithaca: Cornell University Press, 1985.

Hine, Robert V. *Community on the American Frontier: Separate But Not Alone*. Norman: University of Oklahoma Press, 1980.

Hine, Robert V. and John Mack Faragher. *The American West: A New Interpretive History*. New Haven: Yale University Press, 2000.

Hinsdale, B.A. *The Old Northwest*. New York: Townsend MacCoun, 1888.

Hodgson, Adam. *Letters from North America Written During a Tour in the United States and Canada*. Vol. 1. London: Hurst, Robinson, 1824.

Hofstra, Warren R. "'The Extension of His Majesties Dominions': The Virginia Backcountry and the Reconfiguration of Imperial Frontiers," *Journal of American History* 84 (March 1998): 1281-1312.

Holbrook, Stewart. *The Yankee Exodus*. New York: Macmillan, 1950.

Holt, Michael F. *The Fate of Their Country: Politicians, Slavery Extension, and the Coming of the Civil War*. New York: Hill and Wang, 2004.

_____. *The Political Crisis of the 1850s*. New York: John Wiley & Sons, 1978.

Horn, James. "Servant Emigration to the Chesapeake in the Seventeenth Century." In *The Chesapeake in the Seventeenth Century: Essays on Anglo-American Society*, edited by Thad W. Tate and David L. Ammerman, 51-95. Chapel Hill: University of North Carolina Press, 1979.

Horsman, Reginald. *Expansion and American Indian Policy, 1783-1812*. East Lansing: Michigan State University Press, 1967.

_____. *The Frontier in the Formative Years, 1783-1815*. New York: Holt, Rinehart & Winston, 1970.

_____. *Race and Manifest Destiny: The Origins of American Racial Anglo-Saxonism*. Cambridge: Harvard University Press, 1981.

Howard, Robert P. *Illinois: A History of the Prairie State*. Grand Rapids: William E. Eerdsmans, 1972.

Howard, Victor B. *The Evangelical War against Slavery and Caste: The Life and Times of John G. Fee*. Selinsgrove, Pa.: Susquehanna University Press, 1996.

Howells, William C. *Recollections of Life in Ohio, from 1813 to 1840*. Cincinnati: Robert Clarke, 1895.

Hudson, John C. "Migration to an American Frontier," *Annals of the Association of American Geographers* 66 (June 1976): 242-65.

_____. "The Middle West as a Cultural Hybrid," *Pioneer American Society Transactions* 7 (1984): 35-46.

Hughes, Jonathan and Louis P. Cain. *American Economic History*. 4th ed. New York: HarperCollins, 1994.

Hurt, R. Douglas. *Agriculture and Slavery in Missouri's Little Dixie*. Columbia: University of Missouri Press, 1992.

_____. *Indian Agriculture in America: Prehistory to the Present*. Lawrence: University of Kansas Press, 1987.

_____. *The Indian Frontier, 1763-1846*. Albuquerque: University of New Mexico Press, 2002.

_____. "Planters and Slavery in Little Dixie," *Missouri Historical Review* 88 (July 1994): 397-415.

Ingraham, John H. *The Southwest: By a Yankee*. Vol. 2. New York: Harper & Brothers, 1835.

Inman, Ethel G. "Pioneer Days in Northwest Missouri — Harrison County, 1837-1873," *Missouri Historical Review* 22 (April 1928): 307-30.

Isaac, Rhys. *The Transformation of Virginia, 1740-1790*. Chapel Hill: University of North Carolina Press, 1982.

Jefferson, Thomas. *Notes on the State of Virginia*. Edited by William Peden. Chapel Hill: University of North Carolina Press, 1955.

_____. *Writings*. New York: Library of America, 1984.

Jimerson, Randall C. *The Private Civil War: Popular Thought During the Sectional Conflict.* Baton Rouge: Louisiana State University Press, 1988.

Johannsen, Robert W. *Frontier Politics and the Sectional Conflict: The Pacific Northwest on the Eve of the Civil War.* Seattle: University of Washington Press, 1955.

_____. *The Frontier, the Union, and Stephen A. Douglas.* Urbana: University of Illinois Press, 1989.

Johnson, John A. "Overland Journey to the Pacific Coast." WA MSS S-710, Collection of Western Americana, Beinecke Library, Yale University.

Johnson, Overton and William H. Winter. *Route Across the Rocky Mountains.* Princeton: Princeton University Press, 1932.

Johnson, Patricia G. *James Patton and the Appalachian Colonists.* Verona, Va.: McClure Press, 1973.

Jones, Landon Y. *William Clark and the Shaping of the West.* New York: Hill and Wang, 2004.

Jones, Maldwyn A. "Ulster Emigration, 1783-1815." In *Essays in Scotch-Irish History*, edited by E.R.R. Greene, 46-68. London: Routledge & Kegan Paul, 1969.

Jones, Mary Ellen. *Daily Life on the Nineteenth Century American Frontier.* Westport: Greenwood, 1998.

Jordan, Winthrop D. *The White Man's Burden.* New York: Oxford University Press, 1974.

_____. *White Over Black: American Attitudes toward the Negro, 1550-1812.* Chapel Hill: University of North Carolina Press, 1968.

Josephy, Alvin M., Jr. *The Civil War in the American West.* New York: Knopf, 1991.

Journal of the Constitutional Convention of the State of Oregon. Salem: W.H. Byars, 1882.

Journal of the Convention to Form a Constitution for the State of Wisconsin. Madison: B. Brown, 1847.

Journal of the House of Representatives of the Extra-Session of the First General Assembly of the State of Missouri. St. Charles: Robert McCloud, 1821.

Kalm, Peter. *Peter Kalm's Travels in North America: The English Version of 1770.* Vol. 1. Edited by Adolph B. Benson. New York: Wilson-Erickson, 1937.

Kamphoefner, Walter D. *The Westfalians: From Germany to Missouri.* Princeton: Princeton University Press, 1987.

Kansas Constitutional Convention: A Reprint of the Proceedings and Debates of the Convention Which Framed the Constitution of Kansas at Wyandotte in July, 1859. Topeka: Kansas State Printing Plant, 1920.

Katz, William L. *The Black West.* rev. ed. Garden City: Anchor Press, 1987.

Kelly, Kevin P. "'In dispers'd Country Plantations': Settlement Patterns in Seventeenth-Century Surry County, Virginia." In *The Chesapeake in the Seventeenth Century: Essays on Anglo-American Society*, edited by Thad W. Tate and David L. Ammerman, 183-205. Chapel Hill: University of North Carolina Press, 1979.

Kharif, Wali R. 1999. "'To Be Free and Black in the Upper Cumberland." Paper presented at the Ohio Valley History Conference, 22 October, Cookeville, Tenn.

Klein, Herbert S. *The Atlantic Slave Trade.* Cambridge: Cambridge University Press, 1999.

Kulikoff, Allan. *Tobacco and Slaves: The Development of Southern Cultures in the Chesapeake, 1680-1800.* Chapel Hill: University of North Carolina Press, 1986.

_____. "A 'Prolifick' People: Black Population Growth in the Chesapeake Colonies, 1700-1790." In *Colonial Southern Slavery*, edited by Paul Finkelman, 125-63. New York: Garland, 1977.

_____. "The Origins of Afro-American Society in Tidewater Maryland and Virginia, 1700 to 1790," *William and Mary Quarterly* 35 (April 1978): 226-59.

LaLande, Jeff. "'Dixie' of the Pacific Northwest: Southern Oregon's Civil War," *Oregon Historical Quarterly* 100 (Spring 1999): 32-54.

Land, Aubrey C. "Economic Base and Social Structure: The Northern Chesapeake in the Eighteenth Century," *Journal of Economic History* 25 (December 1965): 639-59.

Lapp, Rudolph. *Blacks in Gold Rush California.* New Haven: Yale University Press, 1977.

Latrobe, Charles J. *The Rambler in North America, 1832-1833.* New York: Harper & Brothers, 1835.

Lavender, David. *Land of Giants: The Drive to the Pacific Northwest, 1750-1950.* Garden City: Doubleday, 1956.

Lawlis, Chelsea L. "Migration to the Whitewater Valley, 1820-1830," *Indiana Magazine of History* 33 (September 1947): 225-39.

Lawrence, Barbara and Nedra Branz, eds. *The Flagg Correspondence: Selected Letters, 1816-1854.* Carbondale: Southern Illinois University Press, 1986.

Lee, Everett L., et al. *Population Redistribution and Economic Growth, United States, 1870-1950.* Vol 1, Methodological Considerations and Reference Tables. Philadelphia: American Philosophical Society, 1957.

Lee, George R. "Slavery and Emancipation in Lewis County, Missouri," *Missouri Historical Review* 65 (April 1971): 294-317.

Leopold, Lewis A., ed. *Greater Cincinnati and Its People: A History.* New York: Lewis Historical Publishing Co., 1927.

Levine, Bruce. *Half Slave and Half Free: The Roots of Civil War.* New York: Hill and Wang, 1992.

Lewis, Kenneth E. *The American Frontier: An Archaeological Study of Settlement Pattern and Process.* Orlando: Academic Press, 1984.

Limerick, Patricia N. *The Legacy of Conquest: The Unbroken Past of the American West.* New York: Norton, 1987.

Linden, Fabian. "Economic Democracy in the Slave South: An Appraisal of the Some Recent Views," *Journal of Negro History* 31 (April 1946): 140-89.

Lindley, Harlow, ed. *Indiana as Seen by Early Travelers: A Collection of Reprints from Books of Travel, Letters and Diaries Prior to 1830.* Indianapolis: Indiana Historical Commission, 1916.

Linn, Elizabeth A. *The Life and Public Services of Dr. Lewis F. Linn.* New York: D. Appleton, 1857.

Litwack, Leon F. *North of Slavery: The Negro in the Free States, 1790-1860.* Chicago: University of Chicago Press, 1961.

Lockley, Fred. "Some Documentary Records of Slavery in Oregon," *Oregon Historical Quarterly* 17 (March 1916): 107-15.

Lockley, Timothy J. *Lines in the Sand: Race and Class in Lowcountry Georgia, 1750-1860.* Athens: University of Georgia Press, 2001.

Lofton, Williston H. "Abolition and Labor," *Journal of Negro History* 33 (July 1948): 249-83.

Lucas, Marion B. *A History of Slavery in Kentucky.* Vol. 1, *From Slavery to Segregation, 1760-1891.* Frankfort: Kentucky Historical Society, 1992.

Lyell, Charles. *A Second Visit to the United States of North America.* Vol. 2. New York: Harper & Brothers, 1849.

Lynch, William O. "Anti-Slavery Tendencies of the Democratic Party in the Northwest, 1848-50," *Mississippi Valley Historical Review* 11 (December 1924): 319-31.

_____. "The Influence of Population Movements on Missouri Before 1861," *Missouri Historical Review* 16 (July 1922): 506-16.

_____. "The Westward Flow of Southern Colonists before 1861," *Journal of History* 9 (August 1943): 303-27.

Magill, John. *The Pioneer to the Kentucky Emigrant: A Brief Topographical and Historical Description of the State of Kentucky.* Lexington: University Press of Kentucky, 1942.

Majewski, John. *A House Dividing: Economic Development in Pennsylvania and Virginia Before the Civil War.* Cambridge: Cambridge University Press, 2000.

Malone, Michael P., ed. *Historians and the American West.* Lincoln: University of Nebraska Press, 1983.

Mandel, Bernard. *Labor: Free and Slave, Workingmen and the Anti-Slavery Movement in the United States.* New York: Associated Authors, 1955.

Mapp, Alf J., Jr. *The Virginia Experiment: The Old Dominion's Role in the Making of America, 1607-1781.* 3rd ed. New York: Hamilton Press, 1987.

Marambaud, Pierre. *William Byrd of Westover, 1674-1744.* Charlottesville: University Press of Virginia, 1971.

March, David D. *The History of Missouri.* Vol. 1. New York: Lewis Historical Publishing, 1967.

McClelland, Peter D. and Richard J. Zeckhauser. *Demographic Dimensions of the New Republic: American Interregional Migration, Vital Statistics, and Manumissions, 1800-1860.* Cambridge: Cambridge University Press, 1982.

McDermott, John Francis, ed. *The Frontier Re-examined*. Urbana: University of Illinois Press, 1967.

McGettigan, James W., Jr. "Boone County Slaves: Sales, Estate Divisions, and Families, 1820-1865," Part 1, *Missouri Historical Review* 72 (January 1978): 176-97.

McKivigan John R., ed. *Abolitionism and American Politics and Government*. New York: Garland, 1999.

McManus, Michael J. *Political Abolitionism in Wisconsin, 1840-1861*. Kent, Ohio: Kent State University Press, 1998.

McMurtry, R. Gerald, "The Lincoln Migration from Kentucky to Indiana," *Indiana Magazine of History* 33 (December 1937): 385-421.

McPherson, James M. *For Cause and Comrades: Why Men Fought in the Civil War*. New York: Oxford University Press, 1997.

_____. *The Struggle for Equality: Abolitionists and the Negro in the Civil War and Reconstruction*. Princeton: Princeton University Press, 1964.

Mehlinger, Louis R. "The Attitude of the Free Negro Toward African Colonization," *Journal of Negro History* 1 (June 1916): 276-301.

Meinig, D.W. *The Shaping of America: A Geographical Perspective on 500 Years of History*. Vol. 2, *Continental America, 1800-1867*. New Haven: Yale University Press, 1993.

Memorial and Resolutions of the Legislature of the Missouri Territory. Washington, D.C.: Gales & Seaton, 1819.

Menard, Russell R. "From Servants to Slaves: The Transformation of the Chesapeake Labor System," *Southern Studies* 16 (Winter 1977): 355-90.

_____. *British Migration to the Chesapeake Colonies in the Seventeenth Century*. In *Colonial Chesapeake Society*, edited by Louis G. Carr, Philip D. Morgan and Jean B. Russo, 99-132. Chapel Hill: University of North Carolina Press, 1988.

_____. "The Tobacco Industry in the Chesapeake Colonies, 1617-1730: An Interpretation," *Research in Economic History* 5 (1980): 109-77.

Merk, Frederick. *History of the Westward Movement*. New York: Knopf, 1978.

_____. *Manifest Destiny and Mission in American History: A Reinterpretation*. New York: Knopf, 1963.

_____. *The Monroe Doctrine and American Expansionism, 1843-1849*. New York: Knopf, 1966.

_____. *Slavery and the Annexation of Texas*. New York: Knopf, 1972.

_____. "A Safety Valve Thesis and Texas Annexation," *Mississippi Valley Historical Review* 49 (December 1962): 413-36.

Meyer, Douglas K. *Making the Heartland Quilt: A Geographical History of Settlement and Migration in Early-Nineteenth-Century Illinois*. Carbondale: Southern Illinois University Press, 2000.

Milford, Anna. *London in Flames: The Capital's History Through its Fires*. London: Comerford & Miller, 1998.

Miller, Chandra. "'Title Page to a Great Tragic Volume': The Impact of the Missouri Crisis on Slavery, Race, and Republicanism in the Thought of John C. Calhoun and John Quincy Adams," *Missouri Historical Review* 94 (July 2000): 365-88.

Miller, William E. *Arguing About Slavery: The Great Battle in the United States Congress.* New York: Knopf, 1996.

_____. "A Note on the Importance of the Interstate Slave Trade of the Ante Bellum South," *Journal of Political Economy* 73 (April 1965): 181-87.

Minto, John. "Antecedents of the Oregon Pioneers and the Light These Throw on their Motives," *Oregon Historical Quarterly* 5 (March 1904): 38-63.

"Missouri in 1822, Reprint from *The Arkansas Gazette*," *Missouri Historical Review* 16 (April 1922): 337-42.

Mitchell, Robert D. "The Shenandoah Valley Frontier," *Annals of the Association of American Geographers* 62 (September 1972): 461-86.

Monks, William. *A History of Southern Missouri and Northern Arkansas: Being an Account of the Early Settlements, the Civil War, the Klu Klux Klan, and Times of Peace.* Edited by John F. Bradbury and Lou Wehmer. Fayetteville: University of Arkansas Press, 2003.

Morgan, Edmund S. *American Slavery/American Freedom: The Ordeal of Colonial Virginia.* New York: Norton, 1975.

_____. *Slavery and Servitude in North America, 1607-1800.* Edinburgh: Edinburgh University Press, 2000.

Morgan, Philip D. *Slave Counterpoint: Black Culture in the Eighteenth-Century Chesapeake and Lowcountry.* Chapel Hill: University of North Carolina Press, 1988.

_____. "Slave Life in Piedmont Virginia, 1720-1800." In *Colonial Chesapeake Society*, edited by Lois G. Carr, Philip D. Morgan and Jean B. Russo, 433-84. Chapel Hill: University of North Carolina Press, 1984.

Morgan, Philip D. and Michael L. Nicholls. "Slaves in Piedmont Virginia, 1720-1790," *William and Mary Quarterly* 46 (April 1989): 211-51.

Morris, Rev. C. A. *Miscellany: Consisting of Essays, Biographical Sketches, and Notes of Travel.* Cincinnati: L. Swormstedt & A. Poe, 1854.

Morrison, Chaplain W. *Democratic Politics and Sectionalism: The Wilmot Proviso Controversy.* Chapel Hill: University of North Carolina Press, 1967.

Morrison, Michael A. *Slavery and the American West: The Eclipse of Manifest Destiny and the Coming of the Civil War.* Chapel Hill: University of North Carolina Press, 1997.

Morton, Richard L. *Westward Expansion and Prelude to Revolution, 1710-1763.* Chapel Hill: University of North Carolina Press, 1960.

Moulton, Benjamin. 1966. Changing Patterns of Population. In *Natural Features of Indiana*, edited by Alton A. Lindsey, 532-46. Indianapolis: Indiana Academy of Science.

Mowrer, J. H. "The Republic of Liberia," *Journal of Negro History* 32 (July 1947): 265-306.

Myers, Jacob W. "History of the Gallatin Salines," *Journal of the Illinois State Historical Society* 14 (October 1921-January 1922): 137-49.

Nagel, Paul C. *Missouri: A Bicentennial History.* New York: Norton, 1977.

Nash, Gary B. *Red, White, and Black: The Peoples of Early America.* Englewood Cliffs, N.J.: Prentice-Hall, 1974.

Nash, Gary B. and Richard Weiss, eds. *The Great Fear: Race in the Mind of America.* New York: Holt, Rinehart & Winston, 1970.

Norton, Margaret C., ed. *Illinois Census Returns, 1810 and 1818.* Baltimore: Genealogical Publishing, 1969.

Nunis, Doyce B., Jr. "The Sublettes of Kentucky: Their Early Contribution to the Opening of the West," *Register of the Kentucky Historical Society* 57 (January 1959): 20-34.

Oberly, James W. "Westward Who? Estimates of Native White Interstate Migration After the War of 1812," *Journal of Economic History* 46 (June 1986): 431-40.

Oliver, Egbert S. "Obed Dickinson and the 'Negro Question' in Salem," *Oregon Historical Quarterly* 92 (Spring 1991): 5-40.

Otto, John S. "Upland South Folk Culture: The Oral Traditional History of a 'Plain Folk' Family," *Mid-America Folklore* 9 (Winter 1981): 73-88.

Owsley, Frank L. *Plain Folk of the Old South.* Baton Rouge: Louisiana State University Press, 1949.

_____. "The Pattern of Migration and Settlement on the Southern Frontier," *Journal of Southern History* 11 (May 1945): 147-76.

Painter, Nell F. *Exodusters: Black Migration to Kansas after Reconstruction.* New York: Knopf, 1976.

Palmer, Joel. *Journal of Travels over the Rocky Mountains.* Ann Arbor: University Microfilms, 1966.

Parent, Anthony S., Jr. *Foul Means: The Formation of a Slave Society in Virginia, 1660-1740.* Chapel Hill: University of North Carolina Press, 2003.

Parker, Samuel. *Journal of an Exploring Trip Beyond the Rocky Mountains.* Ithaca: Andrus, Woodruff & Gauntlett, 1844.

Parramore, Thomas C. *Southampton County Virginia.* Charlottesville: University Press of Virginia, 1978.

Parrish, Randall. *Historic Illinois: The Romance of the Earlier Days.* Chicago: A.C. McClurg, 1905.

Parrish, William E. *Frank Blair: Lincoln's Conservative.* Columbia: University of Missouri Press, 1998.

Paxson, Frederic L. *History of the American Frontier, 1763-1893.* Boston: Houghton, Mifflin, 1924.

Pease, Thomas C. *The Frontier State: 1818-1848.* Urbana: University of Illinois Press, 1987.

Peck, John M. *Forty Years of Pioneer Life: Edited from His Journals and Correspondence by Rufus Babcock*. Carbondale: Southern Illinois University Press, 1965.

Perkins, Elizabeth. "Distinctions and Partitions amongst Us: Identity and Interaction in the Revolutionary Ohio Valley." *In Contact Points: American Frontiers from the Mohawk Valley to the Mississippi, 1750-1850*, edited by Andrew R. L. Cayton and Frederika J. Leute, 205-35. Chapel Hill: University of North Carolina Press, 1998.

Perry, James R. *The Formation of a Society on Virginia's Eastern Shore, 1615-1655*. Chapel Hill: University of North Carolina Press, 1990.

Peters, William. *A More Perfect Union*. New York: Crown, 1987.

Peyton, J. Lewis. *History of Augusta County, Virginia*. 2nd ed. Bridgewater, Va.: C. J. Carrier, 1953.

Philbrick, Francis S. *The Rise of the West, 1754-1830*. New York: Harper & Row, 1965.

Phillips, Ulrich B. *Life and Labor in the Old South*. Boston: Little, Brown, 1951.

_____. *The Slave Economy of the Old South*. Baton Rouge: Louisiana State University Press, 1968.

Pike, C. J. "Petitions of Oregon Settlers, 1838-48," *Oregon Historical Quarterly* 34 (September 1933): 216-35.

Pletcher, David M. *The Diplomacy of Annexation: Texas, Oregon, and the Mexican War*. Columbia: University of Missouri Press, 1973.

Plumer, William J. *The Missouri Compromises and Presidential Politics, 1820-1825*. St. Louis: Missouri Historical Society, 1926.

Porter, Stephen. *The Great Fire of London*. London: Sutton Publishing, 1996.

Potter, David W. *The Impending Crisis, 1848-1861*. New York: Harper & Row, 1976.

_____. *People of Plenty: Economic Abundance and the American Character*. Chicago: University of Chicago Press, 1954.

Power, Richard L. *Planting Corn Belt Culture: The Impress of the Upland Southerner and Yankee in the Old Northwest*. Indianapolis: Indiana Historical Society, 1953.

Power, Tyrone. *Impressions of America During the Years 1833, 1834, and 1835*. Vol. 2. 2nd American ed. Philadelphia: Carey, Lea & Blanchard, 1836.

Price, David A. *Love and Hate in Jamestown: John Smith, Pocahontas, and the Start of a New Nation*. New York: Vintage, 2003.

Price, Edward T. *Dividing the Land: Early American Beginnings of Our Private Property Mosaic*. Chicago: University of Chicago Press, 1995.

Quaife, Milo M. *The Diary of James K. Polk, 1845-1849*. Chicago: A.C. McClurg, 1910.

Quarles, Benjamin. *The Negro in the American Revolution*. Chapel Hill: University of North Carolina Press, 1961.

Rafferty, Milton D. *The Ozarks: Land and Life*. Fayetteville: University of Arkansas Press, 2001.

_____. *Rude Pursuits and Rugged Peaks: Schoolcraft's Ozark Journal, 1818-1819.* Fayetteville: University of Arkansas Press, 1996.

Raitz, Karl B. *Kentucky's Bluegrass: A Regional Profile and Guide.* Chapel Hill: Dept. of Geography, University of North Carolina, 1980.

Ransom, Roger L. and Richard Sutch. "Who Pays for Slavery?" In *The Wealth of Races: The Present Value of Benefits from Past Injustices,* edited by Richard F. America, 31-54. New York: Greenwood, 1990.

Rasmussen, Barbara. *Absentee Landowning and Exploitation in West Virginia, 1760-1920.* Lexington: University Press of Kentucky, 2001.

Ratcliffe, Donald J. "Captain James Riley and Antislavery Sentiment in Ohio, 1819-1824," *Ohio Archaeological and Historical Quarterly* 81 (Spring 1972): 76-94.

Ratner, Lormer. *Powder Keg: Northern Opposition to the Antislavery Movement, 1831-1840.* New York: BasicBooks, 1968.

Rawley, James A. *Race and Politics: 'Bleeding Kansas' and the Coming of the Civil War.* Philadelphia and New York: J.B. Lippincott, 1969.

Rayback, Joseph G. *Free Soil: The Election of 1848.* Lexington: University Press of Kentucky, 1970.

Report of the Debates and Proceedings of the Convention for the Revision of the Constitution of the State of Indiana. Indianapolis: A.H. Brown, 1850.

Report of the Debates and Proceedings of the Convention for the Revision of the Constitution of the State of Ohio. Columbus: A.S. Medary, 1851.

Rice, Otis K. *Frontier Kentucky.* Lexington: University Press of Kentucky, 1975.

Richard, K. Keith. "Unwelcome Settlers: Black and Mulatto Oregon Pioneers," Part 1, *Oregon Historical Quarterly* 84 (Spring 1983): 29-56.

_____. "Unwelcome Settlers: Black and Mulatto Oregon Pioneers," Part 2, *Oregon Historical Quarterly* 84 (Summer 1983): 173-92.

Riddle, A.G. *The Life of Benjamin F. Wade.* Cleveland: William W. Williams, 1886.

Robinson, Donald L. *Slavery in the Structure of American Politics; 1765-1820.* New York: Harcourt Brace Jovanovich, 1971.

Rodney, Thomas. *A Journey through the West: Thomas Rodney's 1803 Journal from Delaware to the Mississippi Territory.* Edited by Douglas L. Smith and Ray Swick. Athens: Ohio University Press, 1997.

Roediger, David and Martin H Blatt, eds. *The Meaning of Slavery in the North.* New York: Garland, 1998.

Savage, William S. *Blacks in the West.* Westport: Greenwood, 1976.

Saxton, Alexander. *The Rise and Fall of the White Republic: Class Politics and Mass Culture in Nineteenth-Century America.* London and New York: Verso, 1990.

Scarpino, Philip V. "Slavery in Callaway County, Missouri: 1845-1855," Part 1, *Missouri Historical Review* 71 (October 1976): 22-43.

_____. "Slavery in Callaway County, Missouri: 1845-1855," Part 2, *Missouri Historical Review* 71 (April 1977): 266-83.

Schaefer, Donald F. "A Model of Migration and Wealth Accumulation: Farmers at the Antebellum Southern Frontier," *Explorations in Economic History* 24 (1987): 130-57.

Schapiro, Morton O. *Filling Up America: An Economic-Demographic Model of the Population Growth and Distribution in the Nineteenth-Century United States.* Greenwich: JAI Press, 1986.

Schlesinger, Arthur M., Jr. *The Age of Jackson.* Boston: Little, Brown, 1945.

Schlissel, Lillian. *Women's Diaries of the Westward Journey.* New York: Schocken, 1982.

Schluter, Herman. *Lincoln, Labor, and Slavery: A Chapter from the Social History of America.* New York: Socialist Literature Co., 1913.

Schoen, Harold. "The Free Negro in the Republic of Texas," *Southwestern Historical Quarterly* 40 (January 1937): 166-99.

Schwarz, Philip J. *Migrants Against Slavery: Virginians and the Nation.* Charlottesville: University of Virginia Press, 2001.

Segal, Charles M. and David C. Stineback. *Puritans, Indians, and Manifest Destiny.* New York: Putnam, 1977.

Semple, Ellen C. *American History and Its Geographic Conditions.* Boston: Houghton, Mifflin, 1904.

Sewell, Richard H. *Ballots for Freedom: Antislavery Politics in the United States, 1837-1860.* New York: Oxford University Press, 1976.

Shambaugh, Benjamin F., ed. *Fragments of the Debates of the Iowa Constitutional Conventions of 1844 and 1846.* Iowa City: State Historical Society of Iowa, 1900.

Sheehan, Bernard W. *Savagism and Civility: Englishmen and Indians in 17th Century Colonial Virginia.* New York: Cambridge University Press, 1980.

Sheridan, Richard B. "From Slavery in Missouri to Freedom in Kansas: The Influx of Black Fugitives and Contrabands Into Kansas, 1854-1865," *Kansas History* 12 (Spring 1989): 28-47.

Sherman, William T. *The Memoirs of Gen. William T. Sherman.* 2nd ed., rev. New York: D. Appleton, 1913.

Sherwood, Henry N. "Early Negro Deportation Schemes," *Mississippi Valley Historical Review* 2 (March 1916): 485-508.

_____. "Movement in Ohio to Deport the Negro," *Quarterly Publication of the Historical and Philosophical Society of Ohio* 7 (June/September 1912): 53-77.

_____. "The Formation of the American Colonization Society," *Journal of Negro History* 2 (July 1917): 209-28.

Shortbridge, James R. "The Expansion of the Settlement Frontier in Missouri," *Missouri Historical Review* 75 (October 1980): 64-90.

Silbey, Joel H. *Martin Van Buren and the Emergence of American Popular Politics.* Lanham: Rowman & Littlefield, 2002.

Simeone, James. *Democracy and Slavery in Frontier Illinois: The Bottomland Republic.* DeKalb: Northern Illinois University Press, 2000.

Slotkin, Richard. *Gunfighter Nation: The Myth of the Frontier in Twentieth-Century America.* New York: Atheneum, 1992.

_____. *Regeneration Through Violence: The Mythology of the American Frontier, 1600-1860.* Middletown: Wesleyan University Press, 1974.

Smith, Abbott E. *Colonists in Bondage: White Servitude and Convict Labor in America, 1606-1776.* Gloucester: Peter Smith, 1965.

Smith, Elbert B. *Magnificent Missourian: The Life of Thomas Hart Benton.* Philadelphia and New York: J.B. Lippincott, 1958.

Smith, Jessie C. and Carrell P. Horton, eds. *Historical Statistics of Black America.* Vol. 2, *Media to Vital Statistics.* New York: Gale Research, 1995.

Smith, Henry N. *Virgin Land: The American West as Symbol and Myth.* Cambridge: Harvard University Press, 1950.

Smith, Theodore C. *The Liberty and Free Soil Parties in the Northwest.* New York: Longmans, Green, 1897.

_____. *Parties and Slavery, 1850-1859.* New York: Haskell House, 1968.

Sosin, Jack M. *The Revolutionary Frontier 1763-1783.* New York: Holt, Rinehart & Winston, 1967.

Sparks, William H. *The Memories of Fifty Years: Containing Brief Biographical Notes of Distinguished Americans and Anecdotes of Remarkable Men.* Philadelphia: Claxton, Remsen & Haffelfinger, 1872.

Sprague, Stuart S. *Kentuckians in Missouri.* Baltimore: Genealogical Publishing, 1983.

Stampp, Kenneth M. *America in 1857: A Nation on the Brink.* New York: Oxford University Press, 1990.

_____. *The Imperiled Union: Essays on the Background of the Civil War.* New York: Oxford University Press, 1980.

_____. *The Peculiar Institution: Slavery in the Ante-Bellum South.* New York: Knopf, 1961.

_____, ed. *Causes of the Civil War.* Englewood Cliffs, N.J.: Prentice-Hall, 1959.

Starkey, Marion L. *The First Plantation: A History of Hampton and Elizabeth City County, Virginia, 1607-1887.* Hampton, Va.: Houston Printing, 1936.

Staudenraus, P.J. *The African Colonization Movement, 1816-1865.* New York: Columbia University Press, 1961.

Steckel, Richard H. "Census Matching and Migration: A Research Strategy," *Historical Methods* 21 (Spring 1988): 52-60.

_____. "The Economic Foundations of East-West Migration during the 19th Century," *Explorations in Economic History* 20 (January 1983): 14-36.

Stephanson, Anders. *Manifest Destiny: American Expansionism and the Empire of Right*. New York: Hill and Wang, 1995.

Stephenson, George M. *The Political History of the Public Lands, from 1840 to 1862*. New York: Russell & Russell, 1917.

Stewart, James B. *Holy Warriors: The Abolitionists and American Slavery*. New York: Hill and Wang, 1976.

Stirling, James. *Letters from the Slave States*. New York: Kraus Reprint, 1969.

Strickland, Arrarh E. "Aspects of Slavery in Missouri, 1821," *Missouri Historical Review* 65 (July 1971): 505-26.

Stuart, James. *Three Years in North America*. Vol. 2; 2nd ed., rev. Edinburgh: Robert Cadell, 1833.

Takaki, Ronald T. *Iron Cages: Race and Culture in Nineteenth-Century America*. New York: Knopf, 1979.

Talpalar, Morris. *The Sociology of Colonial Virginia*. 2nd, ed., rev. New York: Philosophical Library, 1968.

Tappan, Arthur, et al. *Address to the Inhabitants of New Mexico and California on the Omission by Congress to Provide Them with Territorial Governments and on the Social and Political Evils of Slavery*. New York: William Harned, 1849.

Tarbell, Ira M. *In the Footsteps of the Lincolns*. New York: Harper & Brothers, 1924.

Taylor, Henry L., ed. *Race and the City: Work, Community, and Protest in Cincinnati, 1820-1970*. Urbana: University of Illinois Press, 1993.

Taylor, Quintard. *In Search of the Racial Frontier: African Americans in the American West, 1528-1990*. New York: Norton, 1994.

Taylor, Robert M., Jr., ed. *The Northwest Ordinance 1787: A Bicentennial Handbook*. Indianapolis: Indiana Historical Society, 1987.

_____. "Slaves and Free Men: Blacks in the Oregon Country, 1840-1860," *Oregon Historical Quarterly* 83 (Summer 1982): 153-70.

Thornbrough, Emma Lou. *The Negro in Indiana: A Study of a Minority*. Indianapolis: Indiana Historical Review: 1957.

_____. "The Race Issue in Indiana Politics During the Civil War," *Indiana Magazine of History* 47 (June 1951): 165-88.

Thurston, Helen M. "The 1802 Constitutional Convention and Status of the Negro," *Ohio Archaeological and Historical Quarterly* 81 (Spring 1972): 15-37.

Trexler, Harrison A. "Slavery in Missouri Territory," *Missouri Historical Review* 3 (April 1901): 179-98.

_____. "Slavery in Missouri, 1804-1865." In *Slavery in the States: Selected Essays*. New York: Negro Universities Press, 1914.

Turner, Frederick J. *The Frontier in American History*. New York and Chicago: Holt, Rinehart & Winston, 1920.

Ulack, Richard, ed. *Atlas of Kentucky.* Lexington: University Press of Kentucky, 1998.

Unruh, John D., Jr. *The Plains Across: The Overland Emigrants and the Trans-Mississippi West, 1840-1860.* Urbana: University of Illinois Press, 1979.

U.S. Bureau of the Census. *Negro Population in the United States, 1790-1915.* Washington, D.C.: Government Printing Office, 1918.

Utter, William T. *The State of Ohio.* Vol. 2, *The Frontier State, 1803-1825.* Columbus: Ohio State Archaeological and Historical Society, 1942.

Van der Zee, John. *Bound Over: Indentured Servitude and American Conscience.* New York: Simon and Schuster, 1985.

Van Every, Dale. *The Final Challenge: The American Frontier, 1804-1854.* New York: William Morrow, 1964.

_____. *Forth to the Wilderness: The First American Frontier, 1754-1774.* New York: Arno Press, 1974.

Van Zandt, Nicholas B. *A Full Description of the Soil, Water, Timber, and Prairies of Each Lot, or Quarter Section of the Military Lands Between the Mississippi and Illinois Rivers.* Washington, D.C.: General Land Office, 1818.

Vedder, Richard K. and Lowell E. Gallaway. "Migration and the Old Northwest." In *Essays in Nineteenth Century Economic History: The Old Northwest,* edited by David. C. Klingaman and Richard K. Vedder, 159-76. Athens: Ohio University Press, 1975.

Vincent, Stephen A. *Southern Seed, Northern Soil: African-American Farm Communities in the Midwest, 1765-1900.* Bloomington: Indiana University Press, 1999.

Violette, E. M. "Early Settlements in Missouri," *Missouri Historical Review* 1 (October 1906): 38-52.

Voegeli, V. Jacque. "The Northwest and the Race Issue, 1861-1862," *Mississippi Valley Historical Review* 50 (September 1963): 235-51.

_____. *Free But Not Equal: The Midwest and the Negro during the Civil War.* Chicago: University of Chicago Press, 1967.

Walker, Dale L. *Pacific Destiny: The Three-Century Journey to the Oregon Country.* New York: Tom Doherty Associates, 2000.

Walters, Ronald G. *The Antislavery Appeal: American Abolitionism after 1830.* Baltimore: Johns Hopkins University Press, 1976.

Wander, Philip C. "Salvation through Separation: The Image of the Negro in the American Colonization Society," *Quarterly Journal of Speech* 57 (February 1971): 57-67.

Wardell, M. L. "Oregon Immigration Prior to 1846," *Oregon Historical Quarterly* 27 (March 1926): 41-64.

Warren, Louis A. *Lincoln's Parentage and Childhood: A History of the Kentucky Lincolns Supported by Documentary Evidence.* New York: Century, 1926.

Webb, James. *Born Fighting: How the Scots-Irish Shaped America.* New York: Broadway Books, 2004.

Webb, Stephen S. *The End of American Independence.* Cambridge: Harvard University Press, 1985.

Weinberg, Albert K. *Manifest Destiny: A Study of Nationalist Expansionism in American History.* Chicago: Quadrangle Books, 1935.

Wertenbaker, Thomas J. *The Planters of Colonial Virginia.* Princeton: Princeton University Press, 1922.

Wheeler, B. Gordon. *Black California: The History of African-Americans in the Golden State.* New York: Hippocrene Books, 1993.

White, Richard. *'It's Your Misfortune and None of My Own': A History of the American West.* Norman: University of Oklahoma Press, 1991.

_____. "Race Relations in the American West," *American Quarterly* 38 (1986): 396-416.

Wilkie, Jane R. "The United States Population by Race and Urban-Rural Residence 1790-1860: Reference Tables," *Demography* 13 (February 1976): 139-48.

_____. "Urbanization and De-Urbanization of the Black Population before the Civil War," *Demography* 13 (August 1976): 311-28.

Willis, George L. *Kentucky Democracy: A History of the Party and Its Representative Members — Past and Present.* Vol. 1. Louisville: Democratic Historical Society, 1935.

Wilson, Charles J. "The Negro in Early Ohio," *Ohio Archaeological and Historical Quarterly* 39 (October 1930): 717-68.

Wilson, Major L. *The Presidency of Martin Van Buren.* Lawrence: University Press of Kansas, 1984.

Winters, Donald L. "'Plain Folk' of the Old South Reexamined: Economic Democracy in Tennessee," *Journal of Southern History* 53 (November 1987): 565-86.

Woods, John. *Two Years' Residence on the English Prairie of Illinois.* Edited by Paul M. Angle. Chicago: R.R. Donnelley & Sons, 1968.

Woodson, Carter G. "Freedom and Slavery in Appalachian America," *Journal of Negro History* 1 (April 1916): 132-50.

_____. "The Beginnings of the Miscegenation of the Whites and Blacks," *Journal of Negro History* 3 (October 1918): 335-53.

_____. "The Negroes of Cincinnati Prior to the Civil War," *Journal of Negro History* 1 (January 1916): 1-22.

Woodward, C. Vann. *American Counterpoint: Slavery and Racism in the North-South Dialogue.* Boston: Little, Brown, 1971.

_____. "The Antislavery Myth," *American Scholar* 31 (Spring 1962): 312-27.

Woolfolk, George R. "Turner's Safety Valve and Free Negro Westward Migration," *Pacific Northwest Quarterly* 56 (July 1965): 125-30.

Woolsey, Ronald C. "The West Becomes a Problem: The Missouri Controversy and Slavery Expansion as the Southern Dilemma," *Missouri Historical Review* 77 (July 1983): 409-32.

Wright, Gavin. *The Political Economy of the Cotton South: Households, Markets, and Wealth in the Nineteenth Century*. New York: Norton, 1978.

Yates, Paul W. *The Jeffersonian Dream: Studies in the History of American Land Policy and Development*. Albuquerque: University of New Mexico Press, 1996.

Young, Rev. Jacob. *Autobiography of a Pioneer: The Nativity, Experience, Travels, and Ministerial Labors of Rev. Jacob Young*. New York: Hunt and Eaton, 1857.

Zelinsky, Wilbur. "The Population Geography of the Free Negro in Ante-Bellum America," *Population Studies* 4 (March 1950): 386-401.

_____. "Where the South Begins: The Northern Limit of the CIS-Appalachian South in Terms of Settlement Landscape," *Social Forces* 30 (December 1951): 172-8.

Zilversmit, Arthur. *The First Emancipation: The Abolition of Slavery in the North*. Chicago: University of Chicago Press, 1967.

Zimmerman, Edward. "Travel into Missouri in October, 1838," *Missouri Historical Review* 9 (October 1914): 33-43.

Zwelling, Shomer S. *Expansion and Imperialism*. Chicago: Loyola University Press: 1970.

INDEX

Printed in the United States
38464LVS00003B/106-117

9 780875 864228